JOSS WHEDON'S
dollhouse
EPITAPHS

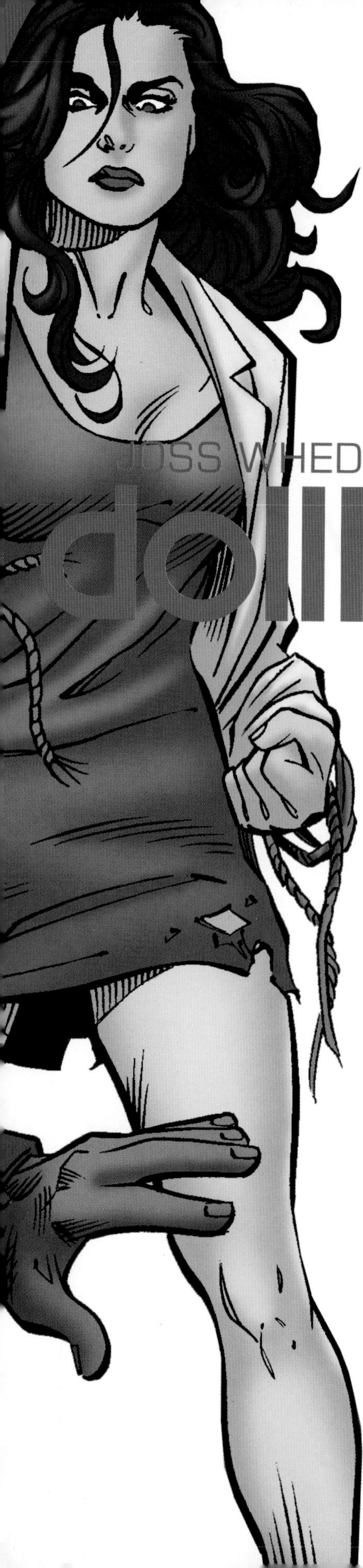

Story and Scripts
ANDREW CHAMBLISS
MAURISSA TANCHAROEN
JED WHEDON

Pencils
CLIFF RICHARDS

Inks
ANDY OWENS
CLIFF RICHARDS

Colors
MICHELLE MADSEN

Letters
NATE PIEKOS OF BLAMBOT®

Cover Art
PHIL NOTO

Dark Horse Books

President & Publisher
Mike Richardson

Editor
Sierra Hahn

Assistant Editor
Freddye Lins

Consulting Editor
Scott Allie

Collection Designer
David Nestelle

Special thanks to Debbie Olshan at Twentieth Century Fox and David Campiti.

Neil Hankerson Executive Vice President • **Tom Weddle** Chief Financial Officer • **Randy Stradley** Vice President of Publishing • **Michael Martens** Vice President of Book Trade Sales • **Anita Nelson** Vice President of Business Affairs • **Micha Hershman** Vice President of Marketing • **David Scroggy** Vice President of Product Development • **Dale LaFountain** Vice President of Information Technology • **Darlene Vogel** Senior Director of Print, Design, and Production • **Ken Lizzi** General Counsel • **Davey Estrada** Editorial Director • **Scott Allie** Senior Managing Editor • **Chris Warner** Senior Books Editor • **Diana Schutz** Executive Editor • **Cary Grazzini** Director of Print and Development • **Lia Ribacchi** Art Director • **Cara Niece** Director of Scheduling

DOLLHOUSE: EPITAPHS

This volume reprints the comic-book series *Dollhouse* #1–#5 and the *Dollhouse* one-shot from Dark Horse Comics.

Published by Dark Horse Books
A division of Dark Horse Comics, Inc.
10956 SE Main Street
Milwaukie, OR 97222

DarkHorse.com

To find a comics shop in your area, call the Comic Shop Locator Service toll-free at (888) 266-4226.

First edition: April 2012
ISBN 978-1-59582-863-7

10 9 8 7 6 5 4 3 2 1
Printed at Midas Printing International, Ltd., Huizhou, China

JOSS WHEDON'S

dollhouse

EPITAPHS

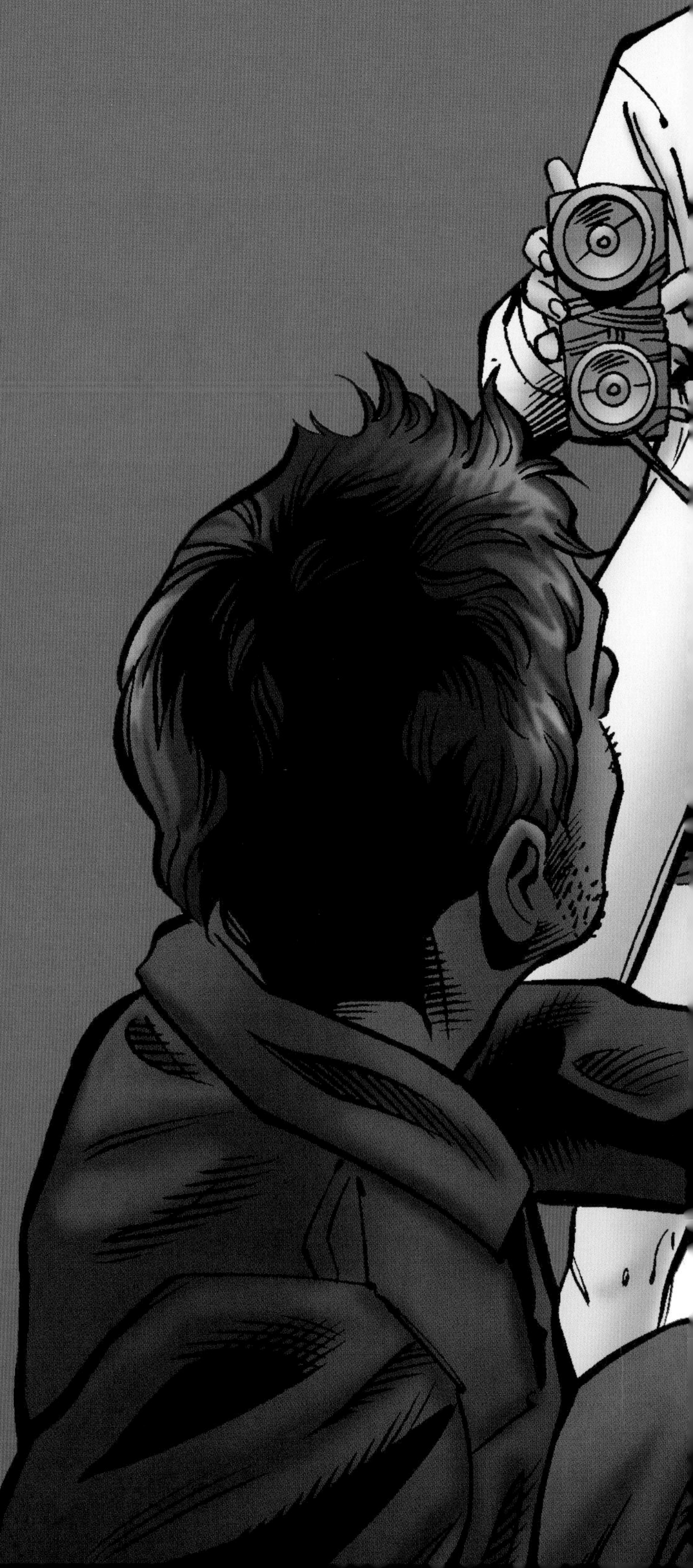

IN EVERY MAJOR CITY, Dollhouses provided wealthy clients with any kind of companionship they required. For a price, beautiful young men and women opted to have their minds wiped clean, turning themselves into "Dolls" who could be imprinted with computer-enhanced personalities and skills—to fit any buyer's request. Now the Dollhouse technology has gone viral . . .

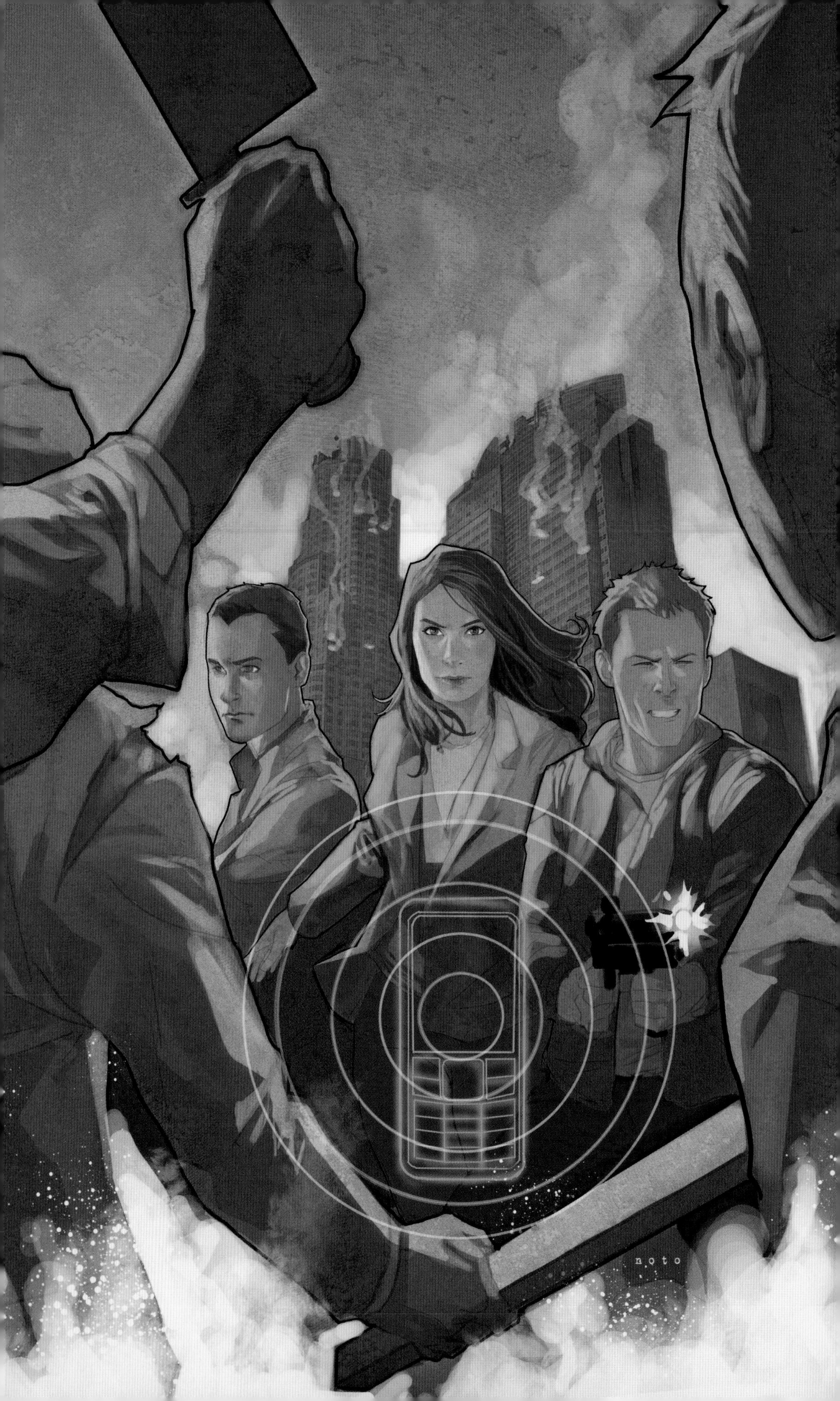
moto

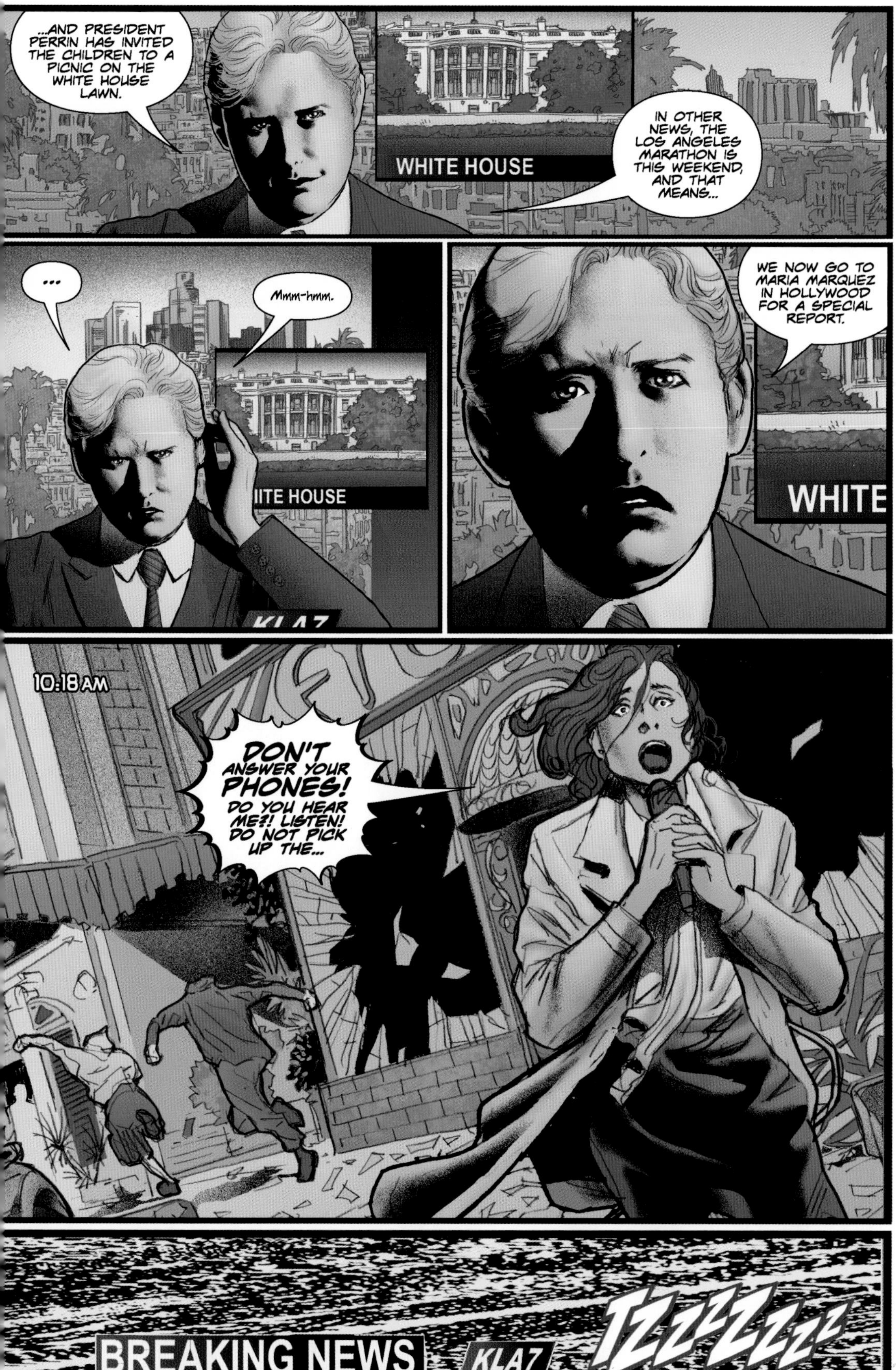

...AND PRESIDENT PERRIN HAS INVITED THE CHILDREN TO A PICNIC ON THE WHITE HOUSE LAWN.
WHITE HOUSE
IN OTHER NEWS, THE LOS ANGELES MARATHON IS THIS WEEKEND, AND THAT MEANS...
...
Mmm-hmm.
IITE HOUSE
WE NOW GO TO MARIA MARQUEZ IN HOLLYWOOD FOR A SPECIAL REPORT.
WHITE
10:18 AM
DON'T ANSWER YOUR PHONES! DO YOU HEAR ME?! LISTEN! DO NOT PICK UP THE...
BREAKING NEWS
KLA7
TZZZZZZ

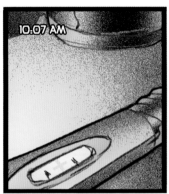

10.07 AM

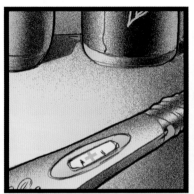

ZONE?

WHAT'S THE VERDICT?

WHAT DOES A **PLUS** MEAN AGAIN?

POSITIVE. AS IN PLUS.

WELL.

I'M...

WE'RE...

WE MADE A PLUS?

WE MADE A PLUS.

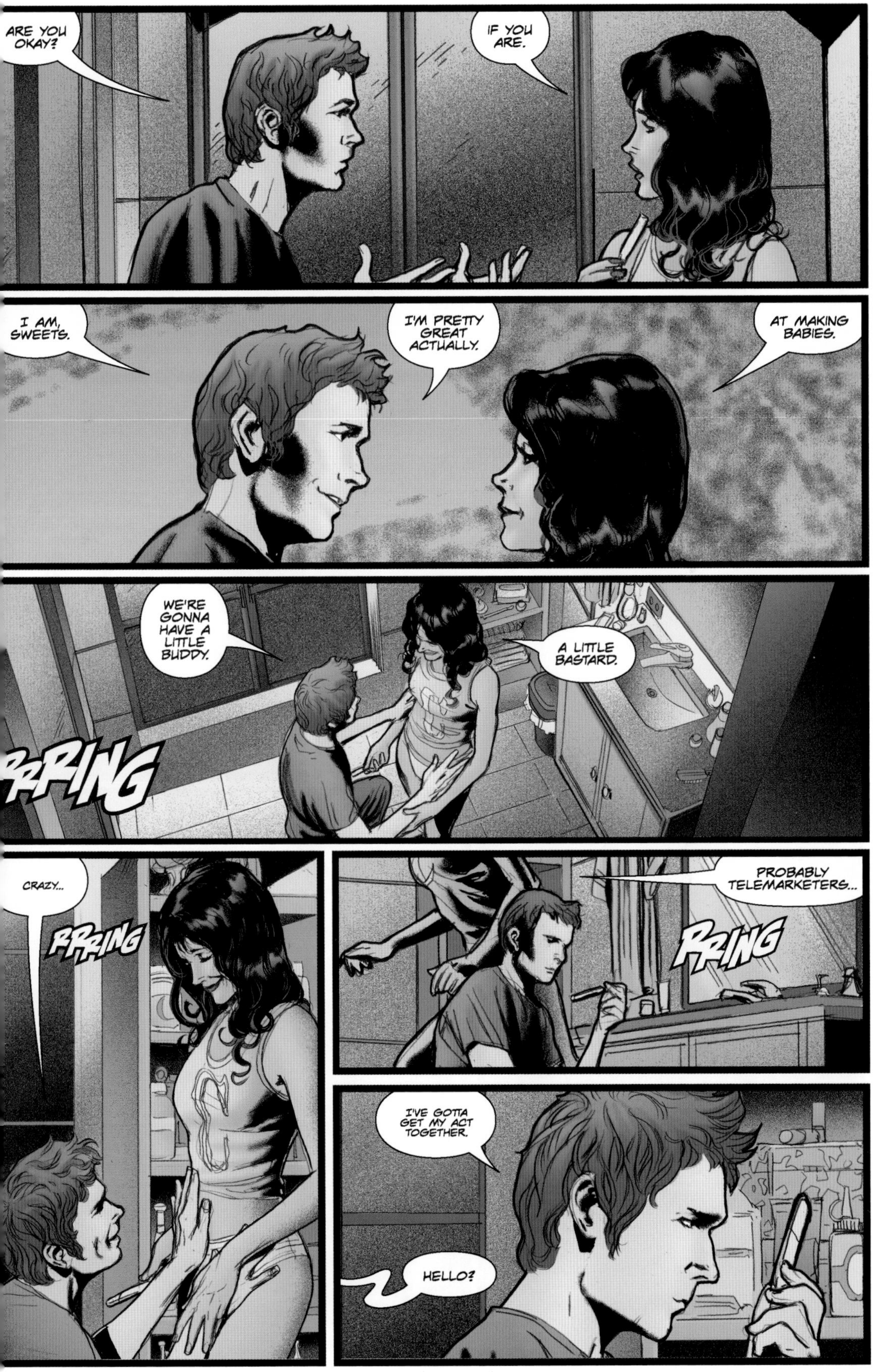

ARE YOU OKAY?
IF YOU ARE.
I AM, SWEETS.
I'M PRETTY GREAT ACTUALLY.
AT MAKING BABIES.
WE'RE GONNA HAVE A LITTLE BUDDY.
A LITTLE BASTARD.
RRRING
CRAZY...
RRRING
PROBABLY TELEMARKETERS...
RRING
I'VE GOTTA GET MY ACT TOGETHER.
HELLO?

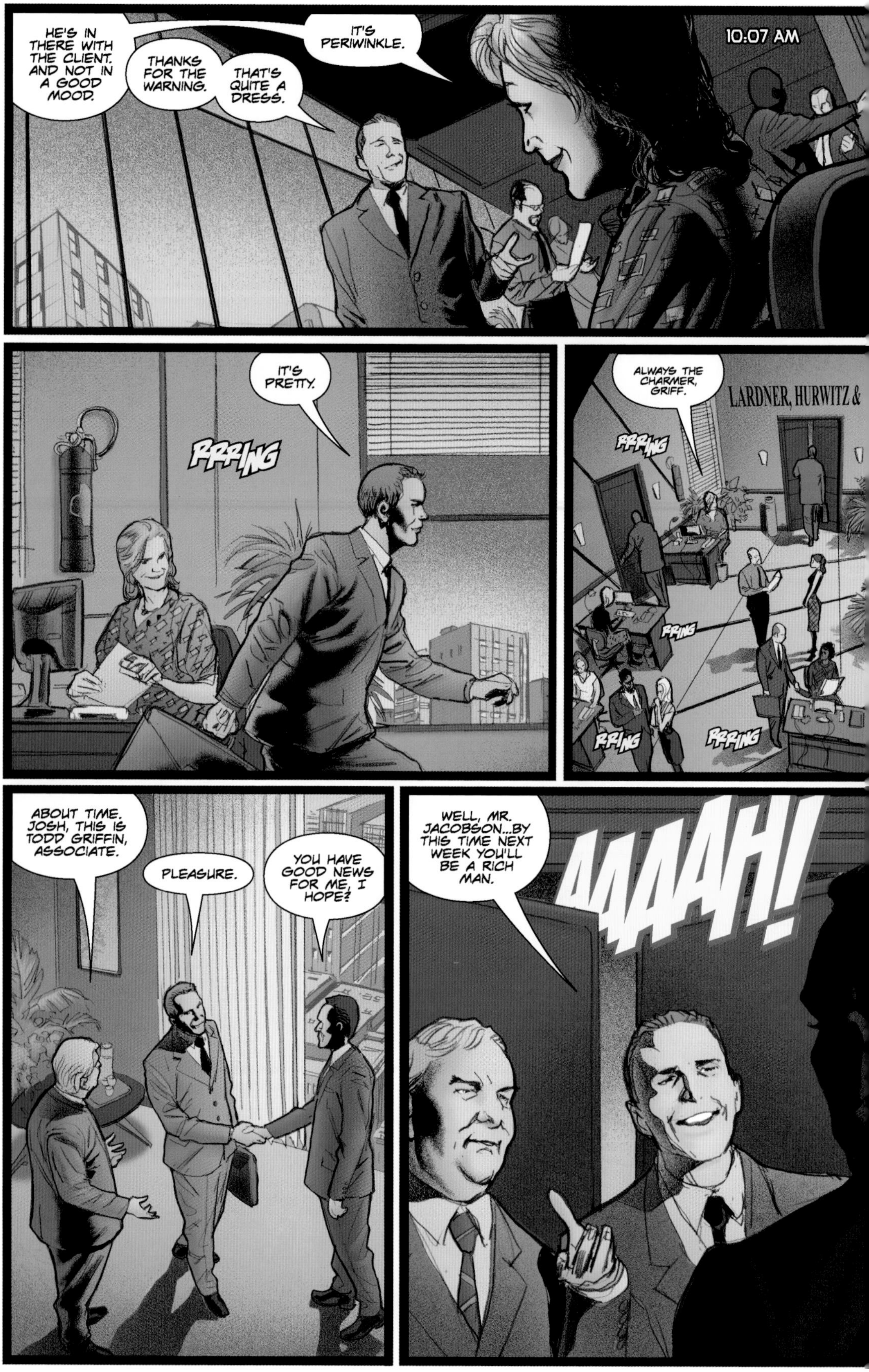
10:07 AM
HE'S IN THERE WITH THE CLIENT. AND NOT IN A GOOD MOOD.
THANKS FOR THE WARNING.
THAT'S QUITE A DRESS.
IT'S PERIWINKLE.
IT'S PRETTY.
RRRING
ALWAYS THE CHARMER, GRIFF.
LARDNER, HURWITZ &
RRRING
RRRING
RRRING
RRRING
ABOUT TIME. JOSH, THIS IS TODD GRIFFIN, ASSOCIATE.
PLEASURE.
YOU HAVE GOOD NEWS FOR ME, I HOPE?
WELL, MR. JACOBSON...BY THIS TIME NEXT WEEK YOU'LL BE A RICH MAN.
AAAAH!

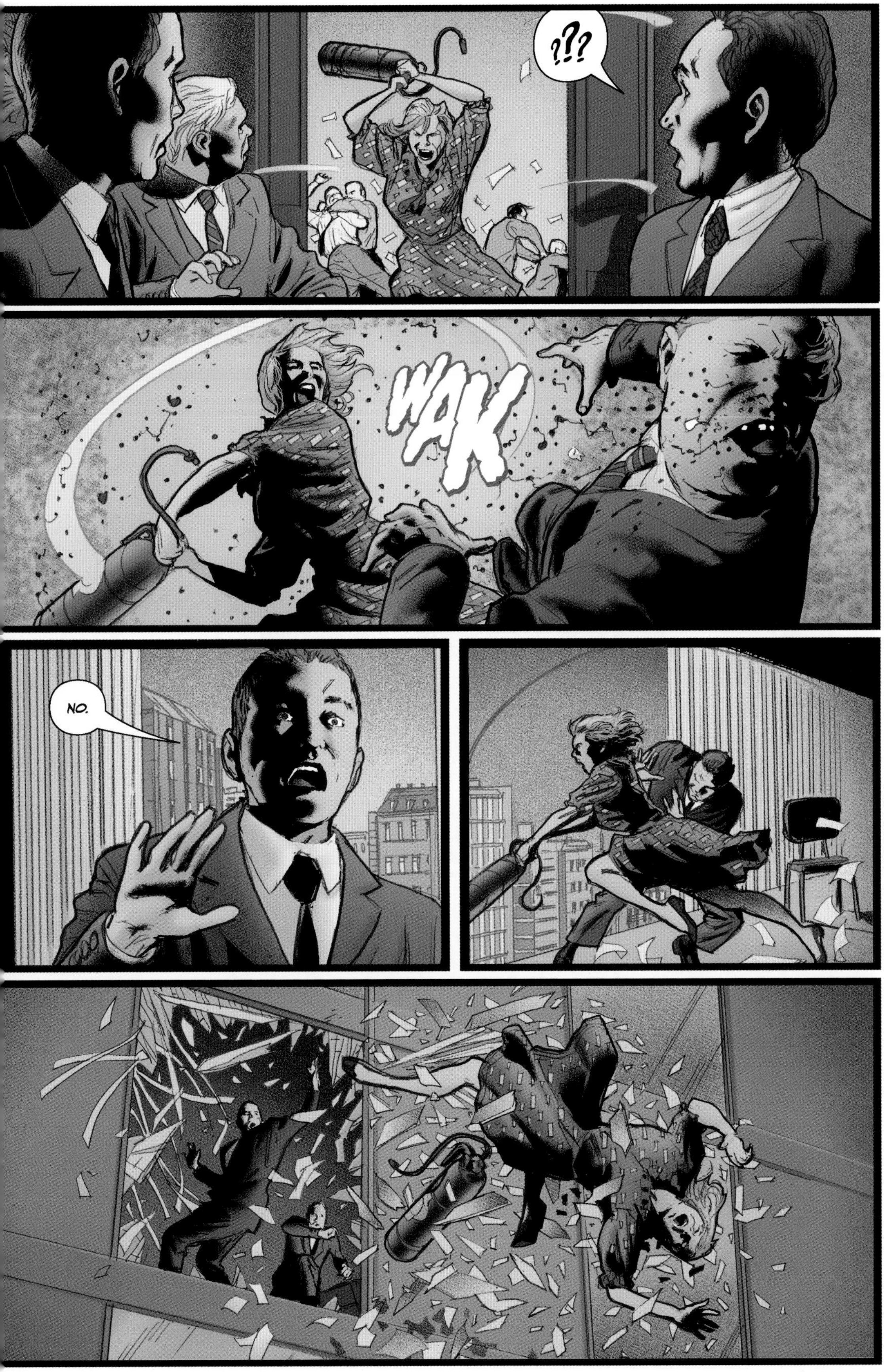
???
WAK
NO.

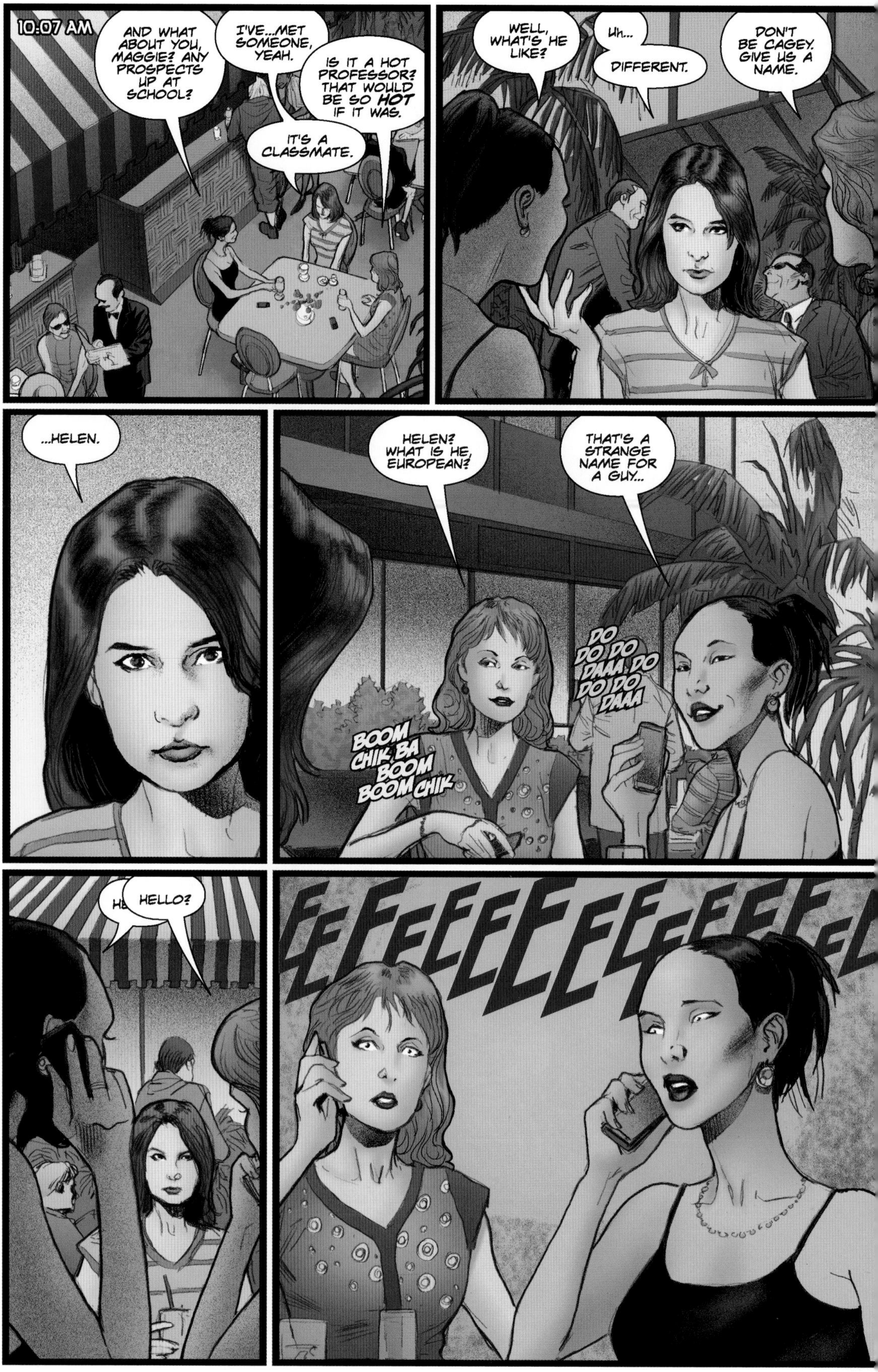
10:07 AM
AND WHAT ABOUT YOU, MAGGIE? ANY PROSPECTS UP AT SCHOOL?
I'VE...MET SOMEONE, YEAH.
IS IT A HOT PROFESSOR? THAT WOULD BE SO **HOT** IF IT WAS.
IT'S A CLASSMATE.
WELL, WHAT'S HE LIKE?
Uh...
DIFFERENT.
DON'T BE CAGEY. GIVE US A NAME.
...HELEN.
HELEN? WHAT IS HE, EUROPEAN?
THAT'S A STRANGE NAME FOR A GUY...
DO DO DO DAAA, DO DO DO DAAA
BOOM CHIK, BA BOOM BOOM CHIK
HELLO?
EEEEEEEEEEEEE

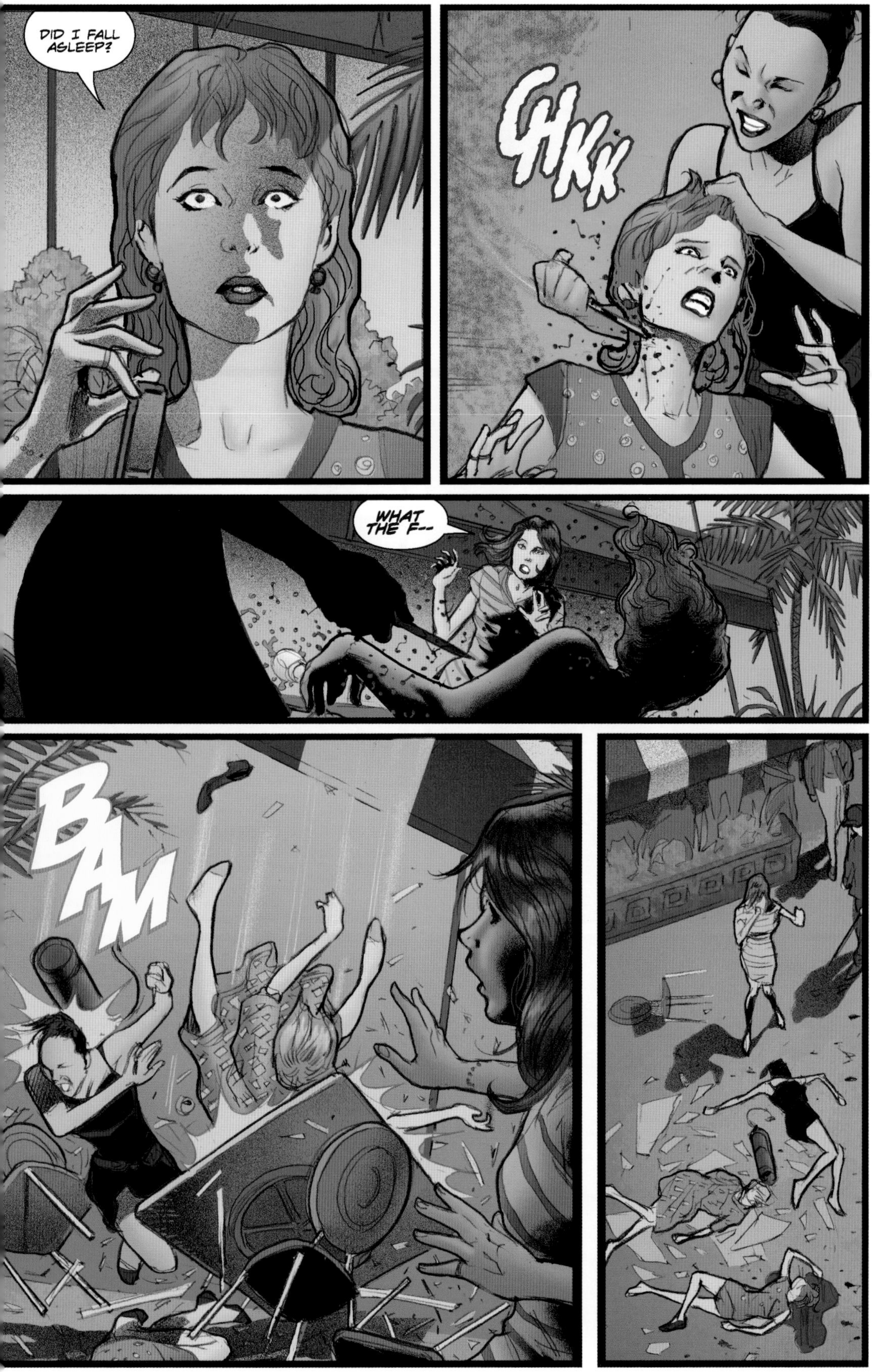
DID I FALL ASLEEP?
CHKK
WHAT THE F--
BAM

COOL?

BASKETBALL'S NOT THE **ONLY** THING THAT CAN MAKE YOU COOL.

HOPE NOT. I ALWAYS GET PICKED LAST. ANDY'S IN MY GRADE AND HE CAN ALREADY DUNK.

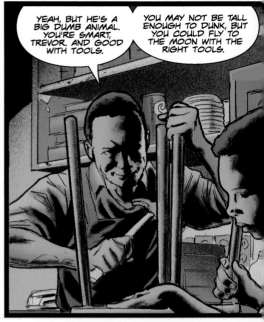

YEAH, BUT HE'S A BIG DUMB ANIMAL. YOU'RE SMART, TREVOR. AND GOOD WITH TOOLS.

YOU MAY NOT BE TALL ENOUGH TO DUNK, BUT YOU COULD FLY TO THE MOON WITH THE RIGHT TOOLS.

IN FACT, YOU CAN'T BE TALLER THAN 6' 3" IF YOU WANT TO BE AN ASTRONAUT.

IS THAT TRUE? LEBRON CAN'T EVEN GO TO SPACE?

NO SIR. THAT SUCKER'S STUCK ON THIS PLANET. BUT YOU, TREVOR? YOU CAN GO ANYWHERE YOU LIKE.

COOL.

AND YOU'RE GOOD WITH THE COMPUTERS. COMPUTERS ARE LIKE THE **ULTIMATE** TOOL.

MY TEACHER SAYS COMPUTERS ARE MAKING US STUPIDER.

BRIING

THAT'S JUST 'CAUSE THEY'RE CHANGING THE WAY WE LIVE. SOME PEOPLE ARE AFRAID OF NEW THINGS, BUT I SAY...

BRIING

YOU GOTTA **EMBRACE** THE NEW OR BE **ERASED** BY THE NEW.

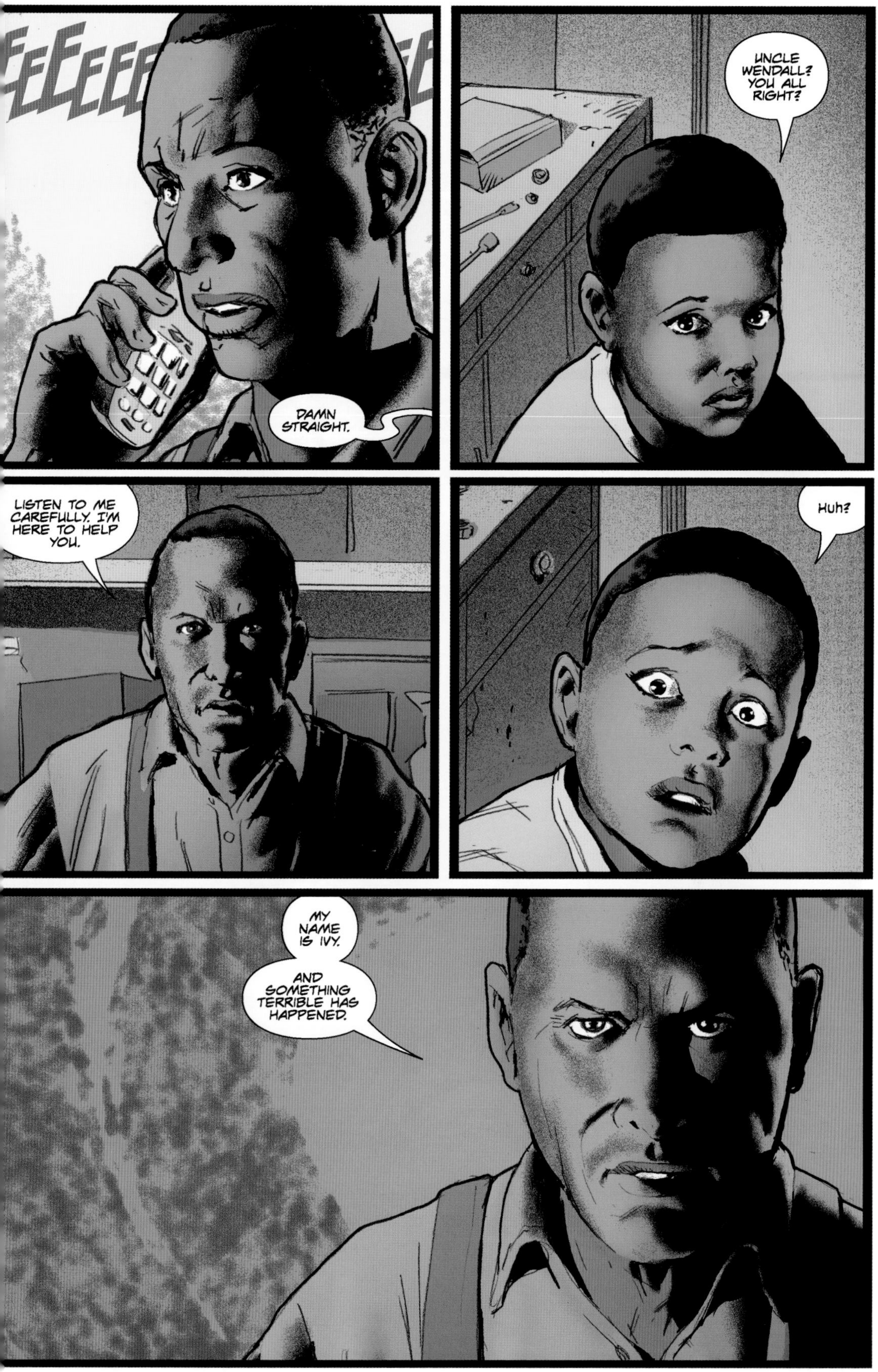
EEEEEE
DAMN STRAIGHT.
UNCLE WENDALL? YOU ALL RIGHT?
LISTEN TO ME CAREFULLY. I'M HERE TO HELP YOU.
Huh?
MY NAME IS IVY.
AND SOMETHING TERRIBLE HAS HAPPENED.

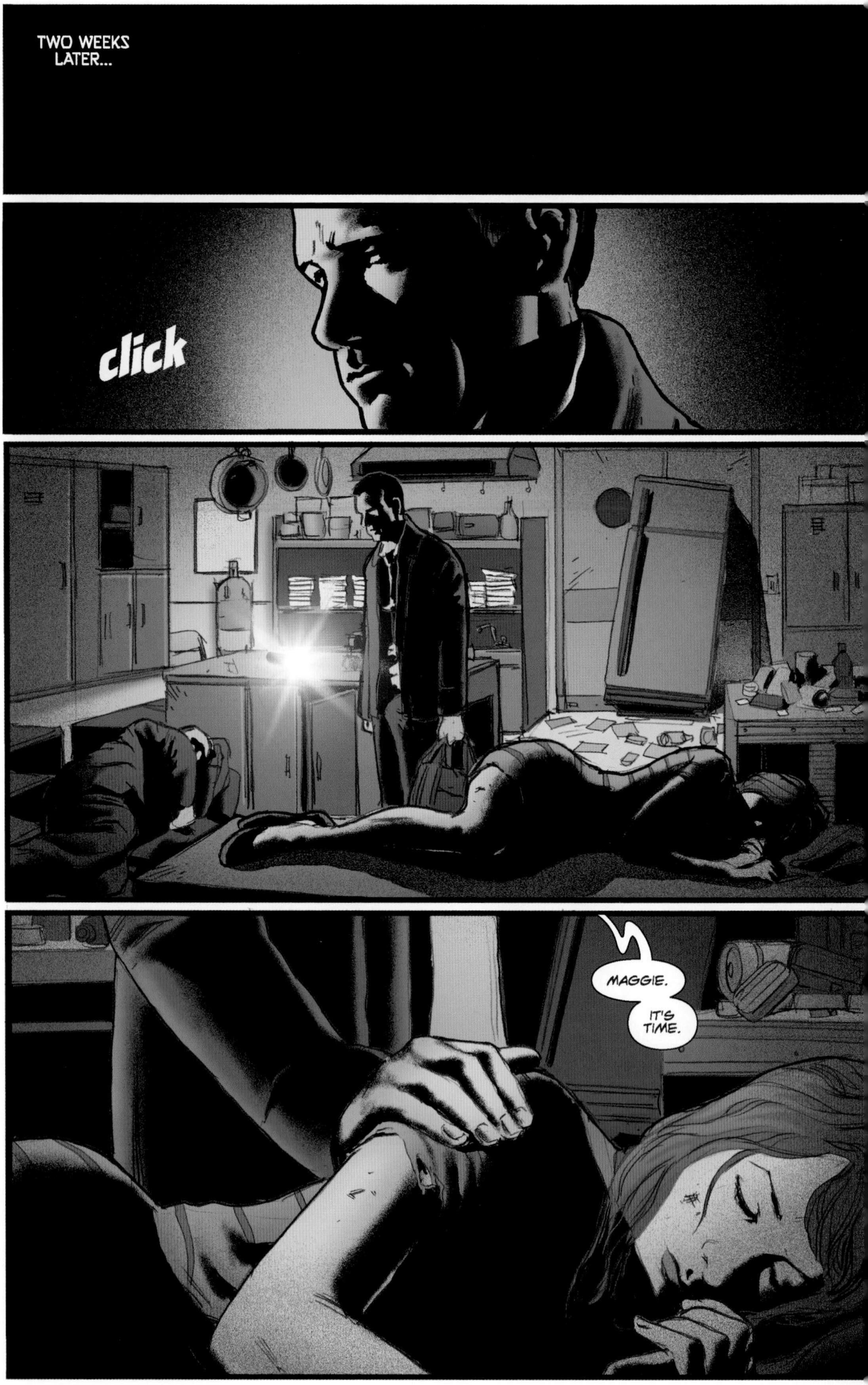
TWO WEEKS LATER...
click
MAGGIE.
IT'S TIME.

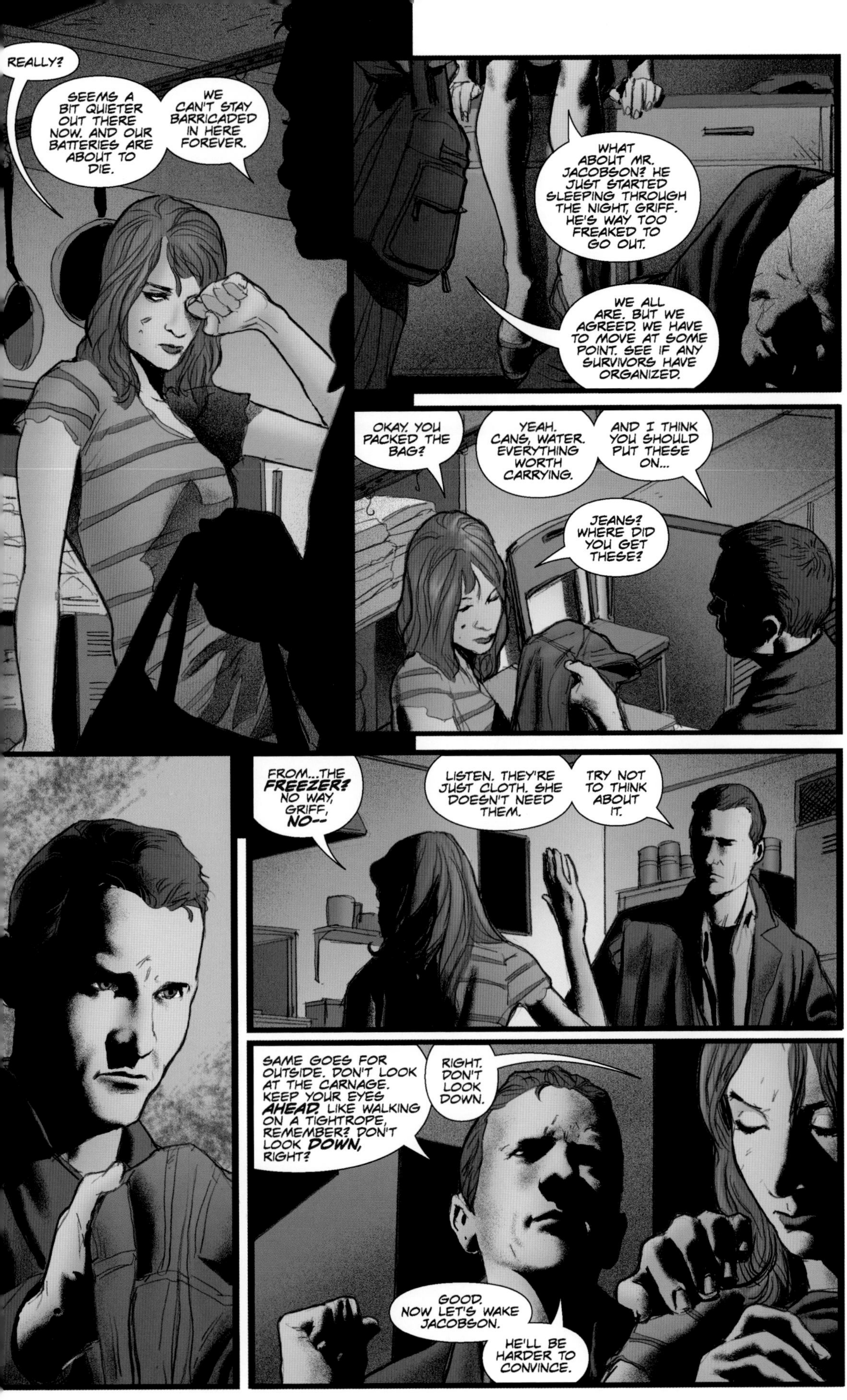

REALLY?
SEEMS A BIT QUIETER OUT THERE NOW. AND OUR BATTERIES ARE ABOUT TO DIE.
WE CAN'T STAY BARRICADED IN HERE FOREVER.
WHAT ABOUT MR. JACOBSON? HE JUST STARTED SLEEPING THROUGH THE NIGHT, GRIFF. HE'S WAY TOO FREAKED TO GO OUT.
WE ALL ARE. BUT WE AGREED. WE HAVE TO MOVE AT SOME POINT. SEE IF ANY SURVIVORS HAVE ORGANIZED.
OKAY. YOU PACKED THE BAG?
YEAH. CANS, WATER. EVERYTHING WORTH CARRYING.
AND I THINK YOU SHOULD PUT THESE ON...
JEANS? WHERE DID YOU GET THESE?
FROM...THE FREEZER? NO WAY, GRIFF, NO--
LISTEN. THEY'RE JUST CLOTH. SHE DOESN'T NEED THEM.
TRY NOT TO THINK ABOUT IT.
SAME GOES FOR OUTSIDE. DON'T LOOK AT THE CARNAGE. KEEP YOUR EYES AHEAD. LIKE WALKING ON A TIGHTROPE, REMEMBER? DON'T LOOK DOWN, RIGHT?
RIGHT. DON'T LOOK DOWN.
GOOD. NOW LET'S WAKE JACOBSON.
HE'LL BE HARDER TO CONVINCE.

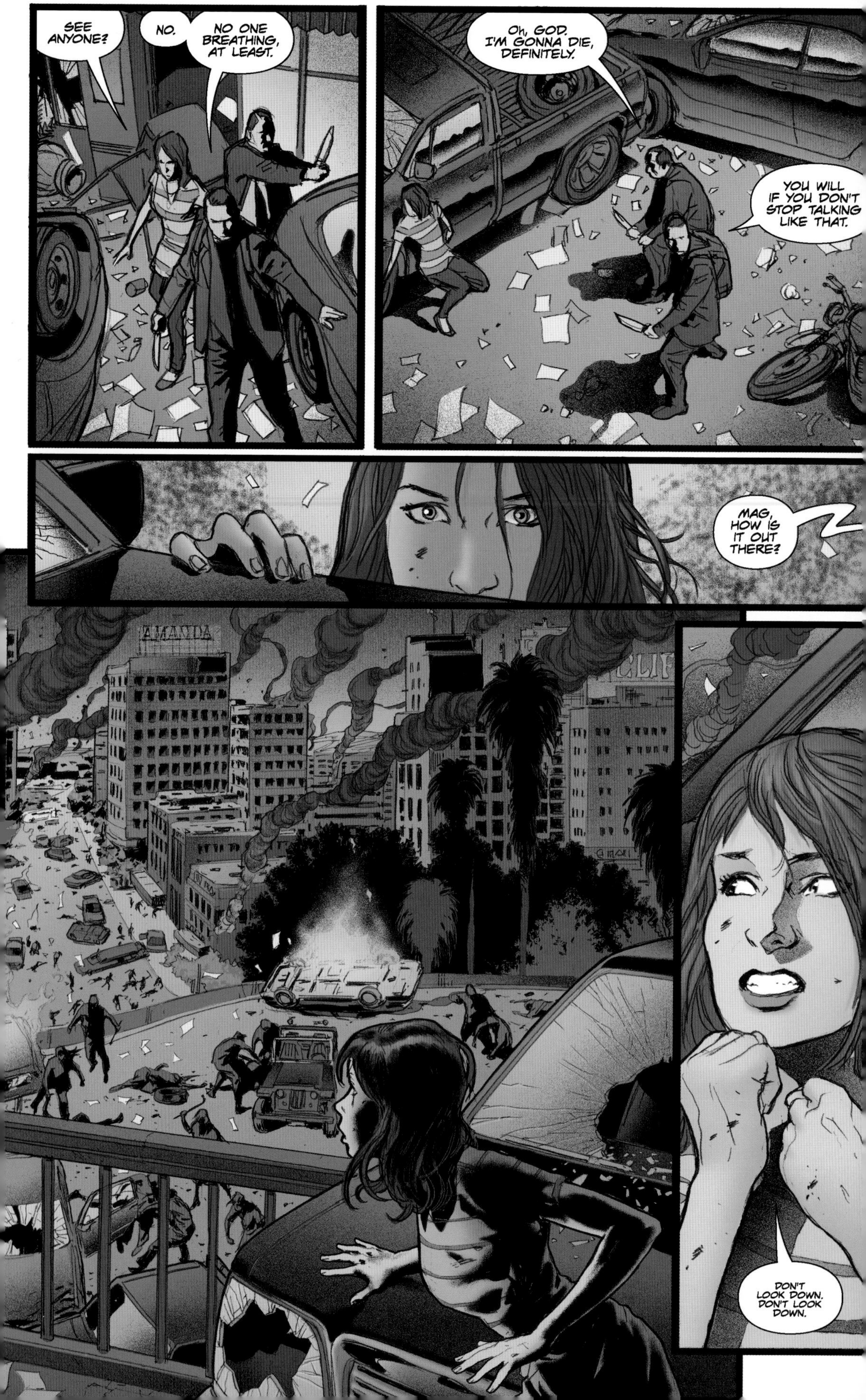

SEE ANYONE?
NO.
NO ONE BREATHING, AT LEAST.
OH, GOD. I'M GONNA DIE, DEFINITELY.
YOU WILL IF YOU DON'T STOP TALKING LIKE THAT.
MAG, HOW IS IT OUT THERE?
AMANDA
DON'T LOOK DOWN. DON'T LOOK DOWN.

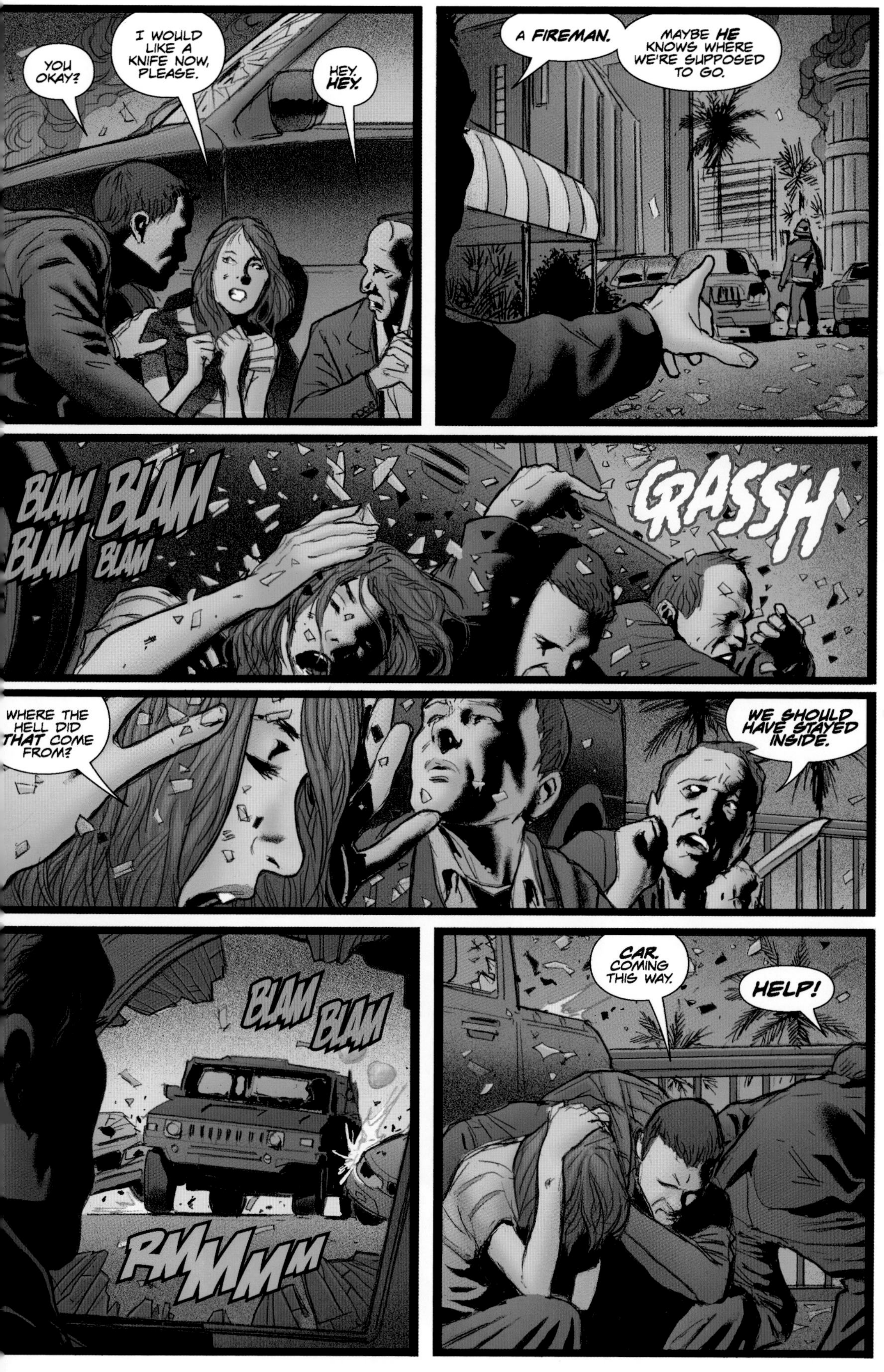

YOU OKAY?
I WOULD LIKE A KNIFE NOW, PLEASE.
HEY. HEY.
A FIREMAN.
MAYBE HE KNOWS WHERE WE'RE SUPPOSED TO GO.
BLAM BLAM BLAM BLAM
GRASSH
WHERE THE HELL DID THAT COME FROM?
WE SHOULD HAVE STAYED INSIDE.
BLAM BLAM
RMMMM
CAR. COMING THIS WAY.
HELP!

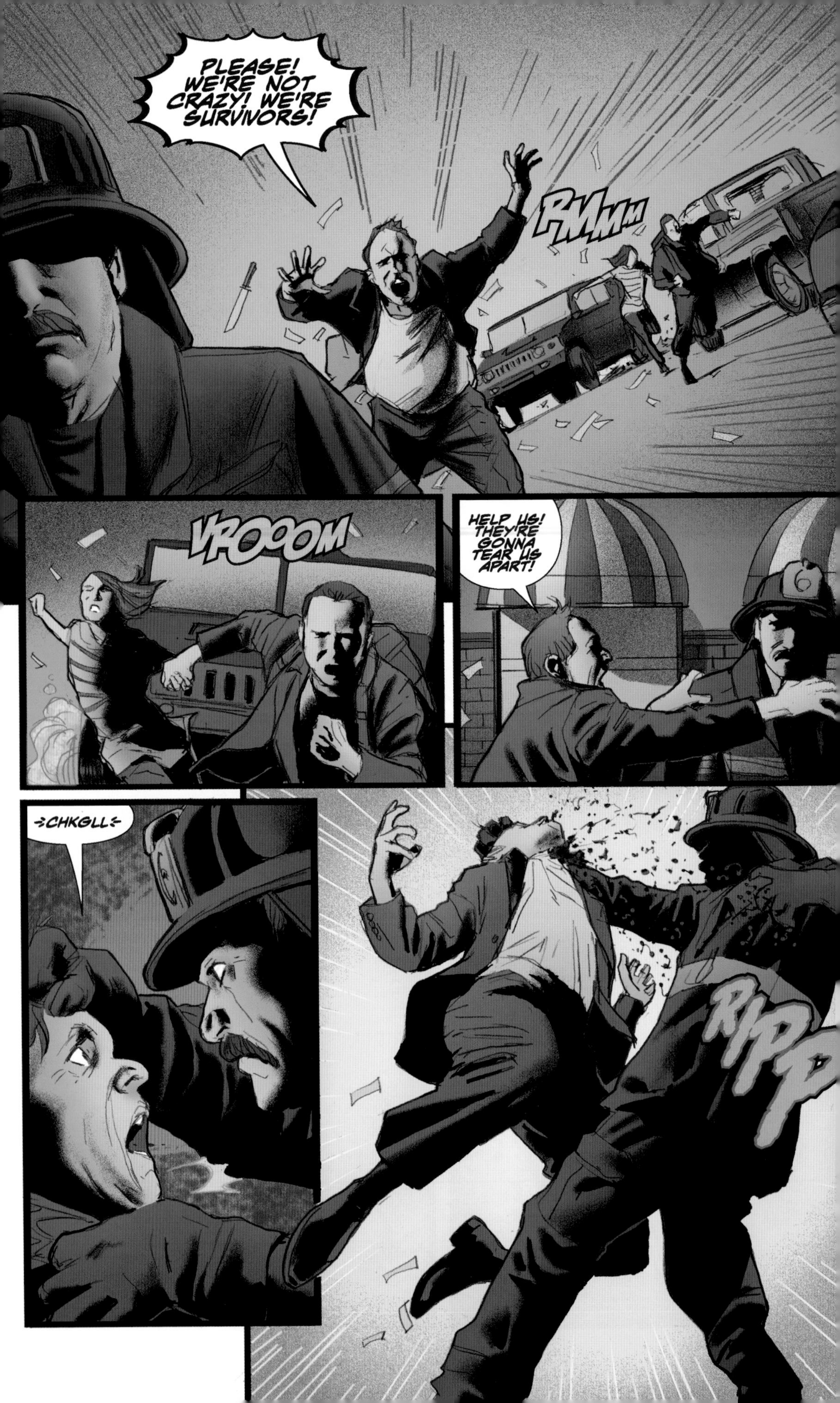
PLEASE! WE'RE NOT CRAZY! WE'RE SURVIVORS!
RMMM
VROOOM
HELP US! THEY'RE GONNA TEAR US APART!
CHKGLL
RIPP

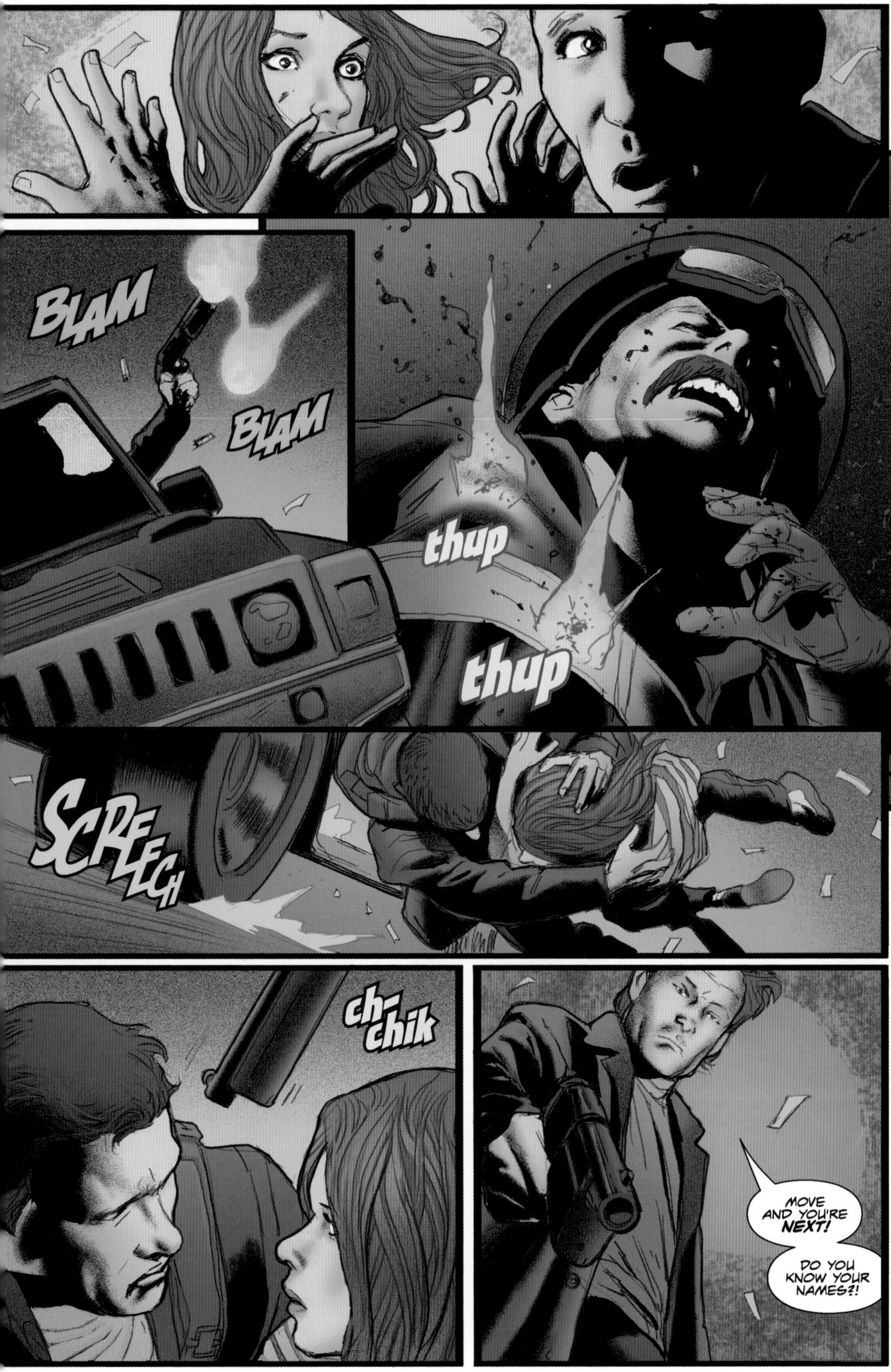
BLAM
BLAM
thup
thup
SCREECH
ch-chik
MOVE AND YOU'RE NEXT!
DO YOU KNOW YOUR NAMES?!

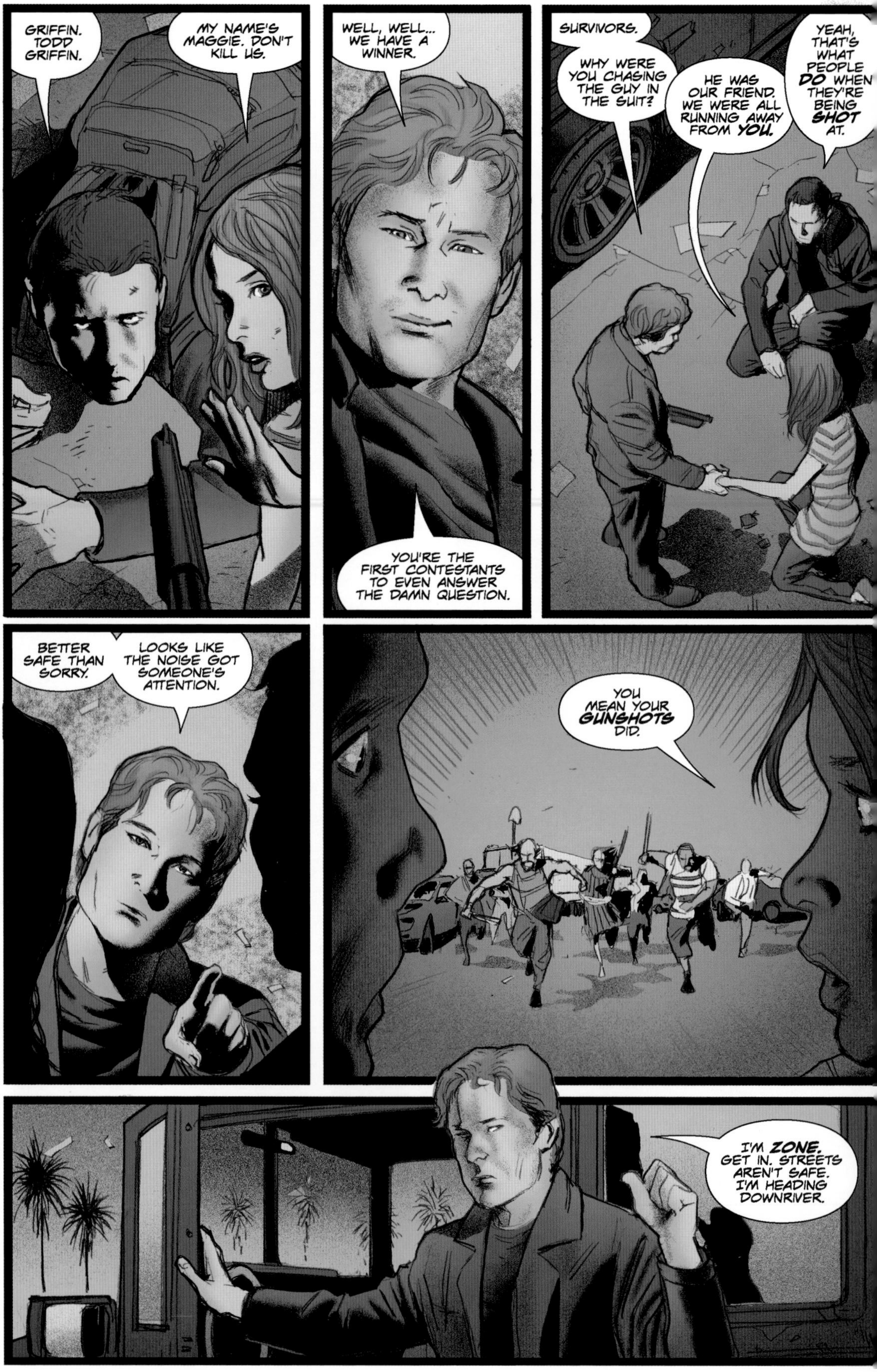
GRIFFIN. TODD GRIFFIN.
MY NAME'S MAGGIE. DON'T KILL US.
WELL, WELL... WE HAVE A WINNER.
YOU'RE THE FIRST CONTESTANTS TO EVEN ANSWER THE DAMN QUESTION.
SURVIVORS.
WHY WERE YOU CHASING THE GUY IN THE SUIT?
HE WAS OUR FRIEND. WE WERE ALL RUNNING AWAY FROM YOU.
YEAH, THAT'S WHAT PEOPLE DO WHEN THEY'RE BEING SHOT AT.
BETTER SAFE THAN SORRY.
LOOKS LIKE THE NOISE GOT SOMEONE'S ATTENTION.
YOU MEAN YOUR GUNSHOTS DID.
I'M ZONE. GET IN. STREETS AREN'T SAFE. I'M HEADING DOWNRIVER.

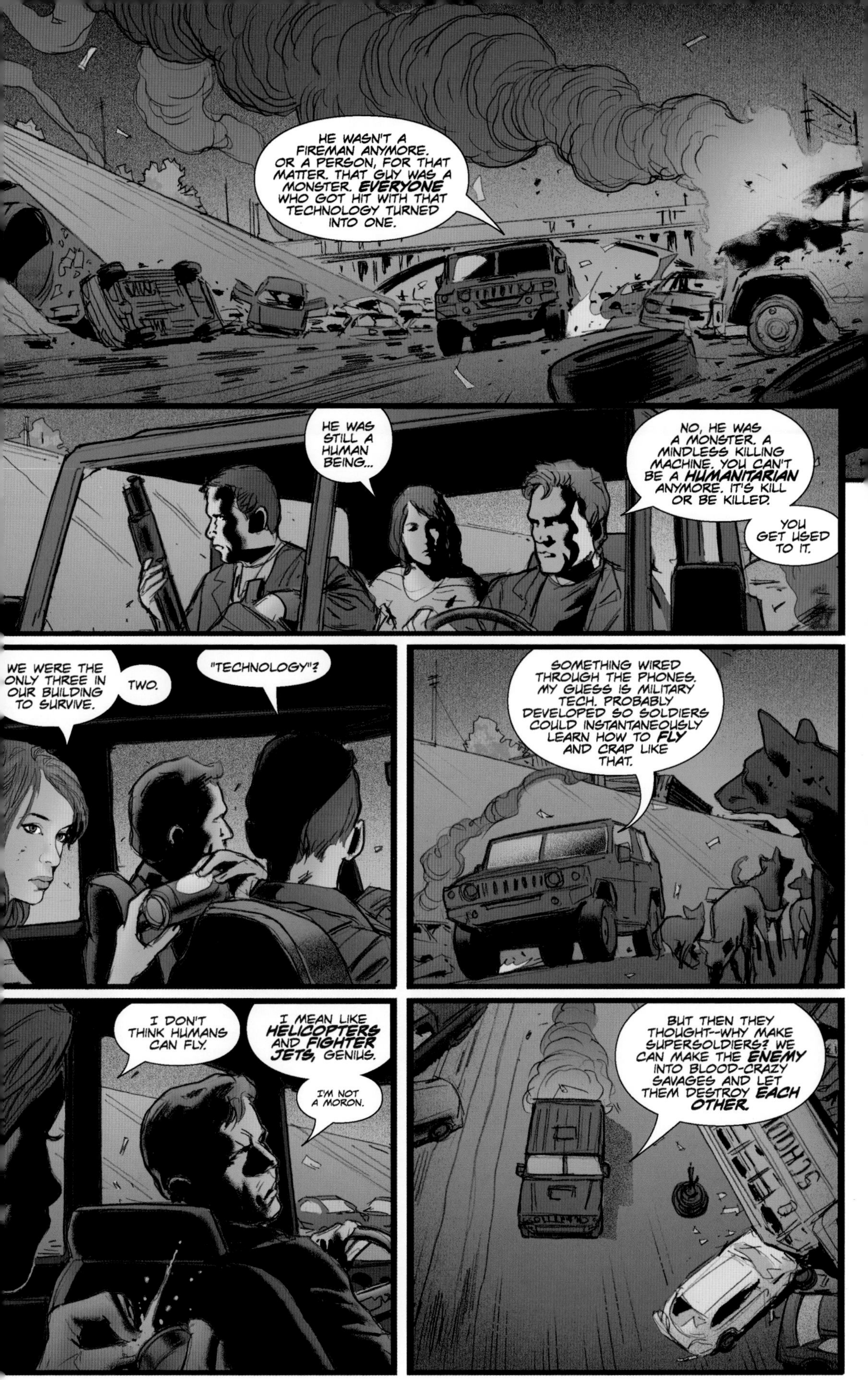
HE WASN'T A FIREMAN ANYMORE. OR A PERSON, FOR THAT MATTER. THAT GUY WAS A MONSTER. EVERYONE WHO GOT HIT WITH THAT TECHNOLOGY TURNED INTO ONE.
HE WAS STILL A HUMAN BEING...
NO, HE WAS A MONSTER. A MINDLESS KILLING MACHINE. YOU CAN'T BE A HUMANITARIAN ANYMORE. IT'S KILL OR BE KILLED.
YOU GET USED TO IT.
WE WERE THE ONLY THREE IN OUR BUILDING TO SURVIVE.
TWO.
"TECHNOLOGY"?
SOMETHING WIRED THROUGH THE PHONES. MY GUESS IS MILITARY TECH. PROBABLY DEVELOPED SO SOLDIERS COULD INSTANTANEOUSLY LEARN HOW TO FLY AND CRAP LIKE THAT.
I DON'T THINK HUMANS CAN FLY.
I MEAN LIKE HELICOPTERS AND FIGHTER JETS, GENIUS.
I'M NOT A MORON.
BUT THEN THEY THOUGHT--WHY MAKE SUPERSOLDIERS? WE CAN MAKE THE ENEMY INTO BLOOD-CRAZY SAVAGES AND LET THEM DESTROY EACH OTHER.

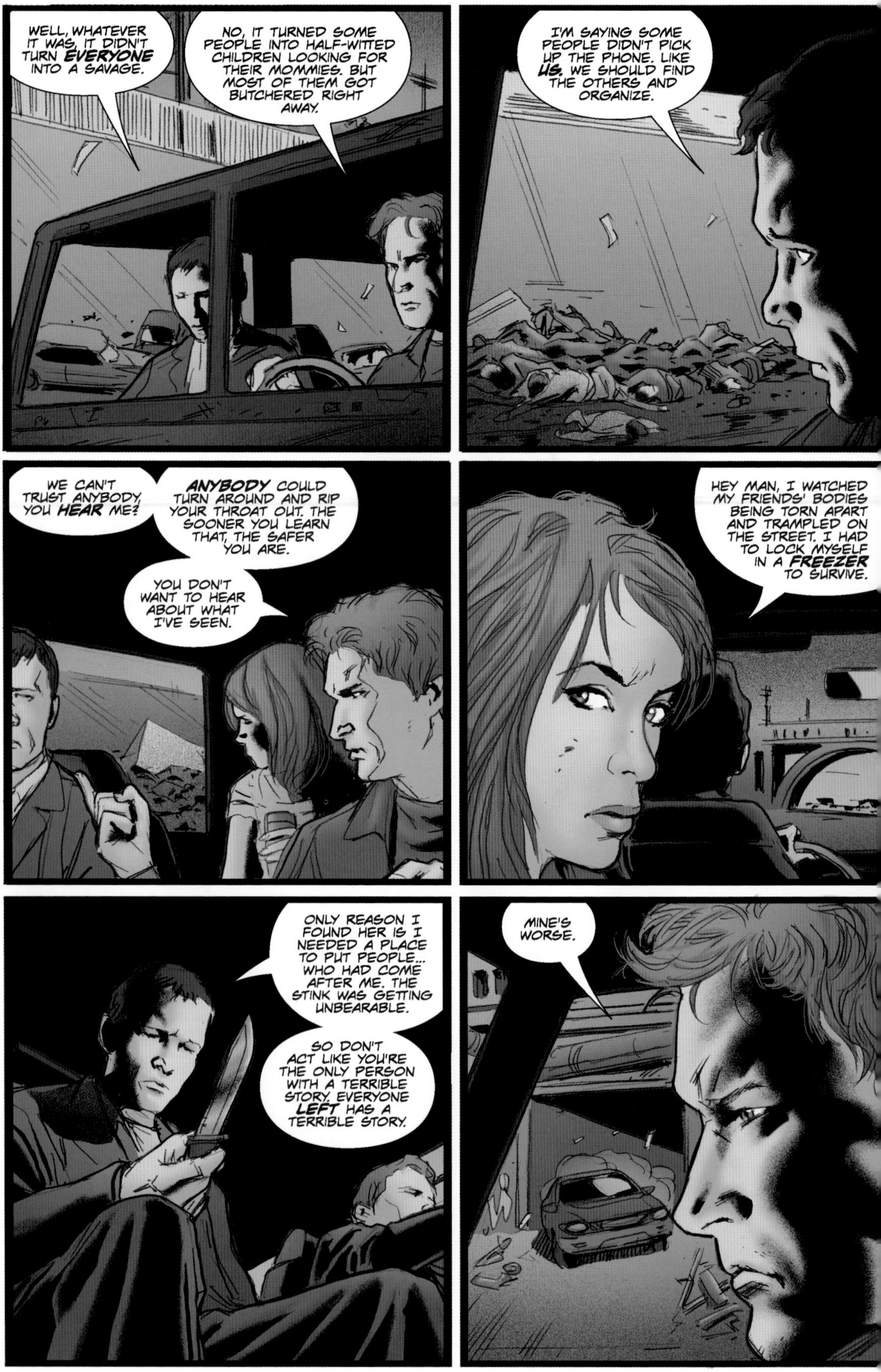
WELL, WHATEVER IT WAS, IT DIDN'T TURN EVERYONE INTO A SAVAGE.
NO, IT TURNED SOME PEOPLE INTO HALF-WITTED CHILDREN LOOKING FOR THEIR MOMMIES. BUT MOST OF THEM GOT BUTCHERED RIGHT AWAY.
I'M SAYING SOME PEOPLE DIDN'T PICK UP THE PHONE. LIKE US. WE SHOULD FIND THE OTHERS AND ORGANIZE.
WE CAN'T TRUST ANYBODY, YOU HEAR ME?
ANYBODY COULD TURN AROUND AND RIP YOUR THROAT OUT. THE SOONER YOU LEARN THAT, THE SAFER YOU ARE.
YOU DON'T WANT TO HEAR ABOUT WHAT I'VE SEEN.
HEY MAN, I WATCHED MY FRIENDS' BODIES BEING TORN APART AND TRAMPLED ON THE STREET. I HAD TO LOCK MYSELF IN A FREEZER TO SURVIVE.
ONLY REASON I FOUND HER IS I NEEDED A PLACE TO PUT PEOPLE... WHO HAD COME AFTER ME. THE STINK WAS GETTING UNBEARABLE.
SO DON'T ACT LIKE YOU'RE THE ONLY PERSON WITH A TERRIBLE STORY. EVERYONE LEFT HAS A TERRIBLE STORY.
MINE'S WORSE.

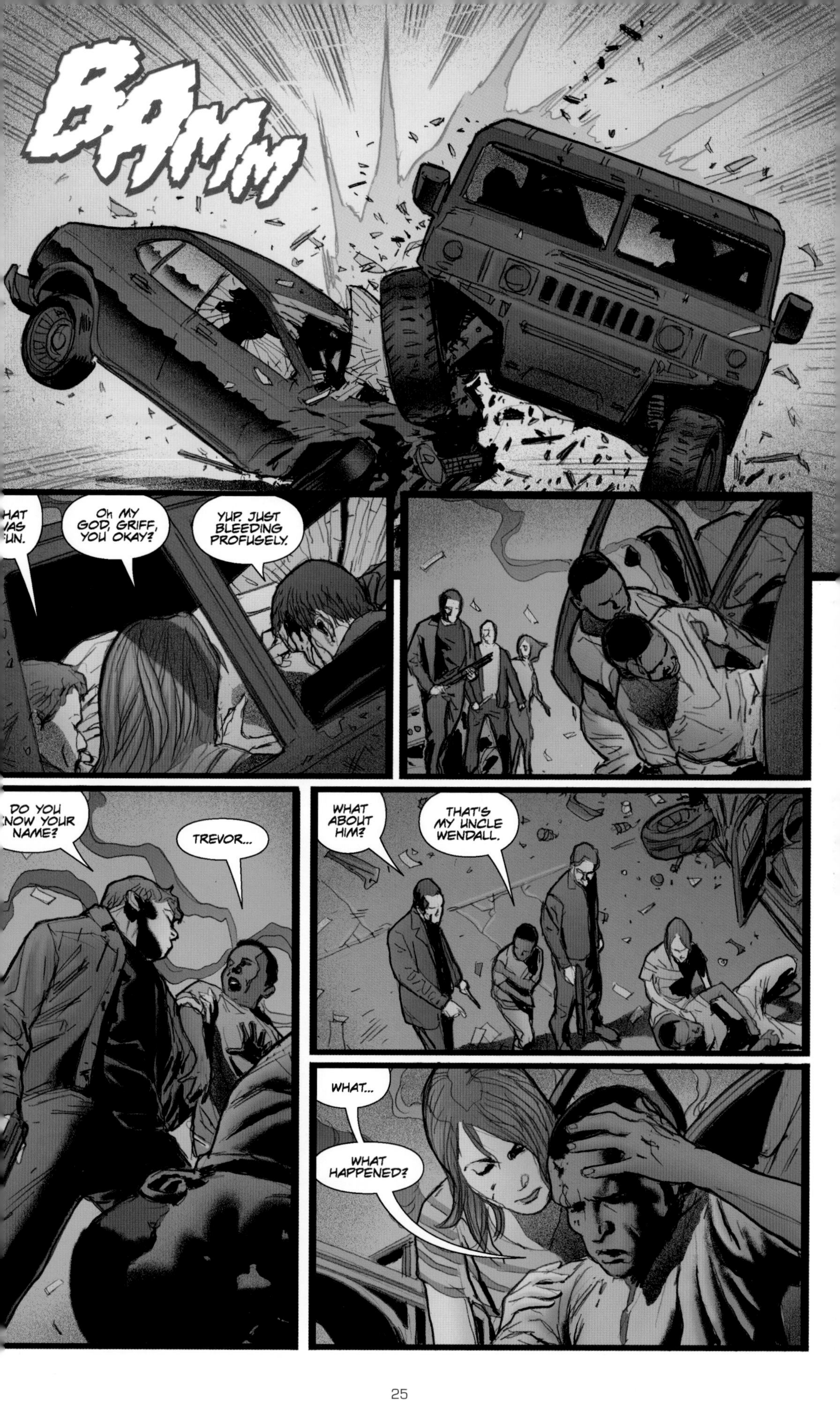
BAMM
HAT
VAS
FUN.
Oh MY GOD, GRIFF, YOU OKAY?
YUP. JUST BLEEDING PROFUSELY.
DO YOU
NOW YOUR NAME?
TREVOR...
WHAT ABOUT HIM?
THAT'S MY UNCLE WENDALL.
WHAT...
WHAT HAPPENED?

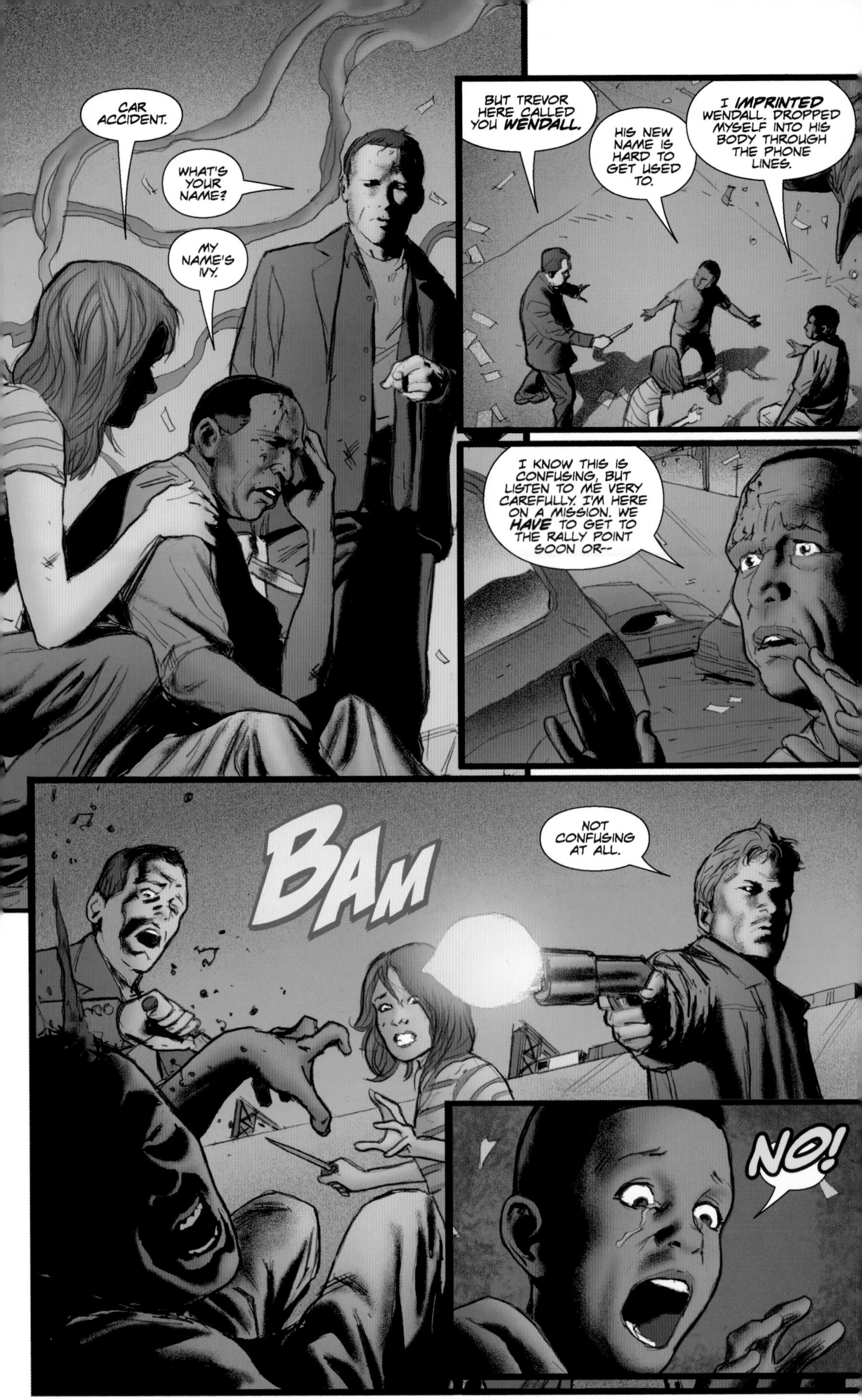
CAR ACCIDENT.
WHAT'S YOUR NAME?
MY NAME'S IVY.
BUT TREVOR HERE CALLED YOU WENDALL.
HIS NEW NAME IS HARD TO GET USED TO.
I IMPRINTED WENDALL. DROPPED MYSELF INTO HIS BODY THROUGH THE PHONE LINES.
I KNOW THIS IS CONFUSING, BUT LISTEN TO ME VERY CAREFULLY. I'M HERE ON A MISSION. WE HAVE TO GET TO THE RALLY POINT SOON OR--
BAM
NOT CONFUSING AT ALL.
NO!

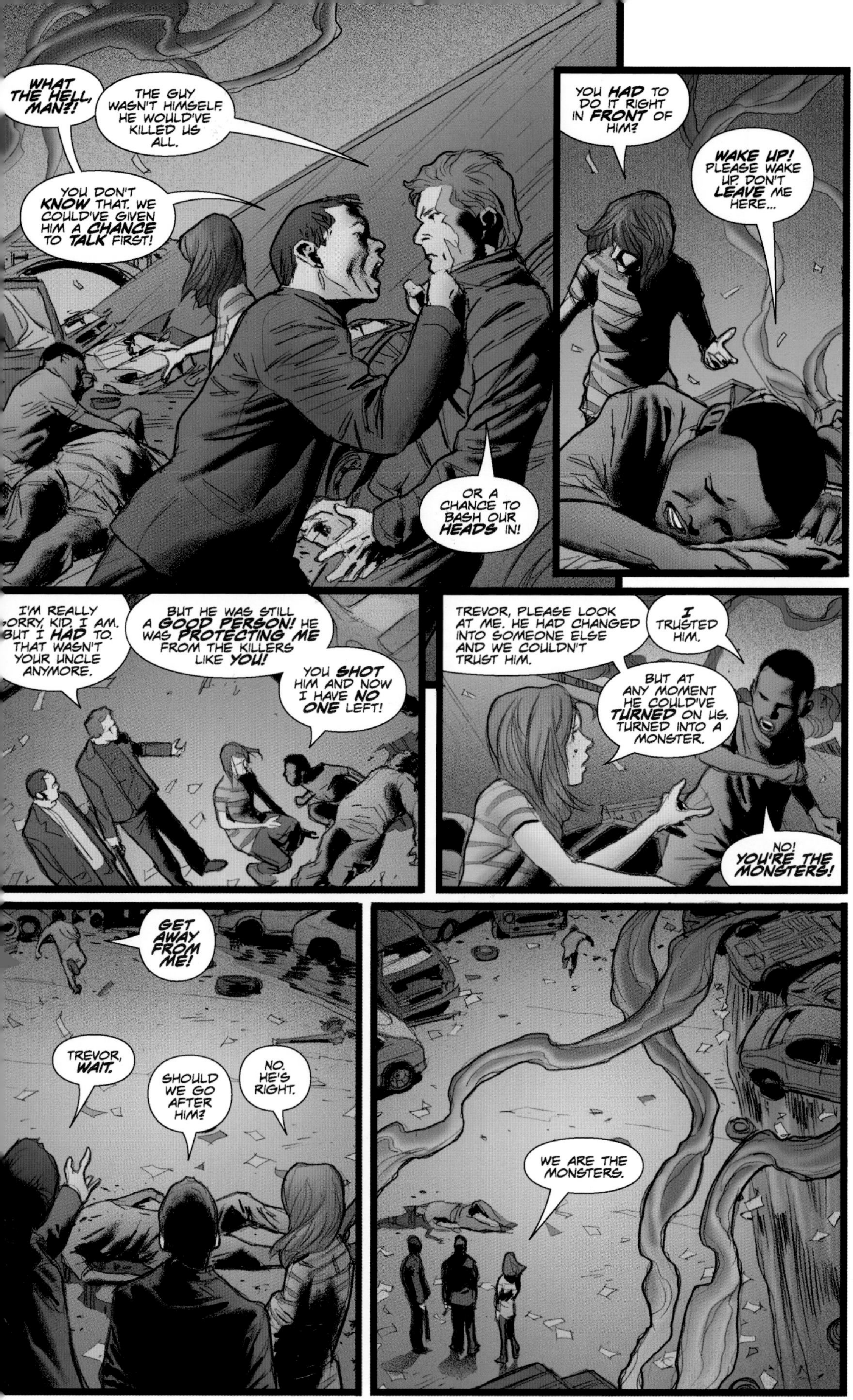

WHAT THE HELL, MAN?!
THE GUY WASN'T HIMSELF. HE WOULD'VE KILLED US ALL.
YOU DON'T KNOW THAT. WE COULD'VE GIVEN HIM A CHANCE TO TALK FIRST!
OR A CHANCE TO BASH OUR HEADS IN!
YOU HAD TO DO IT RIGHT IN FRONT OF HIM?
WAKE UP! PLEASE WAKE UP. DON'T LEAVE ME HERE...
I'M REALLY SORRY, KID. I AM. BUT I HAD TO. THAT WASN'T YOUR UNCLE ANYMORE.
BUT HE WAS STILL A GOOD PERSON! HE WAS PROTECTING ME FROM THE KILLERS LIKE YOU!
YOU SHOT HIM AND NOW I HAVE NO ONE LEFT!
TREVOR, PLEASE LOOK AT ME. HE HAD CHANGED INTO SOMEONE ELSE AND WE COULDN'T TRUST HIM.
I TRUSTED HIM.
BUT AT ANY MOMENT HE COULD'VE TURNED ON US. TURNED INTO A MONSTER.
NO! YOU'RE THE MONSTERS!
GET AWAY FROM ME!
TREVOR, WAIT.
SHOULD WE GO AFTER HIM?
NO. HE'S RIGHT.
WE ARE THE MONSTERS.

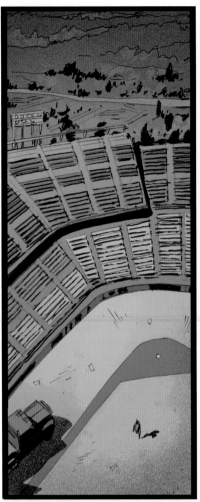

I GOT HERE, JUST LIKE YOU SAID TO, UNCLE WENDALL. NOW WHAT?

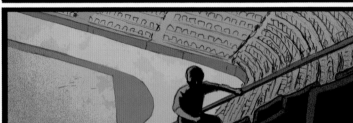

ARE YOU IVY?

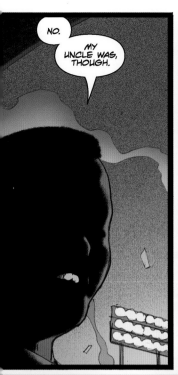

NO.

MY UNCLE WAS, THOUGH.

HE SAID WE WERE SUPPOSED TO COME HERE TO MEET YOU, BUT HE WAS...KILLED.

OR, *SHE* WAS KILLED. I GUESS.

DON'T WORRY. THERE WILL BE OTHERS.

I'M SORRY ABOUT YOUR UNCLE.

HE SAID YOU WANTED TO BUILD AN *ARMY* OR SOMETHING?

AN ARMY WOULD BE NICE. I HAVE A FEELING THIS WILL BE MORE LIKE AN ASSAULT UNIT. SPECIAL FORCES.

COOL.

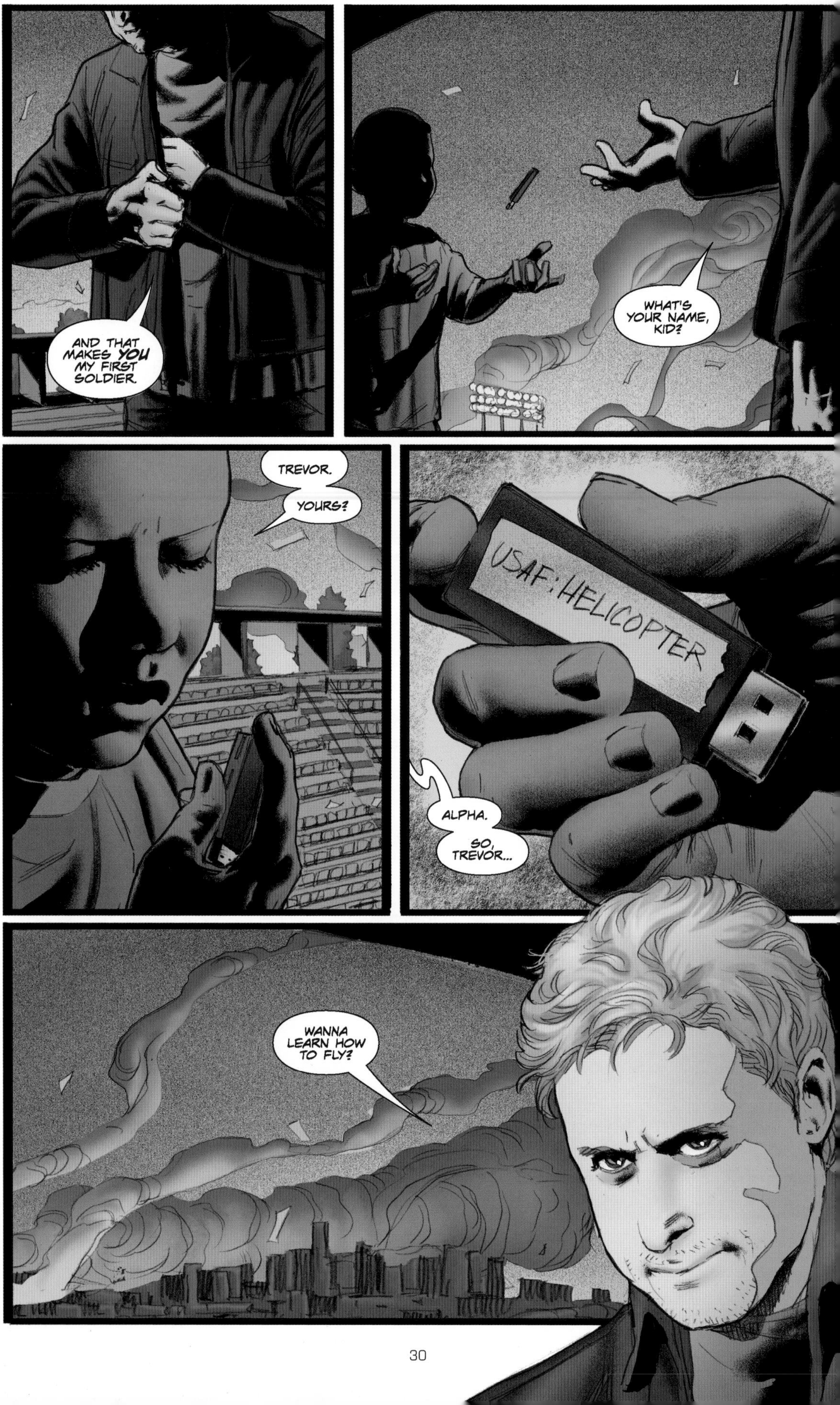
AND THAT MAKES YOU MY FIRST SOLDIER.
WHAT'S YOUR NAME, KID?
TREVOR.
YOURS?
USAF: HELICOPTER
ALPHA.
SO, TREVOR...
WANNA LEARN HOW TO FLY?

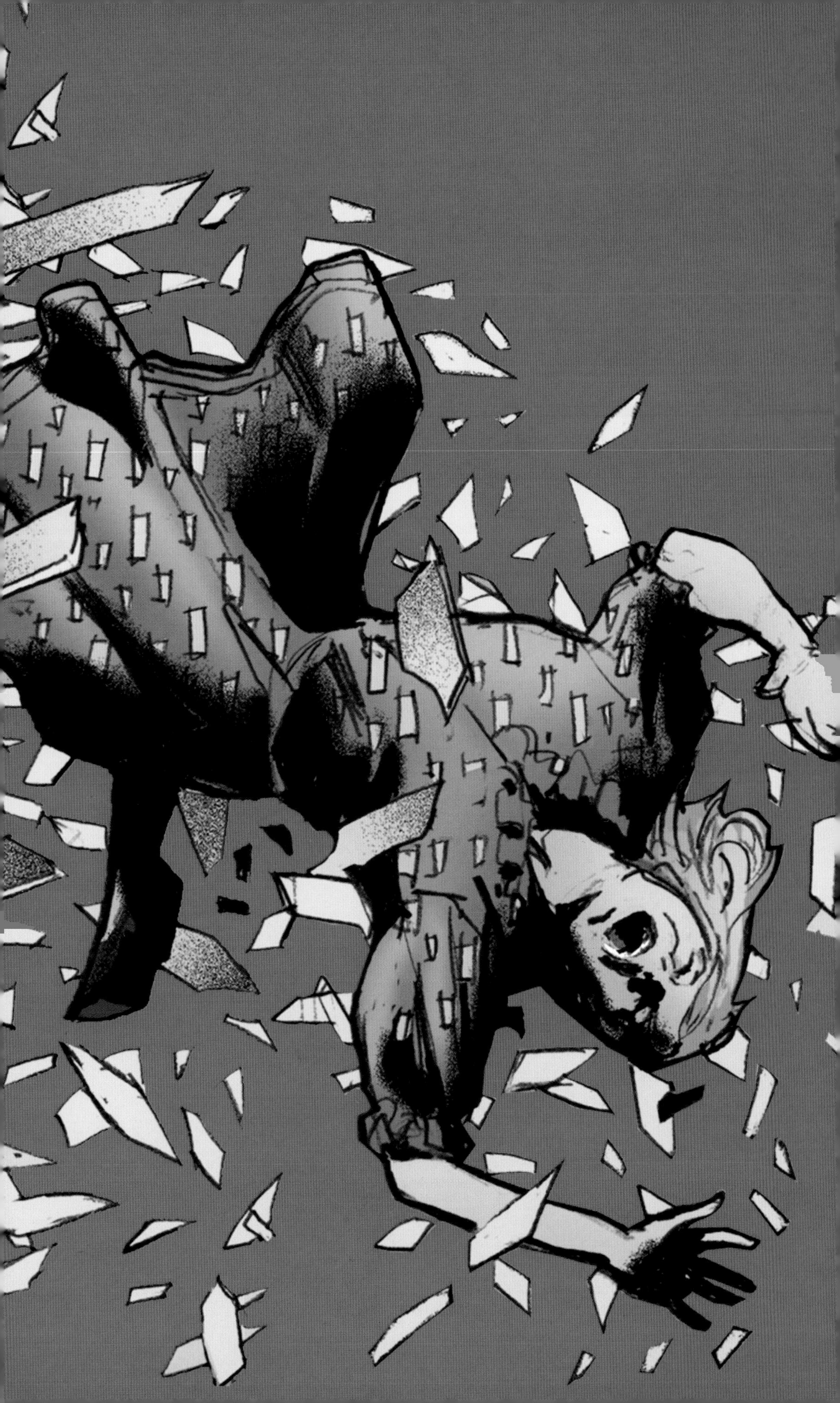

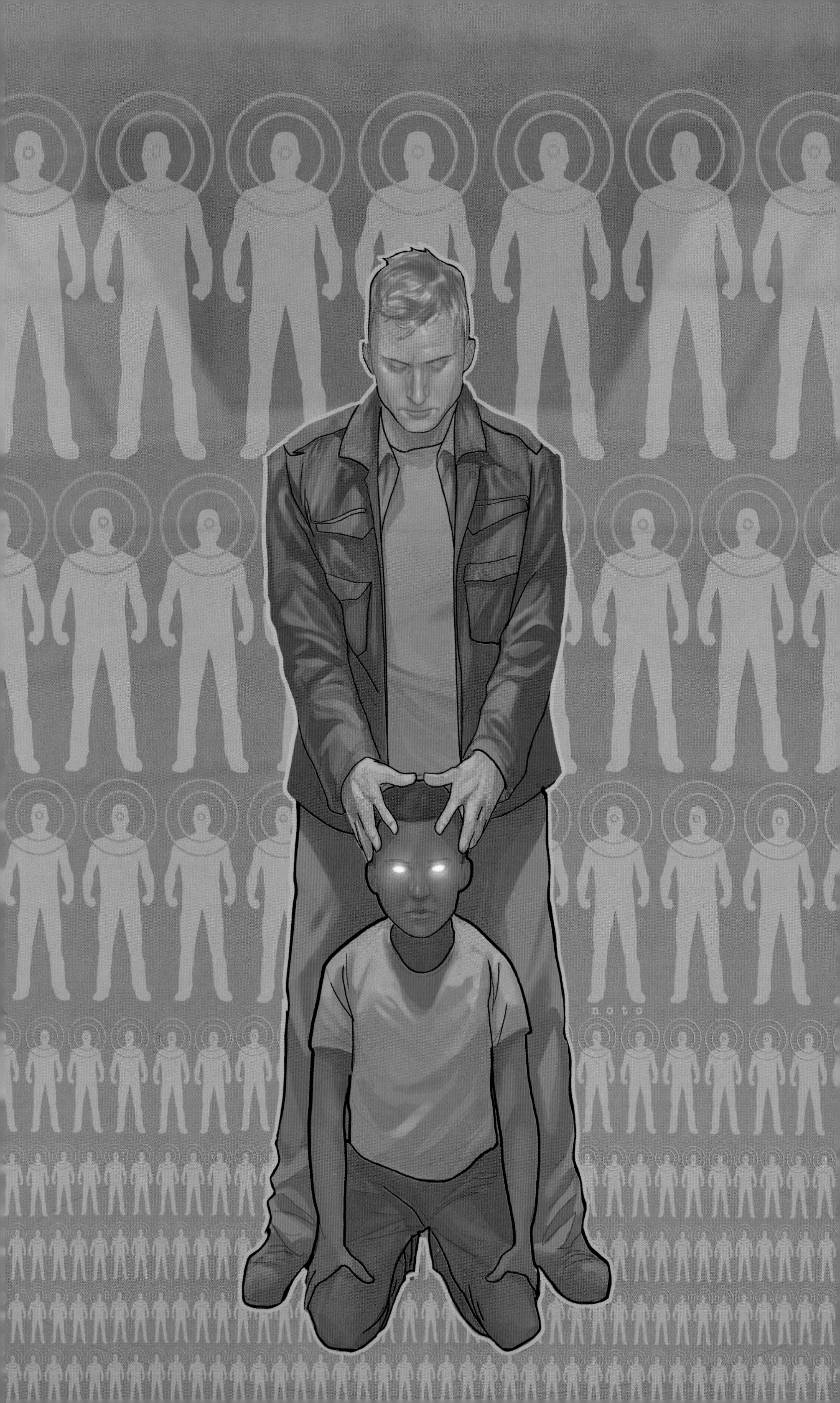
noto

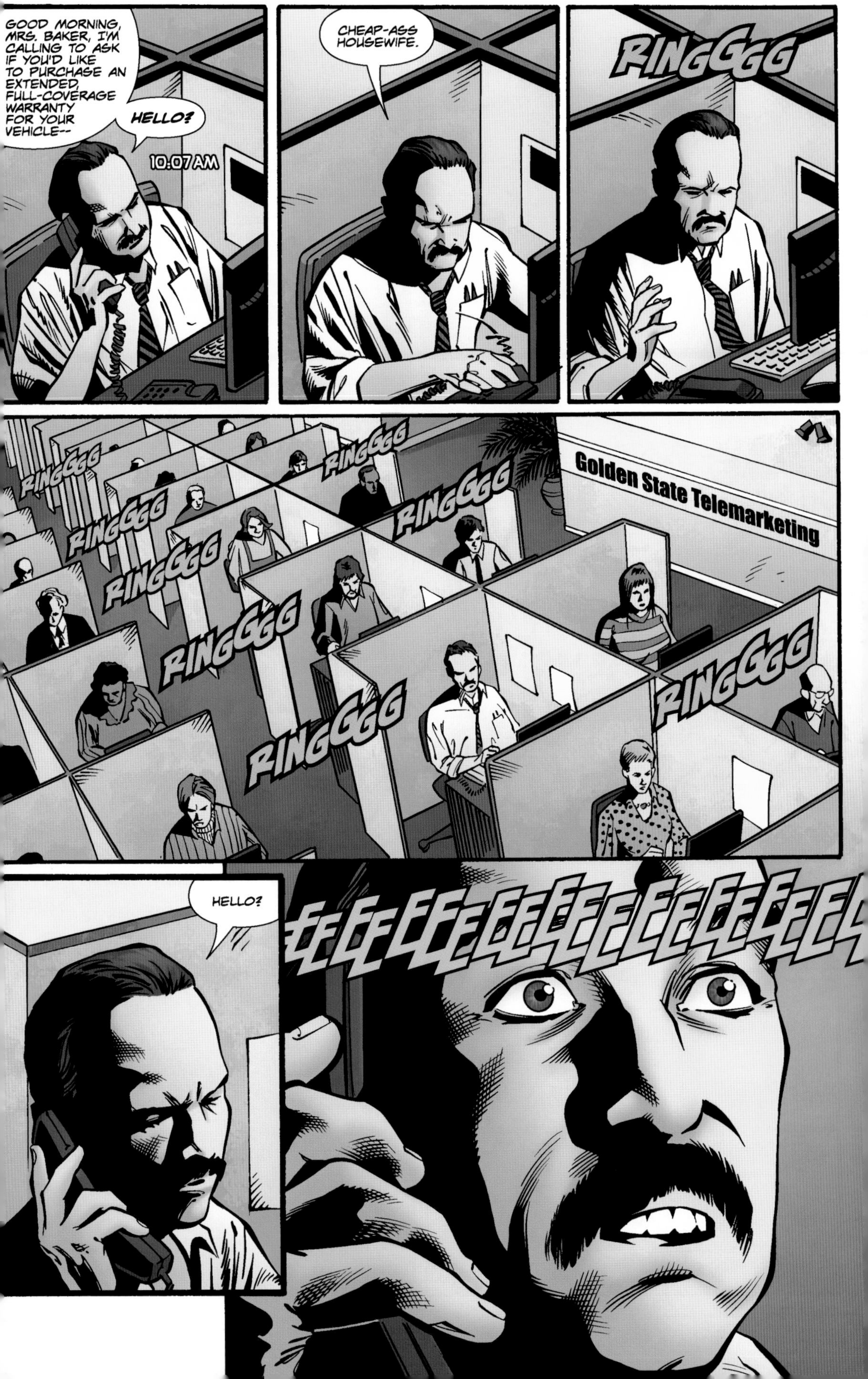
GOOD MORNING, MRS. BAKER, I'M CALLING TO ASK IF YOU'D LIKE TO PURCHASE AN EXTENDED, FULL-COVERAGE WARRANTY FOR YOUR VEHICLE--
HELLO?
10:07AM
CHEAP-ASS HOUSEWIFE.
RINGGGG
RINGGGG
RINGGGG
RINGGGG
RINGGGG
RINGGGG
RINGGGG
RINGGGG
RINGGGG
Golden State Telemarketing
HELLO?
EEEEEEEEEEEEEEEEEEEE

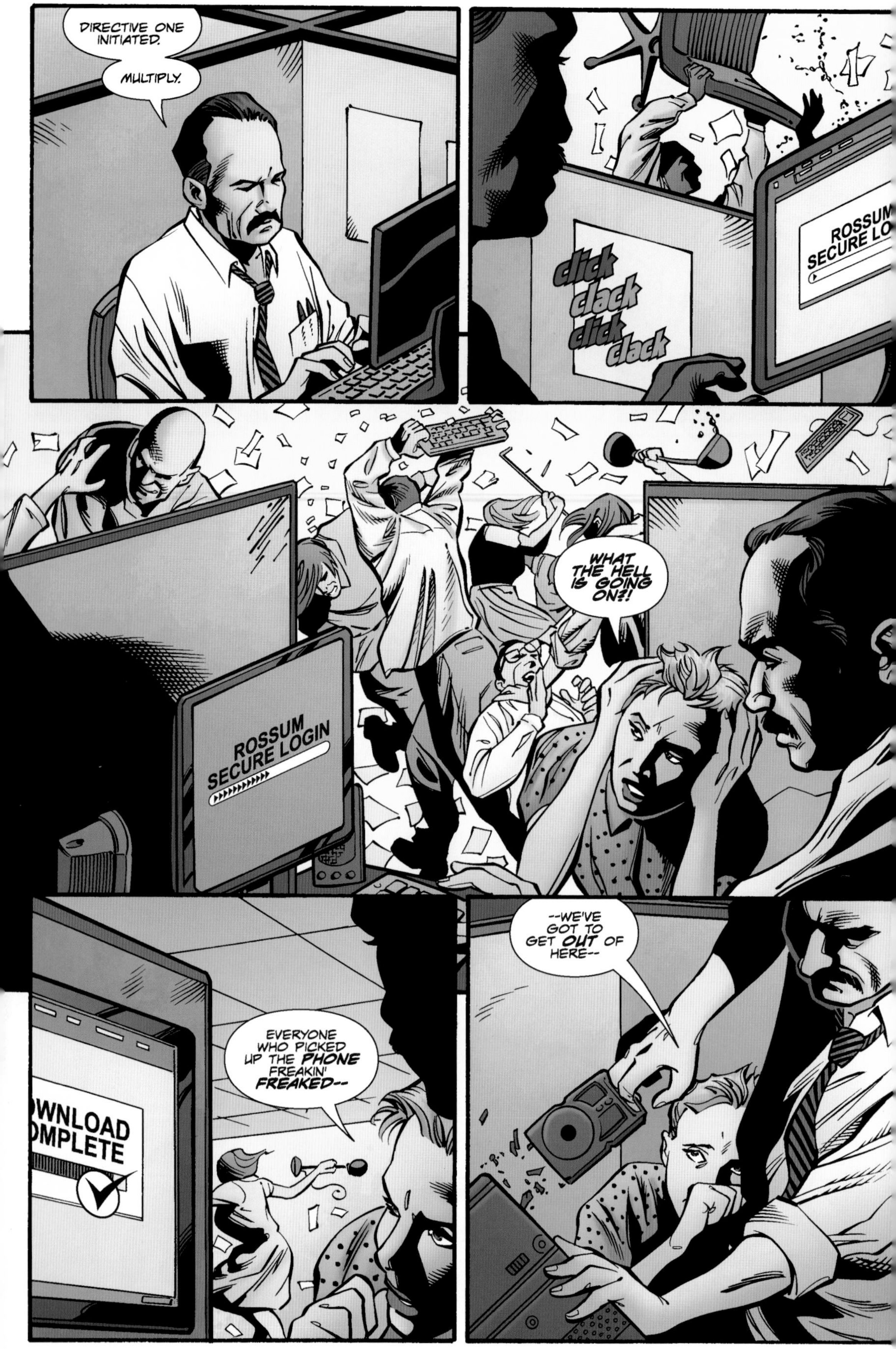

DIRECTIVE ONE INITIATED.
MULTIPLY.
ROSSUM SECURE LO
click clack click clack
WHAT THE HELL IS GOING ON?!
ROSSUM SECURE LOGIN
EVERYONE WHO PICKED UP THE PHONE FREAKIN' FREAKED--
WNLOAD MPLETE
--WE'VE GOT TO GET OUT OF HERE--

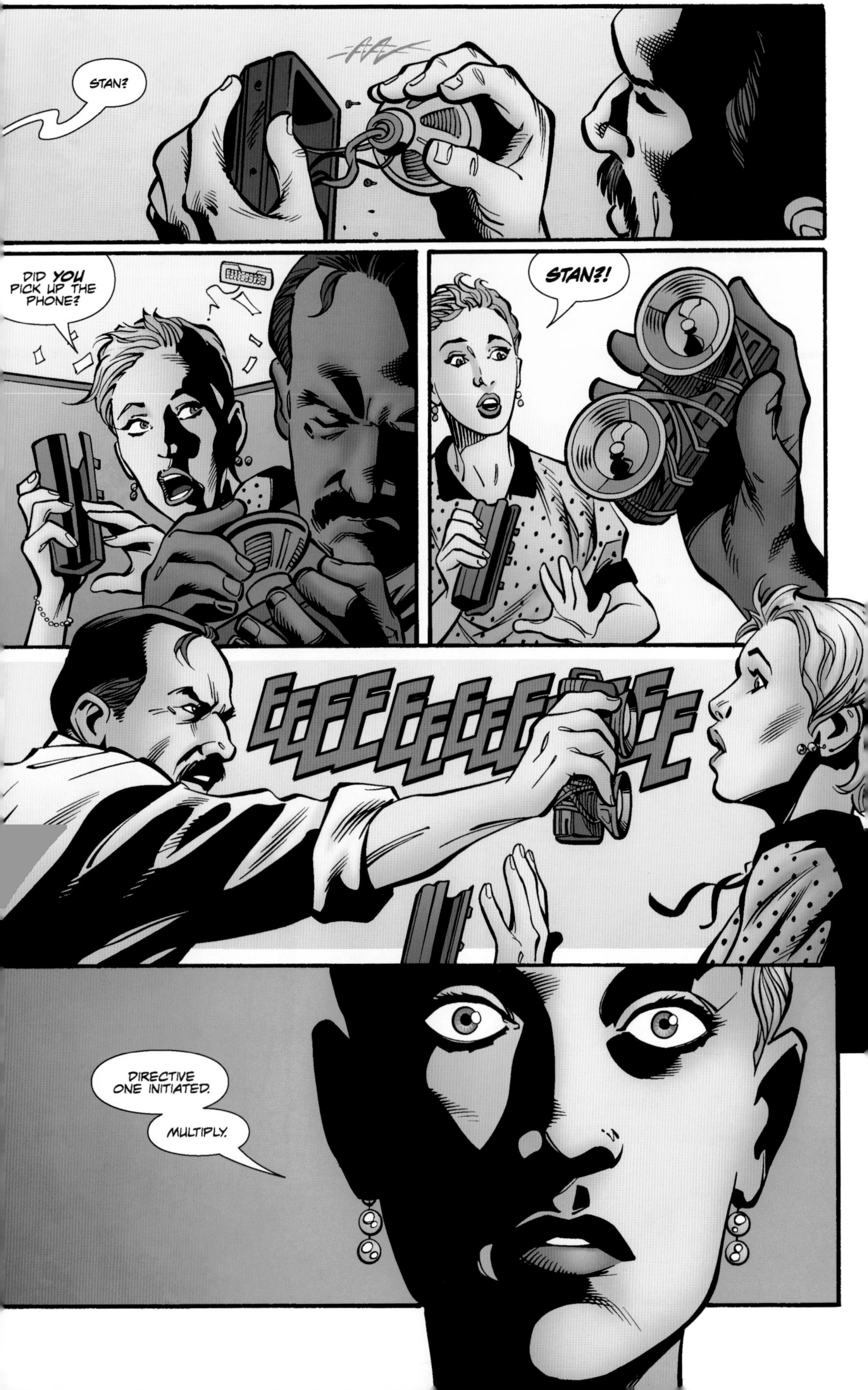
STAN?
DID YOU PICK UP THE PHONE?
STAN?!
EEEEEEEEEEEE
DIRECTIVE ONE INITIATED.
MULTIPLY.

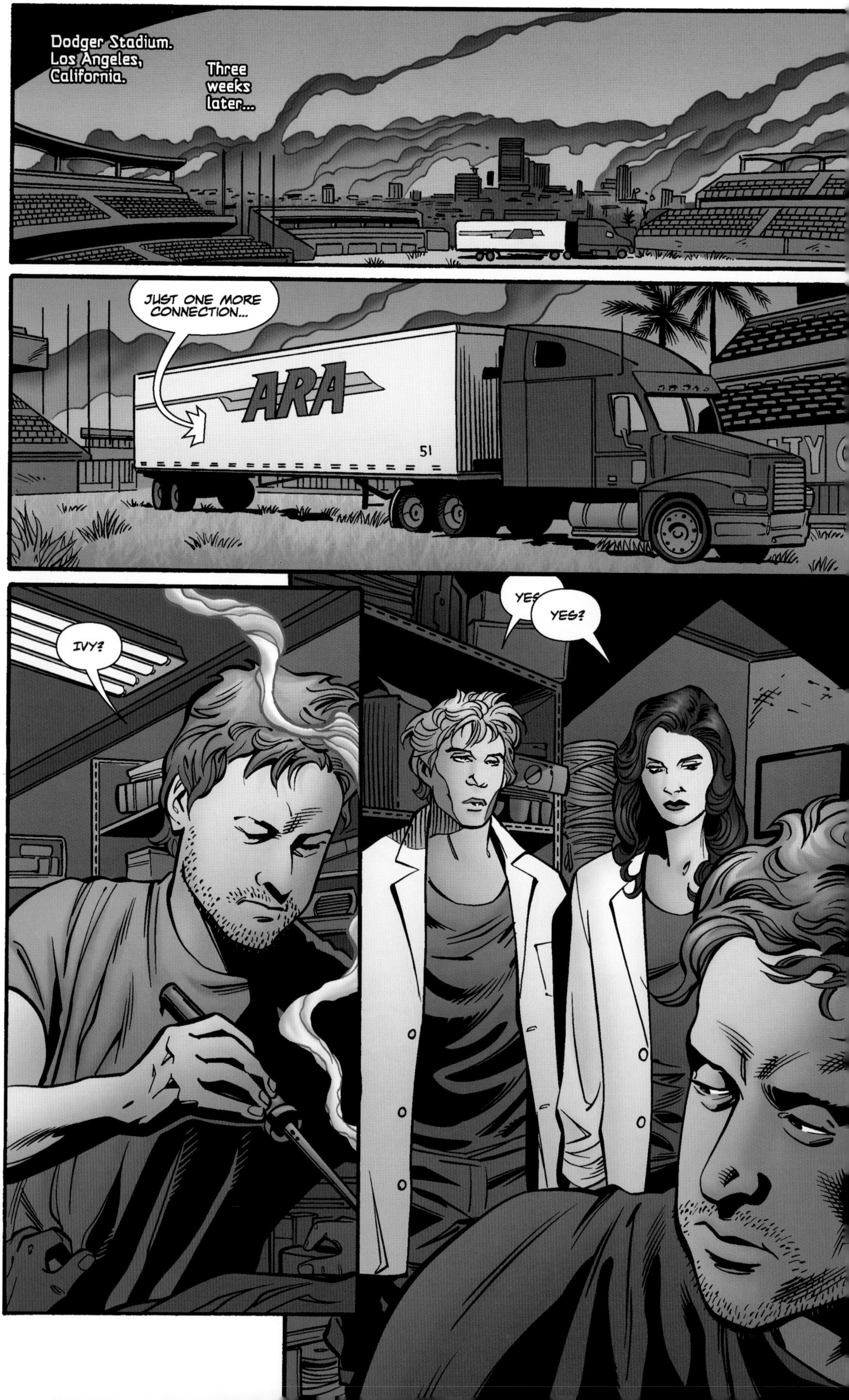

Dodger Stadium. Los Angeles, California.
Three weeks later...
JUST ONE MORE CONNECTION...
ARA
51
IVY?
YES?
YES?

ISN'T THE POINT OF HAVING TWO BODIES IMPRINTED WITH THE SAME PERSONALITY SO YOU CAN BE IN TWO *DIFFERENT* PLACES AT THE SAME TIME?

ONE OF YOU IS REDUNDANT RIGHT NOW.

I WANT BE HER YOU ACT INT

I WANT TO BE HERE WHEN YOU ACTIVATE THE INTERFACE.

SEE WHAT I MEAN?

I'M GOING TO NEED SOME*ONE* TO TEACH HIM HOW TO USE THE TECH.

I'L DO

I'LL DO IT.

IS IT FINISHED? AM I A SUPER-SOLDIER YET?

ALMOST.

BUT I'M AFRAID I HAD TO LEAVE SOME OF THE HARDWARE ON THE OUTSIDE.

COOL.

IF I ONLY HAD THIS *BEFORE* MY UNCLE GOT ATTACKED...

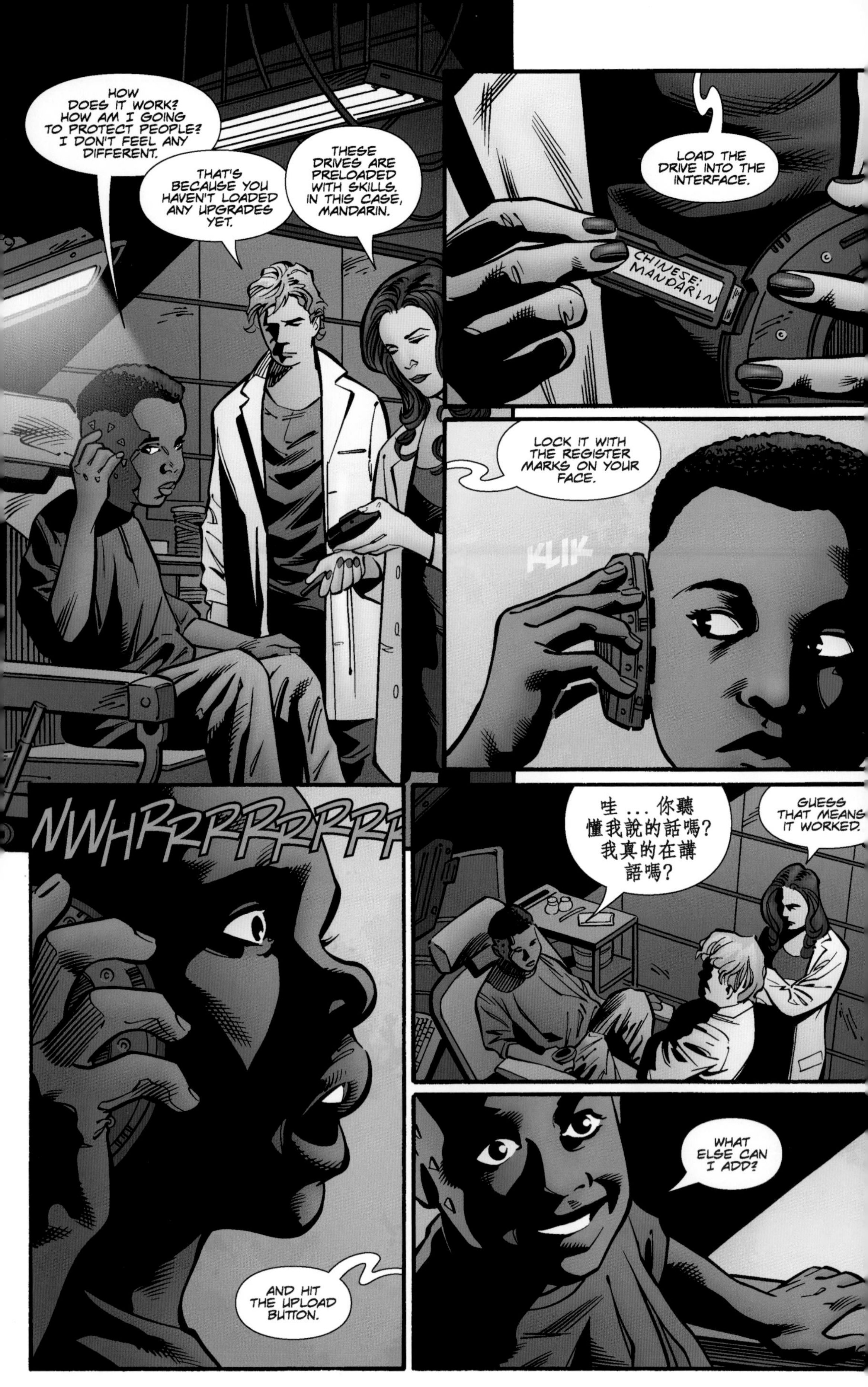
HOW DOES IT WORK? HOW AM I GOING TO PROTECT PEOPLE? I DON'T FEEL ANY DIFFERENT.
THAT'S BECAUSE YOU HAVEN'T LOADED ANY UPGRADES YET.
THESE DRIVES ARE PRELOADED WITH SKILLS. IN THIS CASE, MANDARIN.
LOAD THE DRIVE INTO THE INTERFACE.
CHINESE: MANDARIN
LOCK IT WITH THE REGISTER MARKS ON YOUR FACE.
KLIK
NWHRRRRRRRRR
AND HIT THE UPLOAD BUTTON.
哇...你聽懂我說的話嗎?我真的在講語嗎?
GUESS THAT MEANS IT WORKED.
WHAT ELSE CAN I ADD?

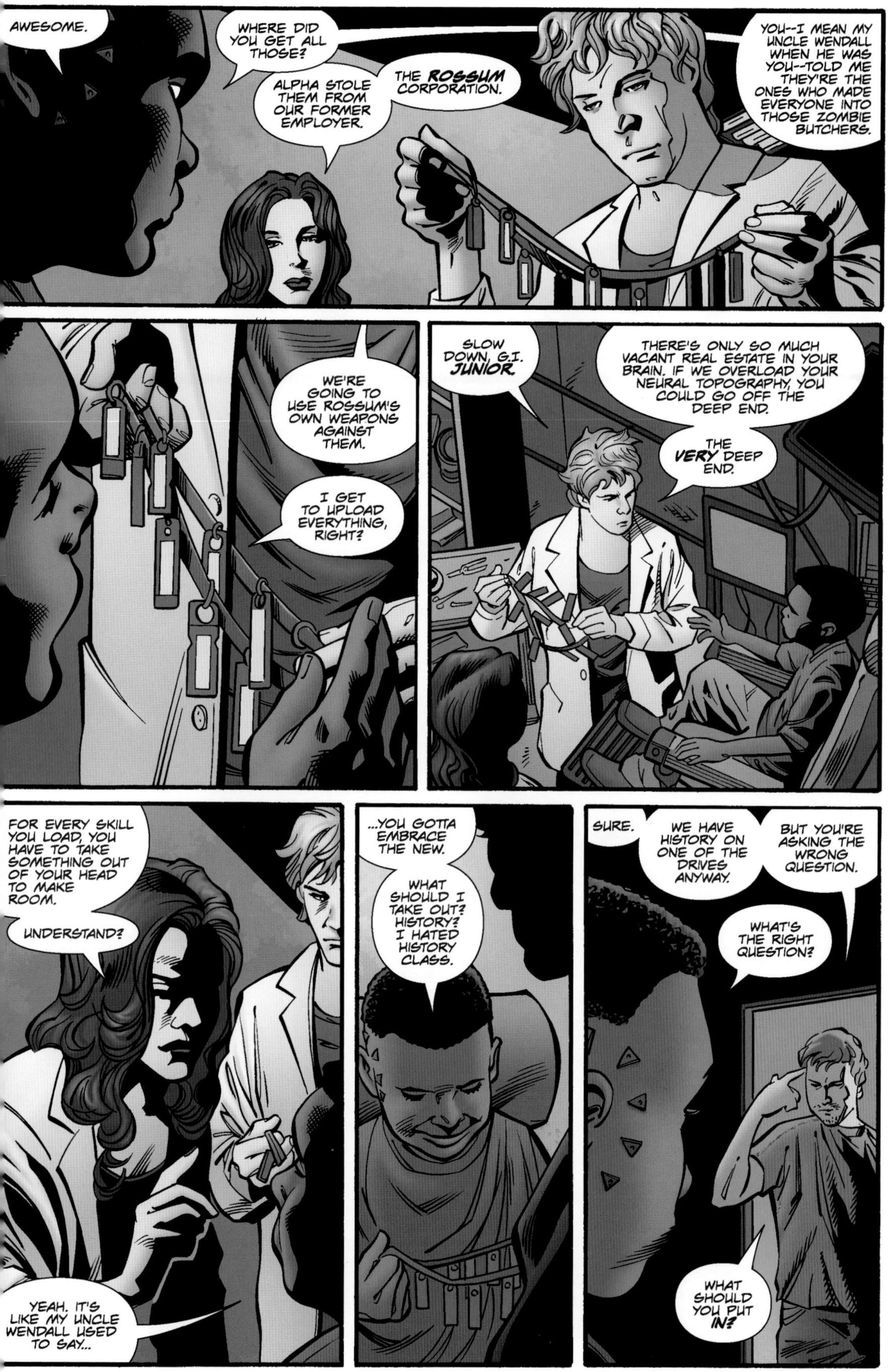
AWESOME.
WHERE DID YOU GET ALL THOSE?
ALPHA STOLE THEM FROM OUR FORMER EMPLOYER.
THE ROSSUM CORPORATION.
YOU--I MEAN MY UNCLE WENDALL WHEN HE WAS YOU--TOLD ME THEY'RE THE ONES WHO MADE EVERYONE INTO THOSE ZOMBIE BUTCHERS.
WE'RE GOING TO USE ROSSUM'S OWN WEAPONS AGAINST THEM.
I GET TO UPLOAD EVERYTHING, RIGHT?
SLOW DOWN, G.I. JUNIOR.
THERE'S ONLY SO MUCH VACANT REAL ESTATE IN YOUR BRAIN. IF WE OVERLOAD YOUR NEURAL TOPOGRAPHY, YOU COULD GO OFF THE DEEP END.
THE VERY DEEP END.
FOR EVERY SKILL YOU LOAD, YOU HAVE TO TAKE SOMETHING OUT OF YOUR HEAD TO MAKE ROOM.
UNDERSTAND?
YEAH. IT'S LIKE MY UNCLE WENDALL USED TO SAY...
...YOU GOTTA EMBRACE THE NEW.
WHAT SHOULD I TAKE OUT? HISTORY? I HATED HISTORY CLASS.
SURE.
WE HAVE HISTORY ON ONE OF THE DRIVES ANYWAY.
BUT YOU'RE ASKING THE WRONG QUESTION.
WHAT'S THE RIGHT QUESTION?
WHAT SHOULD YOU PUT IN?

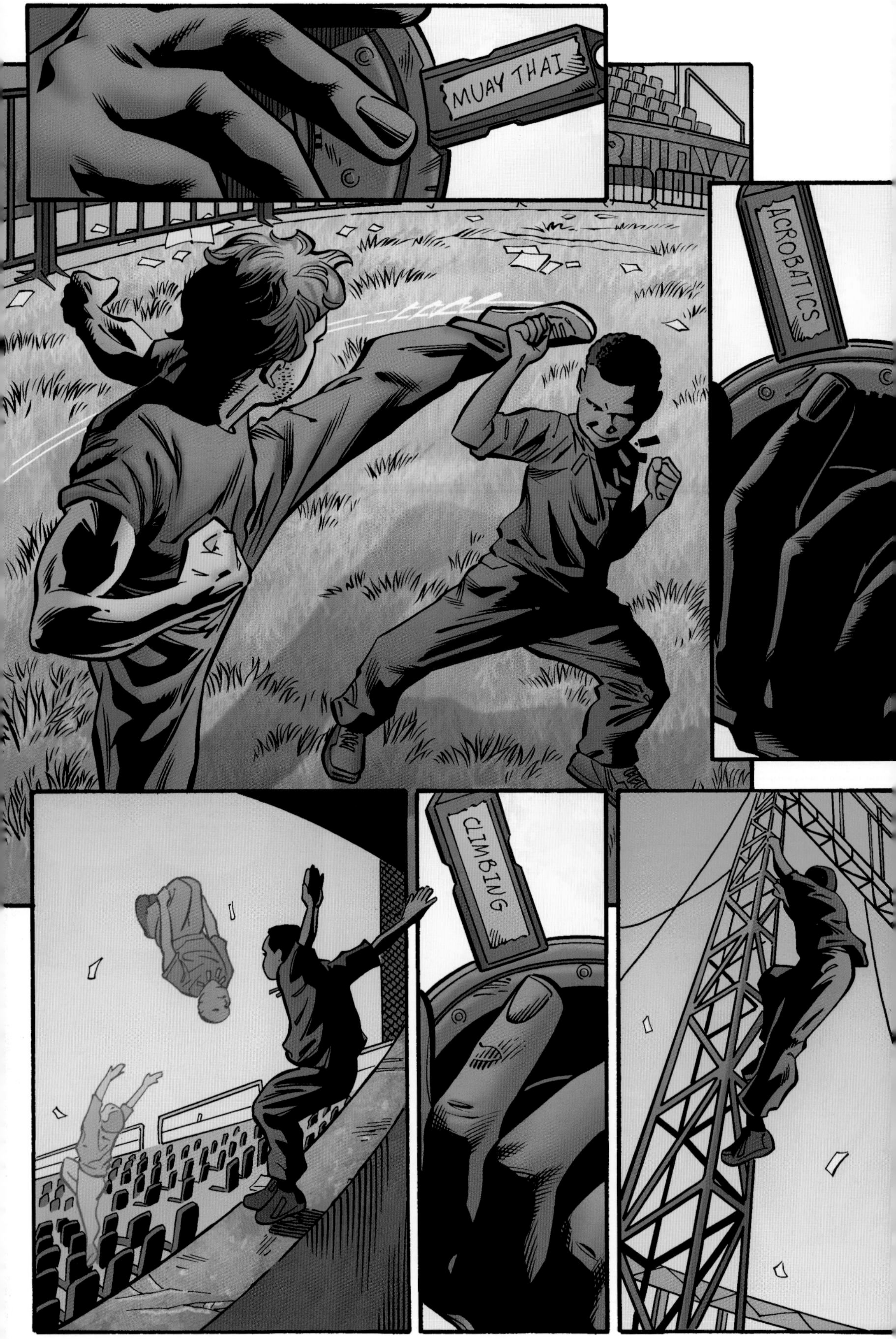
MUAY THAI
ACROBATICS
CLIMBING

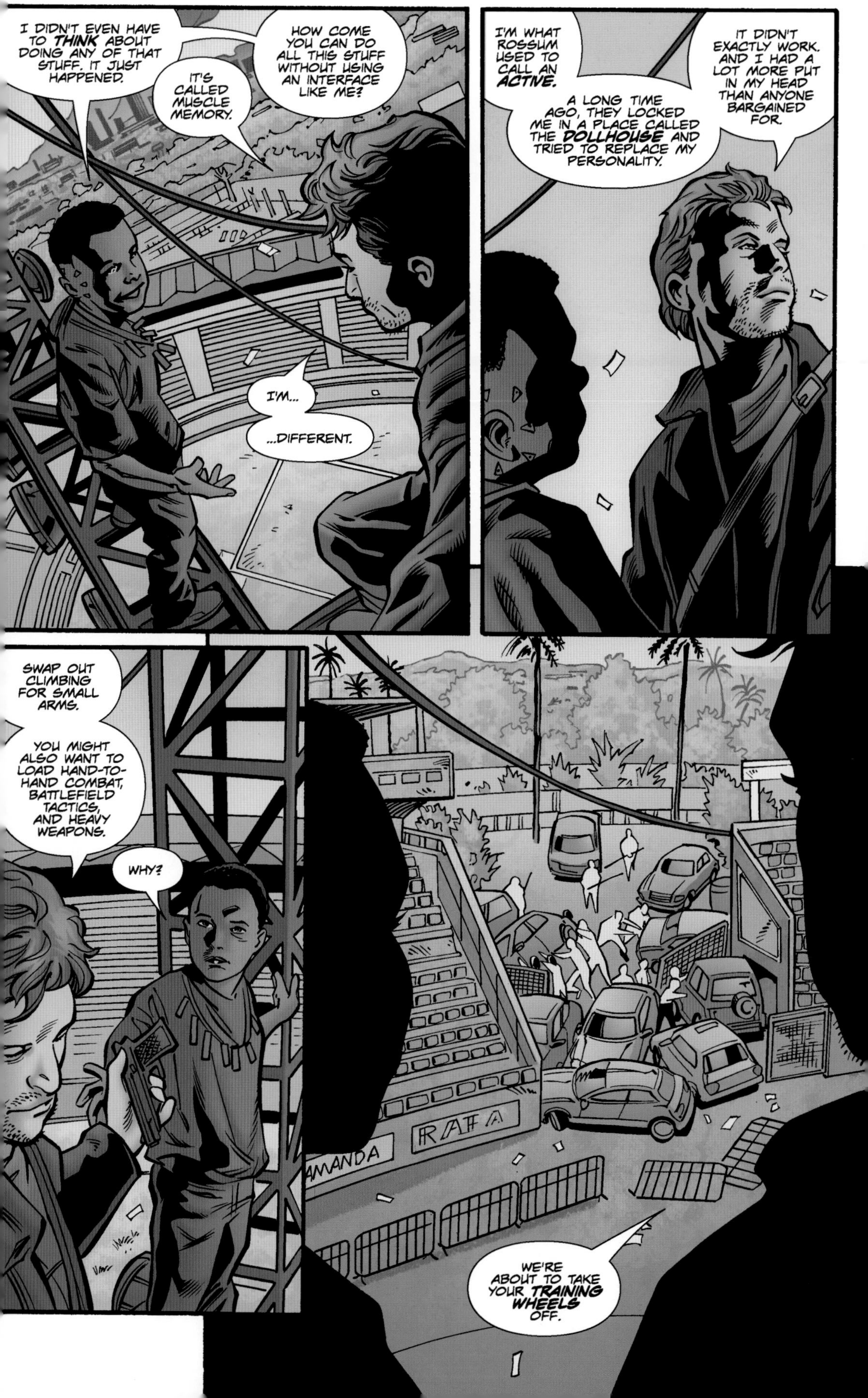
I DIDN'T EVEN HAVE TO THINK ABOUT DOING ANY OF THAT STUFF. IT JUST HAPPENED.
HOW COME YOU CAN DO ALL THIS STUFF WITHOUT USING AN INTERFACE LIKE ME?
IT'S CALLED MUSCLE MEMORY.
I'M...
...DIFFERENT.
I'M WHAT ROSSUM USED TO CALL AN ACTIVE.
A LONG TIME AGO, THEY LOCKED ME IN A PLACE CALLED THE DOLLHOUSE AND TRIED TO REPLACE MY PERSONALITY.
IT DIDN'T EXACTLY WORK. AND I HAD A LOT MORE PUT IN MY HEAD THAN ANYONE BARGAINED FOR.
SWAP OUT CLIMBING FOR SMALL ARMS.
YOU MIGHT ALSO WANT TO LOAD HAND-TO-HAND COMBAT, BATTLEFIELD TACTICS, AND HEAVY WEAPONS.
WHY?
AMANDA
RAFA
WE'RE ABOUT TO TAKE YOUR TRAINING WHEELS OFF.

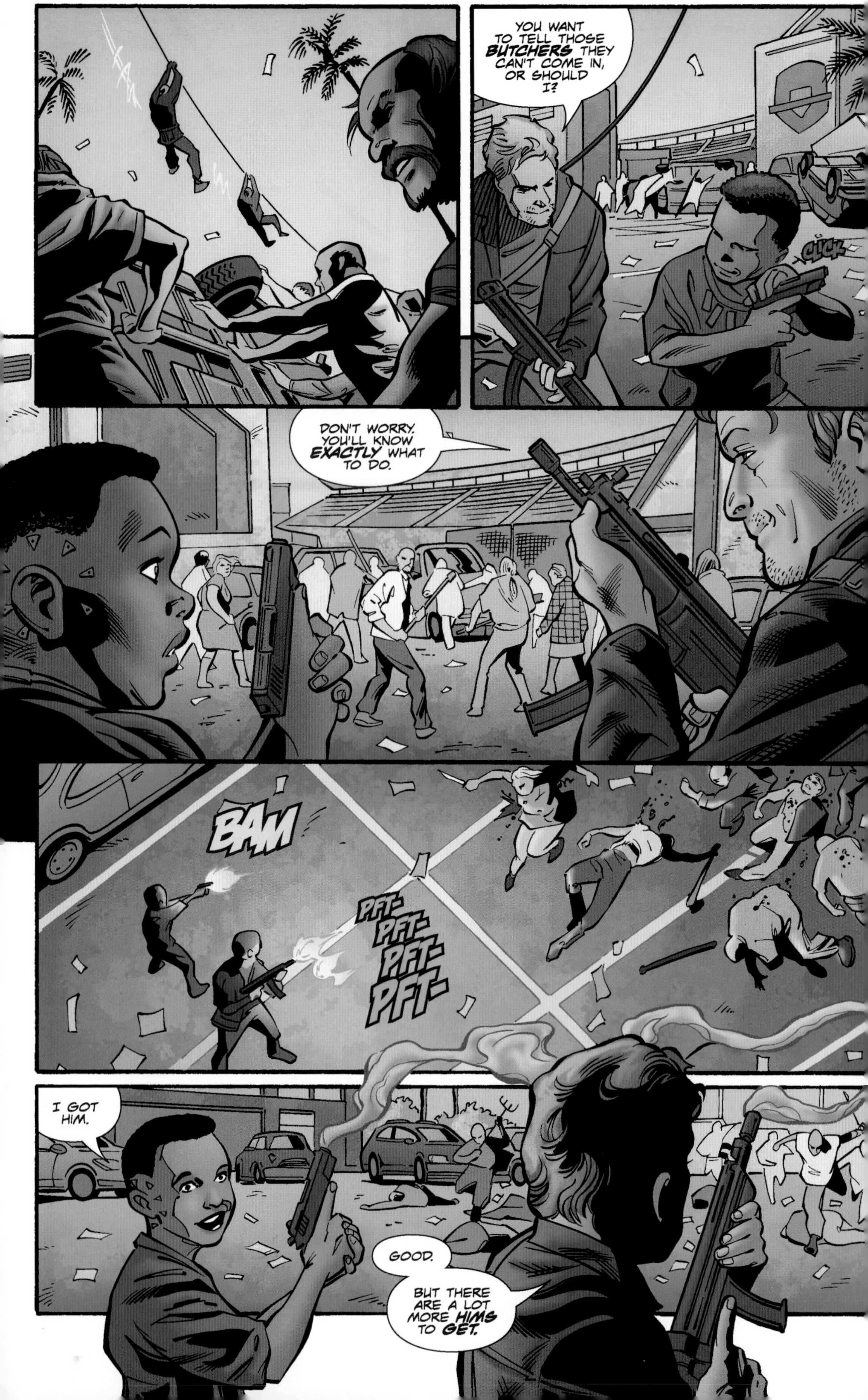
YOU WANT TO TELL THOSE BUTCHERS THEY CAN'T COME IN, OR SHOULD I?
CLICK
DON'T WORRY. YOU'LL KNOW EXACTLY WHAT TO DO.
BAM
PFT- PFT- PFT- PFT-
I GOT HIM.
GOOD.
BUT THERE ARE A LOT MORE HIMS TO GET.

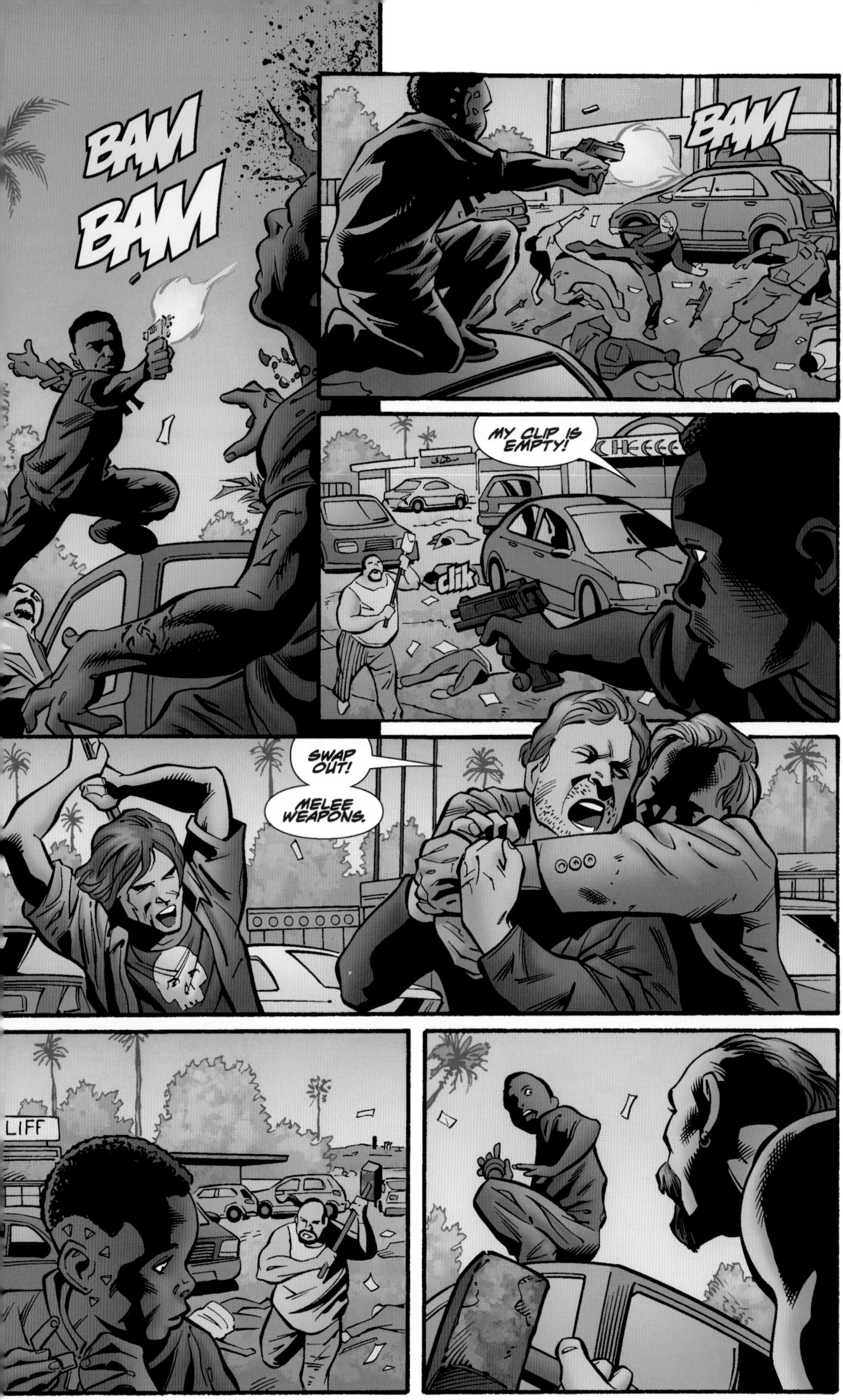
BAM
BAM
BAM
MY CLIP IS EMPTY!
CLIK
SWAP OUT!
MELEE WEAPONS.
LIFF

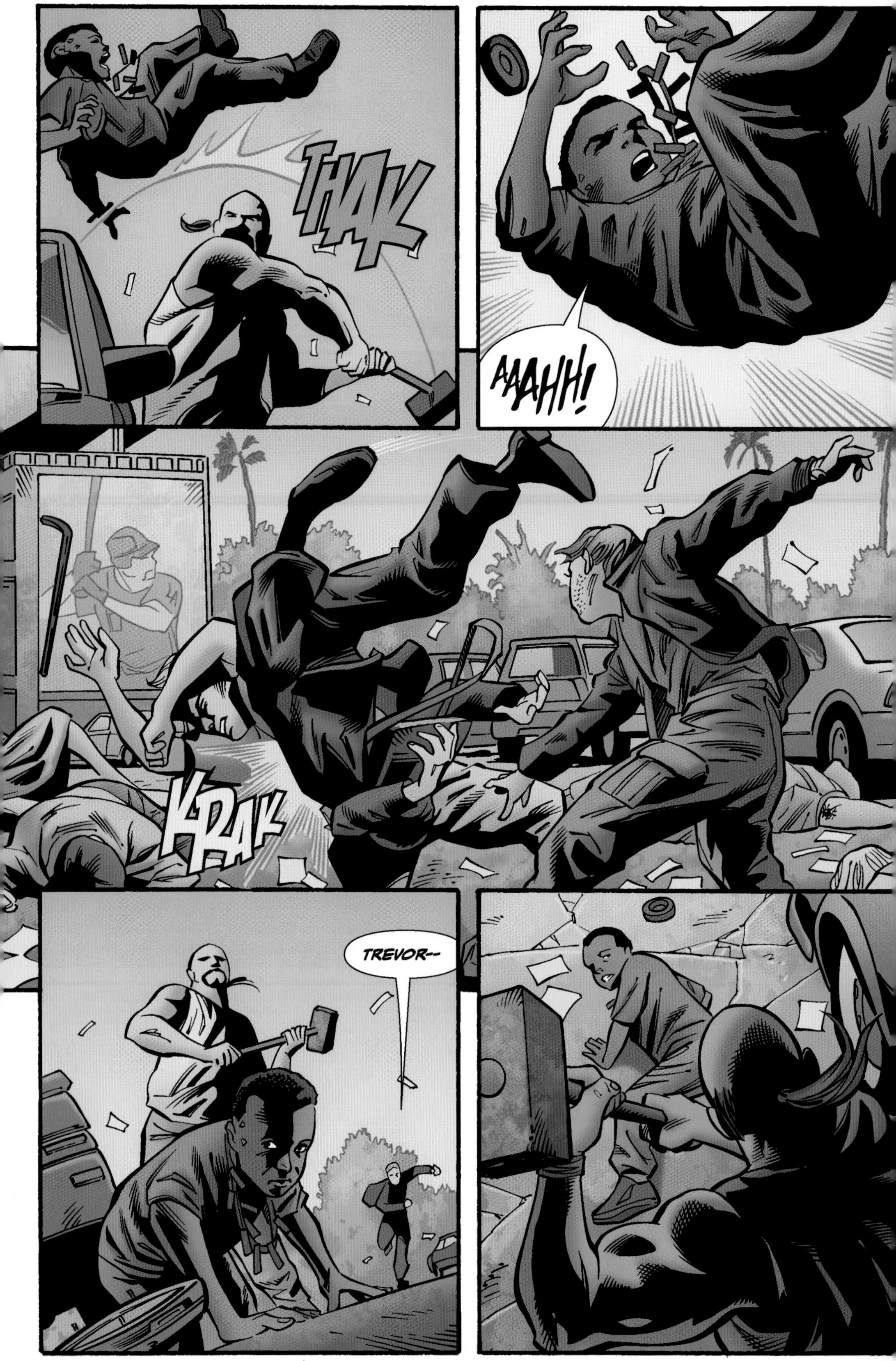
THAK
AAAHH!
KRAK
TREVOR--

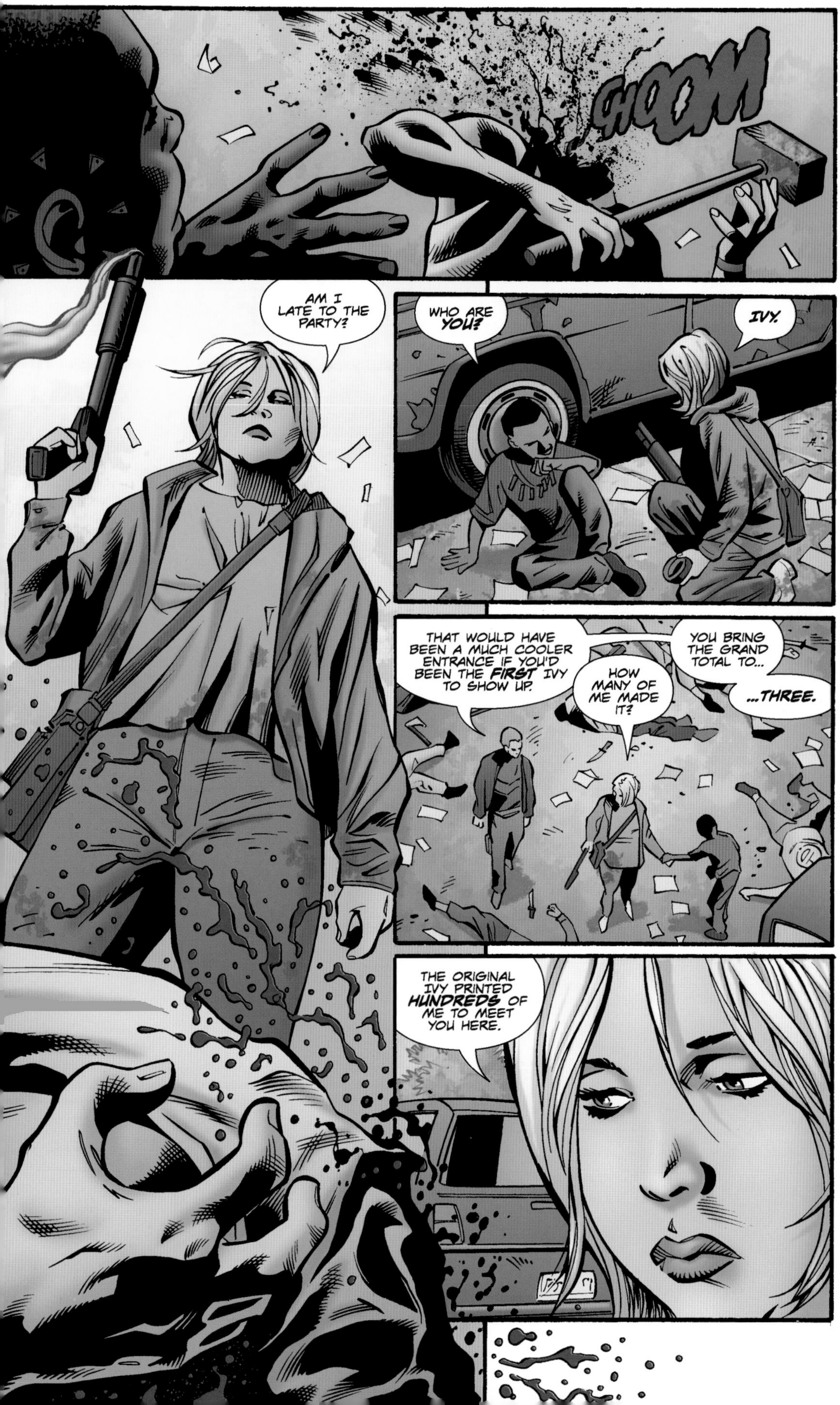
CHOOM
AM I LATE TO THE PARTY?
WHO ARE YOU?
IVY.
THAT WOULD HAVE BEEN A MUCH COOLER ENTRANCE IF YOU'D BEEN THE FIRST IVY TO SHOW UP.
YOU BRING THE GRAND TOTAL TO...
HOW MANY OF ME MADE IT?
...THREE.
THE ORIGINAL IVY PRINTED HUNDREDS OF ME TO MEET YOU HERE.

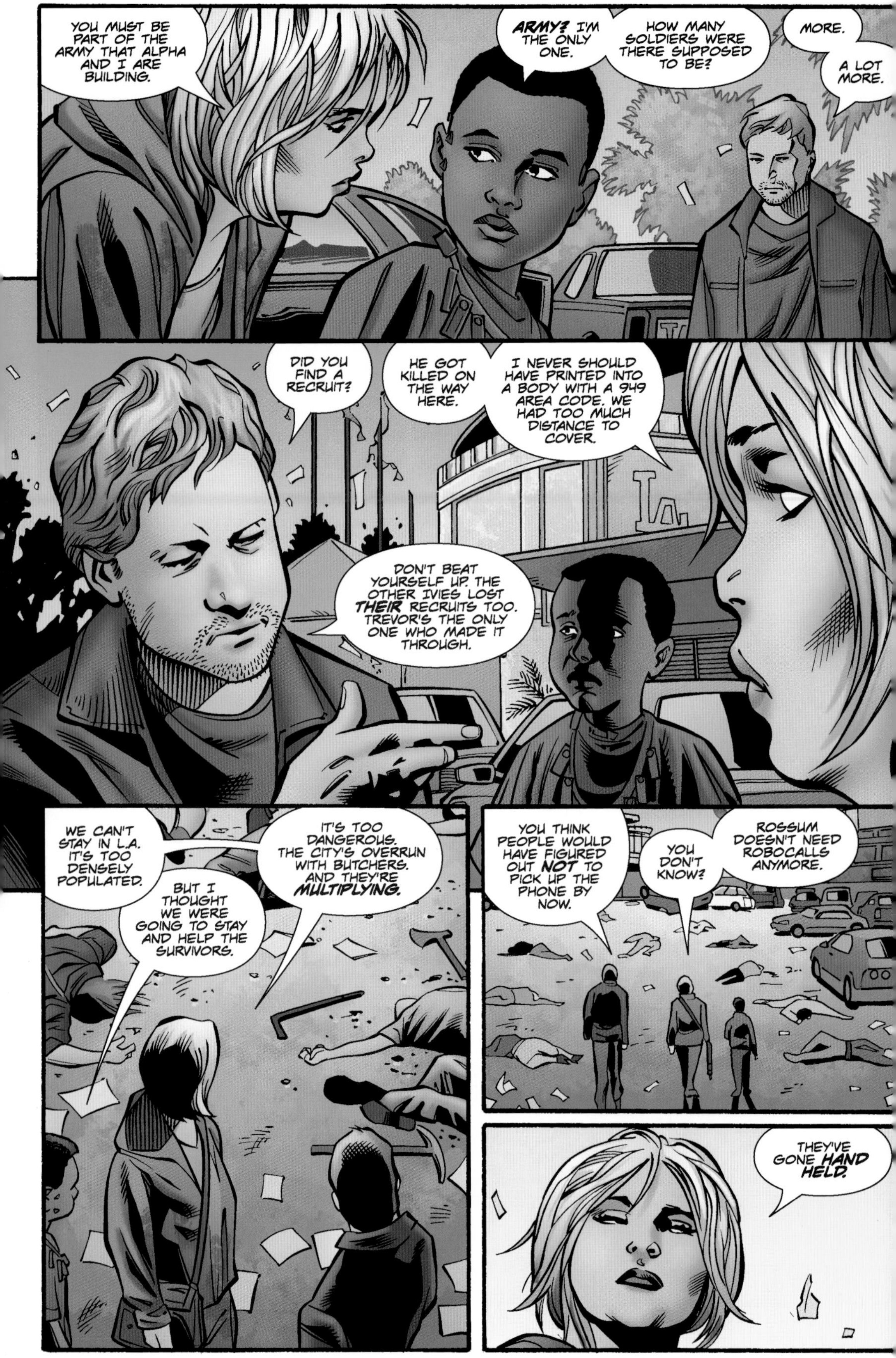
YOU MUST BE PART OF THE ARMY THAT ALPHA AND I ARE BUILDING.
ARMY? I'M THE ONLY ONE.
HOW MANY SOLDIERS WERE THERE SUPPOSED TO BE?
MORE.
A LOT MORE.
DID YOU FIND A RECRUIT?
HE GOT KILLED ON THE WAY HERE.
I NEVER SHOULD HAVE PRINTED INTO A BODY WITH A 949 AREA CODE. WE HAD TOO MUCH DISTANCE TO COVER.
DON'T BEAT YOURSELF UP. THE OTHER IVIES LOST THEIR RECRUITS TOO. TREVOR'S THE ONLY ONE WHO MADE IT THROUGH.
WE CAN'T STAY IN L.A. IT'S TOO DENSELY POPULATED.
BUT I THOUGHT WE WERE GOING TO STAY AND HELP THE SURVIVORS.
IT'S TOO DANGEROUS. THE CITY'S OVERRUN WITH BUTCHERS. AND THEY'RE MULTIPLYING.
YOU THINK PEOPLE WOULD HAVE FIGURED OUT NOT TO PICK UP THE PHONE BY NOW.
YOU DON'T KNOW?
ROSSUM DOESN'T NEED ROBOCALLS ANYMORE.
THEY'VE GONE HAND HELD.

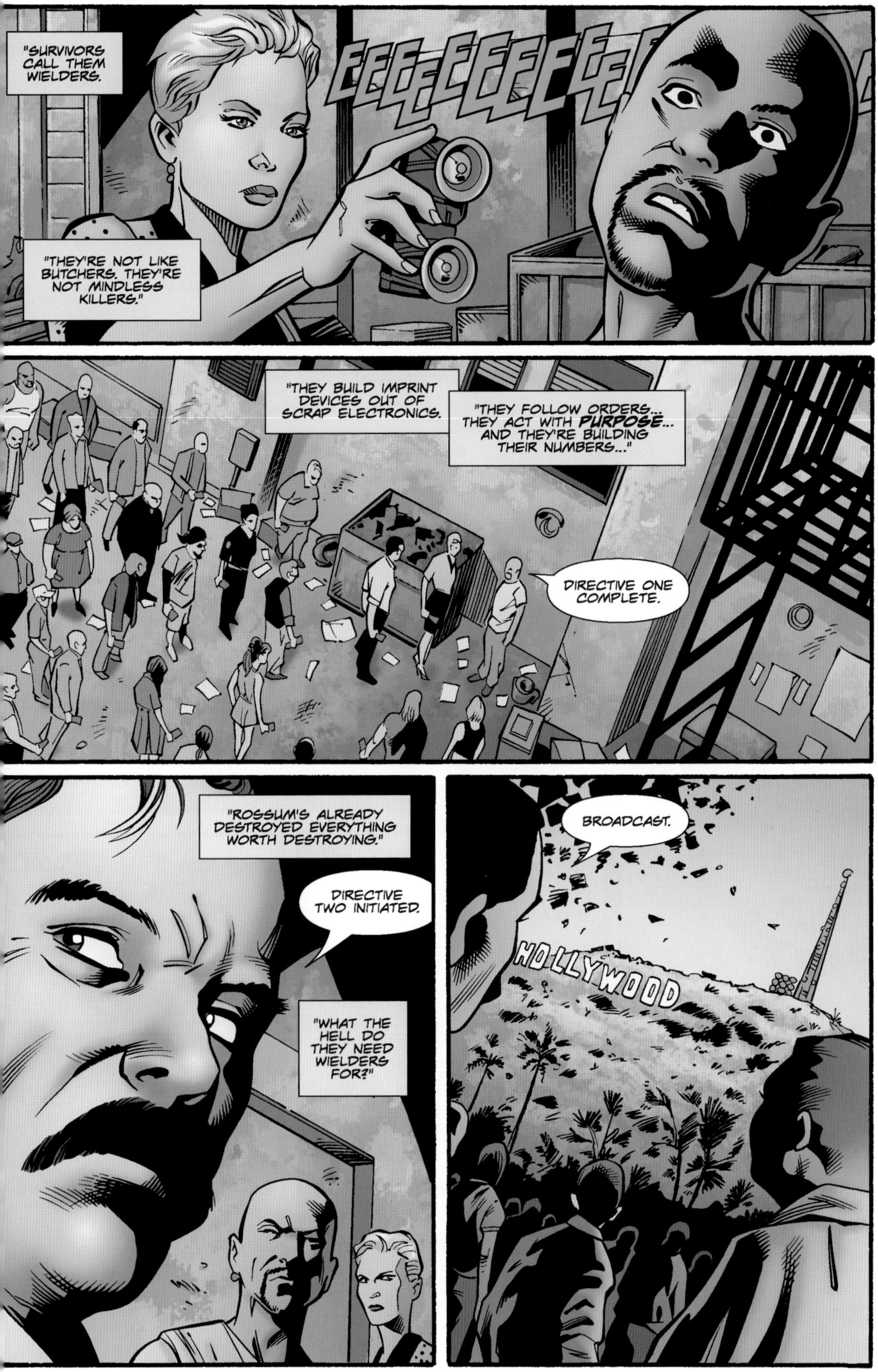
"SURVIVORS CALL THEM WIELDERS.
EEEEEEEEEEEEE
"THEY'RE NOT LIKE BUTCHERS. THEY'RE NOT MINDLESS KILLERS."
"THEY BUILD IMPRINT DEVICES OUT OF SCRAP ELECTRONICS.
"THEY FOLLOW ORDERS... THEY ACT WITH PURPOSE... AND THEY'RE BUILDING THEIR NUMBERS..."
DIRECTIVE ONE COMPLETE.
"ROSSUM'S ALREADY DESTROYED EVERYTHING WORTH DESTROYING."
DIRECTIVE TWO INITIATED.
"WHAT THE HELL DO THEY NEED WIELDERS FOR?"
BROADCAST.
HOLLYWOOD

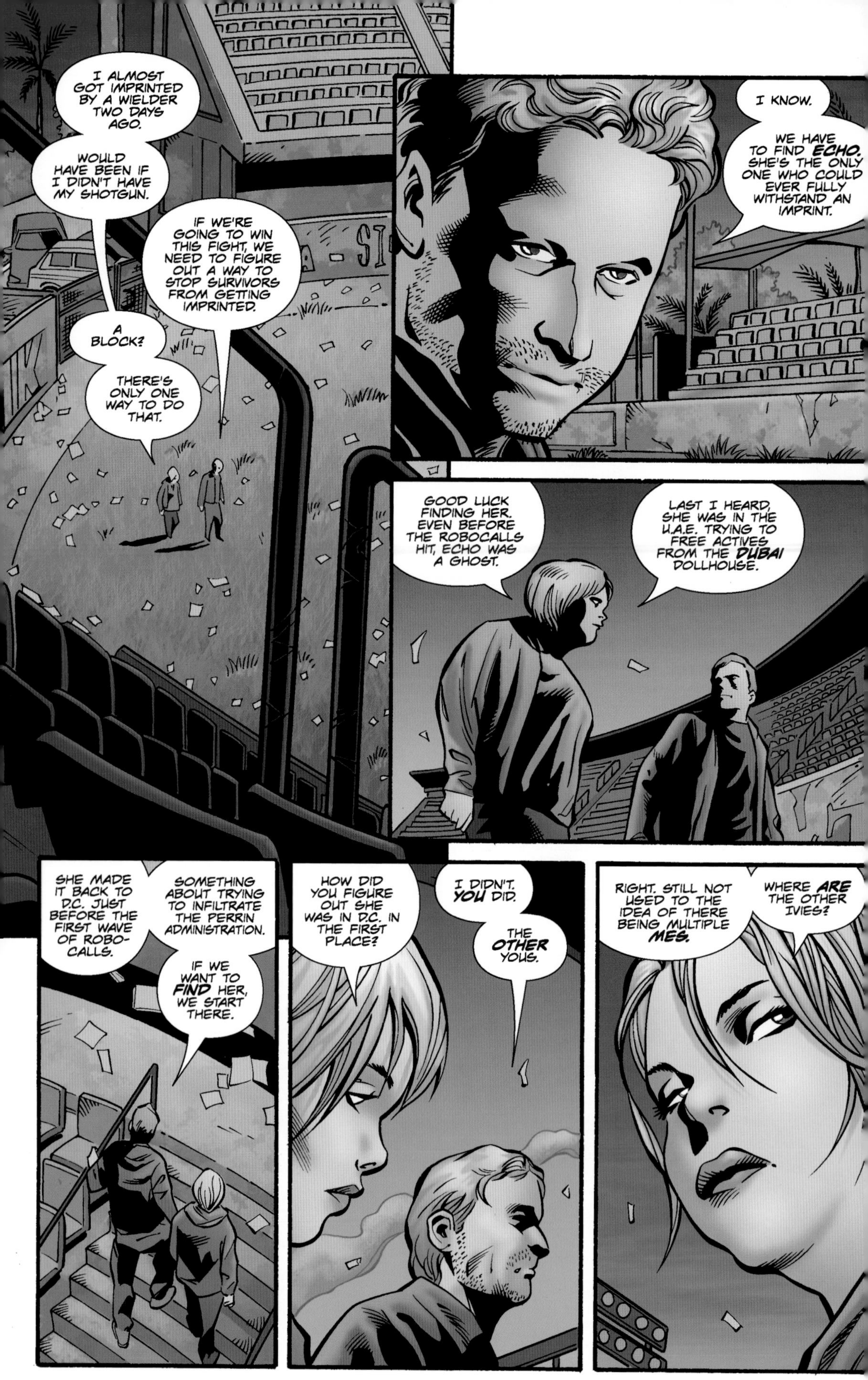

I ALMOST GOT IMPRINTED BY A WIELDER TWO DAYS AGO.
WOULD HAVE BEEN IF I DIDN'T HAVE MY SHOTGUN.
IF WE'RE GOING TO WIN THIS FIGHT, WE NEED TO FIGURE OUT A WAY TO STOP SURVIVORS FROM GETTING IMPRINTED.
A BLOCK?
THERE'S ONLY ONE WAY TO DO THAT.
I KNOW.
WE HAVE TO FIND ECHO. SHE'S THE ONLY ONE WHO COULD EVER FULLY WITHSTAND AN IMPRINT.
GOOD LUCK FINDING HER. EVEN BEFORE THE ROBOCALLS HIT, ECHO WAS A GHOST.
LAST I HEARD, SHE WAS IN THE U.A.E. TRYING TO FREE ACTIVES FROM THE DUBAI DOLLHOUSE.
SHE MADE IT BACK TO D.C. JUST BEFORE THE FIRST WAVE OF ROBO-CALLS.
SOMETHING ABOUT TRYING TO INFILTRATE THE PERRIN ADMINISTRATION.
IF WE WANT TO FIND HER, WE START THERE.
HOW DID YOU FIGURE OUT SHE WAS IN D.C. IN THE FIRST PLACE?
I DIDN'T. YOU DID.
THE OTHER YOUS.
RIGHT. STILL NOT USED TO THE IDEA OF THERE BEING MULTIPLE MES.
WHERE ARE THE OTHER IVIES?

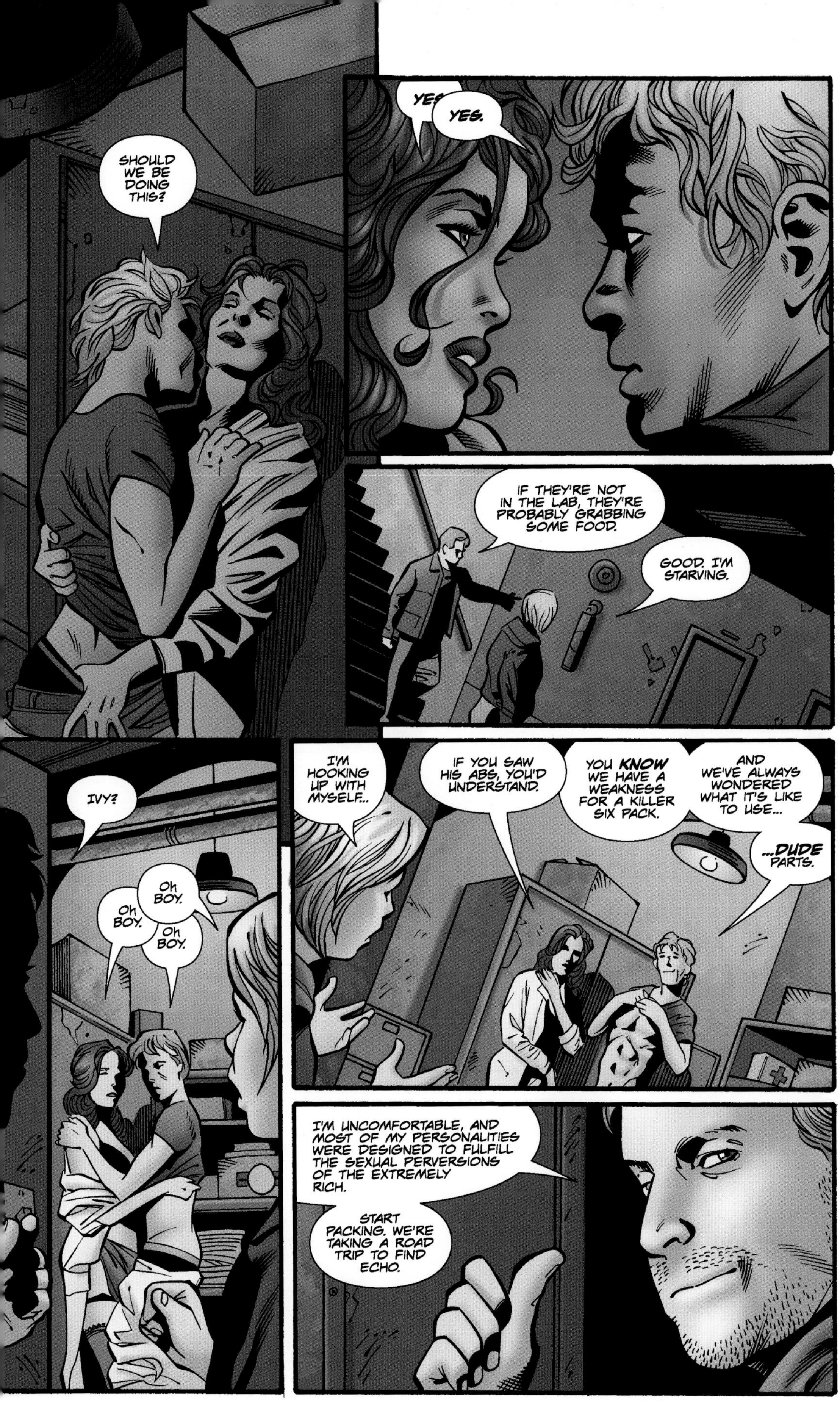
SHOULD WE BE DOING THIS?
YES.
YES.
IF THEY'RE NOT IN THE LAB, THEY'RE PROBABLY GRABBING SOME FOOD.
GOOD. I'M STARVING.
IVY?
Oh BOY.
Oh BOY.
Oh BOY.
I'M HOOKING UP WITH MYSELF...
IF YOU SAW HIS ABS, YOU'D UNDERSTAND.
YOU **KNOW** WE HAVE A WEAKNESS FOR A KILLER SIX PACK.
AND WE'VE ALWAYS WONDERED WHAT IT'S LIKE TO USE...
...**DUDE** PARTS.
I'M UNCOMFORTABLE, AND MOST OF MY PERSONALITIES WERE DESIGNED TO FULFILL THE SEXUAL PERVERSIONS OF THE EXTREMELY RICH.
START PACKING. WE'RE TAKING A ROAD TRIP TO FIND ECHO.

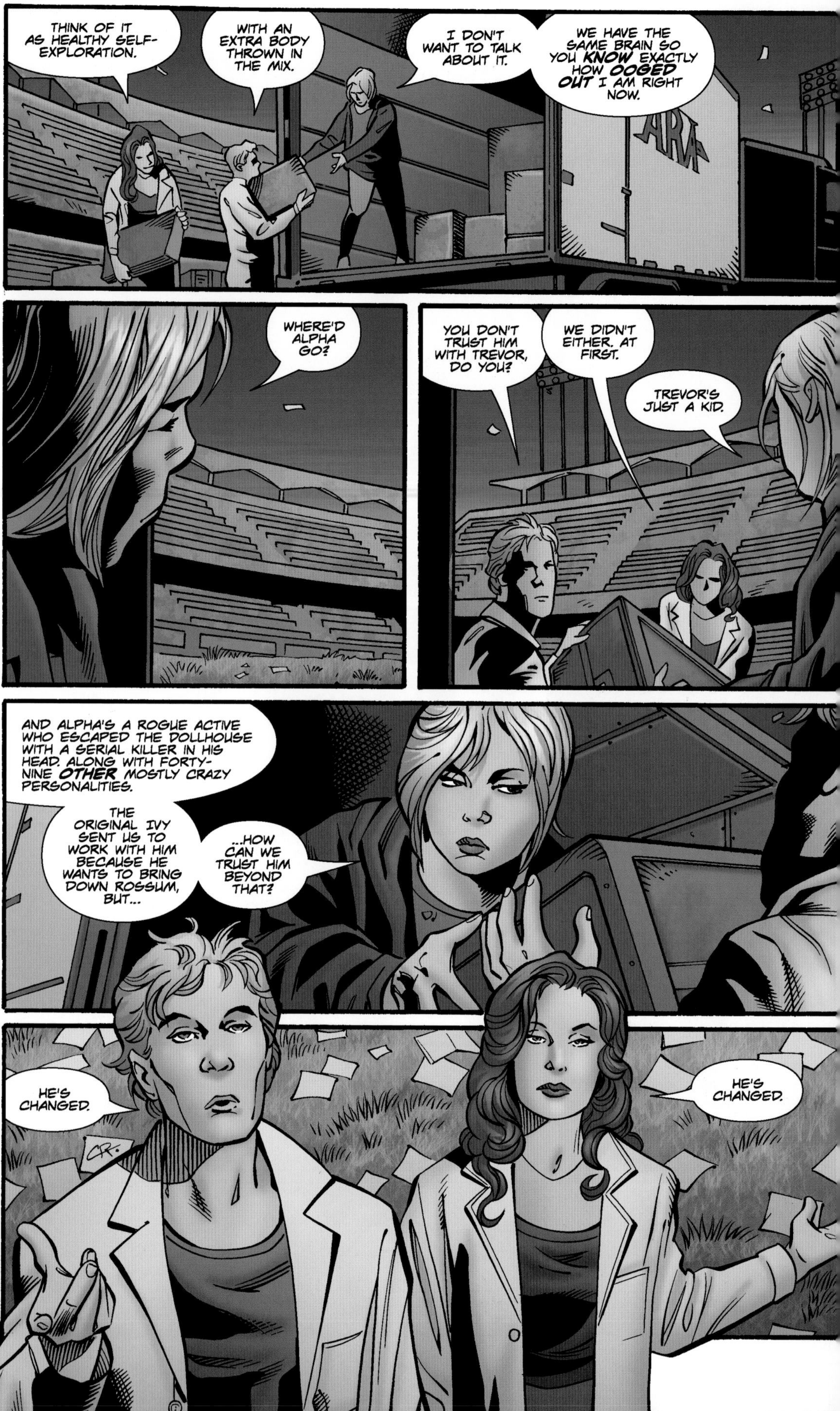
THINK OF IT AS HEALTHY SELF-EXPLORATION.
WITH AN EXTRA BODY THROWN IN THE MIX.
I DON'T WANT TO TALK ABOUT IT.
WE HAVE THE SAME BRAIN SO YOU KNOW EXACTLY HOW OOGED OUT I AM RIGHT NOW.
WHERE'D ALPHA GO?
YOU DON'T TRUST HIM WITH TREVOR, DO YOU?
WE DIDN'T EITHER. AT FIRST.
TREVOR'S JUST A KID.
AND ALPHA'S A ROGUE ACTIVE WHO ESCAPED THE DOLLHOUSE WITH A SERIAL KILLER IN HIS HEAD. ALONG WITH FORTY-NINE OTHER MOSTLY CRAZY PERSONALITIES.
THE ORIGINAL IVY SENT US TO WORK WITH HIM BECAUSE HE WANTS TO BRING DOWN ROSSUM, BUT...
...HOW CAN WE TRUST HIM BEYOND THAT?
HE'S CHANGED.
HE'S CHANGED.

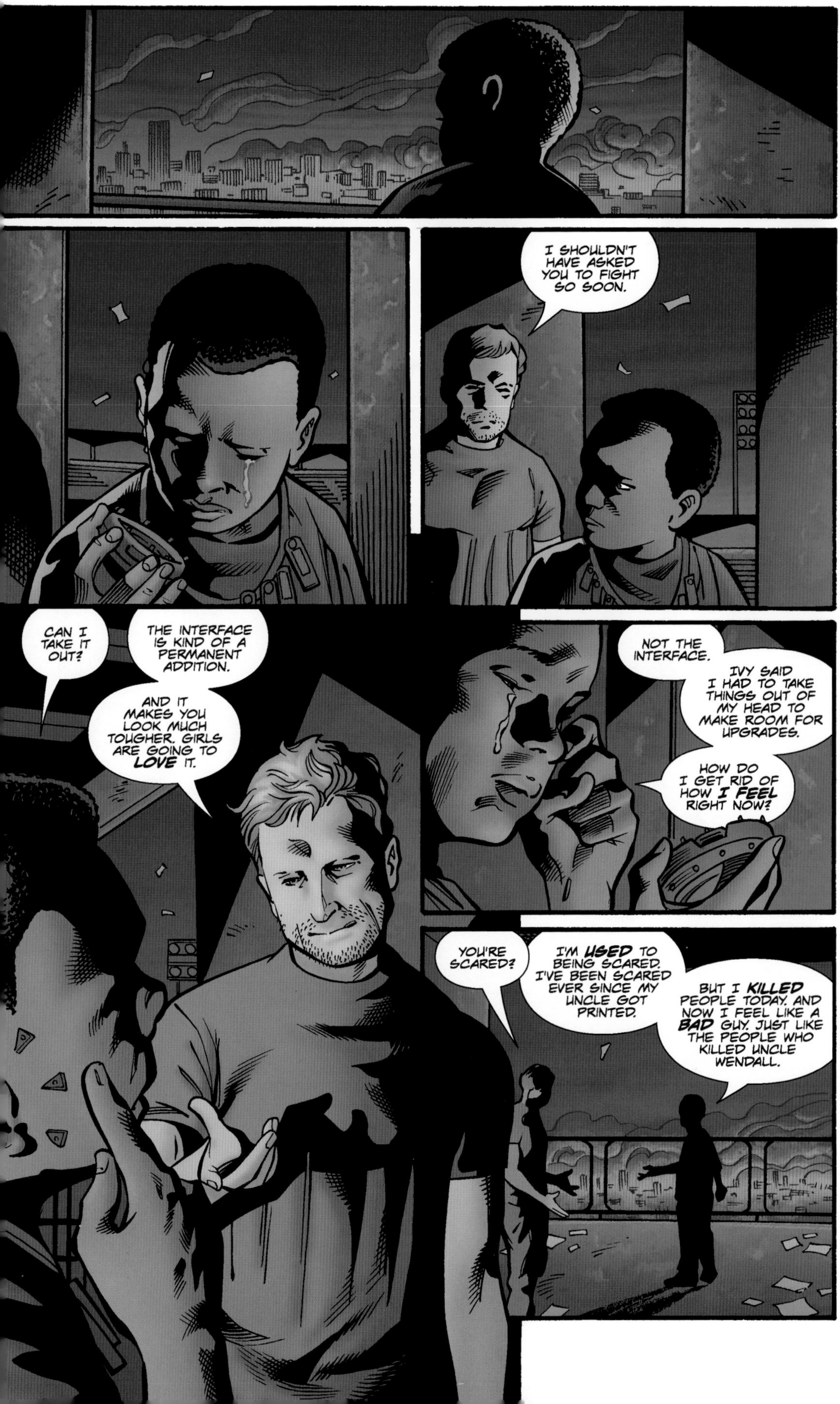

I SHOULDN'T HAVE ASKED YOU TO FIGHT SO SOON.
CAN I TAKE IT OUT?
THE INTERFACE IS KIND OF A PERMANENT ADDITION.
AND IT MAKES YOU LOOK MUCH TOUGHER. GIRLS ARE GOING TO LOVE IT.
NOT THE INTERFACE.
IVY SAID I HAD TO TAKE THINGS OUT OF MY HEAD TO MAKE ROOM FOR UPGRADES.
HOW DO I GET RID OF HOW I FEEL RIGHT NOW?
YOU'RE SCARED?
I'M USED TO BEING SCARED. I'VE BEEN SCARED EVER SINCE MY UNCLE GOT PRINTED.
BUT I KILLED PEOPLE TODAY. AND NOW I FEEL LIKE A BAD GUY. JUST LIKE THE PEOPLE WHO KILLED UNCLE WENDALL.

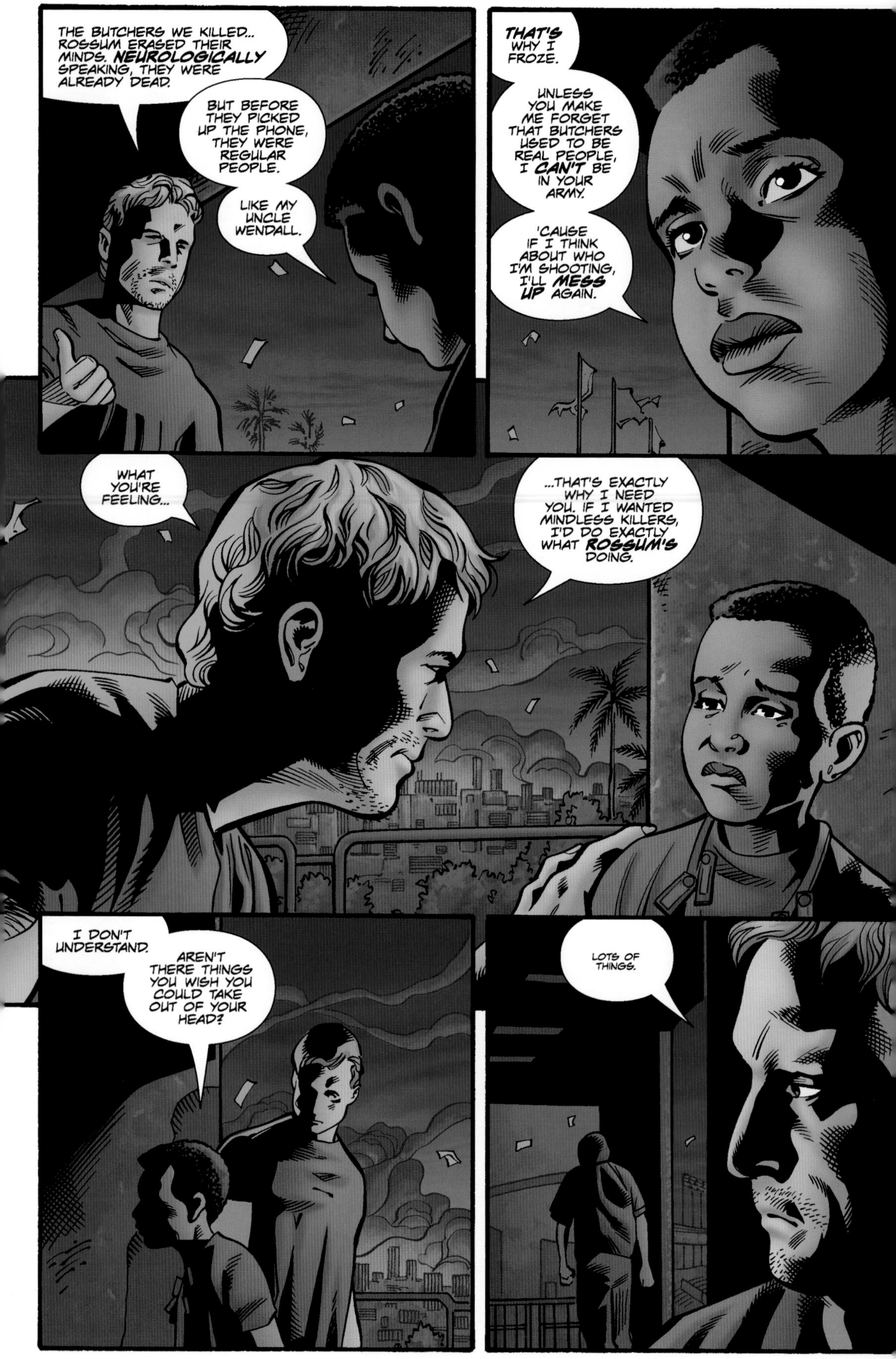
THE BUTCHERS WE KILLED... ROSSUM ERASED THEIR MINDS. NEUROLOGICALLY SPEAKING, THEY WERE ALREADY DEAD.
BUT BEFORE THEY PICKED UP THE PHONE, THEY WERE REGULAR PEOPLE.
LIKE MY UNCLE WENDALL.
THAT'S WHY I FROZE.
UNLESS YOU MAKE ME FORGET THAT BUTCHERS USED TO BE REAL PEOPLE, I CAN'T BE IN YOUR ARMY.
'CAUSE IF I THINK ABOUT WHO I'M SHOOTING, I'LL MESS UP AGAIN.
WHAT YOU'RE FEELING...
...THAT'S EXACTLY WHY I NEED YOU. IF I WANTED MINDLESS KILLERS, I'D DO EXACTLY WHAT ROSSUM'S DOING.
I DON'T UNDERSTAND.
AREN'T THERE THINGS YOU WISH YOU COULD TAKE OUT OF YOUR HEAD?
LOTS OF THINGS.

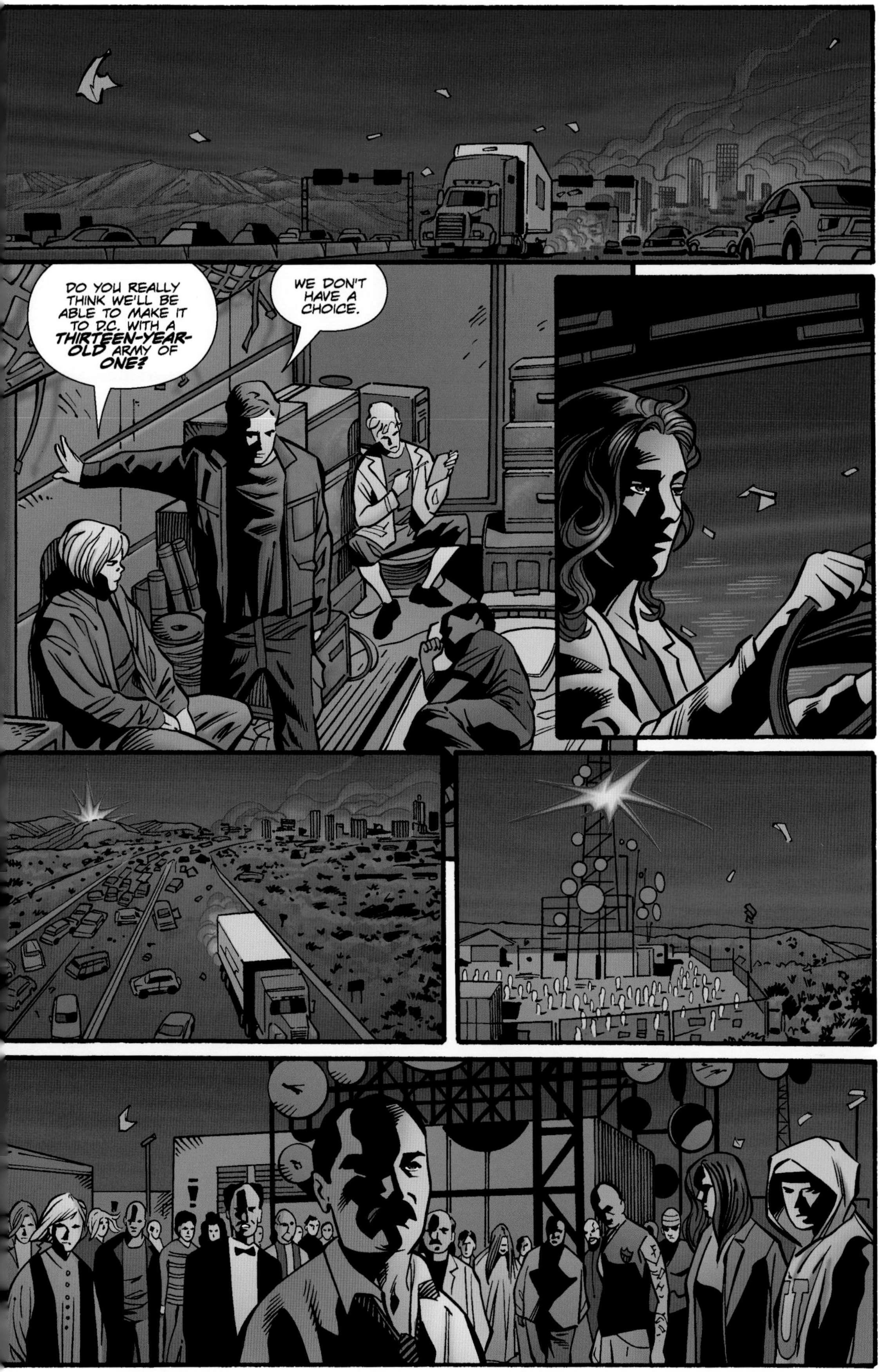
DO YOU REALLY THINK WE'LL BE ABLE TO MAKE IT TO D.C. WITH A THIRTEEN-YEAR-OLD ARMY OF ONE?
WE DON'T HAVE A CHOICE.

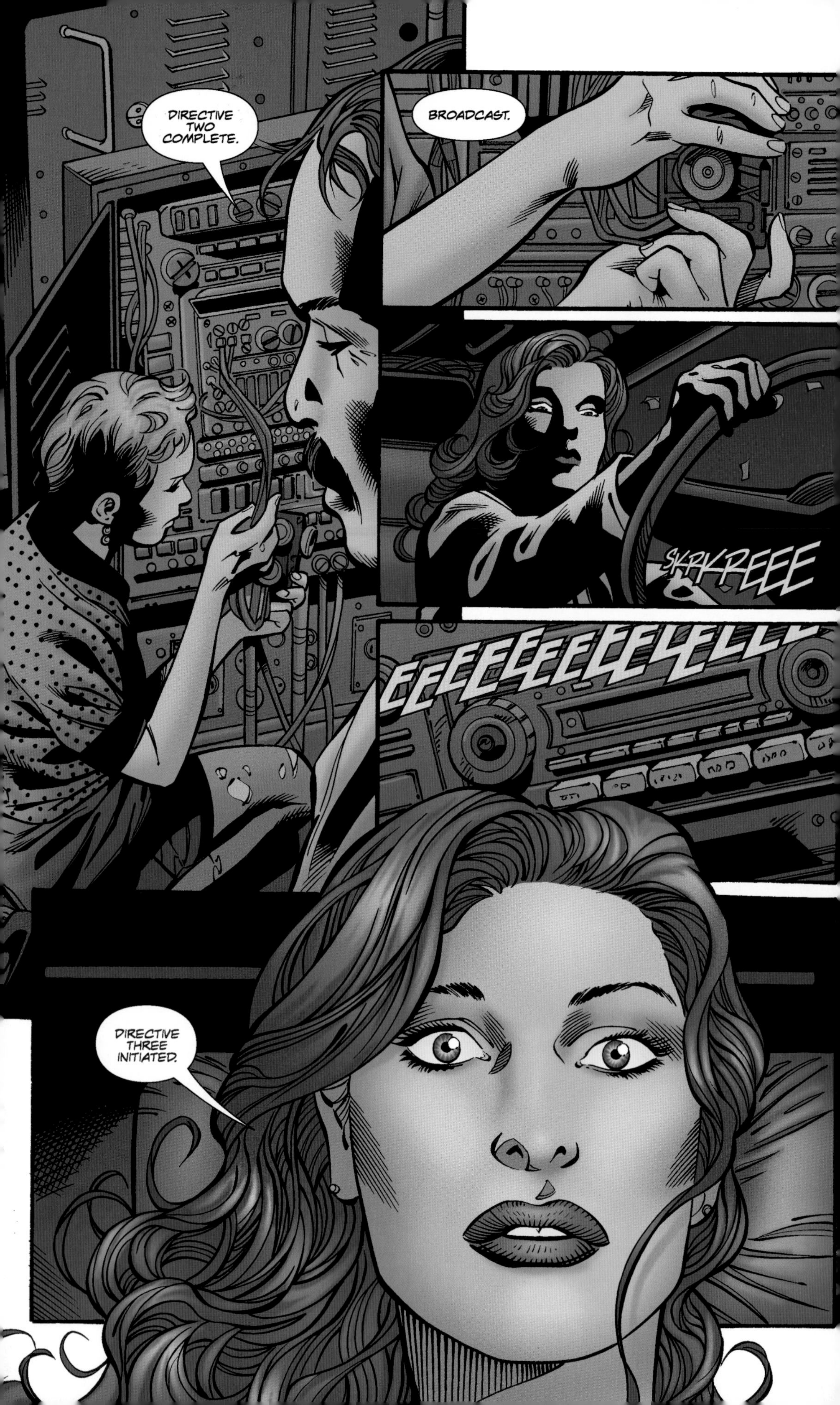

DIRECTIVE TWO COMPLETE.
BROADCAST.
SKRK REEE
EEEEEEEEEEEEE
DIRECTIVE THREE INITIATED.

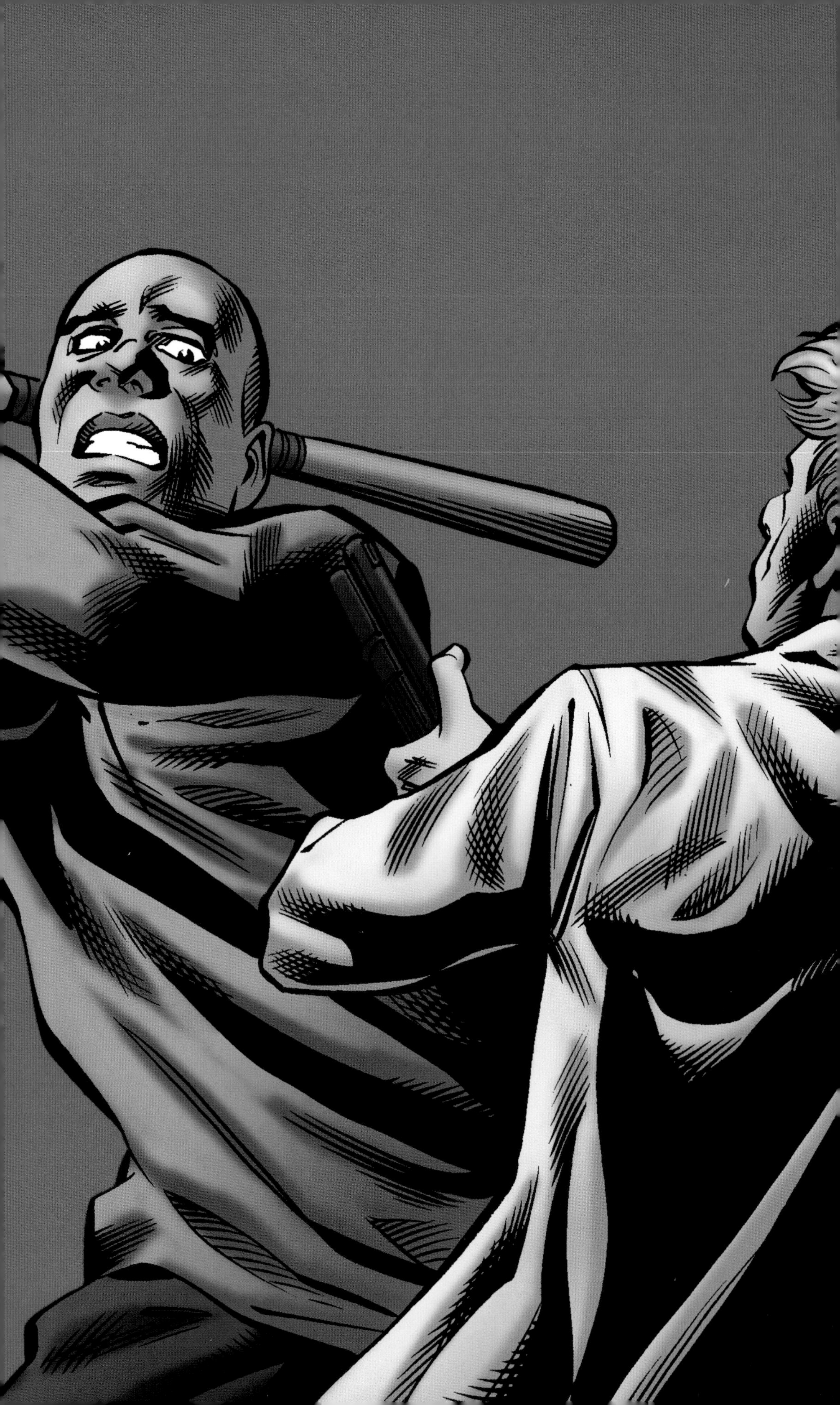

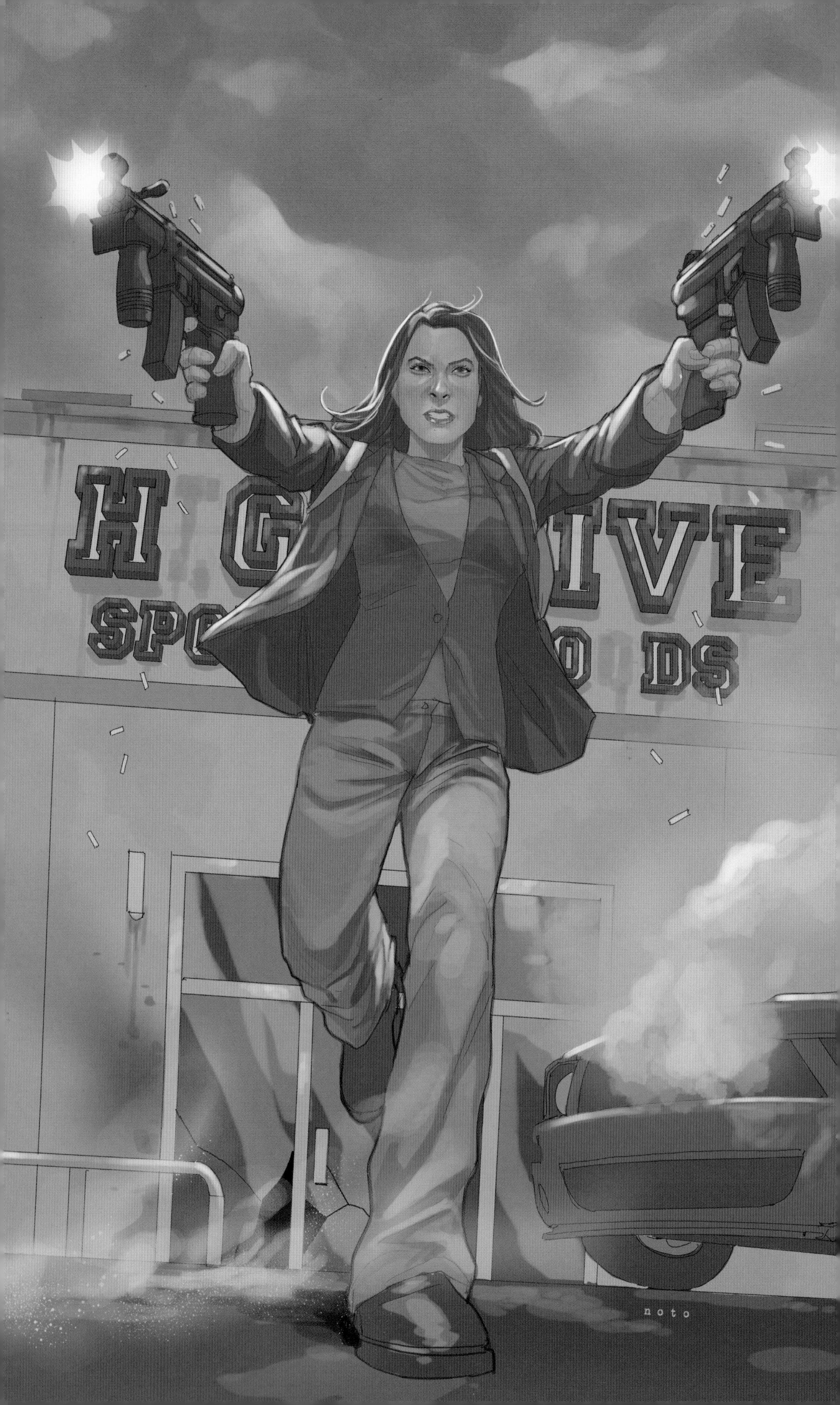
H G IVE
SPO O DS
noto

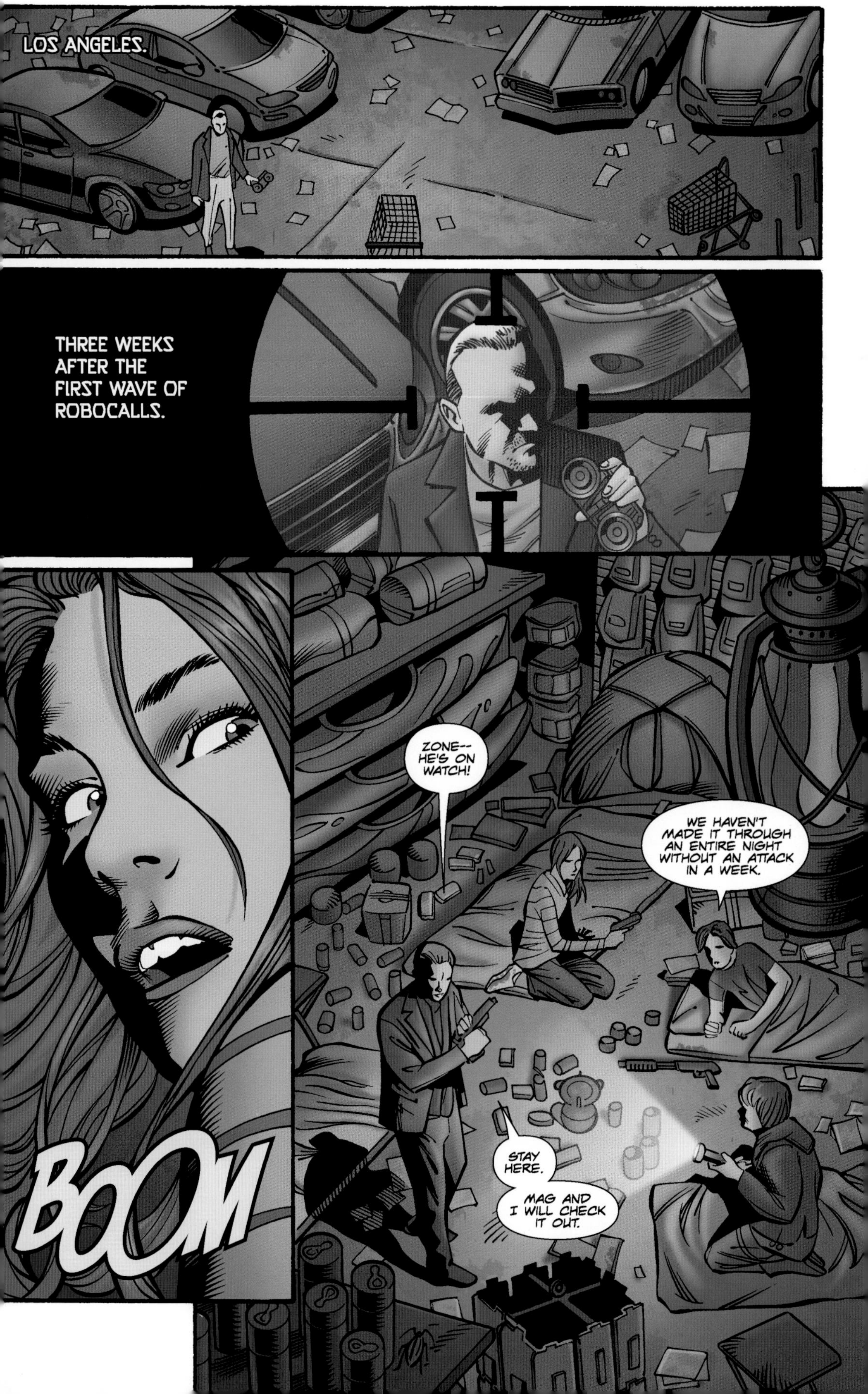
LOS ANGELES.
THREE WEEKS AFTER THE FIRST WAVE OF ROBOCALLS.
BOOM
ZONE-- HE'S ON WATCH!
WE HAVEN'T MADE IT THROUGH AN ENTIRE NIGHT WITHOUT AN ATTACK IN A WEEK.
STAY HERE.
MAG AND I WILL CHECK IT OUT.

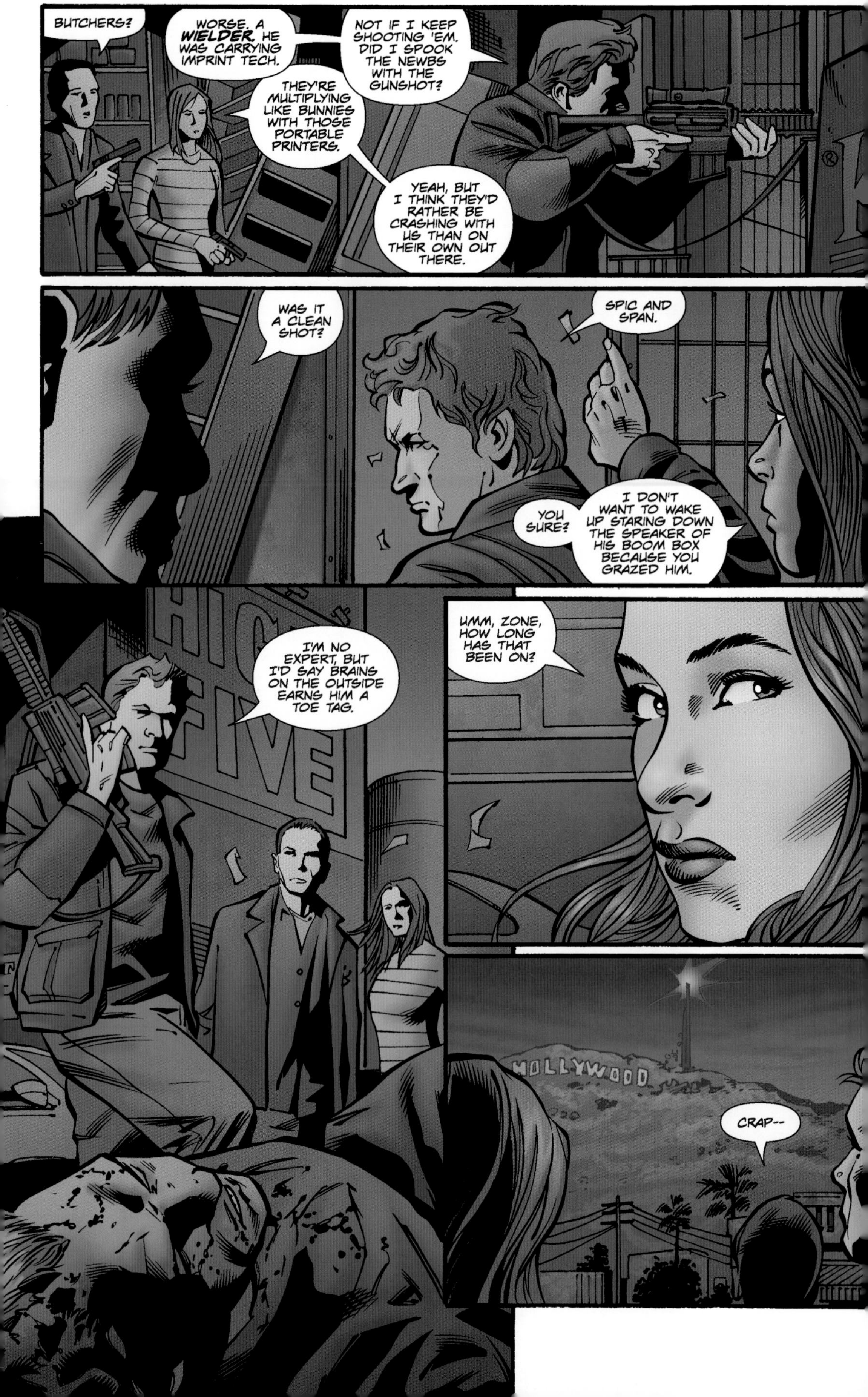
BUTCHERS?
WORSE. A WIELDER. HE WAS CARRYING IMPRINT TECH.
THEY'RE MULTIPLYING LIKE BUNNIES WITH THOSE PORTABLE PRINTERS.
NOT IF I KEEP SHOOTING 'EM. DID I SPOOK THE NEWBS WITH THE GUNSHOT?
YEAH, BUT I THINK THEY'D RATHER BE CRASHING WITH US THAN ON THEIR OWN OUT THERE.
WAS IT A CLEAN SHOT?
SPIC AND SPAN.
YOU SURE?
I DON'T WANT TO WAKE UP STARING DOWN THE SPEAKER OF HIS BOOM BOX BECAUSE YOU GRAZED HIM.
I'M NO EXPERT, BUT I'D SAY BRAINS ON THE OUTSIDE EARNS HIM A TOE TAG.
UMM, ZONE, HOW LONG HAS THAT BEEN ON?
HOLLYWOOD
CRAP--

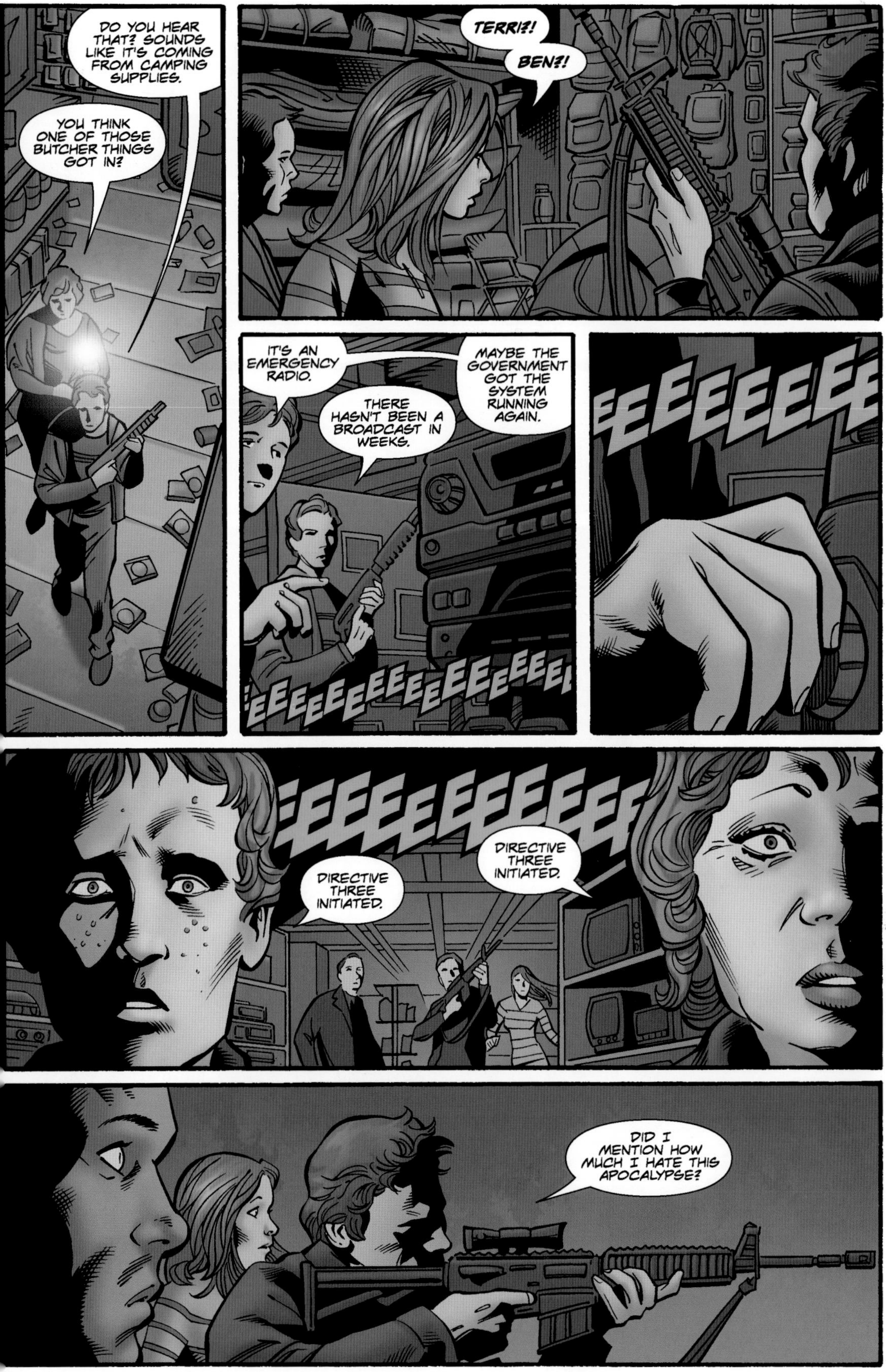
DO YOU HEAR THAT? SOUNDS LIKE IT'S COMING FROM CAMPING SUPPLIES.
YOU THINK ONE OF THOSE BUTCHER THINGS GOT IN?
TERRI?!
BEN?!
IT'S AN EMERGENCY RADIO.
THERE HASN'T BEEN A BROADCAST IN WEEKS.
MAYBE THE GOVERNMENT GOT THE SYSTEM RUNNING AGAIN.
EEEEEEEEEEEEEEE
EEEEEEEE
EEEEEEEEEEEEEE
DIRECTIVE THREE INITIATED.
DIRECTIVE THREE INITIATED.
DID I MENTION HOW MUCH I HATE THIS APOCALYPSE?

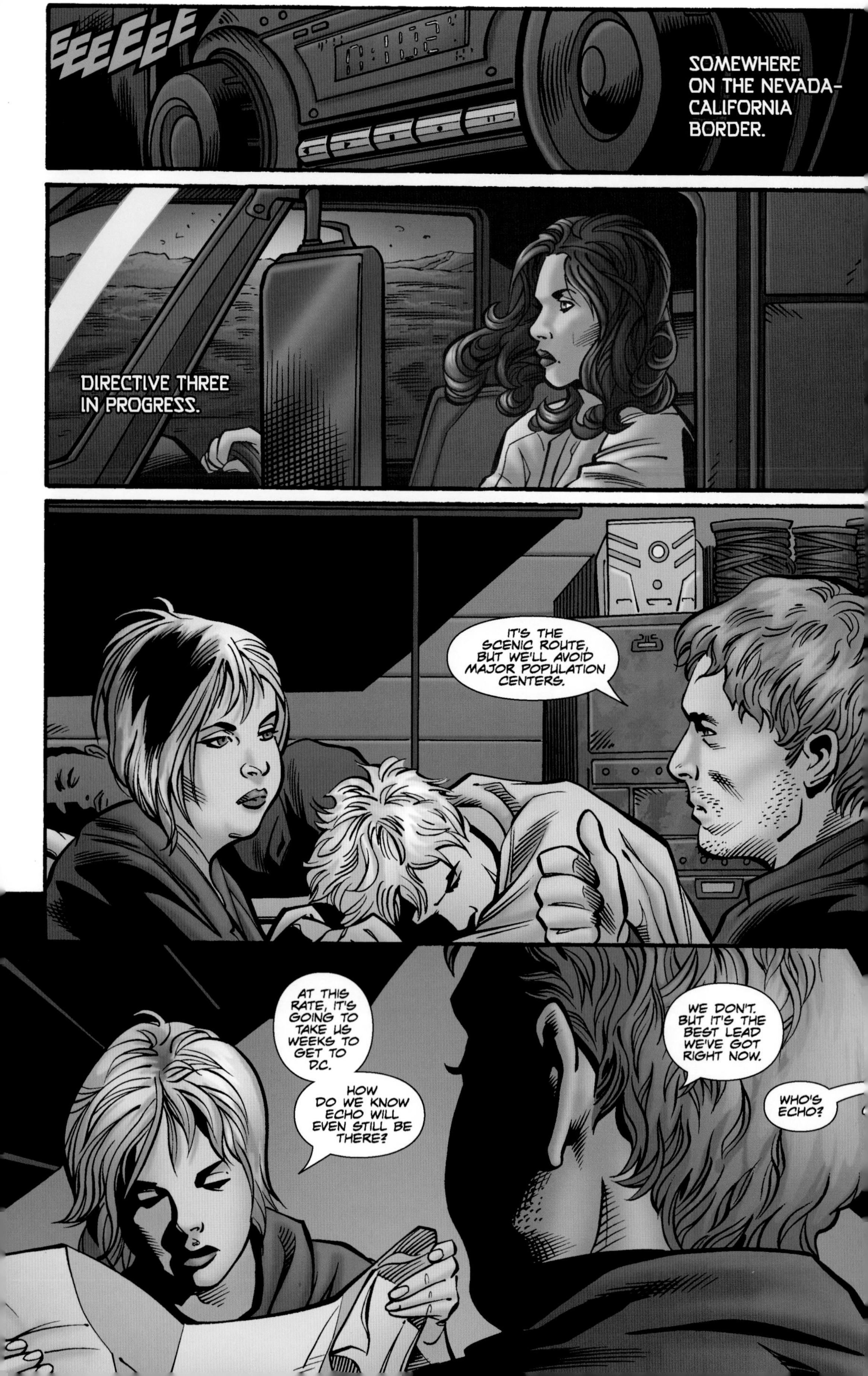
EEEEEE
SOMEWHERE ON THE NEVADA-CALIFORNIA BORDER.
DIRECTIVE THREE IN PROGRESS.
IT'S THE SCENIC ROUTE, BUT WE'LL AVOID MAJOR POPULATION CENTERS.
AT THIS RATE, IT'S GOING TO TAKE US WEEKS TO GET TO D.C.
HOW DO WE KNOW ECHO WILL EVEN STILL BE THERE?
WE DON'T. BUT IT'S THE BEST LEAD WE'VE GOT RIGHT NOW.
WHO'S ECHO?

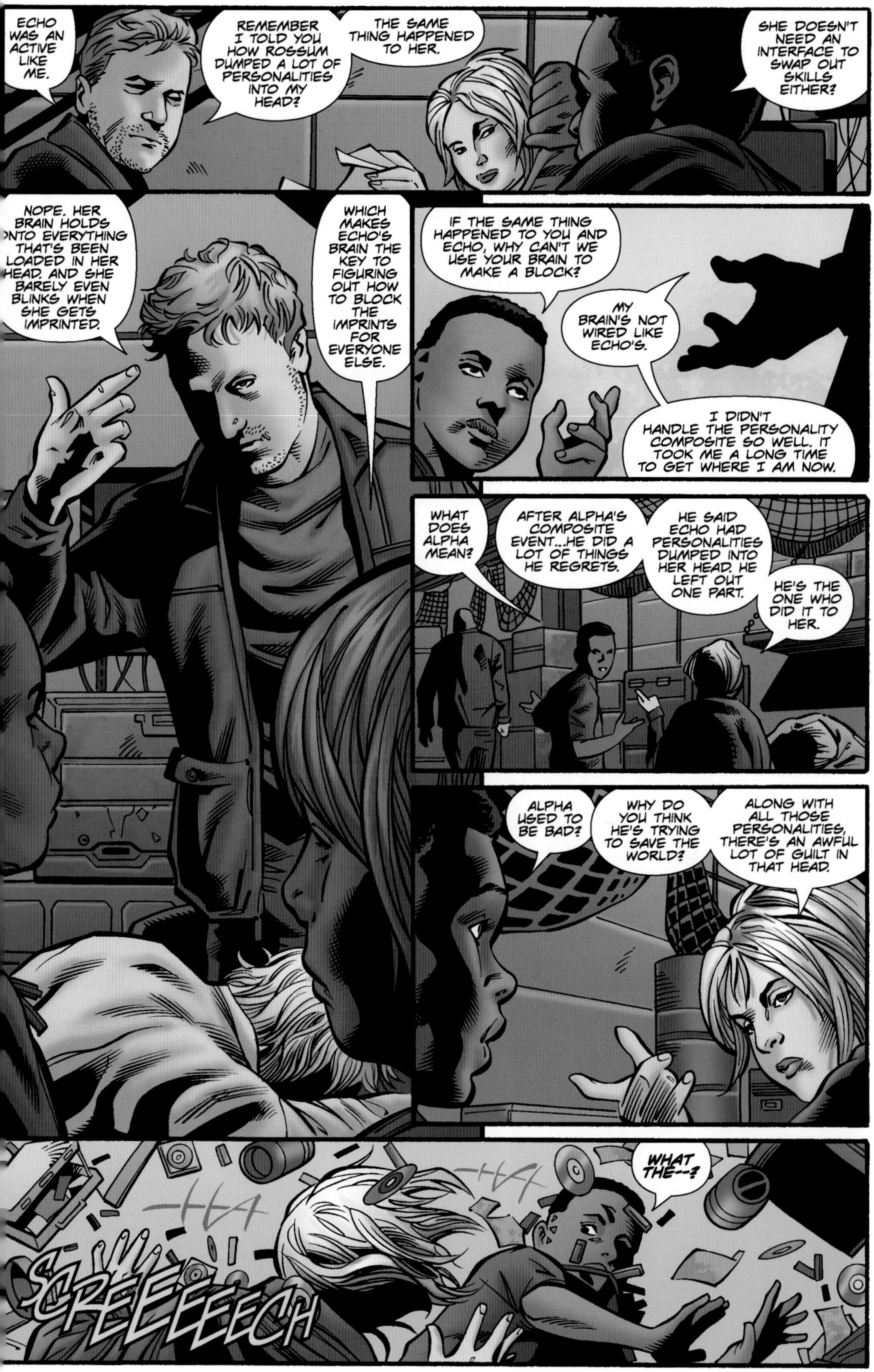
ECHO WAS AN ACTIVE LIKE ME.
REMEMBER I TOLD YOU HOW ROSSUM DUMPED A LOT OF PERSONALITIES INTO MY HEAD?
THE SAME THING HAPPENED TO HER.
SHE DOESN'T NEED AN INTERFACE TO SWAP OUT SKILLS EITHER?
NOPE. HER BRAIN HOLDS ONTO EVERYTHING THAT'S BEEN LOADED IN HER HEAD. AND SHE BARELY EVEN BLINKS WHEN SHE GETS IMPRINTED.
WHICH MAKES ECHO'S BRAIN THE KEY TO FIGURING OUT HOW TO BLOCK THE IMPRINTS FOR EVERYONE ELSE.
IF THE SAME THING HAPPENED TO YOU AND ECHO, WHY CAN'T WE USE YOUR BRAIN TO MAKE A BLOCK?
MY BRAIN'S NOT WIRED LIKE ECHO'S.
I DIDN'T HANDLE THE PERSONALITY COMPOSITE SO WELL. IT TOOK ME A LONG TIME TO GET WHERE I AM NOW.
WHAT DOES ALPHA MEAN?
AFTER ALPHA'S COMPOSITE EVENT...HE DID A LOT OF THINGS HE REGRETS.
HE SAID ECHO HAD PERSONALITIES DUMPED INTO HER HEAD. HE LEFT OUT ONE PART.
HE'S THE ONE WHO DID IT TO HER.
ALPHA USED TO BE BAD?
WHY DO YOU THINK HE'S TRYING TO SAVE THE WORLD?
ALONG WITH ALL THOSE PERSONALITIES, THERE'S AN AWFUL LOT OF GUILT IN THAT HEAD.
WHAT THE--?
SCREEEEECH

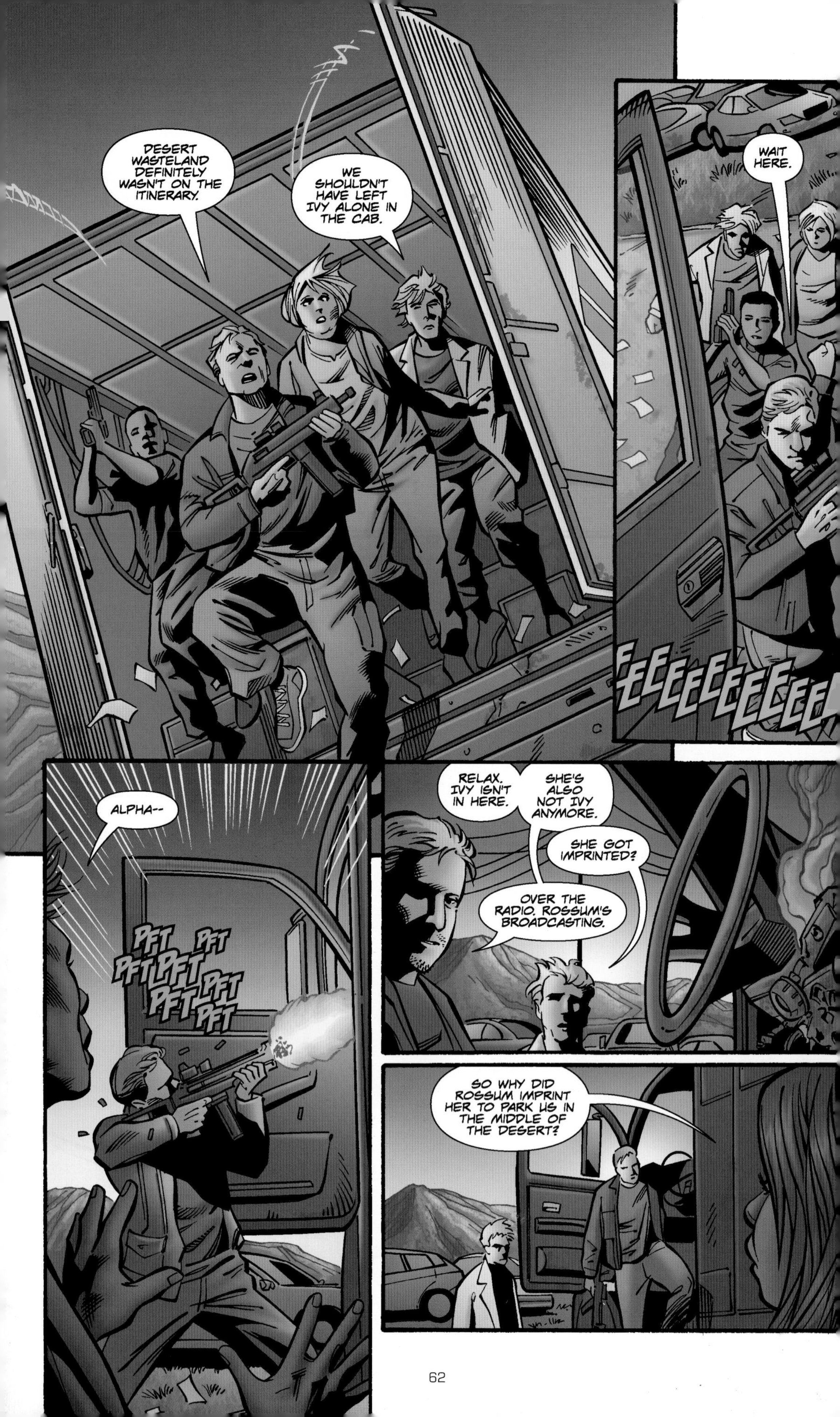

DESERT WASTELAND DEFINITELY WASN'T ON THE ITINERARY.
WE SHOULDN'T HAVE LEFT IVY ALONE IN THE CAB.
WAIT HERE.
EEEEEEEEEEE
ALPHA--
PFT PFT PFT PFT PFT PFT PFT PFT
RELAX. IVY ISN'T IN HERE.
SHE'S ALSO NOT IVY ANYMORE.
SHE GOT IMPRINTED?
OVER THE RADIO. ROSSUM'S BROADCASTING.
SO WHY DID ROSSUM IMPRINT HER TO PARK US IN THE MIDDLE OF THE DESERT?

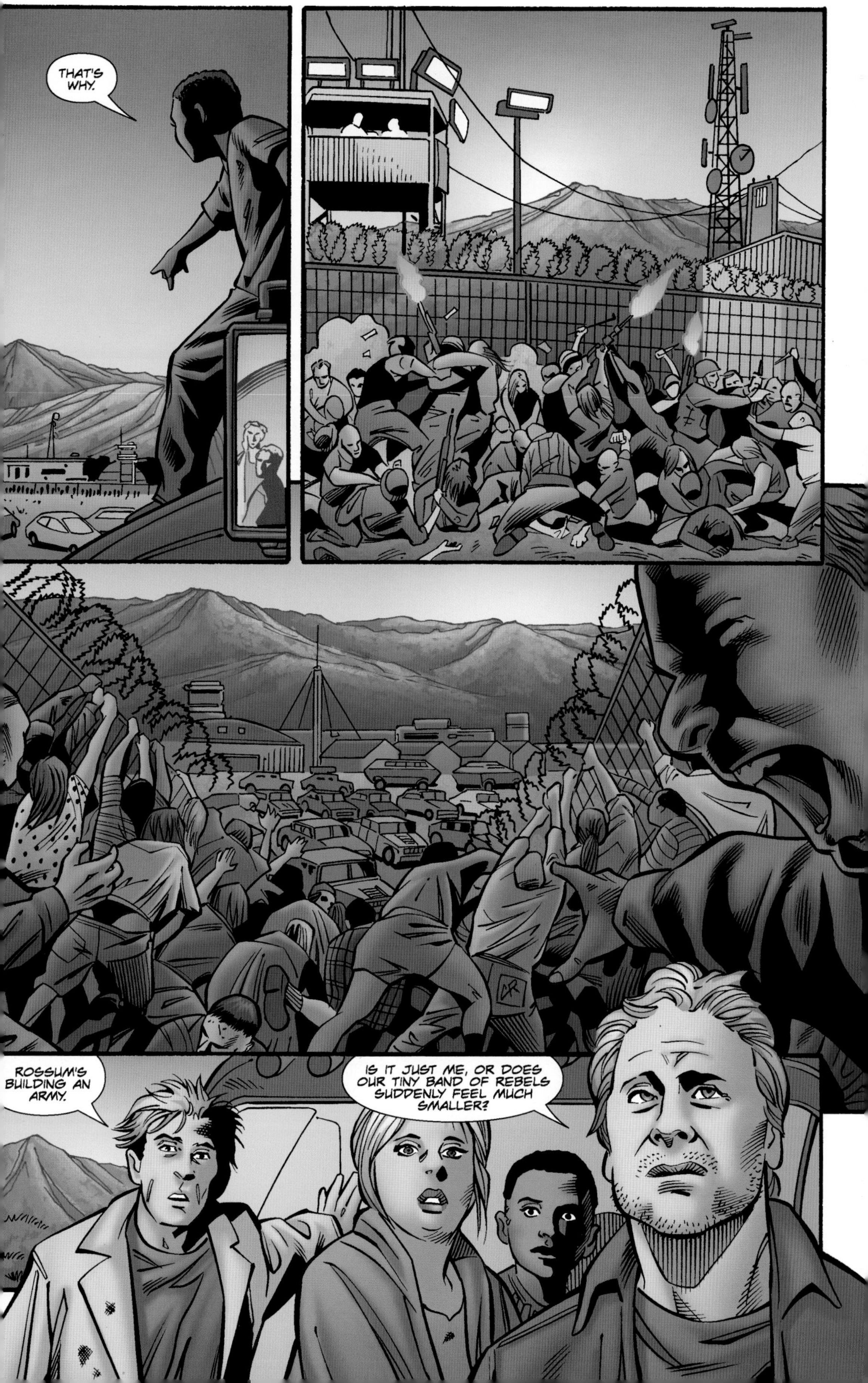
THAT'S WHY.
ROSSUM'S BUILDING AN ARMY.
IS IT JUST ME, OR DOES OUR TINY BAND OF REBELS SUDDENLY FEEL MUCH SMALLER?

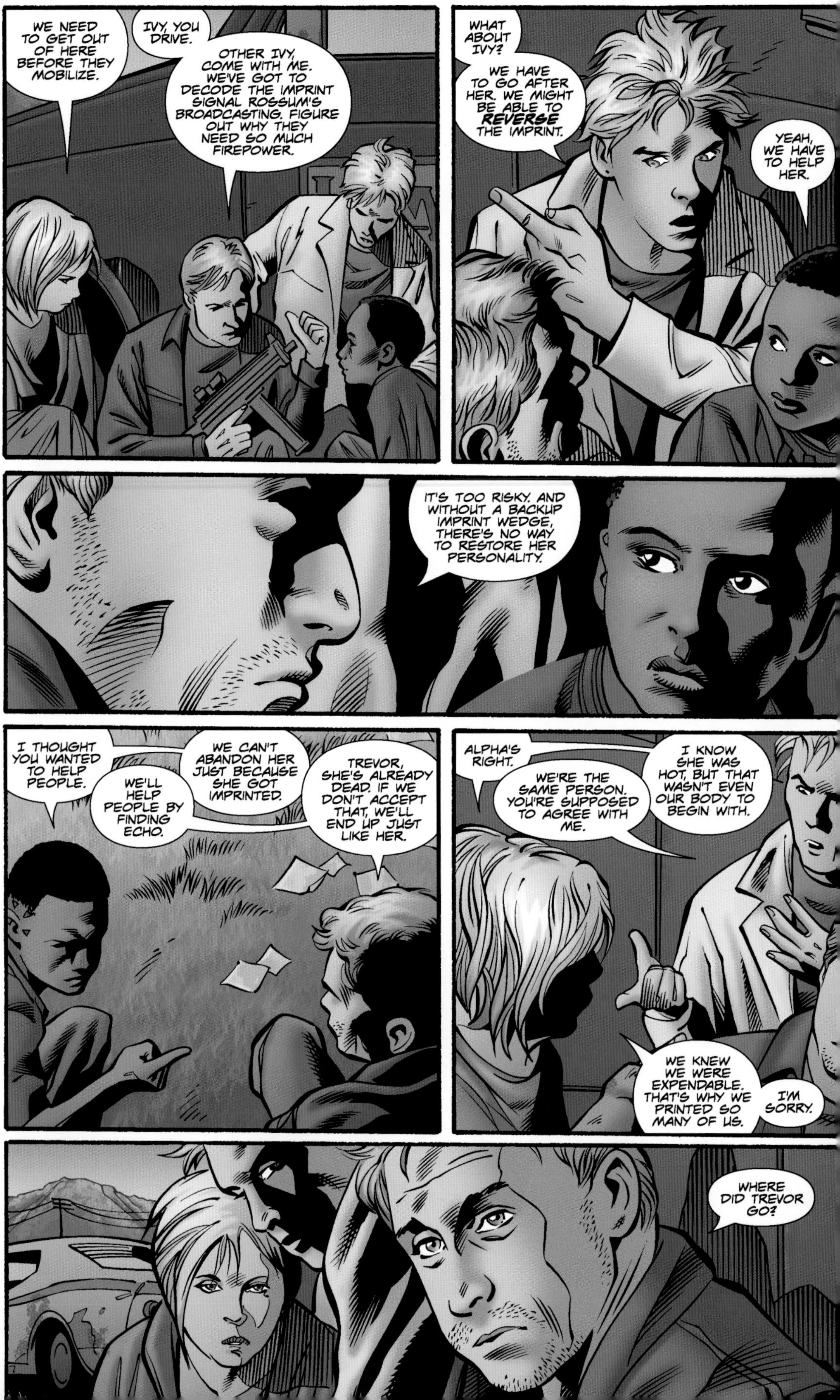

WE NEED TO GET OUT OF HERE BEFORE THEY MOBILIZE.
IVY, YOU DRIVE.
OTHER IVY, COME WITH ME. WE'VE GOT TO DECODE THE IMPRINT SIGNAL ROSSUM'S BROADCASTING. FIGURE OUT WHY THEY NEED SO MUCH FIREPOWER.
WHAT ABOUT IVY?
WE HAVE TO GO AFTER HER. WE MIGHT BE ABLE TO **REVERSE** THE IMPRINT.
YEAH, WE HAVE TO HELP HER.
IT'S TOO RISKY. AND WITHOUT A BACKUP IMPRINT WEDGE, THERE'S NO WAY TO RESTORE HER PERSONALITY.
I THOUGHT YOU WANTED TO HELP PEOPLE.
WE'LL HELP PEOPLE BY FINDING ECHO.
WE CAN'T ABANDON HER JUST BECAUSE SHE GOT IMPRINTED.
TREVOR, SHE'S ALREADY DEAD. IF WE DON'T ACCEPT THAT, WE'LL END UP JUST LIKE HER.
ALPHA'S RIGHT.
WE'RE THE SAME PERSON. YOU'RE SUPPOSED TO AGREE WITH ME.
I KNOW SHE WAS HOT, BUT THAT WASN'T EVEN OUR BODY TO BEGIN WITH.
WE KNEW WE WERE EXPENDABLE. THAT'S WHY WE PRINTED SO MANY OF US.
I'M SORRY.
WHERE DID TREVOR GO?

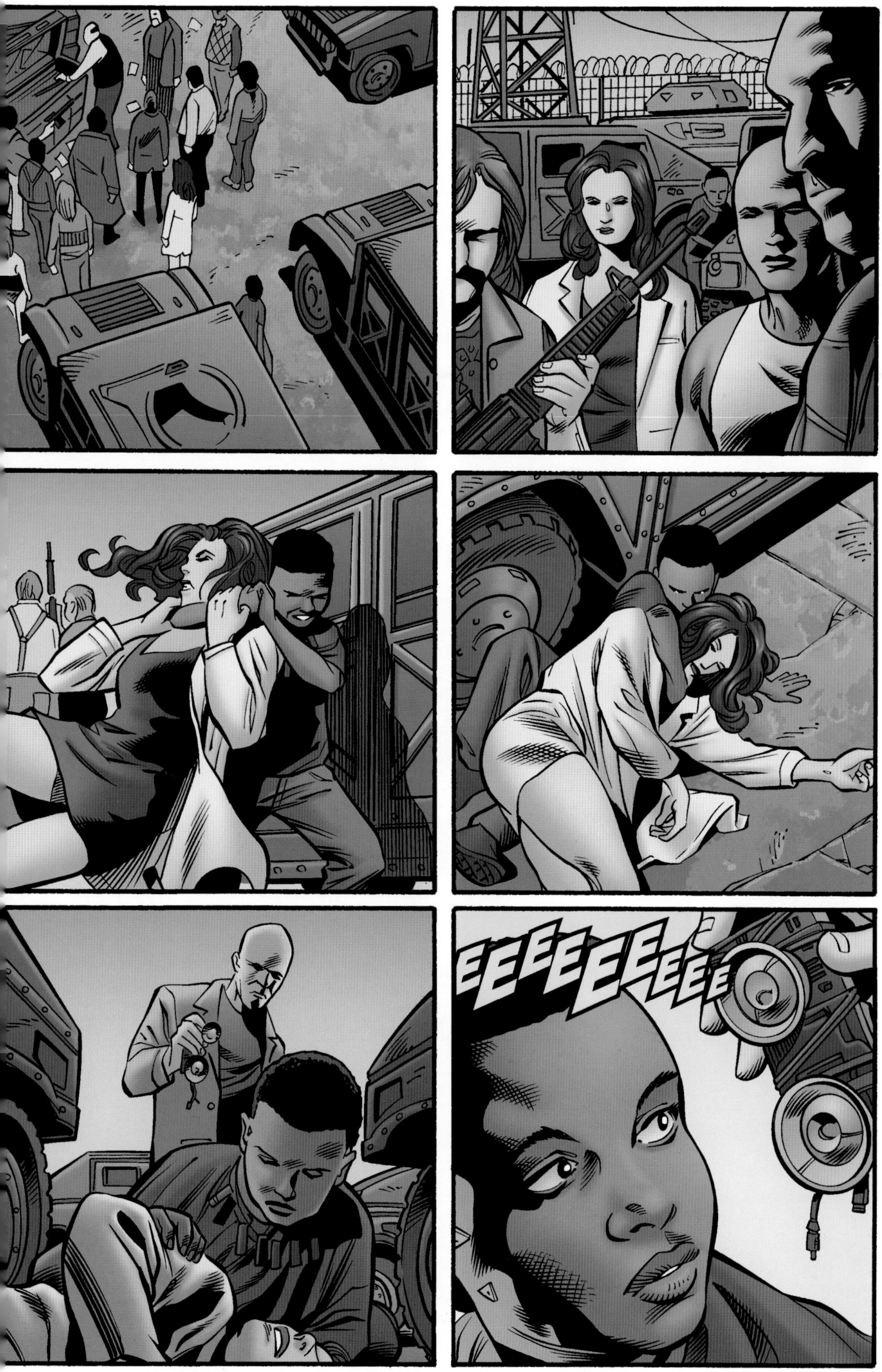
EEEEEEEEE

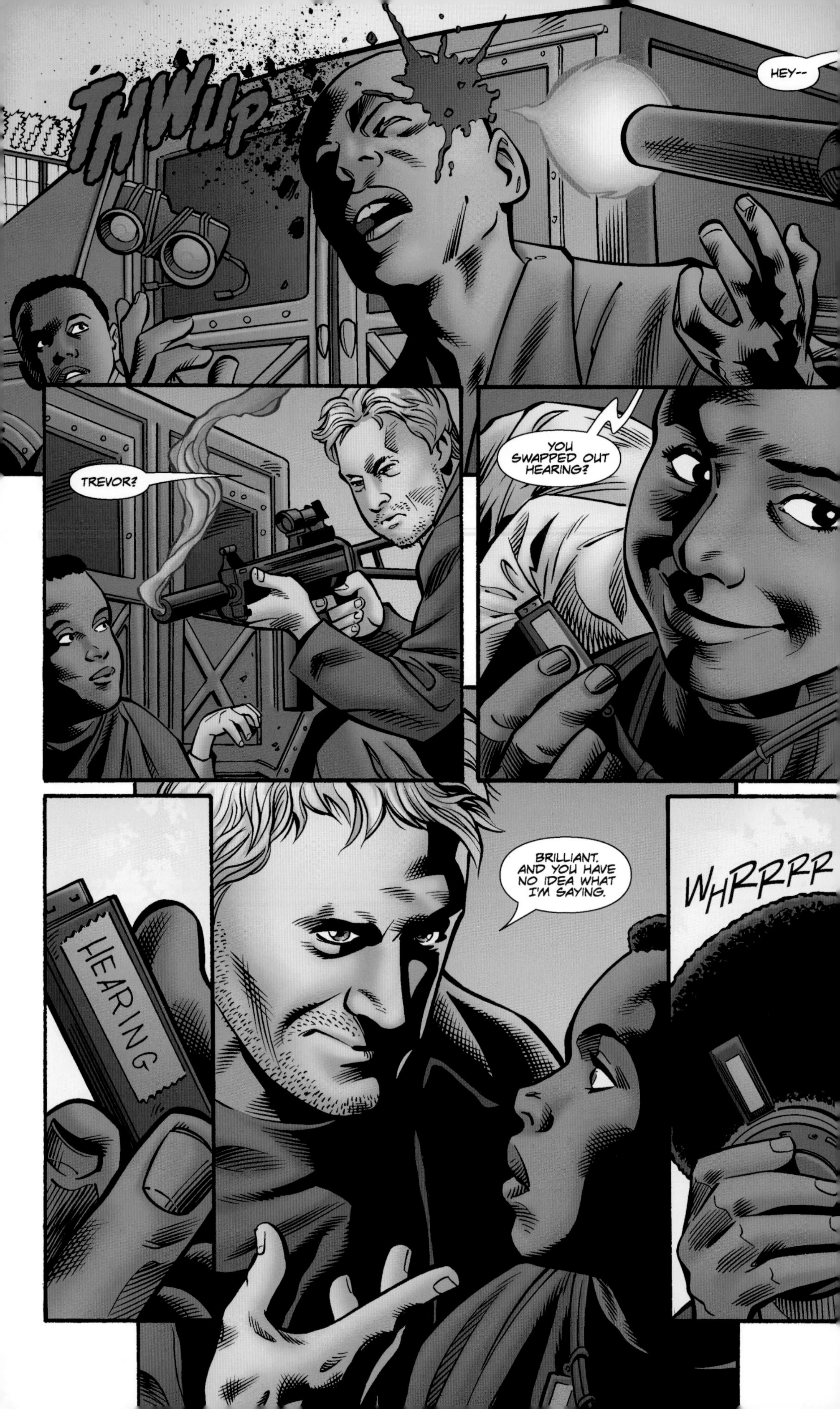
THWUP
HEY--
TREVOR?
YOU SWAPPED OUT HEARING?
HEARING
BRILLIANT. AND YOU HAVE NO IDEA WHAT I'M SAYING.
WHRRRR

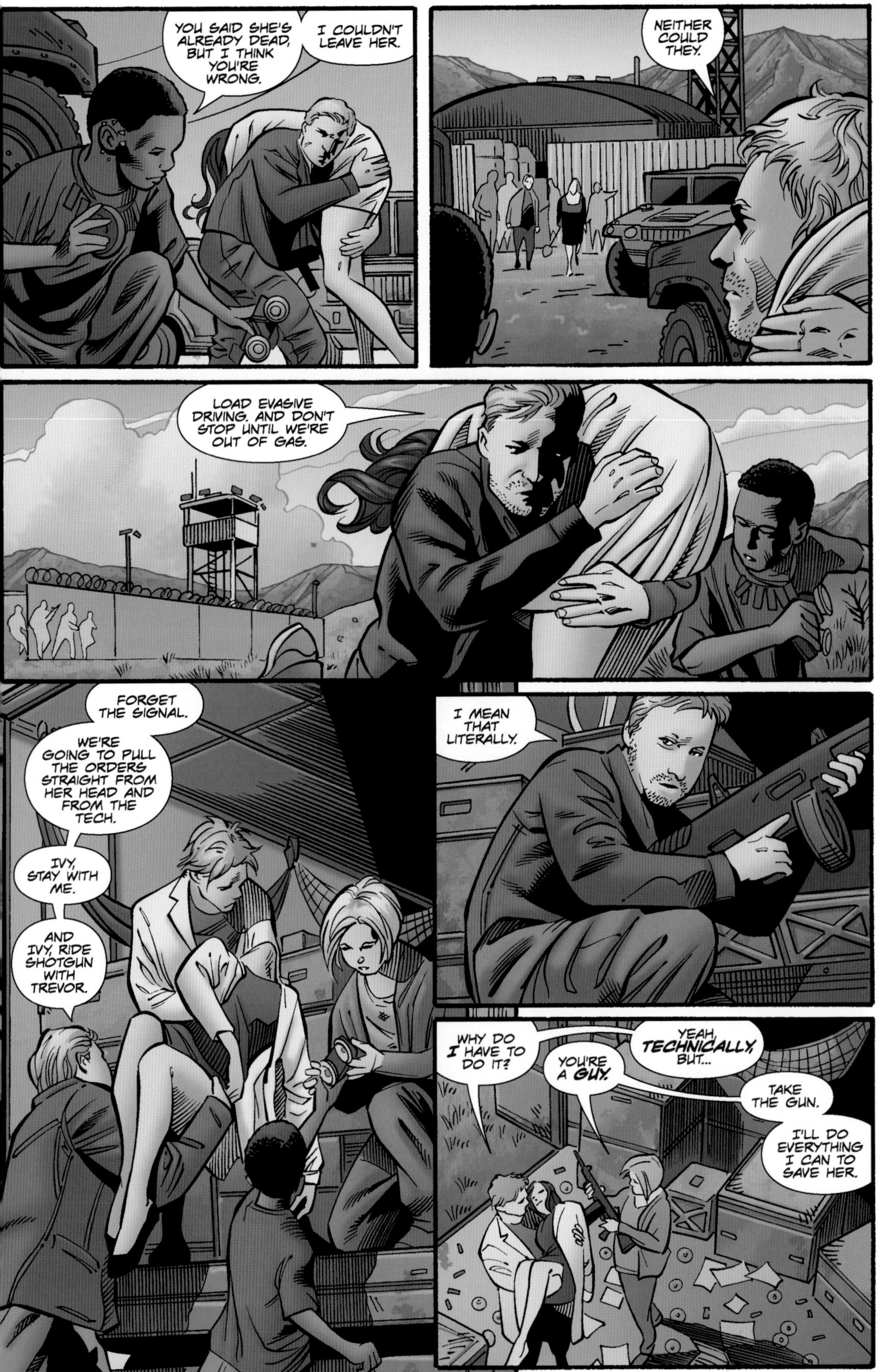
YOU SAID SHE'S ALREADY DEAD, BUT I THINK YOU'RE WRONG.
I COULDN'T LEAVE HER.
NEITHER COULD THEY.
LOAD EVASIVE DRIVING. AND DON'T STOP UNTIL WE'RE OUT OF GAS.
FORGET THE SIGNAL.
WE'RE GOING TO PULL THE ORDERS STRAIGHT FROM HER HEAD AND FROM THE TECH.
IVY, STAY WITH ME.
AND IVY, RIDE SHOTGUN WITH TREVOR.
I MEAN THAT LITERALLY.
WHY DO I HAVE TO DO IT?
YOU'RE A GUY.
YEAH, TECHNICALLY, BUT...
TAKE THE GUN.
I'LL DO EVERYTHING I CAN TO SAVE HER.

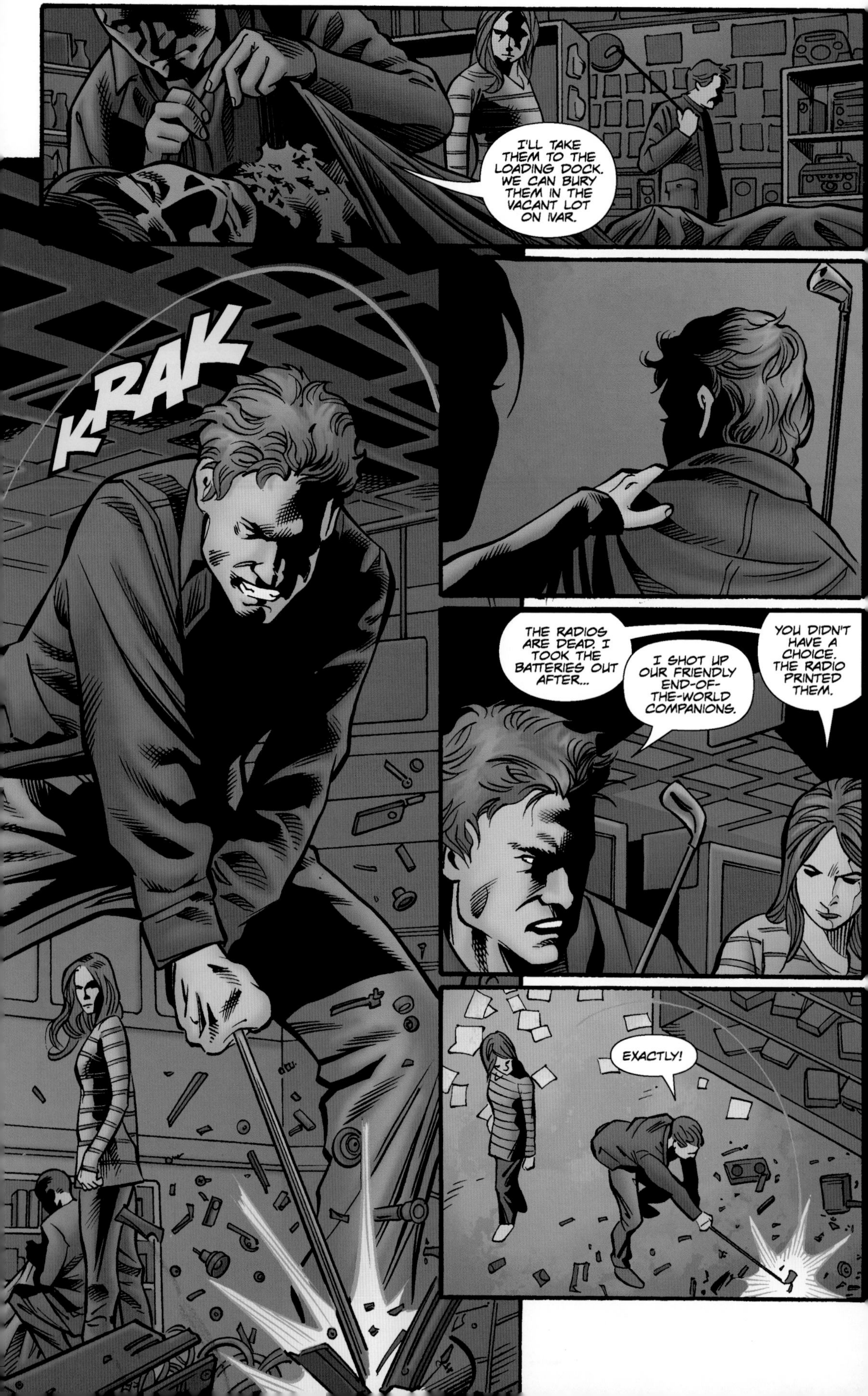
I'LL TAKE THEM TO THE LOADING DOCK. WE CAN BURY THEM IN THE VACANT LOT ON IVAR.
KRAK
THE RADIOS ARE DEAD. I TOOK THE BATTERIES OUT AFTER...
I SHOT UP OUR FRIENDLY END-OF-THE-WORLD COMPANIONS.
YOU DIDN'T HAVE A CHOICE. THE RADIO PRINTED THEM.
EXACTLY!

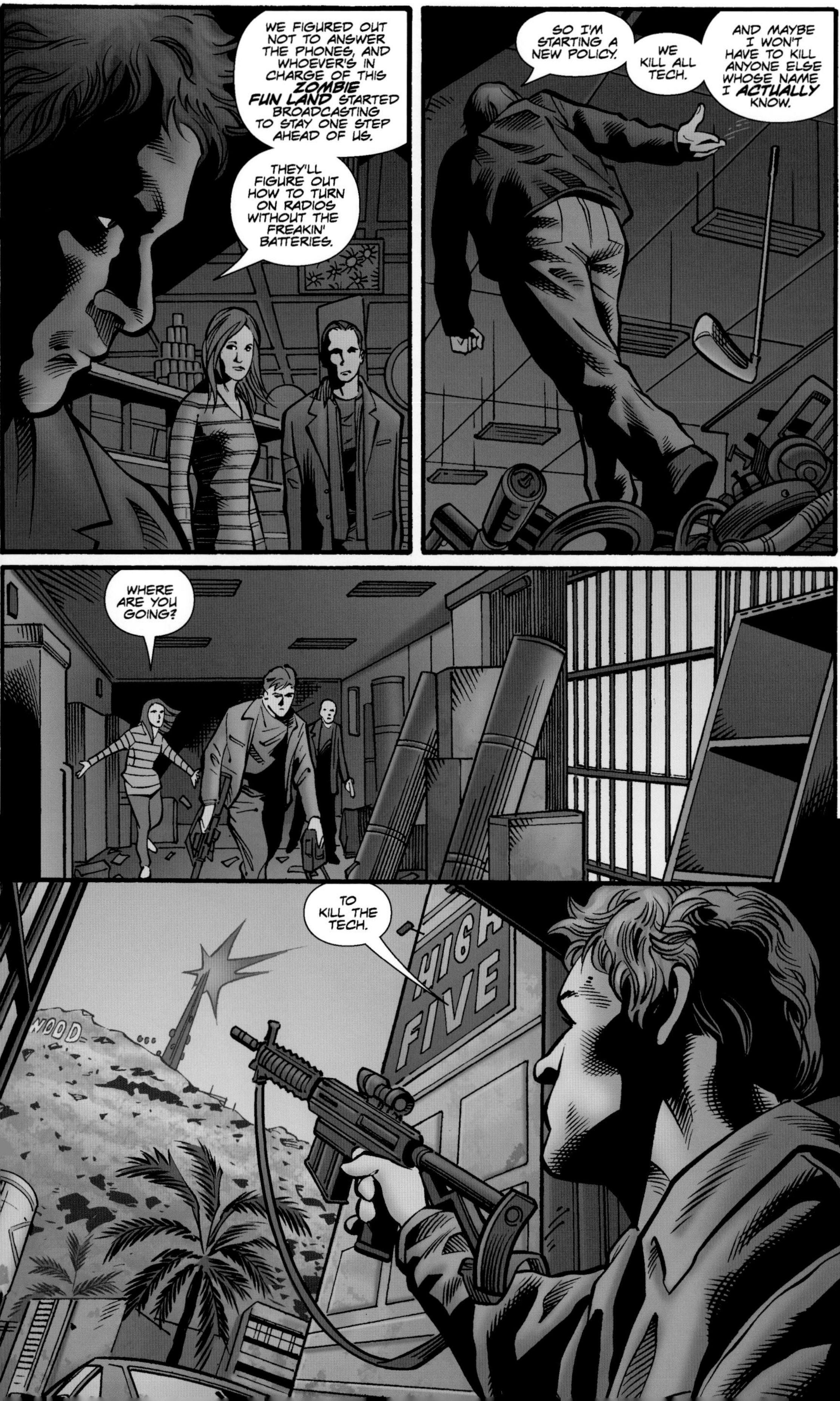
WE FIGURED OUT NOT TO ANSWER THE PHONES, AND WHOEVER'S IN CHARGE OF THIS ZOMBIE FUN LAND STARTED BROADCASTING TO STAY ONE STEP AHEAD OF US.
THEY'LL FIGURE OUT HOW TO TURN ON RADIOS WITHOUT THE FREAKIN' BATTERIES.
SO I'M STARTING A NEW POLICY.
WE KILL ALL TECH.
AND MAYBE I WON'T HAVE TO KILL ANYONE ELSE WHOSE NAME I ACTUALLY KNOW.
WHERE ARE YOU GOING?
TO KILL THE TECH.
HIGH FIVE
WOOD

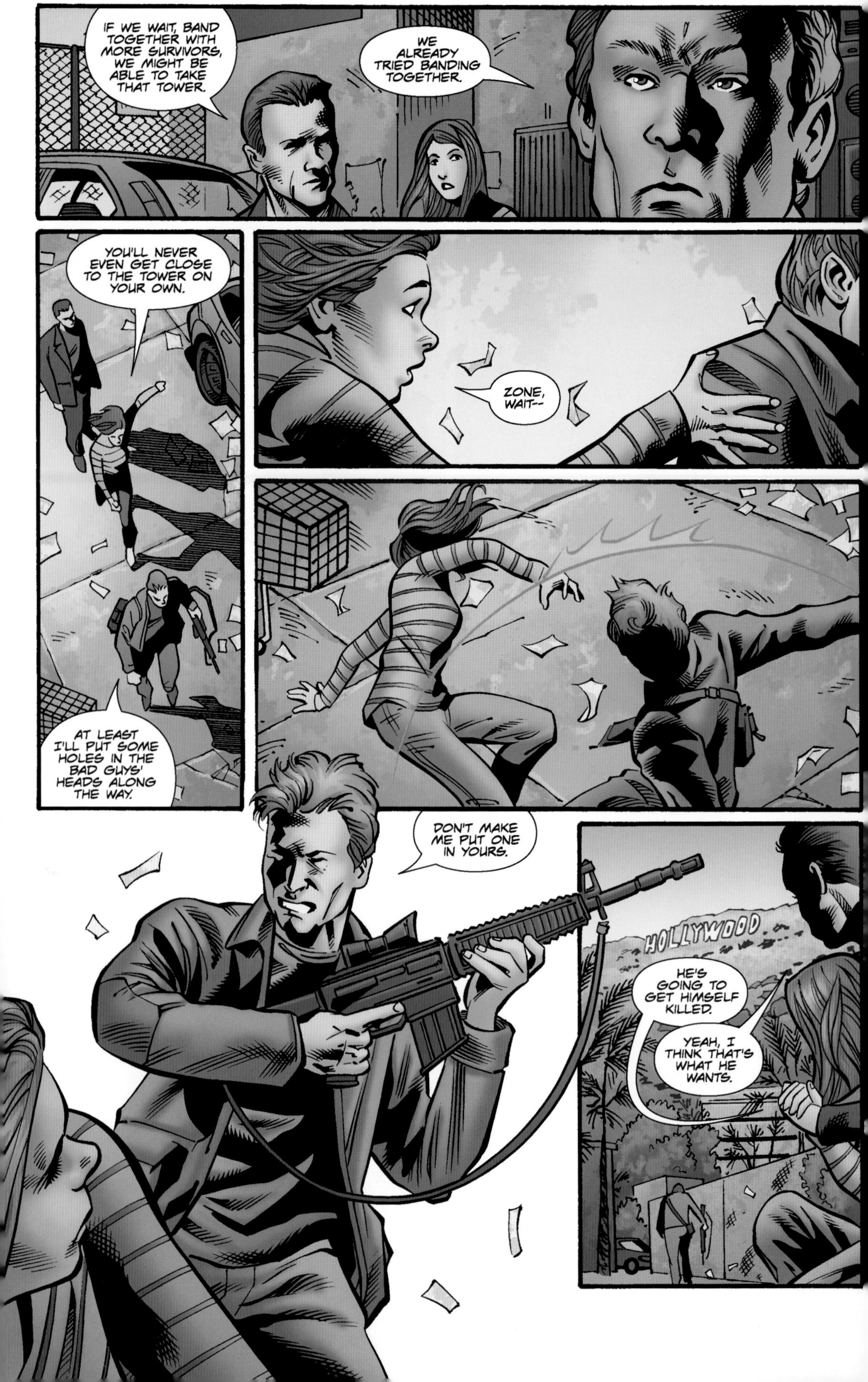
IF WE WAIT, BAND TOGETHER WITH MORE SURVIVORS, WE MIGHT BE ABLE TO TAKE THAT TOWER.
WE ALREADY TRIED BANDING TOGETHER.
YOU'LL NEVER EVEN GET CLOSE TO THE TOWER ON YOUR OWN.
AT LEAST I'LL PUT SOME HOLES IN THE BAD GUYS' HEADS ALONG THE WAY.
ZONE, WAIT--
DON'T MAKE ME PUT ONE IN YOURS.
HOLLYWOOD
HE'S GOING TO GET HIMSELF KILLED.
YEAH, I THINK THAT'S WHAT HE WANTS.

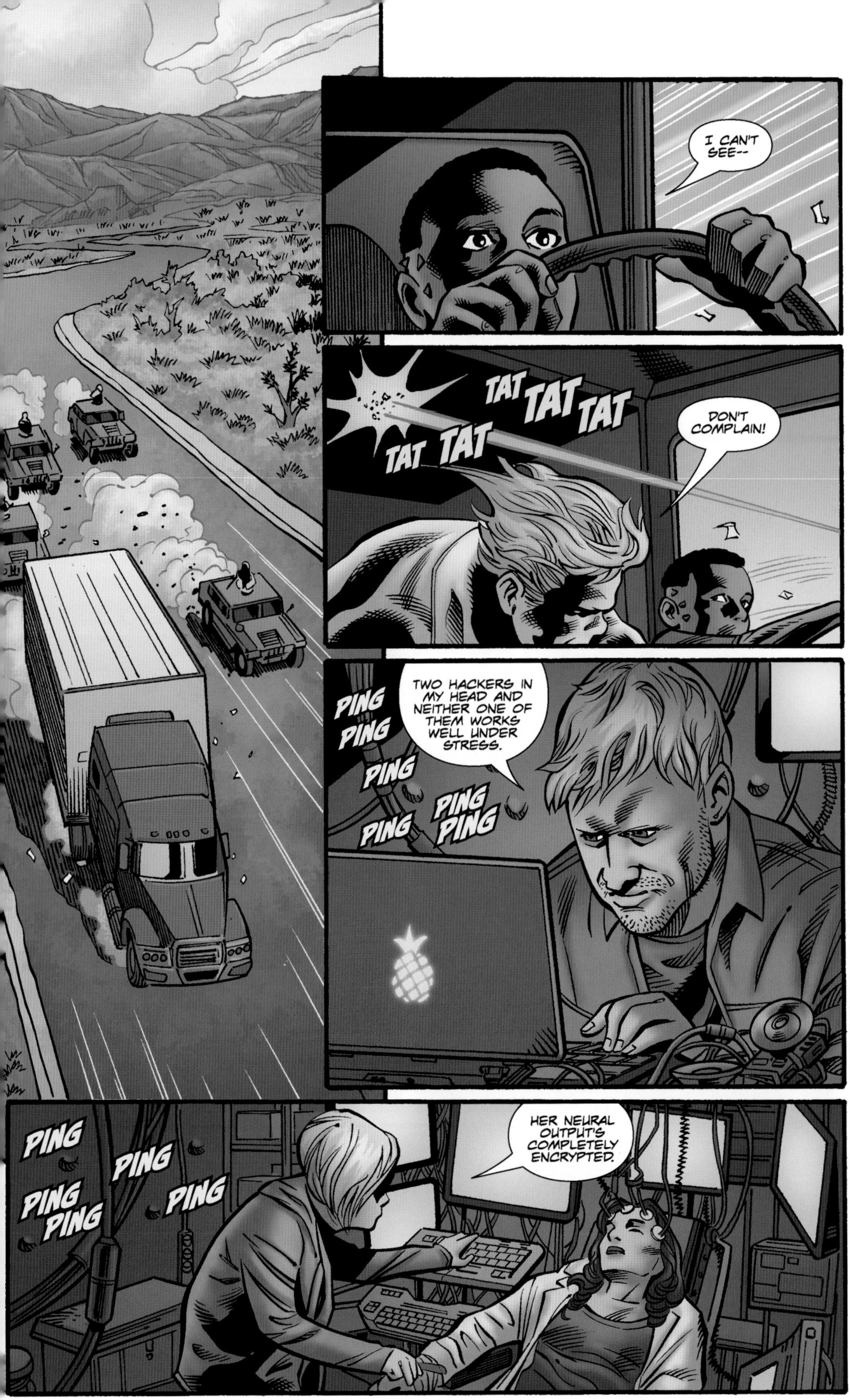
I CAN'T SEE--
TAT TAT TAT TAT TAT
DON'T COMPLAIN!
PING PING PING PING PING PING
TWO HACKERS IN MY HEAD AND NEITHER ONE OF THEM WORKS WELL UNDER STRESS.
PING PING PING PING PING
HER NEURAL OUTPUT'S COMPLETELY ENCRYPTED.

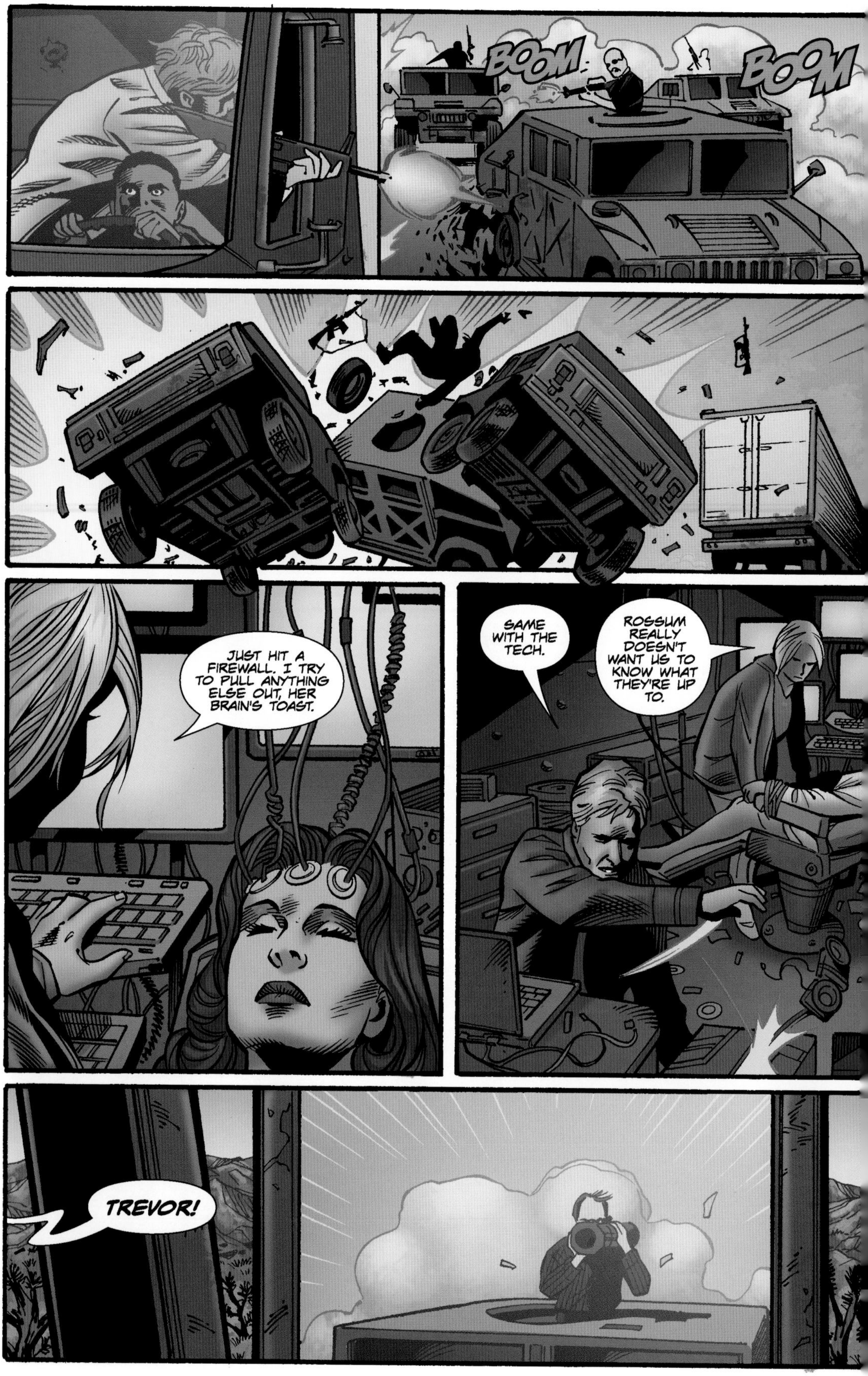
BOOM
BOOM
JUST HIT A FIREWALL. I TRY TO PULL ANYTHING ELSE OUT, HER BRAIN'S TOAST.
SAME WITH THE TECH.
ROSSUM REALLY DOESN'T WANT US TO KNOW WHAT THEY'RE UP TO.
TREVOR!

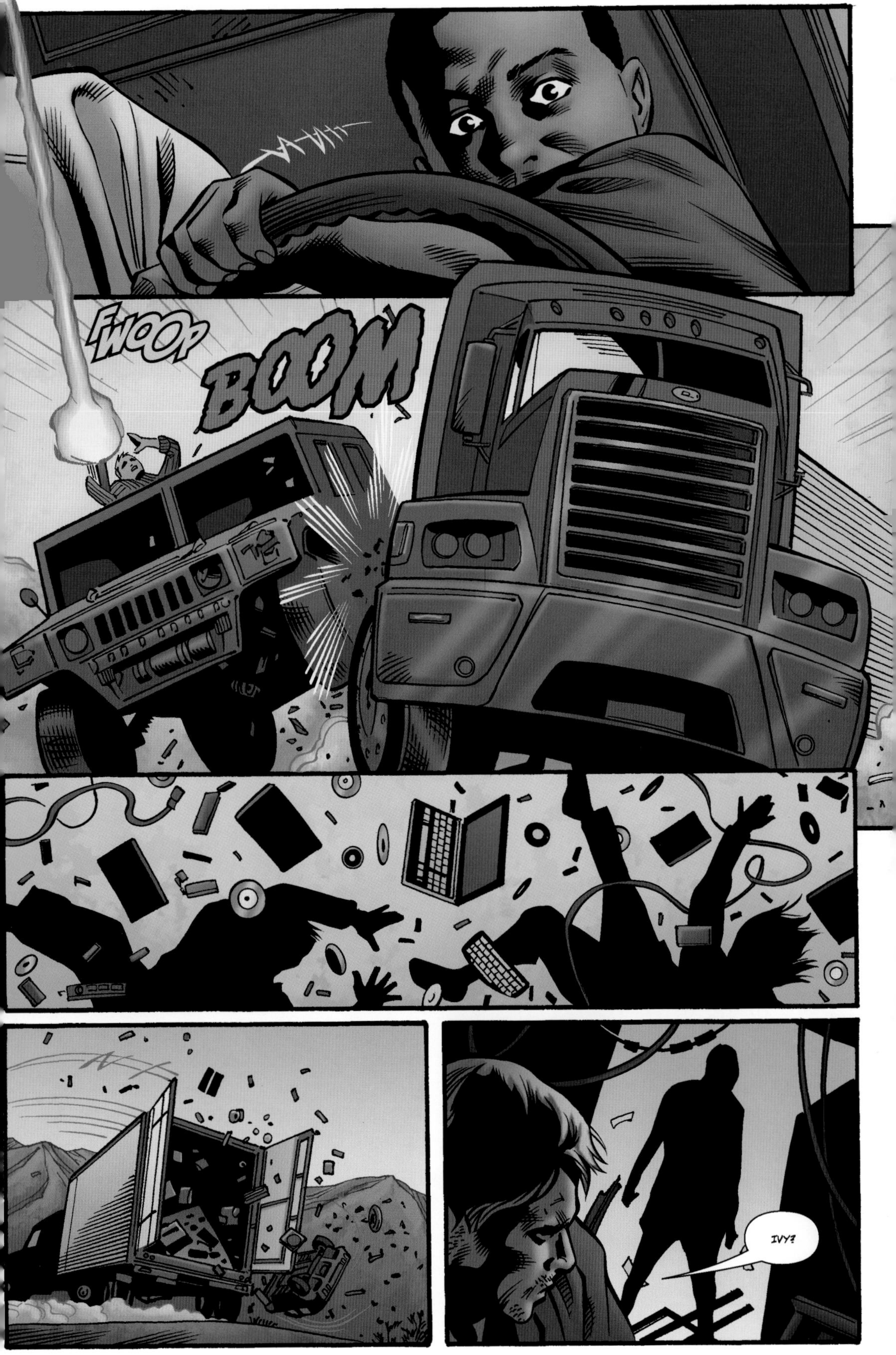
FWOOP
BOOM
IVY?

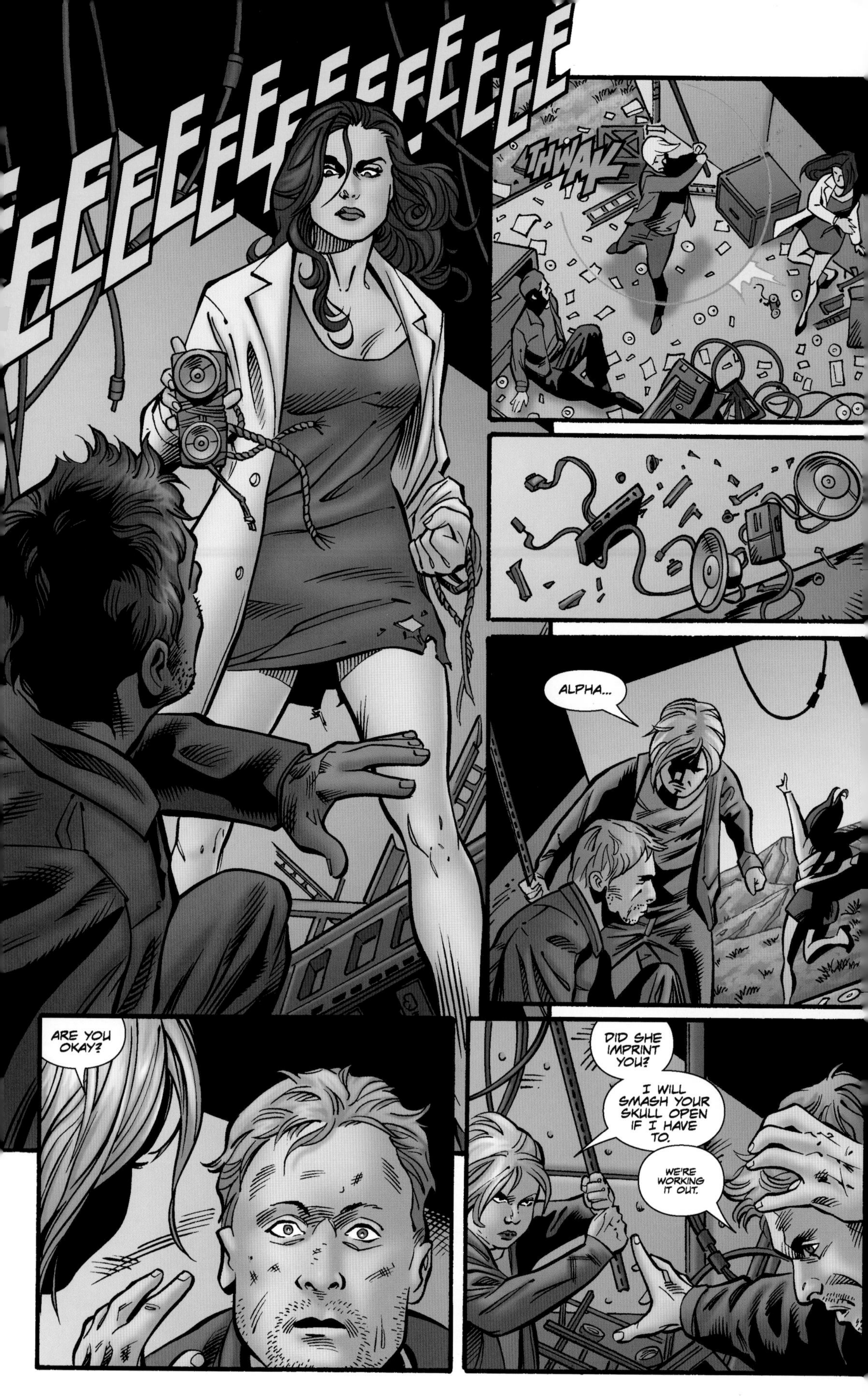
EEEEEEEEEEEEEEEE
THWAK
ALPHA...
ARE YOU OKAY?
DID SHE IMPRINT YOU?
I WILL SMASH YOUR SKULL OPEN IF I HAVE TO.
WE'RE WORKING IT OUT.

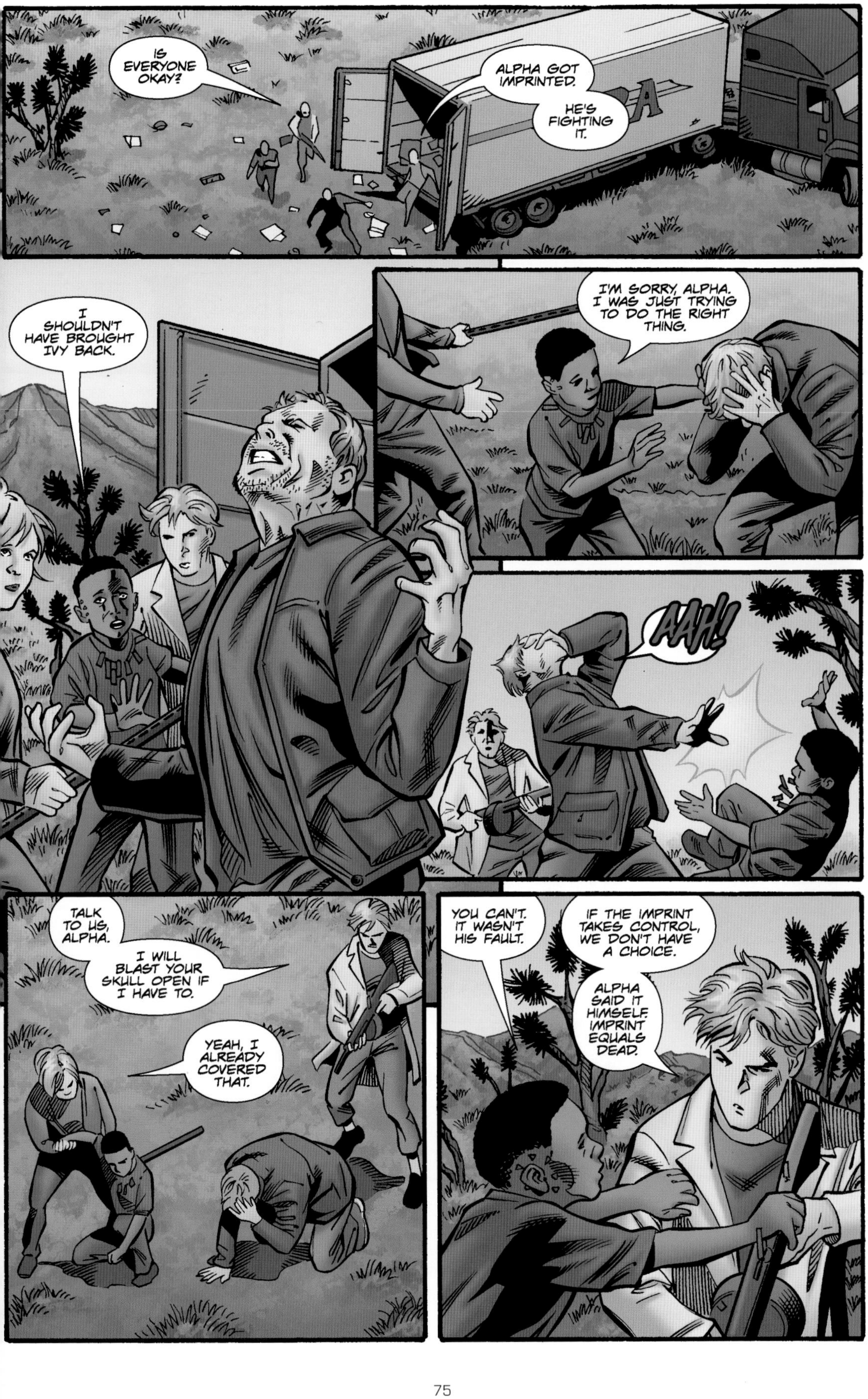
IS EVERYONE OKAY?
ALPHA GOT IMPRINTED.
HE'S FIGHTING IT.
I SHOULDN'T HAVE BROUGHT IVY BACK.
I'M SORRY, ALPHA. I WAS JUST TRYING TO DO THE RIGHT THING.
AAH!
TALK TO US, ALPHA.
I WILL BLAST YOUR SKULL OPEN IF I HAVE TO.
YEAH, I ALREADY COVERED THAT.
YOU CAN'T. IT WASN'T HIS FAULT.
IF THE IMPRINT TAKES CONTROL, WE DON'T HAVE A CHOICE.
ALPHA SAID IT HIMSELF. IMPRINT EQUALS DEAD.

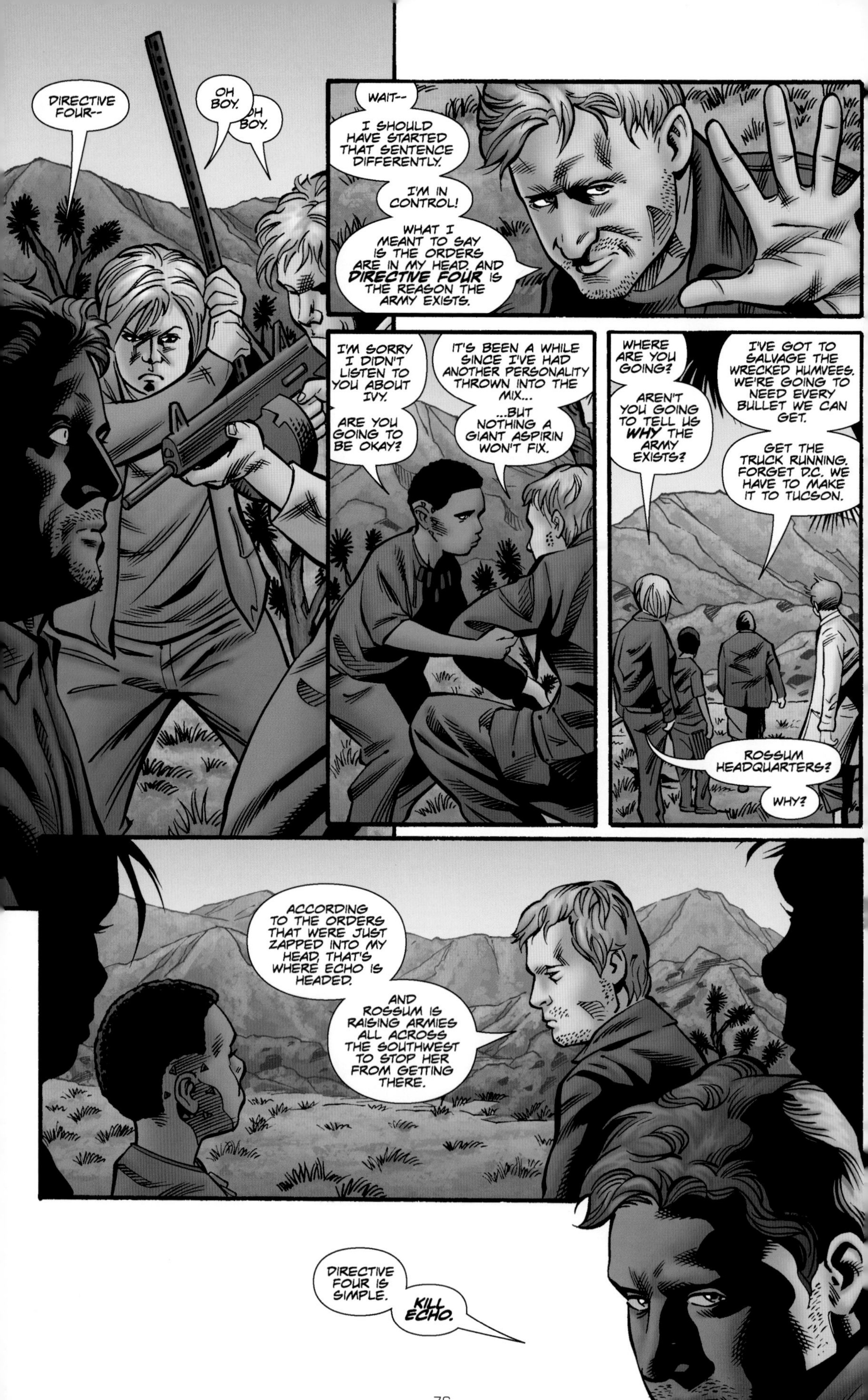
DIRECTIVE FOUR--
OH BOY.
OH BOY.
WAIT--
I SHOULD HAVE STARTED THAT SENTENCE DIFFERENTLY.
I'M IN CONTROL!
WHAT I MEANT TO SAY IS THE ORDERS ARE IN MY HEAD, AND DIRECTIVE FOUR IS THE REASON THE ARMY EXISTS.
I'M SORRY I DIDN'T LISTEN TO YOU ABOUT IVY.
ARE YOU GOING TO BE OKAY?
IT'S BEEN A WHILE SINCE I'VE HAD ANOTHER PERSONALITY THROWN INTO THE MIX...
...BUT NOTHING A GIANT ASPIRIN WON'T FIX.
WHERE ARE YOU GOING?
AREN'T YOU GOING TO TELL US WHY THE ARMY EXISTS?
I'VE GOT TO SALVAGE THE WRECKED HUMVEES. WE'RE GOING TO NEED EVERY BULLET WE CAN GET.
GET THE TRUCK RUNNING. FORGET D.C. WE HAVE TO MAKE IT TO TUCSON.
ROSSUM HEADQUARTERS?
WHY?
ACCORDING TO THE ORDERS THAT WERE JUST ZAPPED INTO MY HEAD, THAT'S WHERE ECHO IS HEADED.
AND ROSSUM IS RAISING ARMIES ALL ACROSS THE SOUTHWEST TO STOP HER FROM GETTING THERE.
DIRECTIVE FOUR IS SIMPLE.
KILL ECHO.

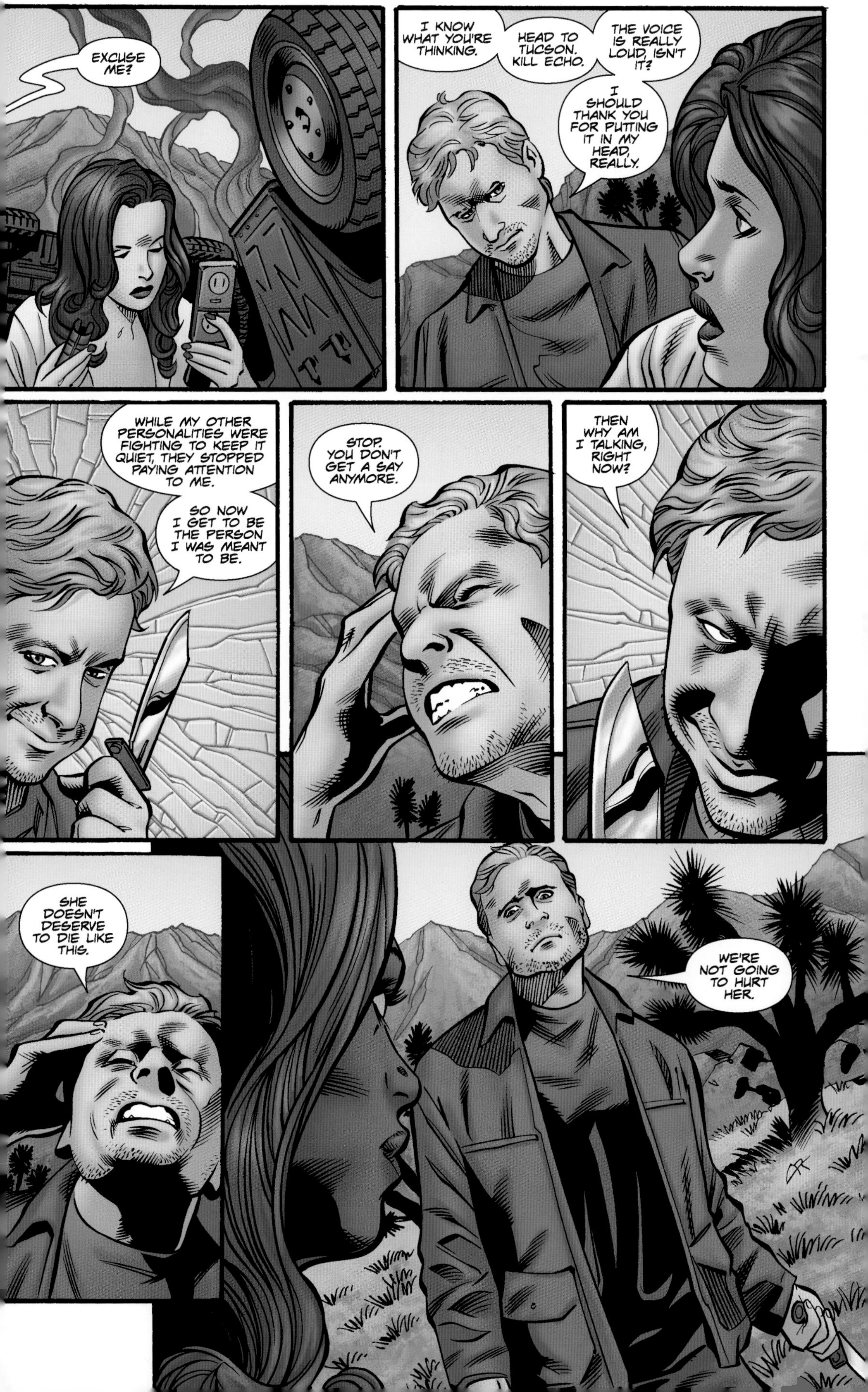
EXCUSE ME?
I KNOW WHAT YOU'RE THINKING.
HEAD TO TUCSON. KILL ECHO.
THE VOICE IS REALLY LOUD, ISN'T IT?
I SHOULD THANK YOU FOR PUTTING IT IN MY HEAD, REALLY.
WHILE MY OTHER PERSONALITIES WERE FIGHTING TO KEEP IT QUIET, THEY STOPPED PAYING ATTENTION TO ME.
SO NOW I GET TO BE THE PERSON I WAS MEANT TO BE.
STOP. YOU DON'T GET A SAY ANYMORE.
THEN WHY AM I TALKING, RIGHT NOW?
SHE DOESN'T DESERVE TO DIE LIKE THIS.
WE'RE NOT GOING TO HURT HER.

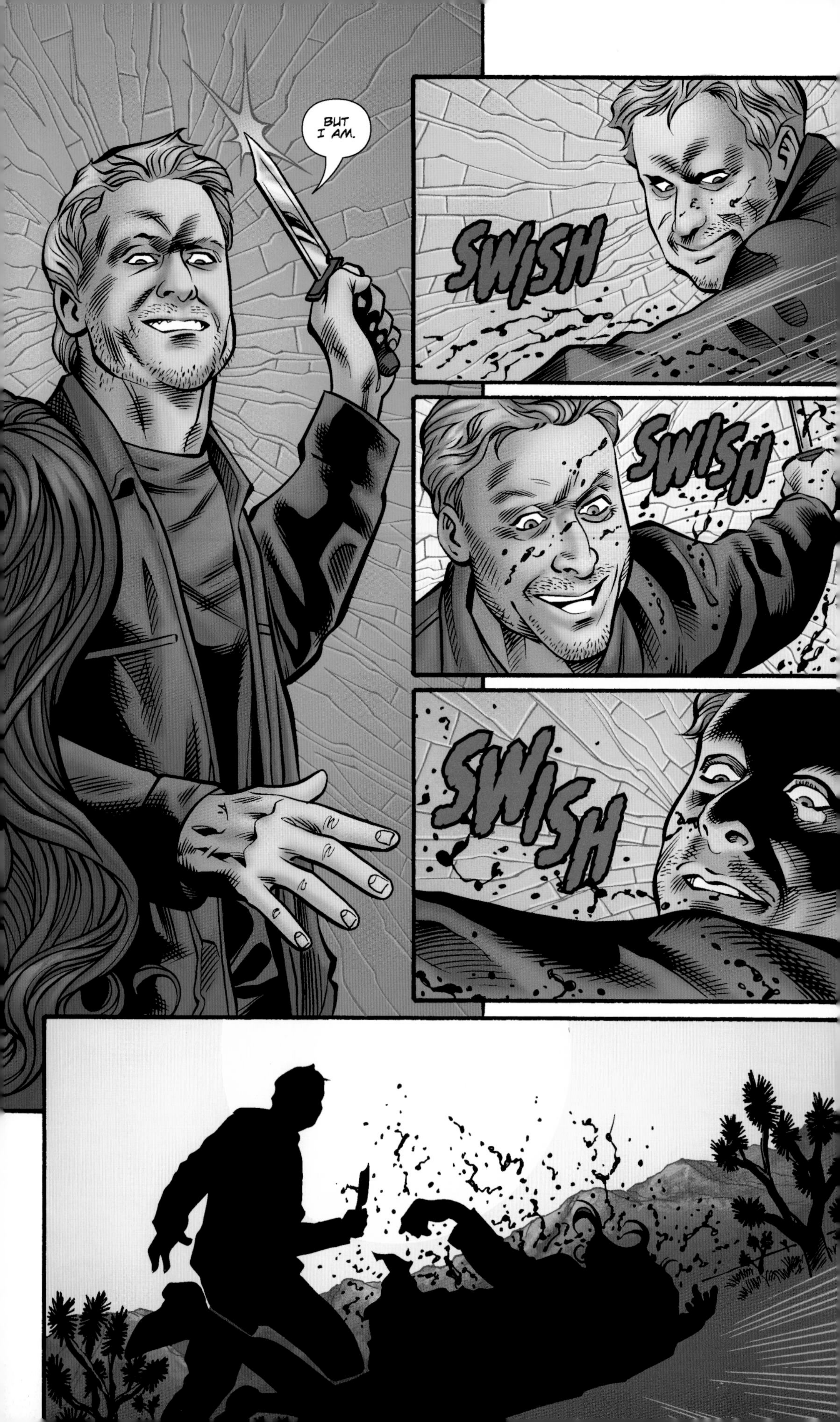
BUT I AM.
SWISH
SWISH
SWISH

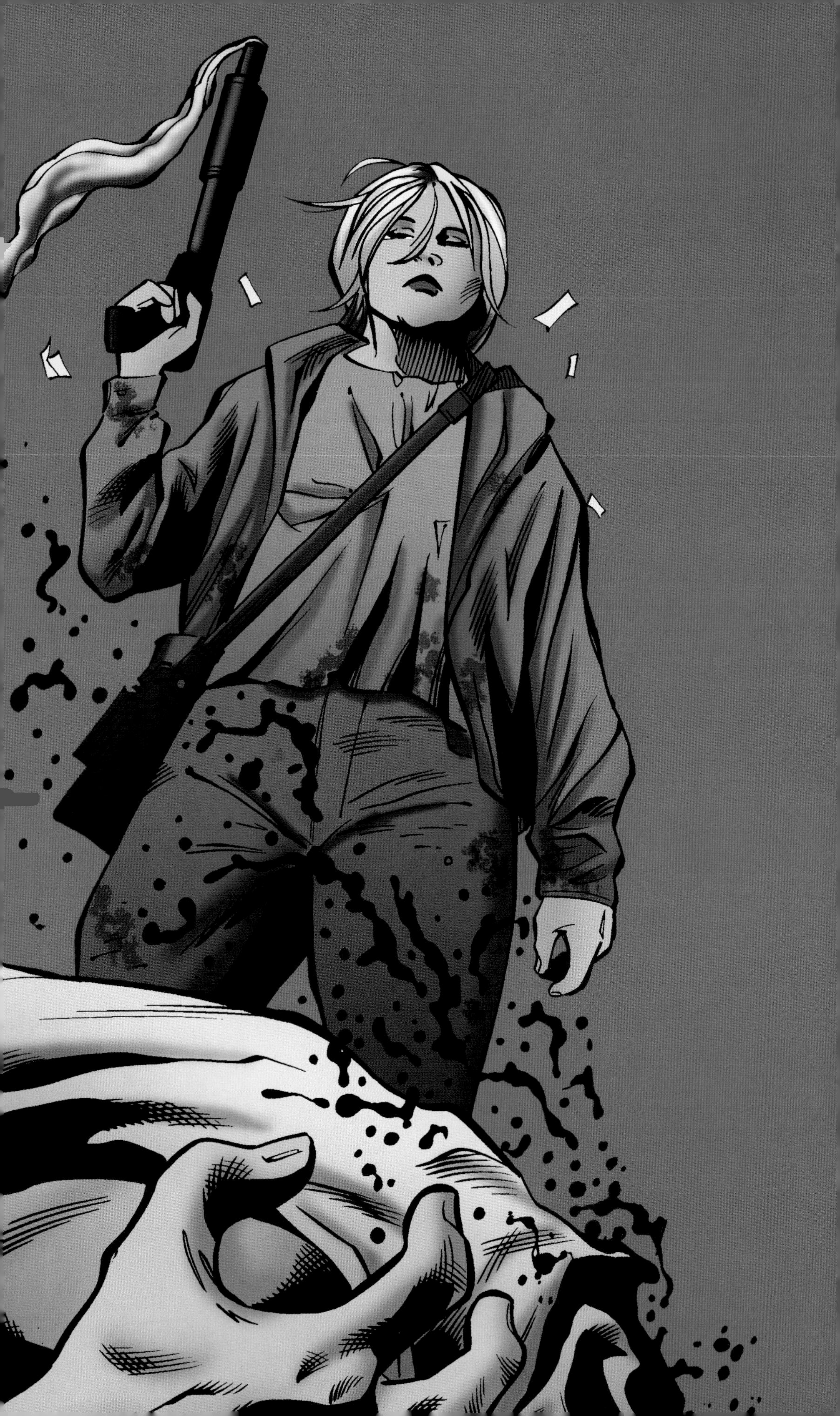

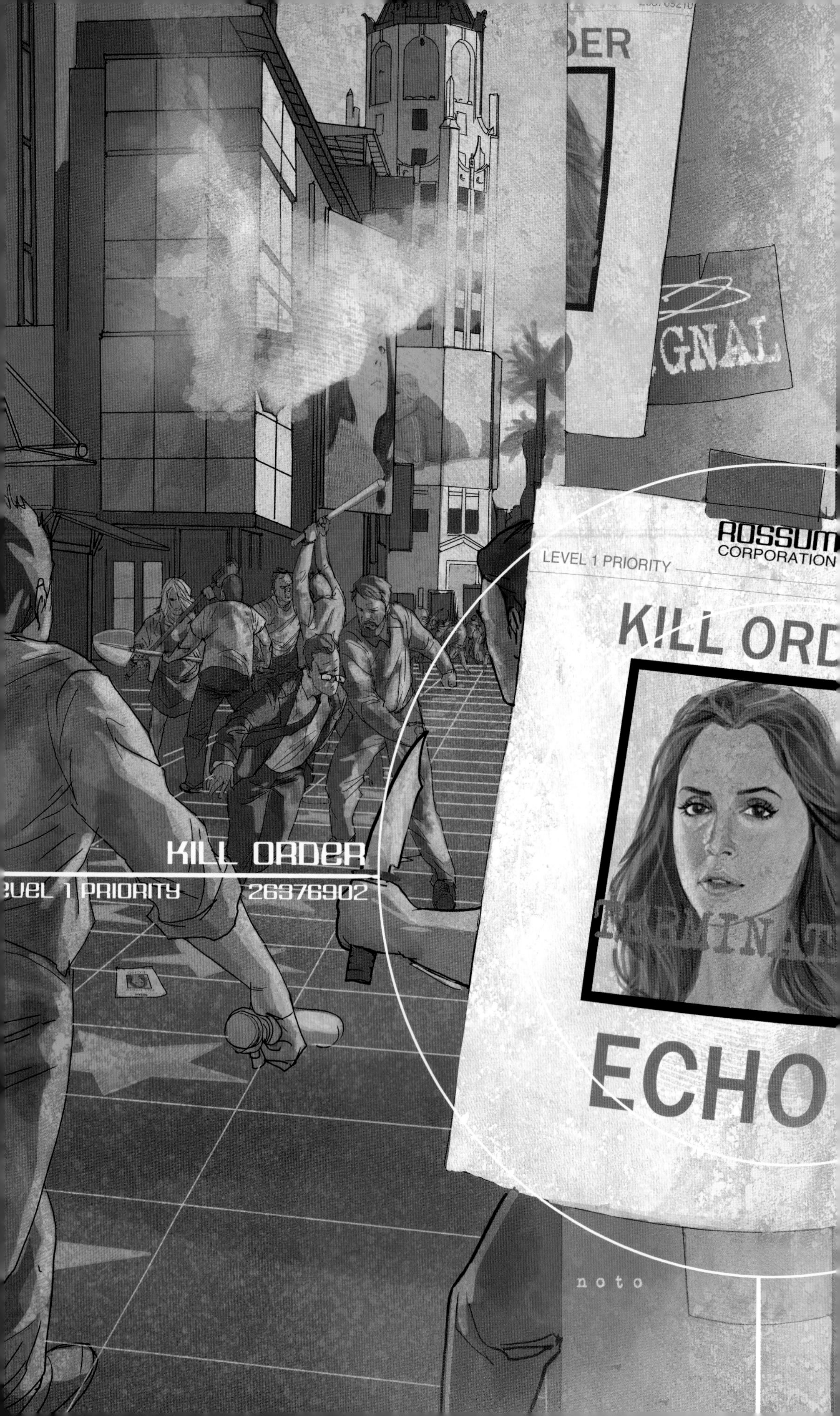

KILL ORDER
EVEL 1 PRIORITY 26376902
ROSSUM CORPORATION
LEVEL 1 PRIORITY
KILL ORD
ECHO
noto

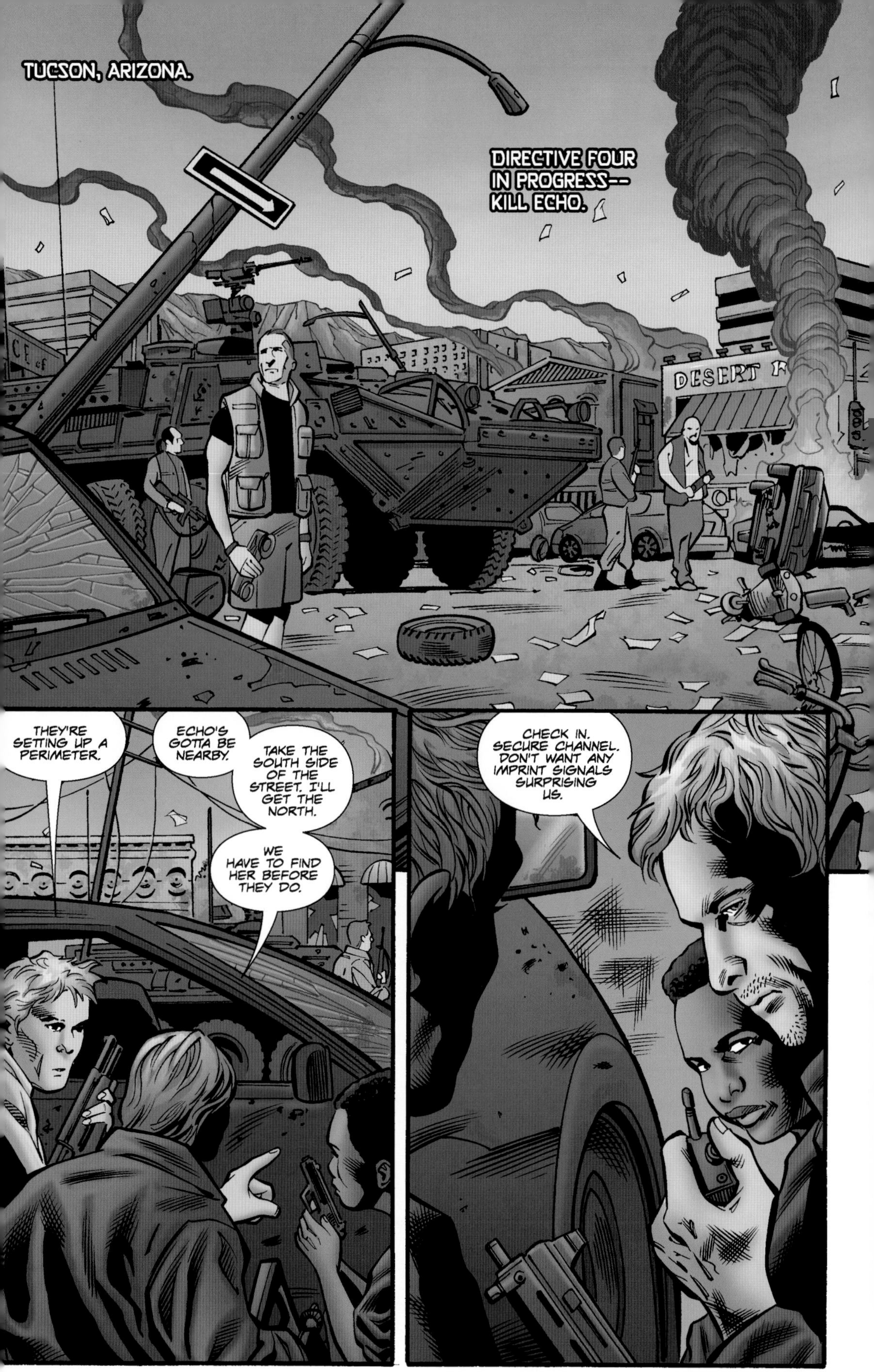
TUCSON, ARIZONA.
DIRECTIVE FOUR IN PROGRESS-- KILL ECHO.
DESERT
THEY'RE SETTING UP A PERIMETER.
ECHO'S GOTTA BE NEARBY.
TAKE THE SOUTH SIDE OF THE STREET. I'LL GET THE NORTH.
WE HAVE TO FIND HER BEFORE THEY DO.
CHECK IN. SECURE CHANNEL. DON'T WANT ANY IMPRINT SIGNALS SURPRISING US.

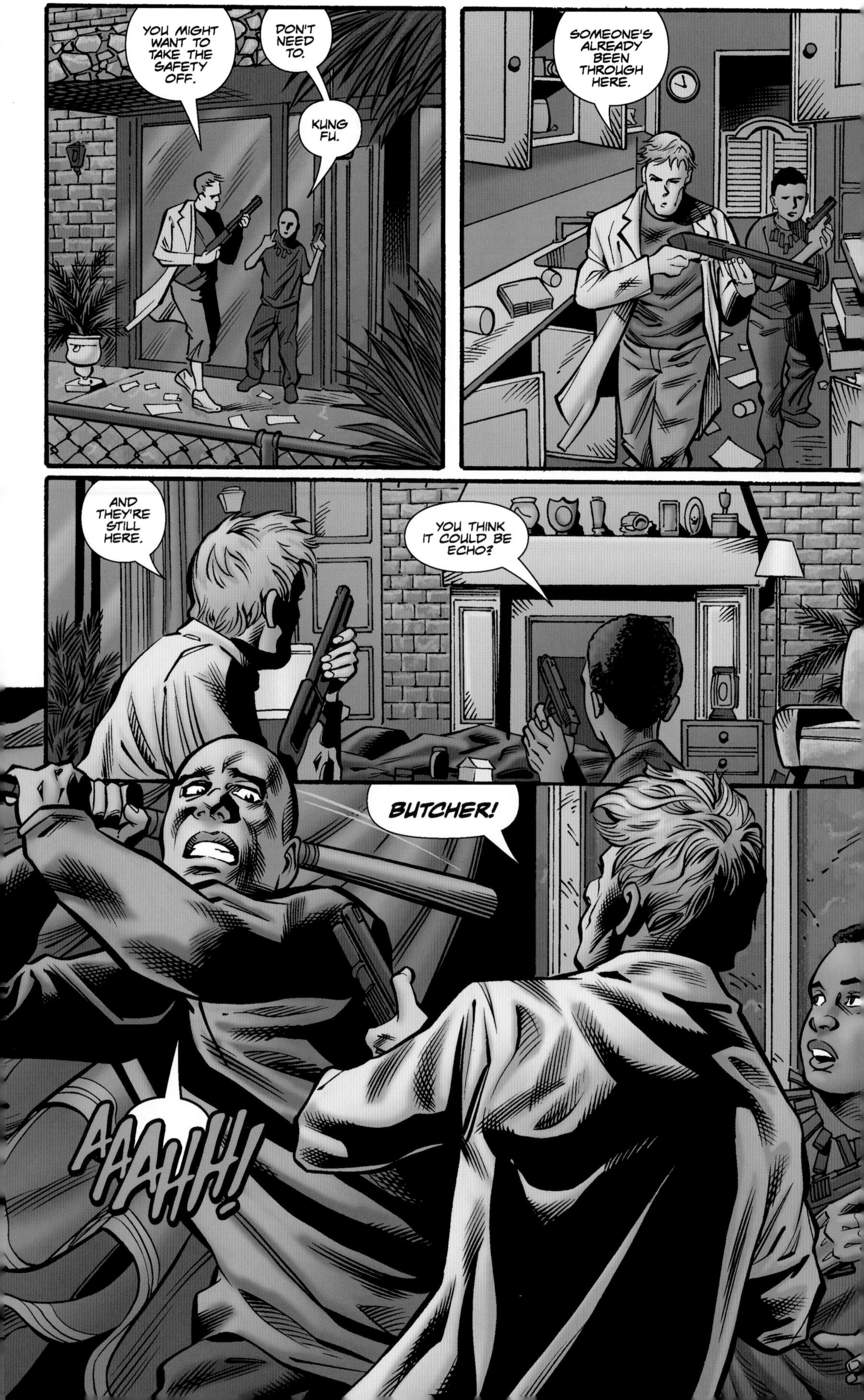
YOU MIGHT WANT TO TAKE THE SAFETY OFF.
DON'T NEED TO.
KUNG FU.
SOMEONE'S ALREADY BEEN THROUGH HERE.
AND THEY'RE STILL HERE.
YOU THINK IT COULD BE ECHO?
BUTCHER!
AAAHH!

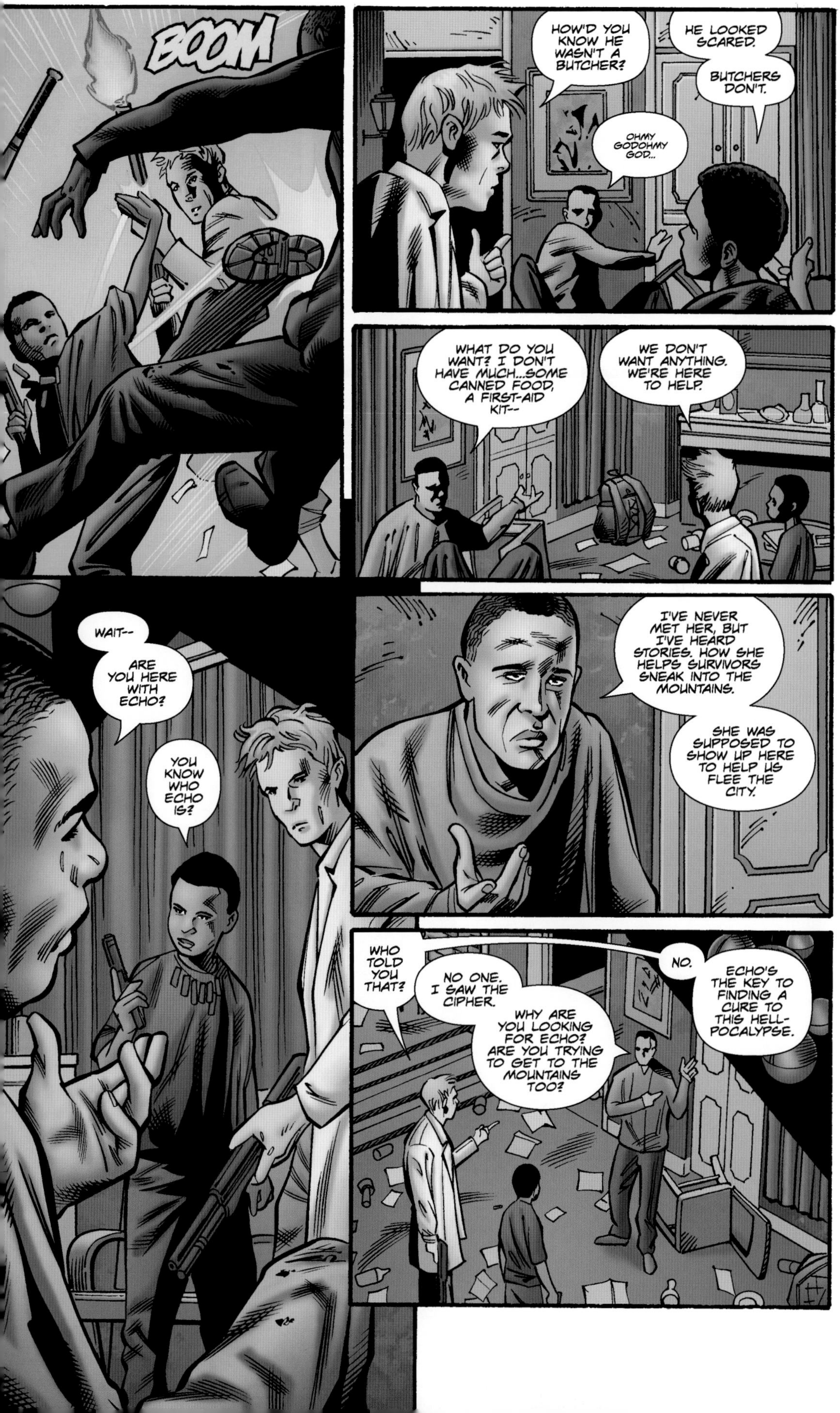

BOOM
HOW'D YOU KNOW HE WASN'T A BUTCHER?
HE LOOKED SCARED.
BUTCHERS DON'T.
OHMY GODOHMY GOD...
WHAT DO YOU WANT? I DON'T HAVE MUCH...SOME CANNED FOOD, A FIRST-AID KIT--
WE DON'T WANT ANYTHING. WE'RE HERE TO HELP.
WAIT--
ARE YOU HERE WITH ECHO?
YOU KNOW WHO ECHO IS?
I'VE NEVER MET HER, BUT I'VE HEARD STORIES. HOW SHE HELPS SURVIVORS SNEAK INTO THE MOUNTAINS.
SHE WAS SUPPOSED TO SHOW UP HERE TO HELP US FLEE THE CITY.
WHO TOLD YOU THAT?
NO ONE. I SAW THE CIPHER.
NO.
WHY ARE YOU LOOKING FOR ECHO? ARE YOU TRYING TO GET TO THE MOUNTAINS TOO?
ECHO'S THE KEY TO FINDING A CURE TO THIS HELL-POCALYPSE.

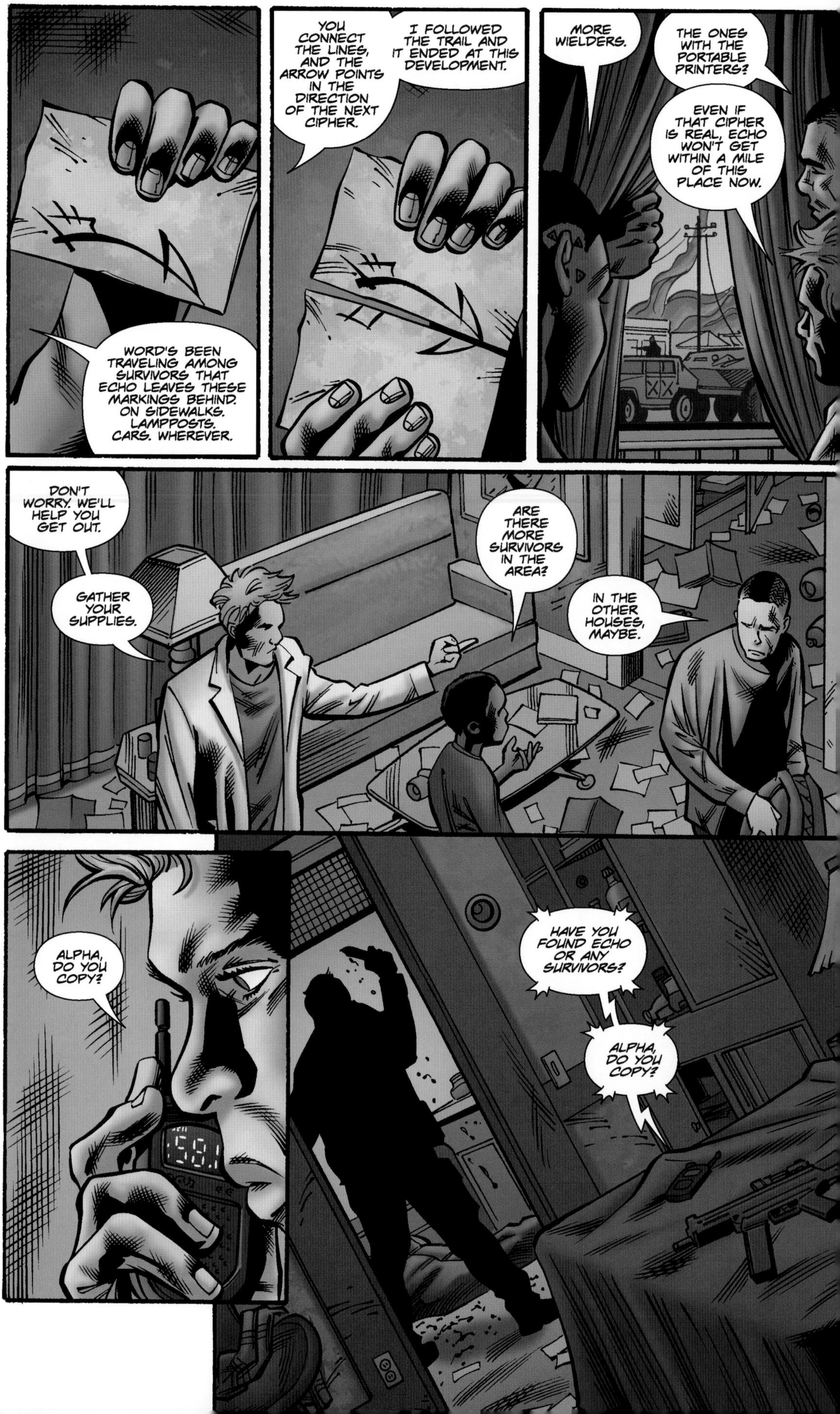
WORD'S BEEN TRAVELING AMONG SURVIVORS THAT ECHO LEAVES THESE MARKINGS BEHIND. ON SIDEWALKS. LAMPPOSTS. CARS. WHEREVER.
YOU CONNECT THE LINES, AND THE ARROW POINTS IN THE DIRECTION OF THE NEXT CIPHER.
I FOLLOWED THE TRAIL AND IT ENDED AT THIS DEVELOPMENT.
MORE WIELDERS.
THE ONES WITH THE PORTABLE PRINTERS?
EVEN IF THAT CIPHER IS REAL, ECHO WON'T GET WITHIN A MILE OF THIS PLACE NOW.
DON'T WORRY. WE'LL HELP YOU GET OUT.
GATHER YOUR SUPPLIES.
ARE THERE MORE SURVIVORS IN THE AREA?
IN THE OTHER HOUSES, MAYBE.
ALPHA, DO YOU COPY?
HAVE YOU FOUND ECHO OR ANY SURVIVORS?
ALPHA, DO YOU COPY?

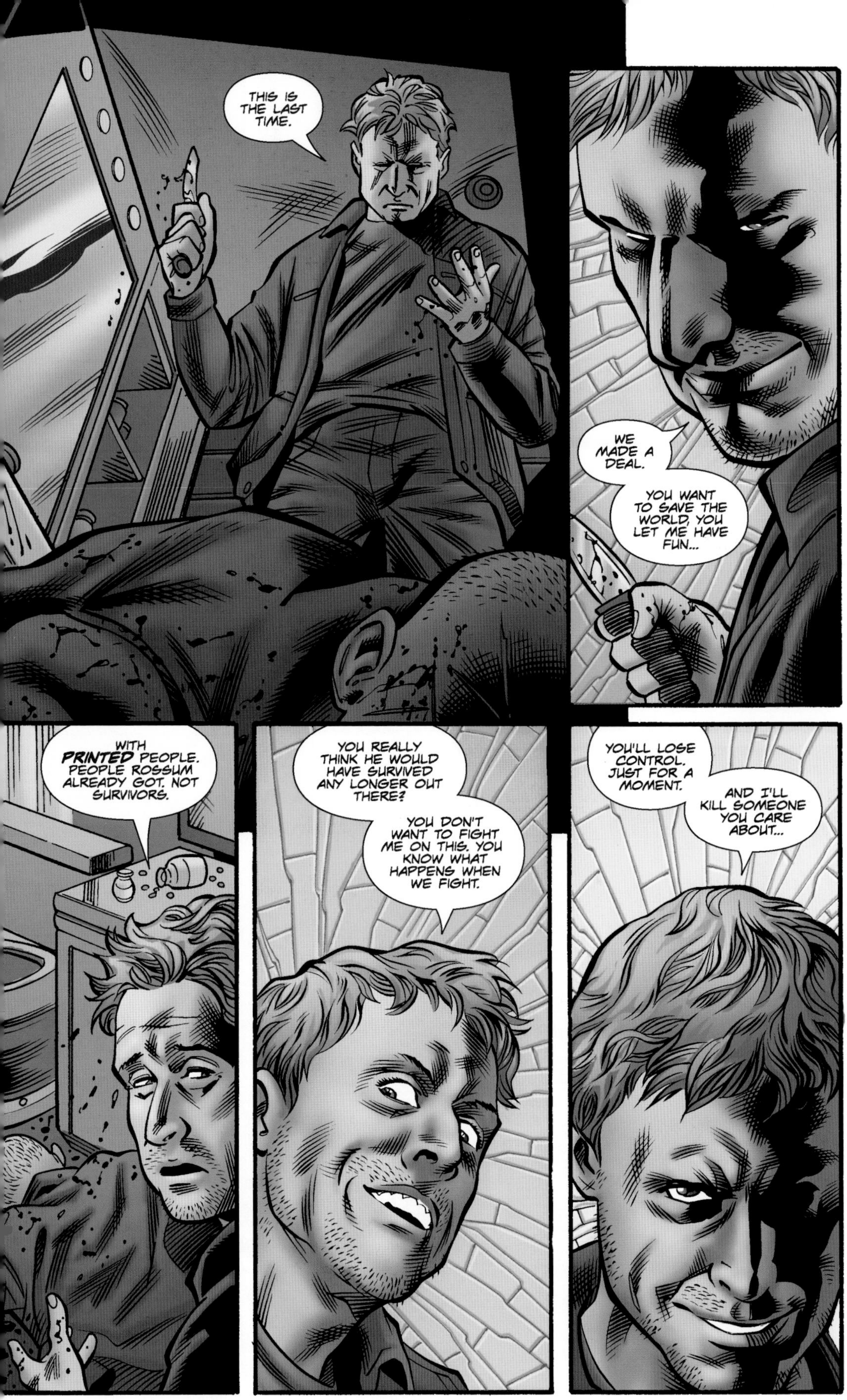
THIS IS THE LAST TIME.
WE MADE A DEAL.
YOU WANT TO SAVE THE WORLD, YOU LET ME HAVE FUN...
WITH PRINTED PEOPLE. PEOPLE ROSSUM ALREADY GOT. NOT SURVIVORS.
YOU REALLY THINK HE WOULD HAVE SURVIVED ANY LONGER OUT THERE?
YOU DON'T WANT TO FIGHT ME ON THIS. YOU KNOW WHAT HAPPENS WHEN WE FIGHT.
YOU'LL LOSE CONTROL. JUST FOR A MOMENT.
AND I'LL KILL SOMEONE YOU CARE ABOUT...

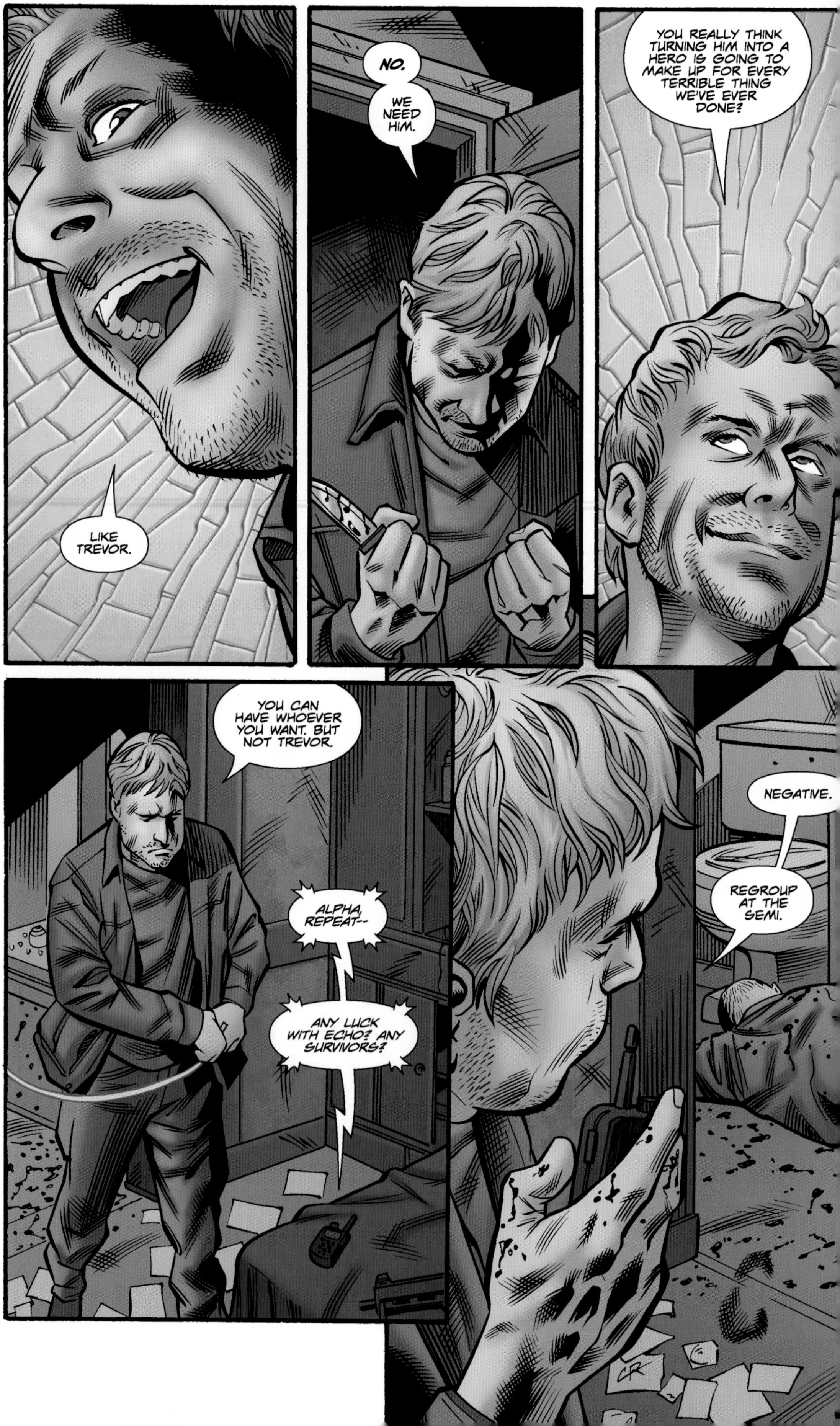

LIKE TREVOR.
NO.
WE NEED HIM.
YOU REALLY THINK TURNING HIM INTO A HERO IS GOING TO MAKE UP FOR EVERY TERRIBLE THING WE'VE EVER DONE?
YOU CAN HAVE WHOEVER YOU WANT. BUT NOT TREVOR.
ALPHA, REPEAT--
ANY LUCK WITH ECHO? ANY SURVIVORS?
NEGATIVE.
REGROUP AT THE SEMI.

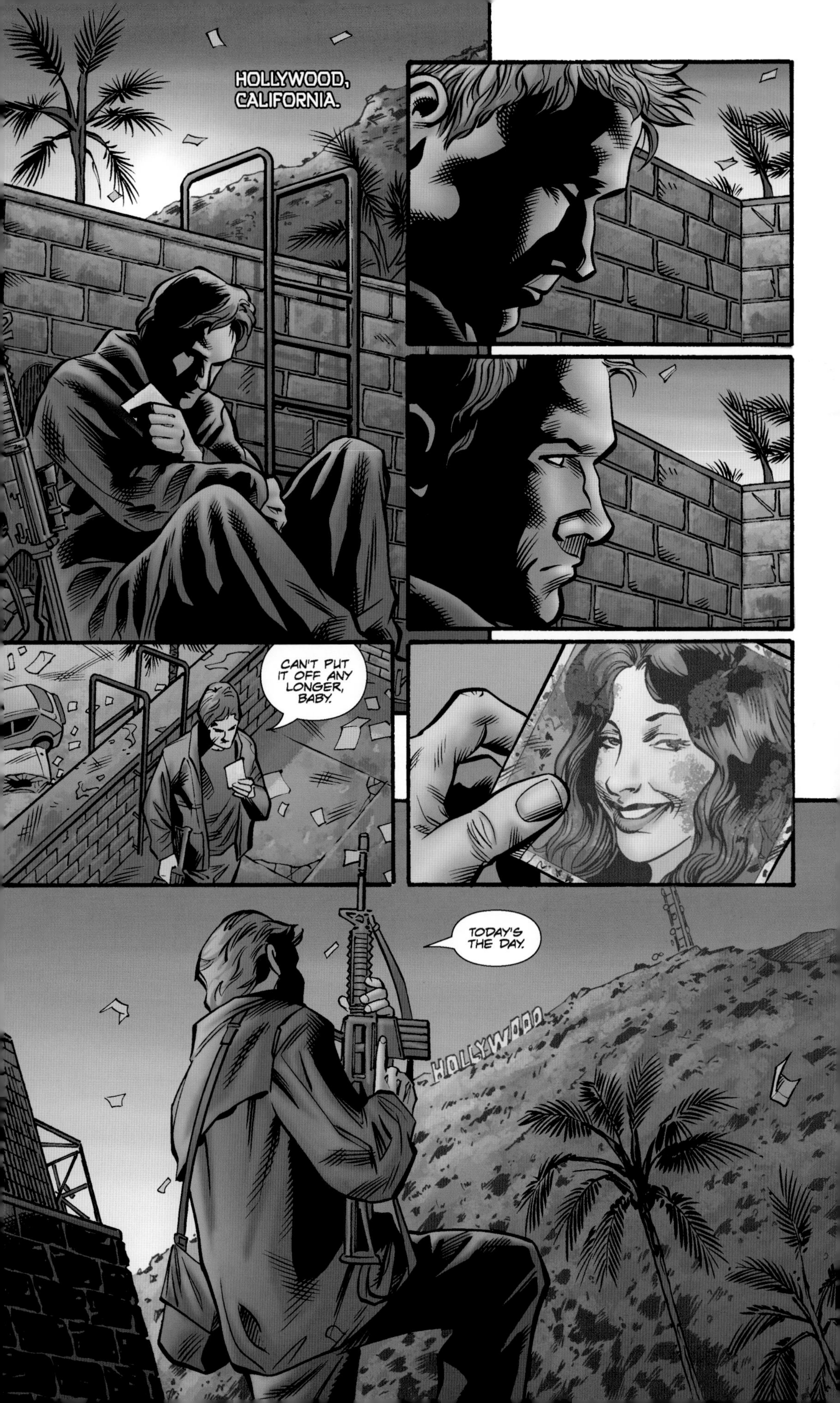
HOLLYWOOD, CALIFORNIA.
CAN'T PUT IT OFF ANY LONGER, BABY.
TODAY'S THE DAY.
HOLLYWOOD

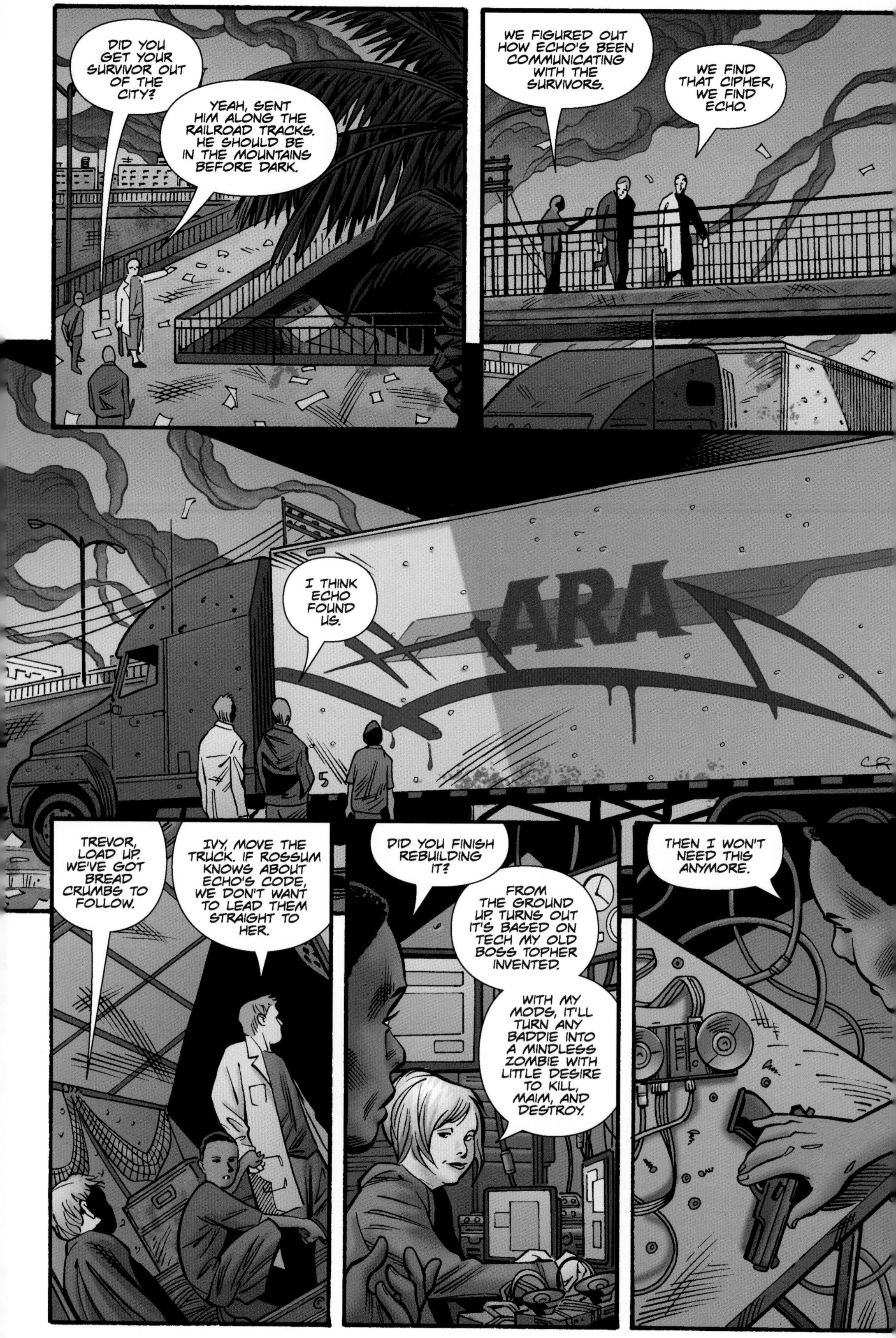

DID YOU GET YOUR SURVIVOR OUT OF THE CITY?
YEAH, SENT HIM ALONG THE RAILROAD TRACKS. HE SHOULD BE IN THE MOUNTAINS BEFORE DARK.
WE FIGURED OUT HOW ECHO'S BEEN COMMUNICATING WITH THE SURVIVORS.
WE FIND THAT CIPHER, WE FIND ECHO.
I THINK ECHO FOUND US.
ARA
TREVOR, LOAD UP. WE'VE GOT BREAD CRUMBS TO FOLLOW.
IVY, MOVE THE TRUCK. IF ROSSUM KNOWS ABOUT ECHO'S CODE, WE DON'T WANT TO LEAD THEM STRAIGHT TO HER.
DID YOU FINISH REBUILDING IT?
FROM THE GROUND UP. TURNS OUT IT'S BASED ON TECH MY OLD BOSS TOPHER INVENTED.
WITH MY MODS, IT'LL TURN ANY BADDIE INTO A MINDLESS ZOMBIE WITH LITTLE DESIRE TO KILL, MAIM, AND DESTROY.
THEN I WON'T NEED THIS ANYMORE.

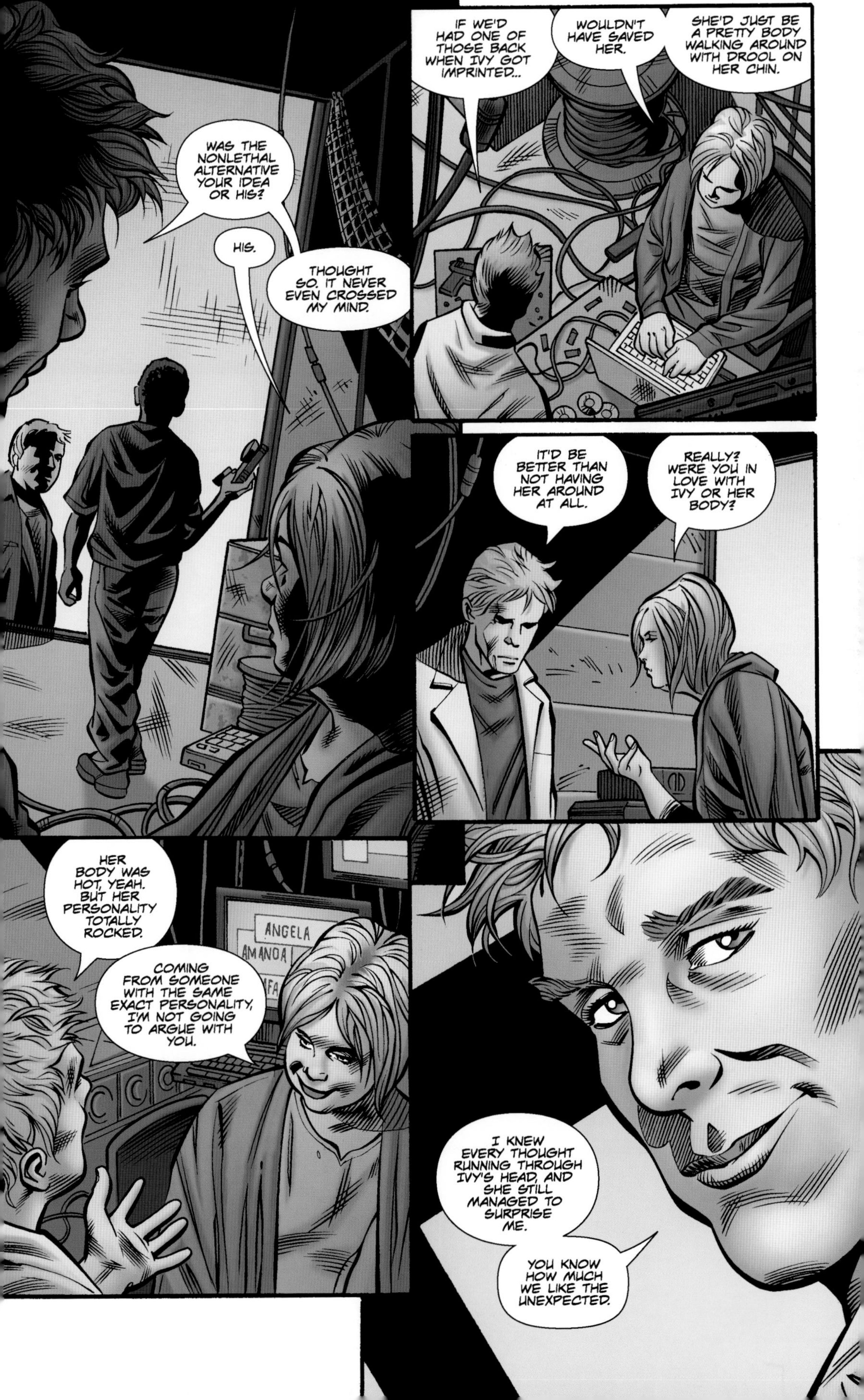
WAS THE NONLETHAL ALTERNATIVE YOUR IDEA OR HIS?
HIS.
THOUGHT SO. IT NEVER EVEN CROSSED MY MIND.
IF WE'D HAD ONE OF THOSE BACK WHEN IVY GOT IMPRINTED...
WOULDN'T HAVE SAVED HER.
SHE'D JUST BE A PRETTY BODY WALKING AROUND WITH DROOL ON HER CHIN.
IT'D BE BETTER THAN NOT HAVING HER AROUND AT ALL.
REALLY? WERE YOU IN LOVE WITH IVY OR HER BODY?
HER BODY WAS HOT, YEAH. BUT HER PERSONALITY TOTALLY ROCKED.
ANGELA
AMANDA
COMING FROM SOMEONE WITH THE SAME EXACT PERSONALITY, I'M NOT GOING TO ARGUE WITH YOU.
I KNEW EVERY THOUGHT RUNNING THROUGH IVY'S HEAD, AND SHE STILL MANAGED TO SURPRISE ME.
YOU KNOW HOW MUCH WE LIKE THE UNEXPECTED.

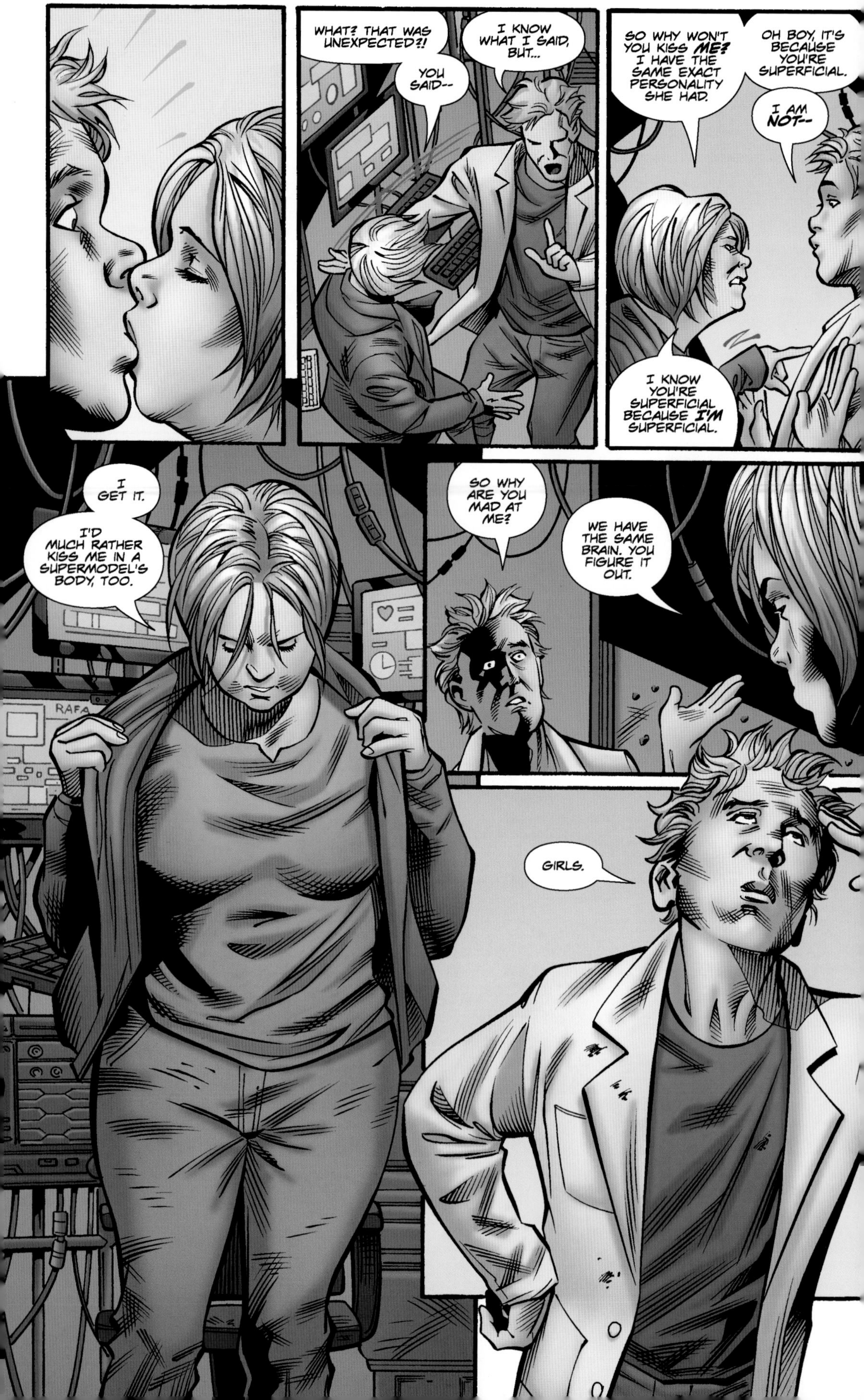
WHAT? THAT WAS UNEXPECTED?!
YOU SAID--
I KNOW WHAT I SAID, BUT...
SO WHY WON'T YOU KISS ME? I HAVE THE SAME EXACT PERSONALITY SHE HAD.
OH BOY, IT'S BECAUSE YOU'RE SUPERFICIAL.
I AM NOT--
I KNOW YOU'RE SUPERFICIAL BECAUSE I'M SUPERFICIAL.
I GET IT.
I'D MUCH RATHER KISS ME IN A SUPERMODEL'S BODY, TOO.
RAFA
SO WHY ARE YOU MAD AT ME?
WE HAVE THE SAME BRAIN. YOU FIGURE IT OUT.
GIRLS.

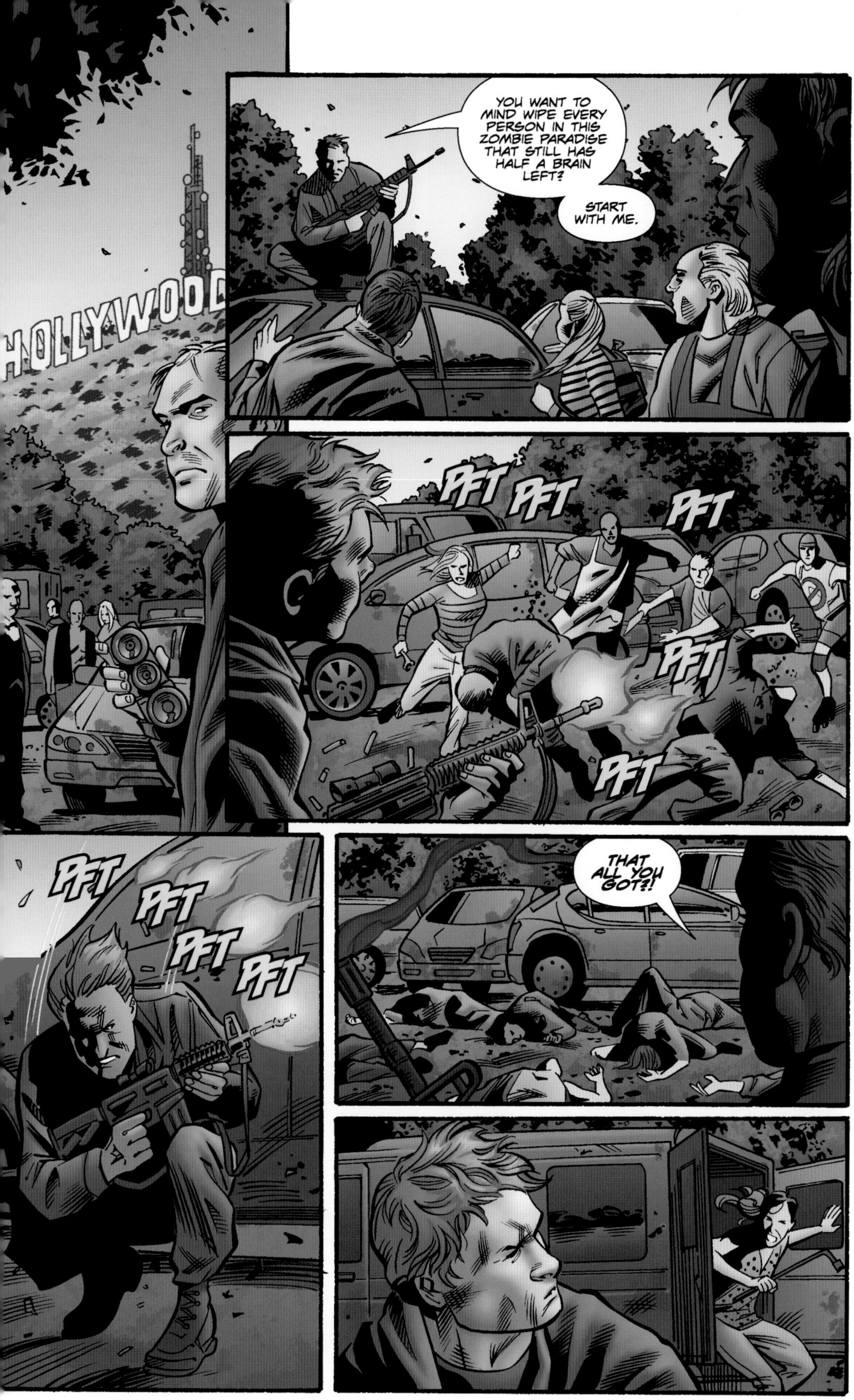
HOLLYWOOD
YOU WANT TO MIND WIPE EVERY PERSON IN THIS ZOMBIE PARADISE THAT STILL HAS HALF A BRAIN LEFT?
START WITH ME.
PFT
PFT
PFT
PFT
PFT
PFT
PFT
PFT
PFT
THAT ALL YOU GOT?!

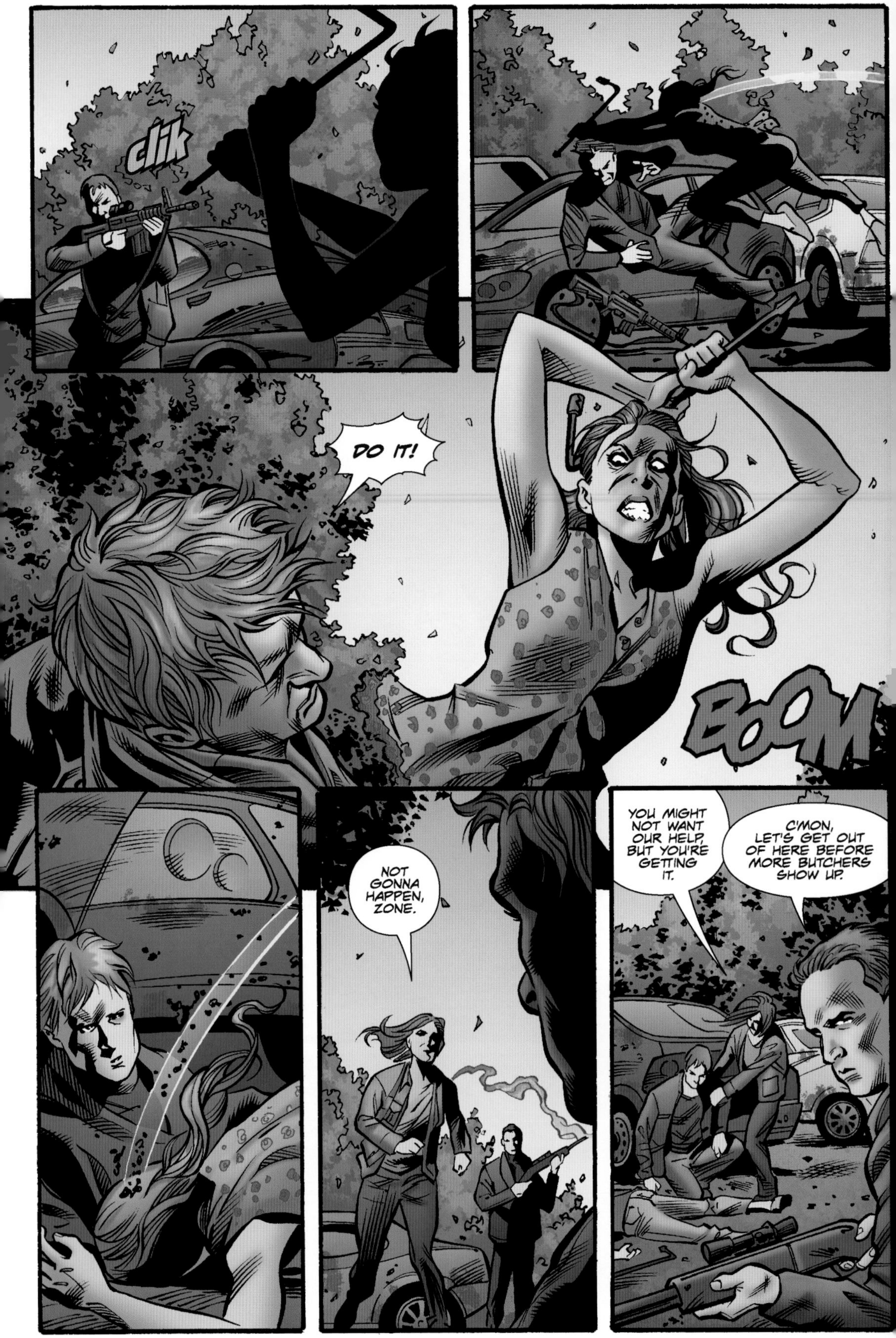
clik
DO IT!
BOOM
NOT GONNA HAPPEN, ZONE.
YOU MIGHT NOT WANT OUR HELP, BUT YOU'RE GETTING IT.
C'MON, LET'S GET OUT OF HERE BEFORE MORE BUTCHERS SHOW UP.

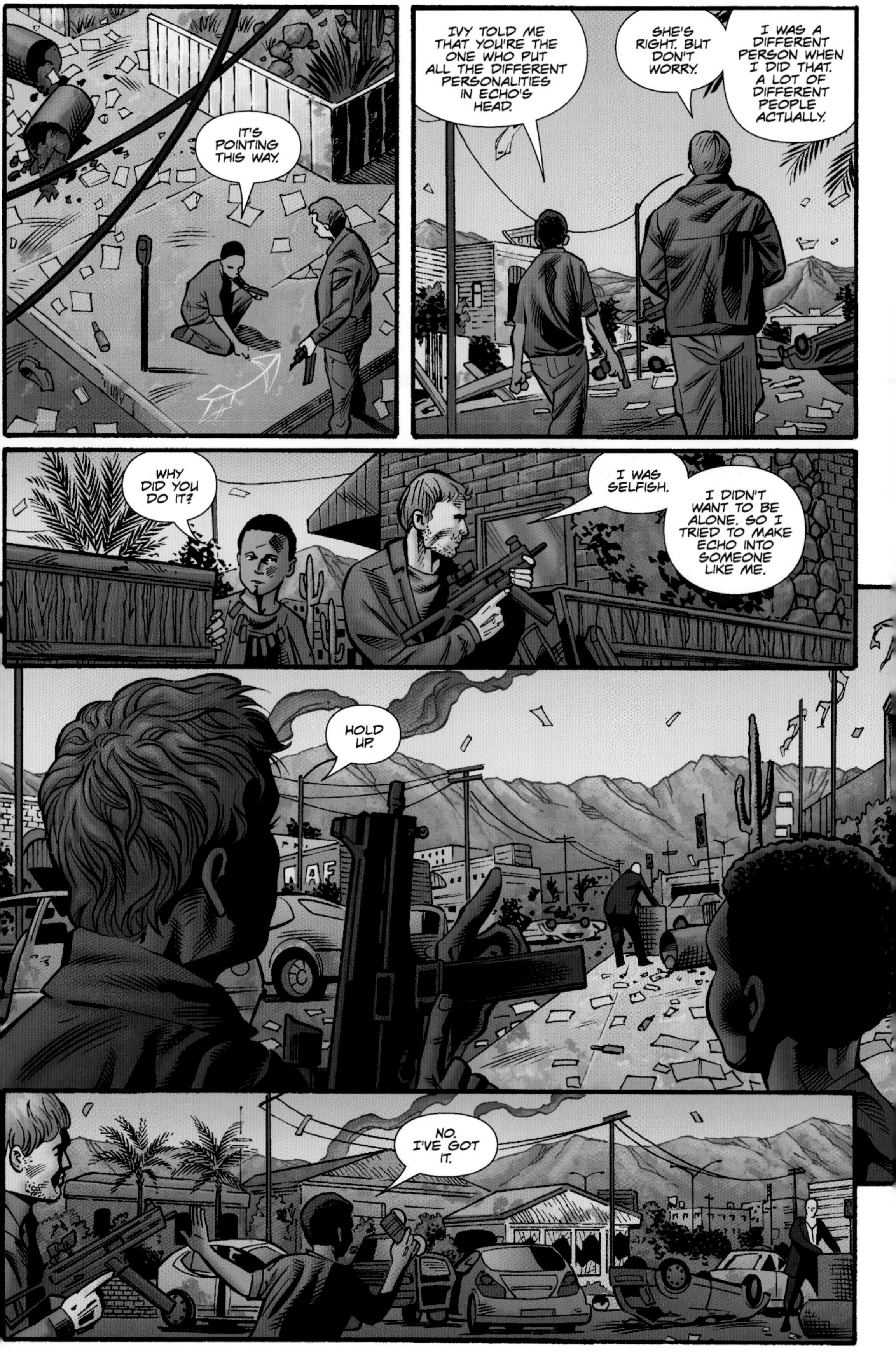
IT'S POINTING THIS WAY.
IVY TOLD ME THAT YOU'RE THE ONE WHO PUT ALL THE DIFFERENT PERSONALITIES IN ECHO'S HEAD.
SHE'S RIGHT. BUT DON'T WORRY.
I WAS A DIFFERENT PERSON WHEN I DID THAT. A LOT OF DIFFERENT PEOPLE ACTUALLY.
WHY DID YOU DO IT?
I WAS SELFISH.
I DIDN'T WANT TO BE ALONE. SO I TRIED TO MAKE ECHO INTO SOMEONE LIKE ME.
HOLD UP.
NO. I'VE GOT IT.

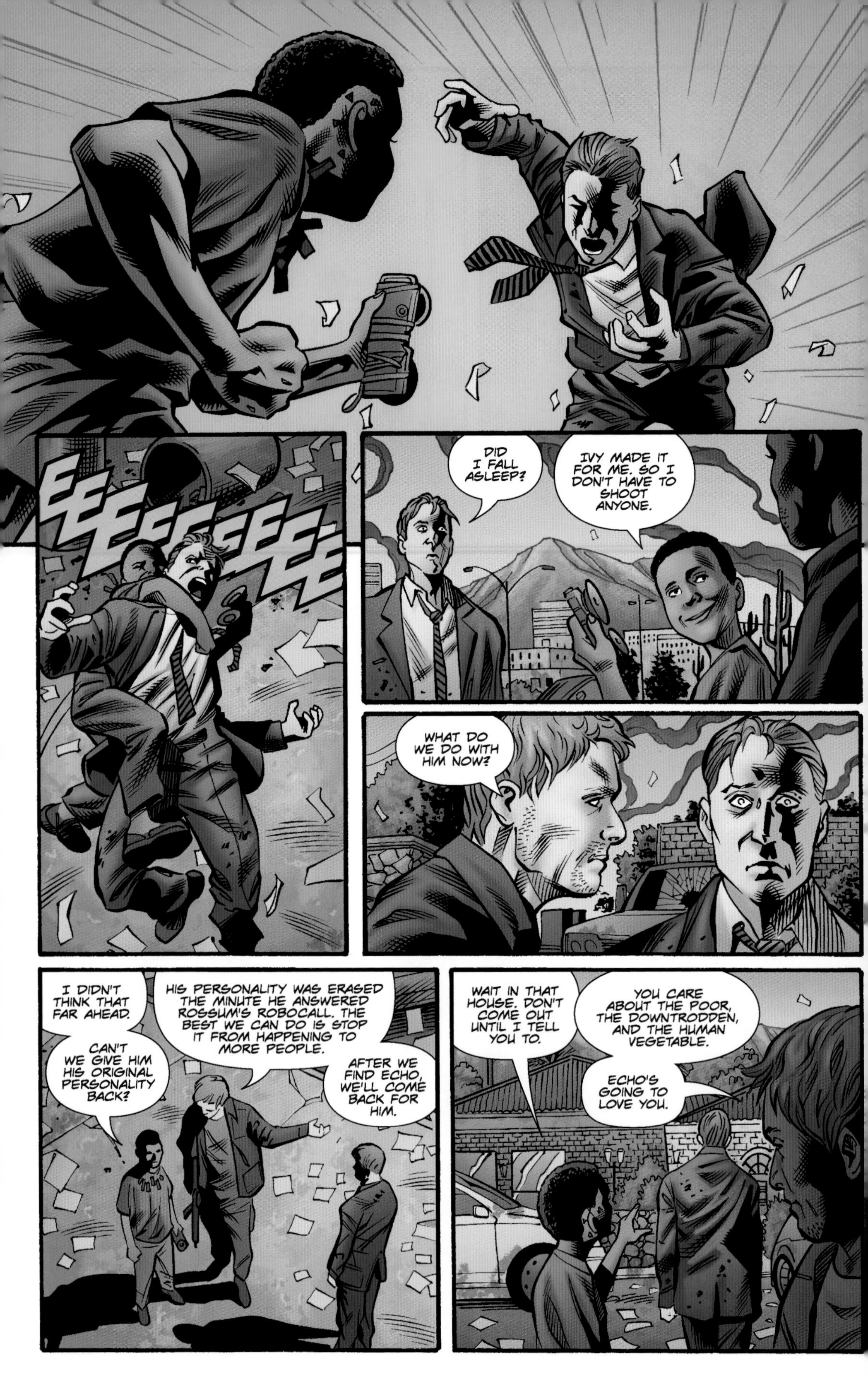
EEEEEEEEEEE
DID I FALL ASLEEP?
IVY MADE IT FOR ME. SO I DON'T HAVE TO SHOOT ANYONE.
WHAT DO WE DO WITH HIM NOW?
I DIDN'T THINK THAT FAR AHEAD.
CAN'T WE GIVE HIM HIS ORIGINAL PERSONALITY BACK?
HIS PERSONALITY WAS ERASED THE MINUTE HE ANSWERED ROSSUM'S ROBOCALL. THE BEST WE CAN DO IS STOP IT FROM HAPPENING TO MORE PEOPLE.
AFTER WE FIND ECHO, WE'LL COME BACK FOR HIM.
WAIT IN THAT HOUSE. DON'T COME OUT UNTIL I TELL YOU TO.
YOU CARE ABOUT THE POOR, THE DOWNTRODDEN, AND THE HUMAN VEGETABLE.
ECHO'S GOING TO LOVE YOU.

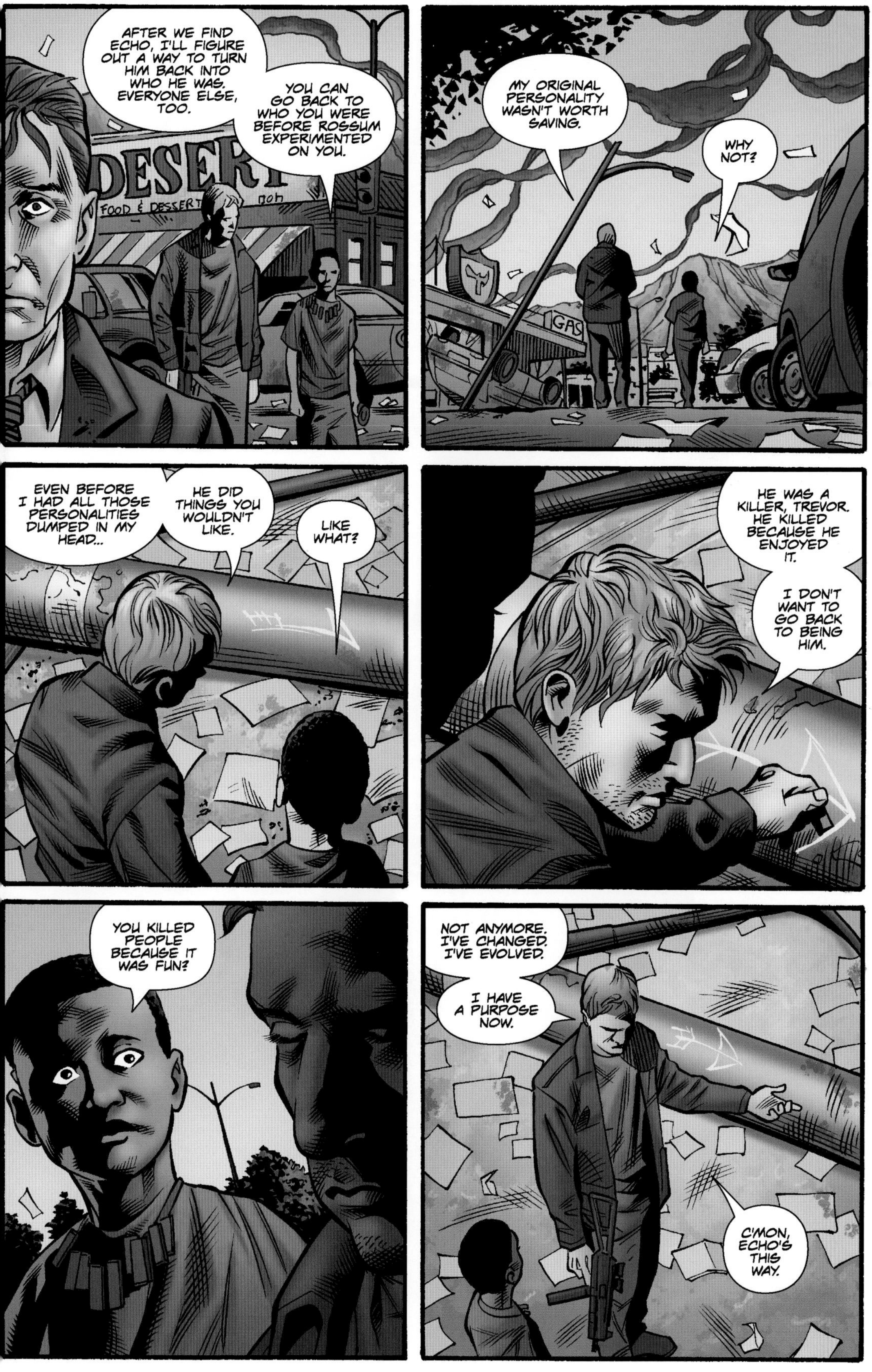
AFTER WE FIND ECHO, I'LL FIGURE OUT A WAY TO TURN HIM BACK INTO WHO HE WAS. EVERYONE ELSE, TOO.
YOU CAN GO BACK TO WHO YOU WERE BEFORE ROSSUM EXPERIMENTED ON YOU.
DESERT
FOOD & DESSERT
MY ORIGINAL PERSONALITY WASN'T WORTH SAVING.
WHY NOT?
GAS
EVEN BEFORE I HAD ALL THOSE PERSONALITIES DUMPED IN MY HEAD...
HE DID THINGS YOU WOULDN'T LIKE.
LIKE WHAT?
HE WAS A KILLER, TREVOR. HE KILLED BECAUSE HE ENJOYED IT.
I DON'T WANT TO GO BACK TO BEING HIM.
YOU KILLED PEOPLE BECAUSE IT WAS FUN?
NOT ANYMORE. I'VE CHANGED. I'VE EVOLVED.
I HAVE A PURPOSE NOW.
C'MON, ECHO'S THIS WAY.

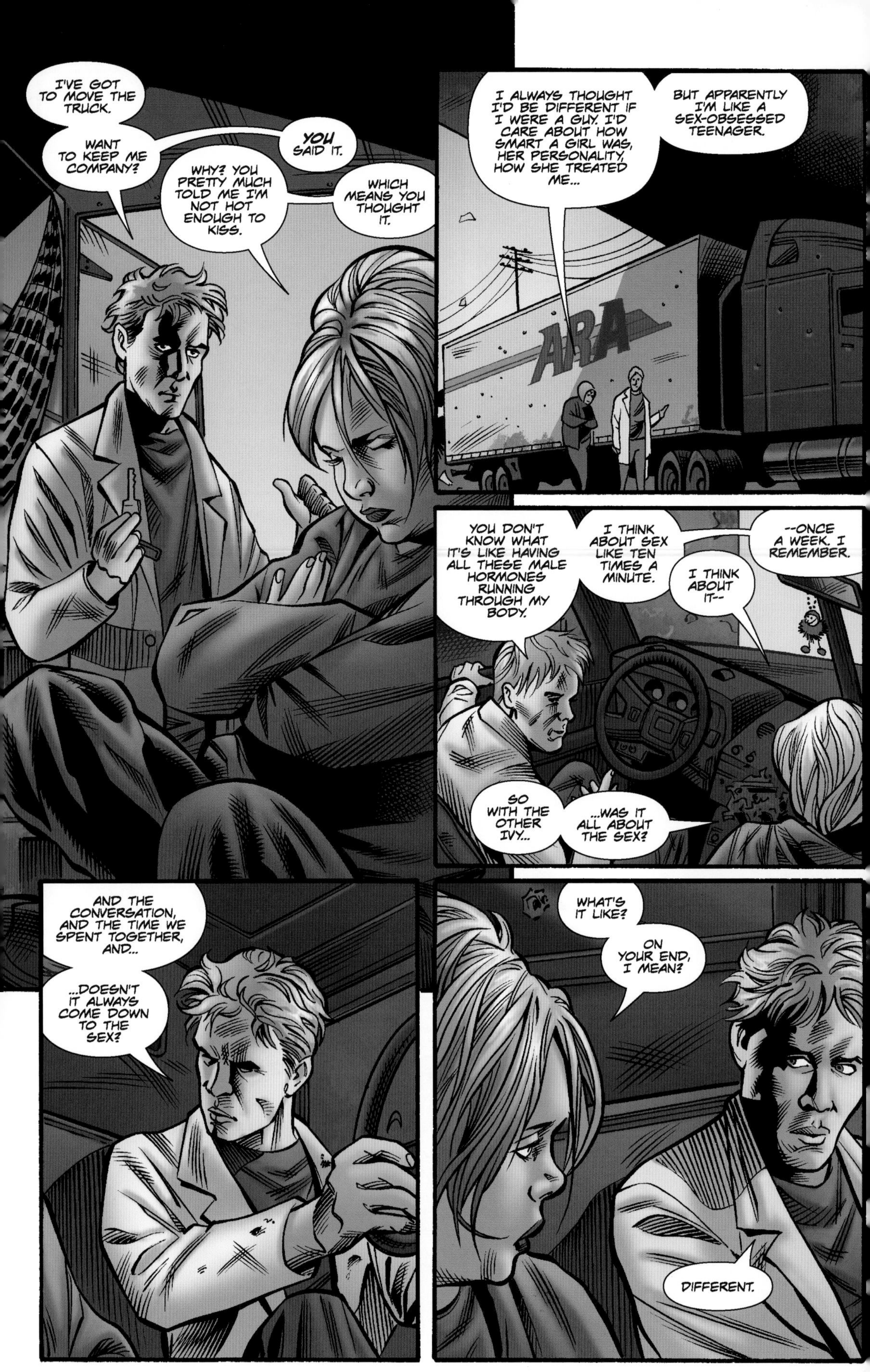
I'VE GOT TO MOVE THE TRUCK.
WANT TO KEEP ME COMPANY?
WHY? YOU PRETTY MUCH TOLD ME I'M NOT HOT ENOUGH TO KISS.
YOU SAID IT.
WHICH MEANS YOU THOUGHT IT.
I ALWAYS THOUGHT I'D BE DIFFERENT IF I WERE A GUY. I'D CARE ABOUT HOW SMART A GIRL WAS, HER PERSONALITY, HOW SHE TREATED ME...
BUT APPARENTLY I'M LIKE A SEX-OBSESSED TEENAGER.
ARA
YOU DON'T KNOW WHAT IT'S LIKE HAVING ALL THESE MALE HORMONES RUNNING THROUGH MY BODY.
I THINK ABOUT SEX LIKE TEN TIMES A MINUTE.
I THINK ABOUT IT--
--ONCE A WEEK. I REMEMBER.
SO WITH THE OTHER IVY...
...WAS IT ALL ABOUT THE SEX?
AND THE CONVERSATION, AND THE TIME WE SPENT TOGETHER, AND...
...DOESN'T IT ALWAYS COME DOWN TO THE SEX?
WHAT'S IT LIKE?
ON YOUR END, I MEAN?
DIFFERENT.

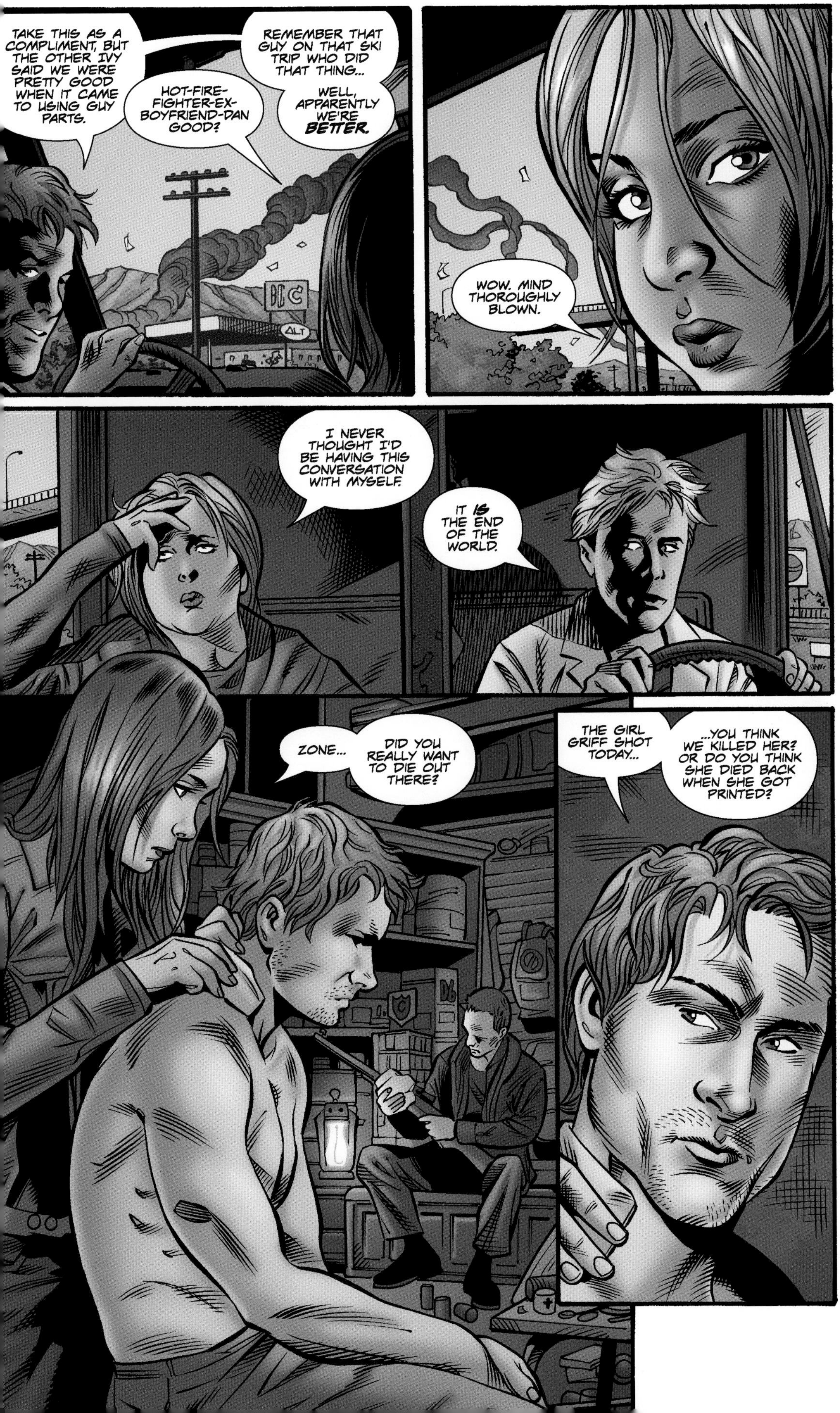

TAKE THIS AS A COMPLIMENT, BUT THE OTHER IVY SAID WE WERE PRETTY GOOD WHEN IT CAME TO USING GUY PARTS.
HOT-FIRE-FIGHTER-EX-BOYFRIEND-DAN GOOD?
REMEMBER THAT GUY ON THAT SKI TRIP WHO DID THAT THING...
WELL, APPARENTLY WE'RE **BETTER.**
WOW. MIND THOROUGHLY BLOWN.
I NEVER THOUGHT I'D BE HAVING THIS CONVERSATION WITH MYSELF.
IT **IS** THE END OF THE WORLD.
ZONE...
DID YOU REALLY WANT TO DIE OUT THERE?
THE GIRL GRIFF SHOT TODAY...
...YOU THINK WE KILLED HER? OR DO YOU THINK SHE DIED BACK WHEN SHE GOT PRINTED?

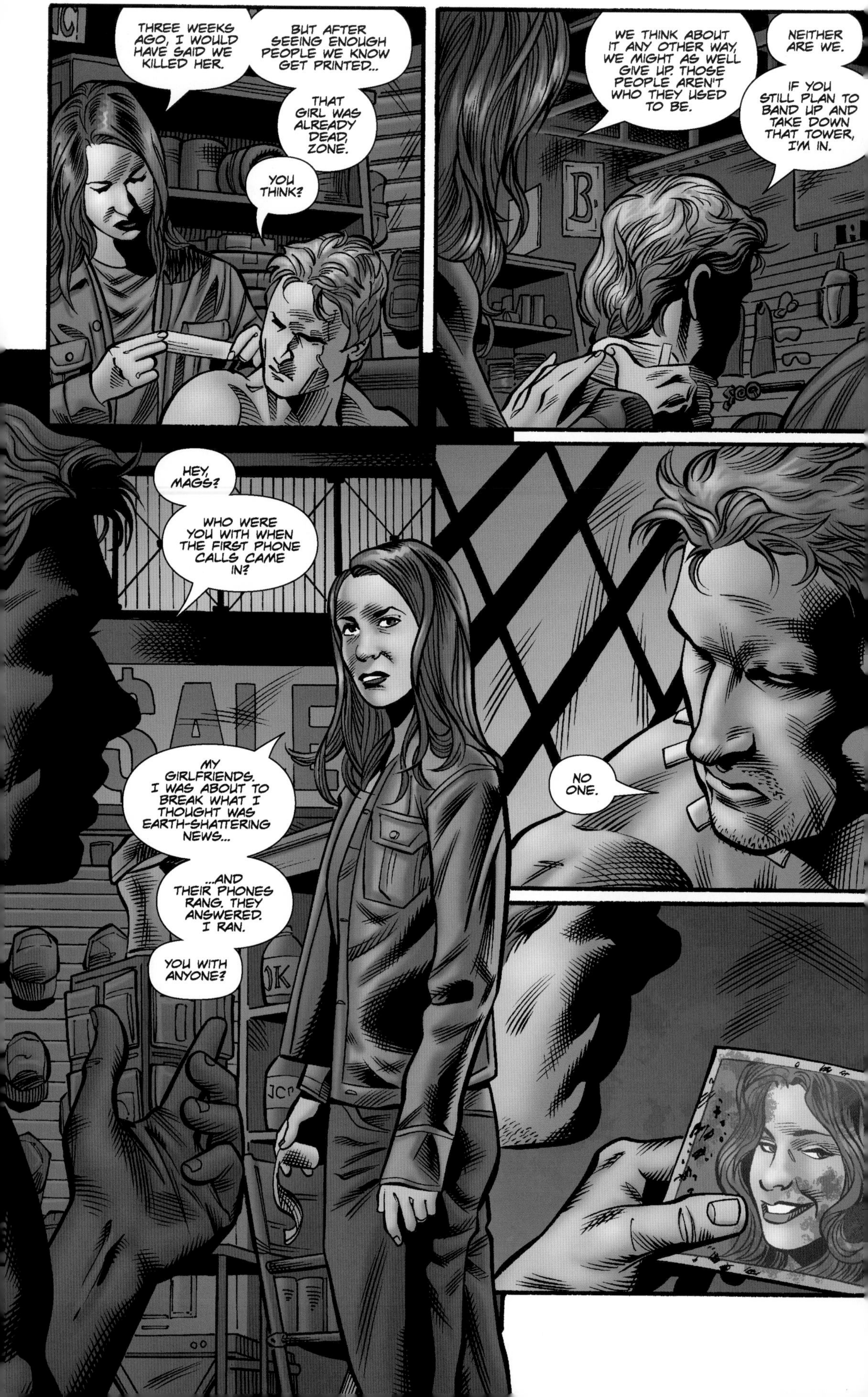
THREE WEEKS AGO, I WOULD HAVE SAID WE KILLED HER.
BUT AFTER SEEING ENOUGH PEOPLE WE KNOW GET PRINTED...
THAT GIRL WAS ALREADY DEAD, ZONE.
YOU THINK?
WE THINK ABOUT IT ANY OTHER WAY, WE MIGHT AS WELL GIVE UP. THOSE PEOPLE AREN'T WHO THEY USED TO BE.
NEITHER ARE WE.
IF YOU STILL PLAN TO BAND UP AND TAKE DOWN THAT TOWER, I'M IN.
HEY, MAGS?
WHO WERE YOU WITH WHEN THE FIRST PHONE CALLS CAME IN?
MY GIRLFRIENDS. I WAS ABOUT TO BREAK WHAT I THOUGHT WAS EARTH-SHATTERING NEWS...
...AND THEIR PHONES RANG. THEY ANSWERED. I RAN.
YOU WITH ANYONE?
NO ONE.

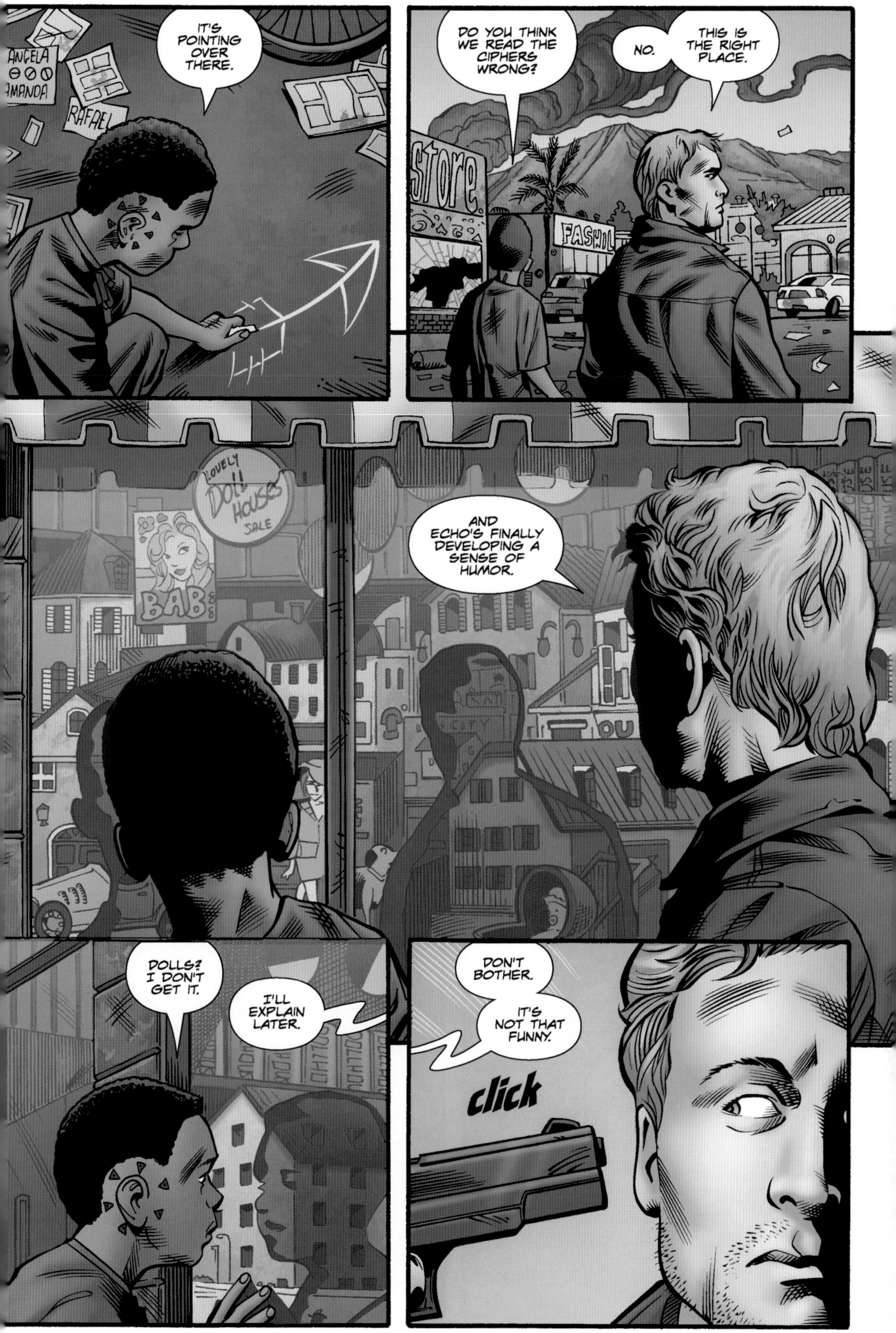
ANGELA
AMANDA
RAFAEL
IT'S POINTING OVER THERE.
DO YOU THINK WE READ THE CIPHERS WRONG?
NO.
THIS IS THE RIGHT PLACE.
STORE
FASHI
LOVELY DOLL HOUSES SALE
BAB
AND ECHO'S FINALLY DEVELOPING A SENSE OF HUMOR.
DOLLS? I DON'T GET IT.
I'LL EXPLAIN LATER.
DON'T BOTHER.
IT'S NOT THAT FUNNY.
click

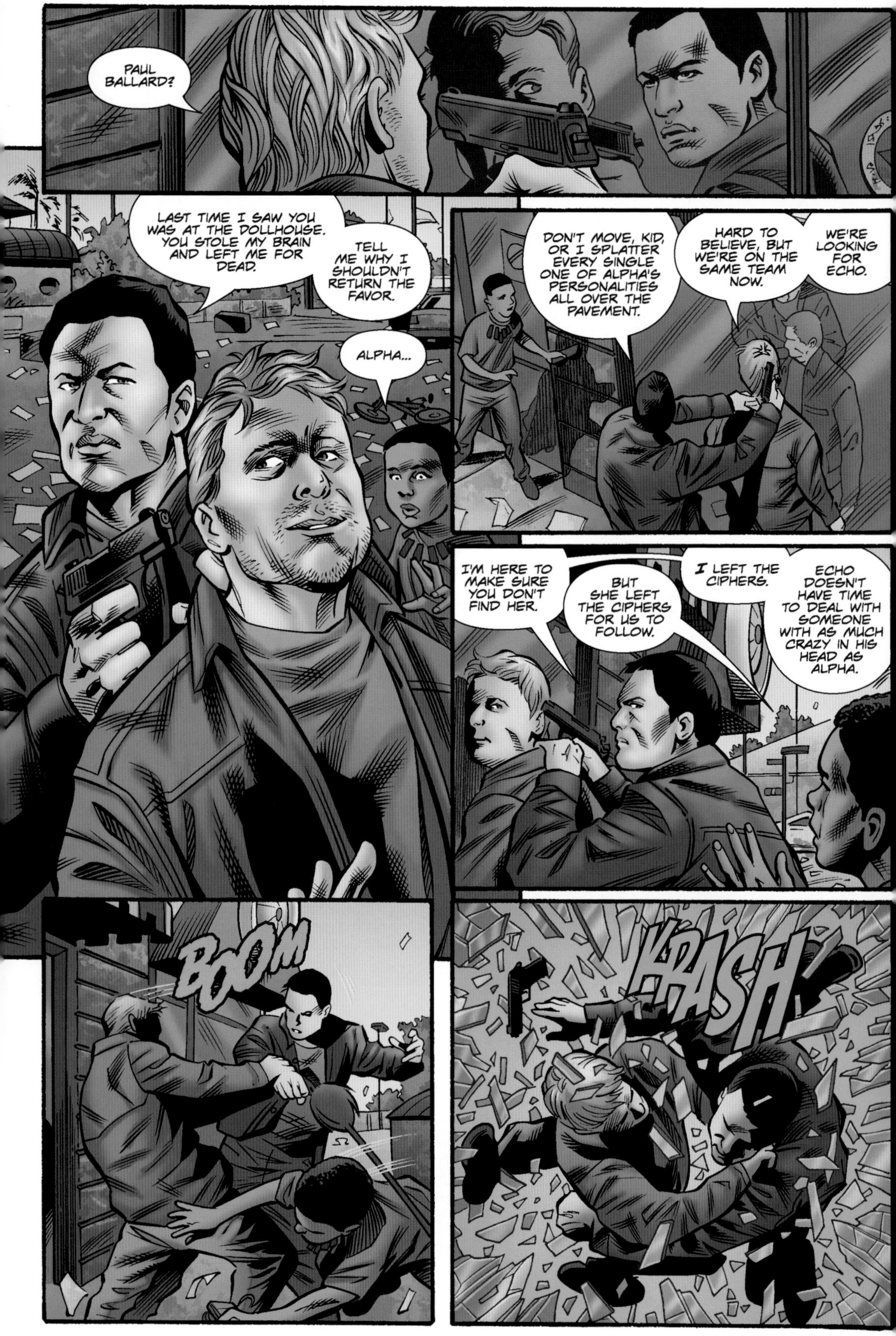
PAUL BALLARD?
LAST TIME I SAW YOU WAS AT THE DOLLHOUSE. YOU STOLE MY BRAIN AND LEFT ME FOR DEAD.
TELL ME WHY I SHOULDN'T RETURN THE FAVOR.
ALPHA...
DON'T MOVE, KID, OR I SPLATTER EVERY SINGLE ONE OF ALPHA'S PERSONALITIES ALL OVER THE PAVEMENT.
HARD TO BELIEVE, BUT WE'RE ON THE SAME TEAM NOW.
WE'RE LOOKING FOR ECHO.
I'M HERE TO MAKE SURE YOU DON'T FIND HER.
BUT SHE LEFT THE CIPHERS FOR US TO FOLLOW.
I LEFT THE CIPHERS.
ECHO DOESN'T HAVE TIME TO DEAL WITH SOMEONE WITH AS MUCH CRAZY IN HIS HEAD AS ALPHA.
BOOM
KRASH

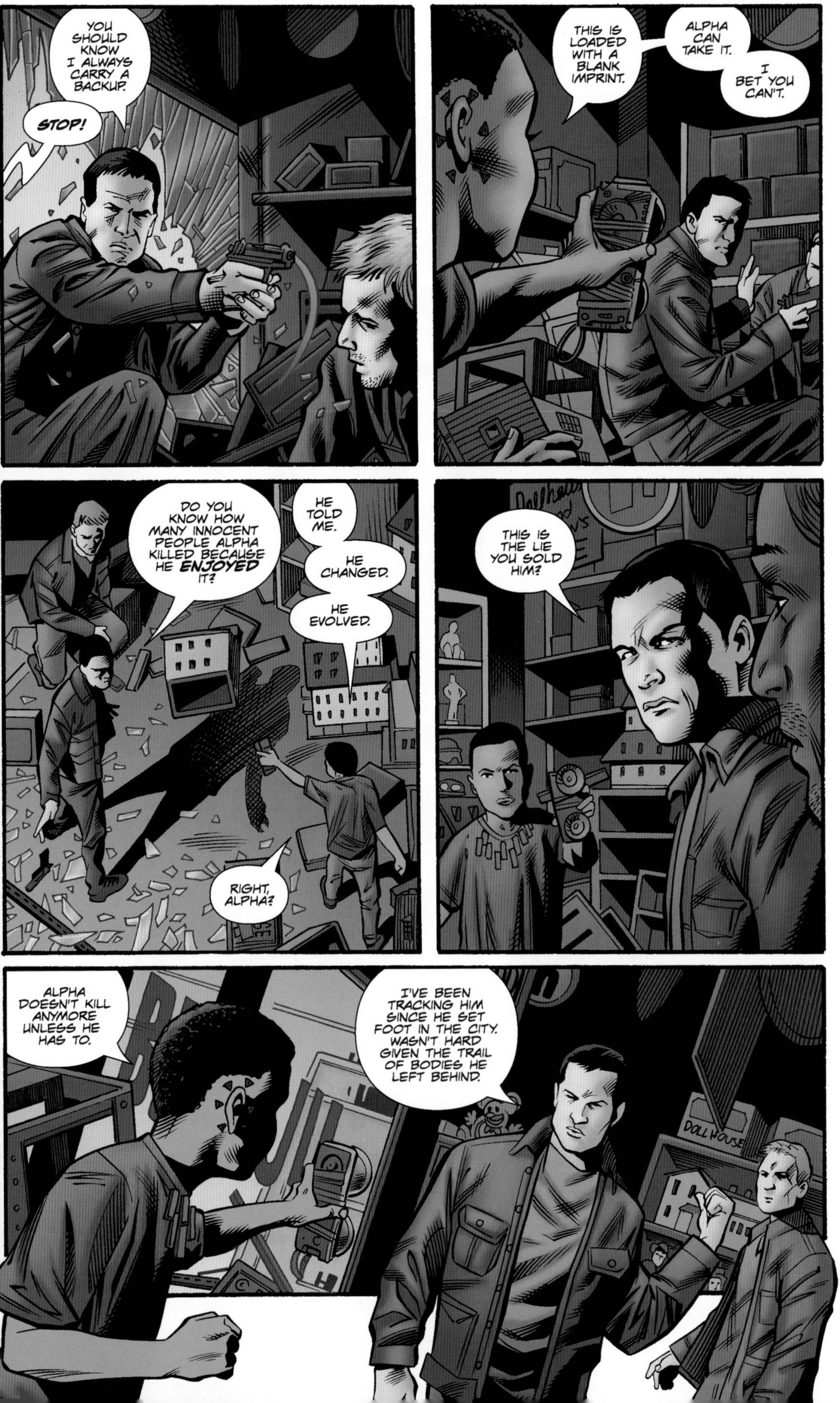
YOU SHOULD KNOW I ALWAYS CARRY A BACKUP.
STOP!
THIS IS LOADED WITH A BLANK IMPRINT.
ALPHA CAN TAKE IT.
I BET YOU CAN'T.
DO YOU KNOW HOW MANY INNOCENT PEOPLE ALPHA KILLED BECAUSE HE ENJOYED IT?
HE TOLD ME.
HE CHANGED.
HE EVOLVED.
RIGHT, ALPHA?
THIS IS THE LIE YOU SOLD HIM?
ALPHA DOESN'T KILL ANYMORE UNLESS HE HAS TO.
I'VE BEEN TRACKING HIM SINCE HE SET FOOT IN THE CITY. WASN'T HARD GIVEN THE TRAIL OF BODIES HE LEFT BEHIND.
DOLLHOUSE

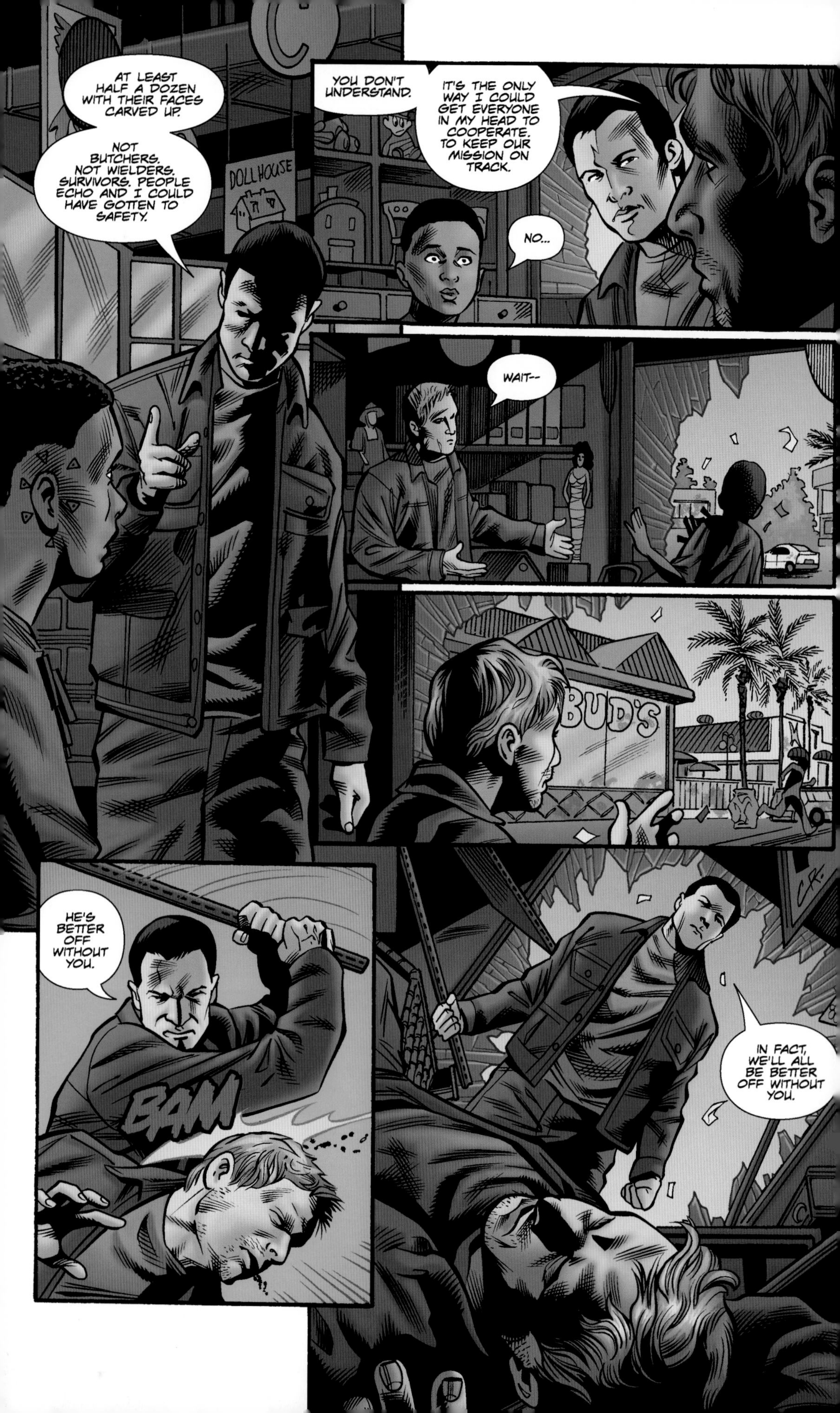
AT LEAST HALF A DOZEN WITH THEIR FACES CARVED UP.
NOT BUTCHERS. NOT WIELDERS. SURVIVORS. PEOPLE ECHO AND I COULD HAVE GOTTEN TO SAFETY.
DOLLHOUSE
YOU DON'T UNDERSTAND.
IT'S THE ONLY WAY I COULD GET EVERYONE IN MY HEAD TO COOPERATE. TO KEEP OUR MISSION ON TRACK.
NO...
WAIT--
BUD'S
HE'S BETTER OFF WITHOUT YOU.
BAM
IN FACT, WE'LL ALL BE BETTER OFF WITHOUT YOU.

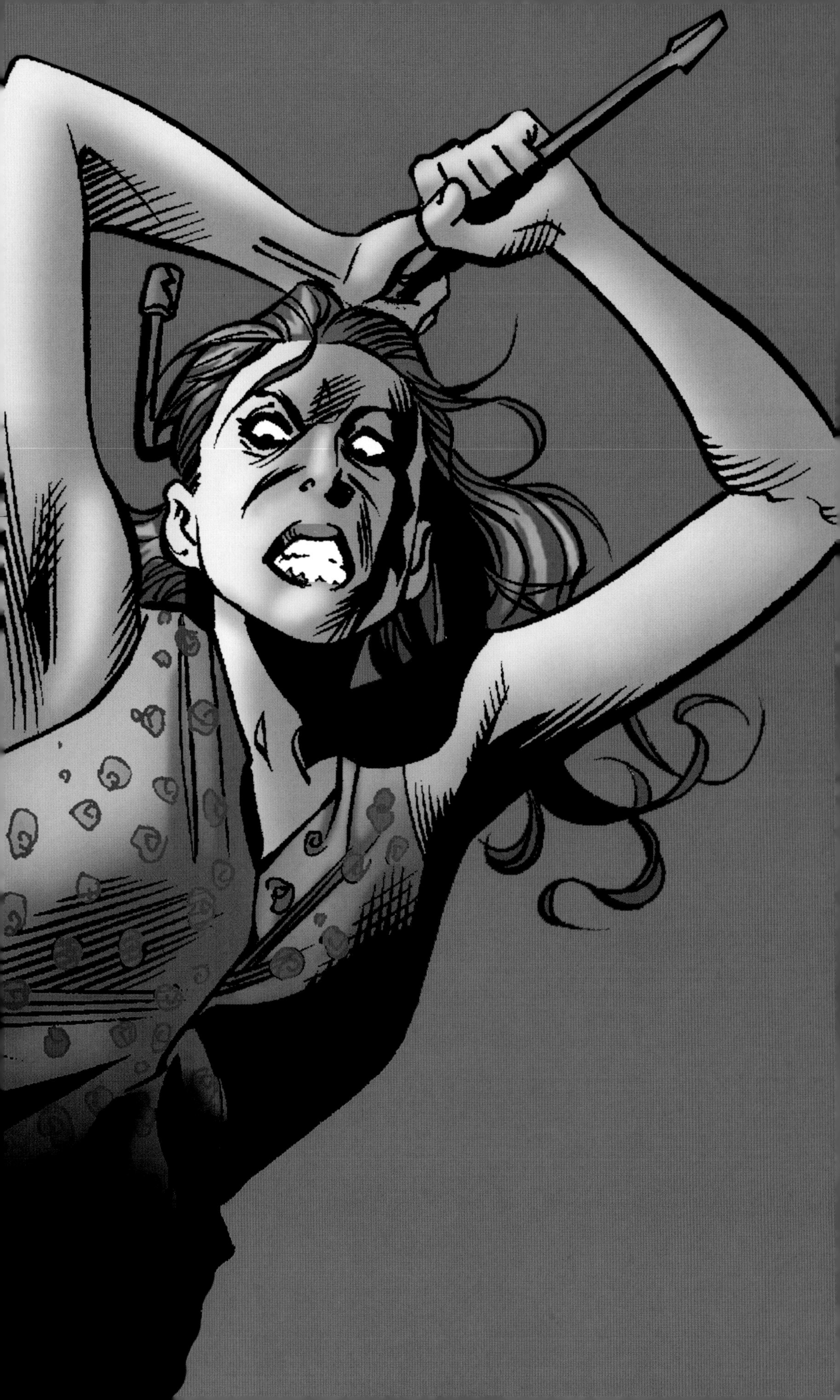

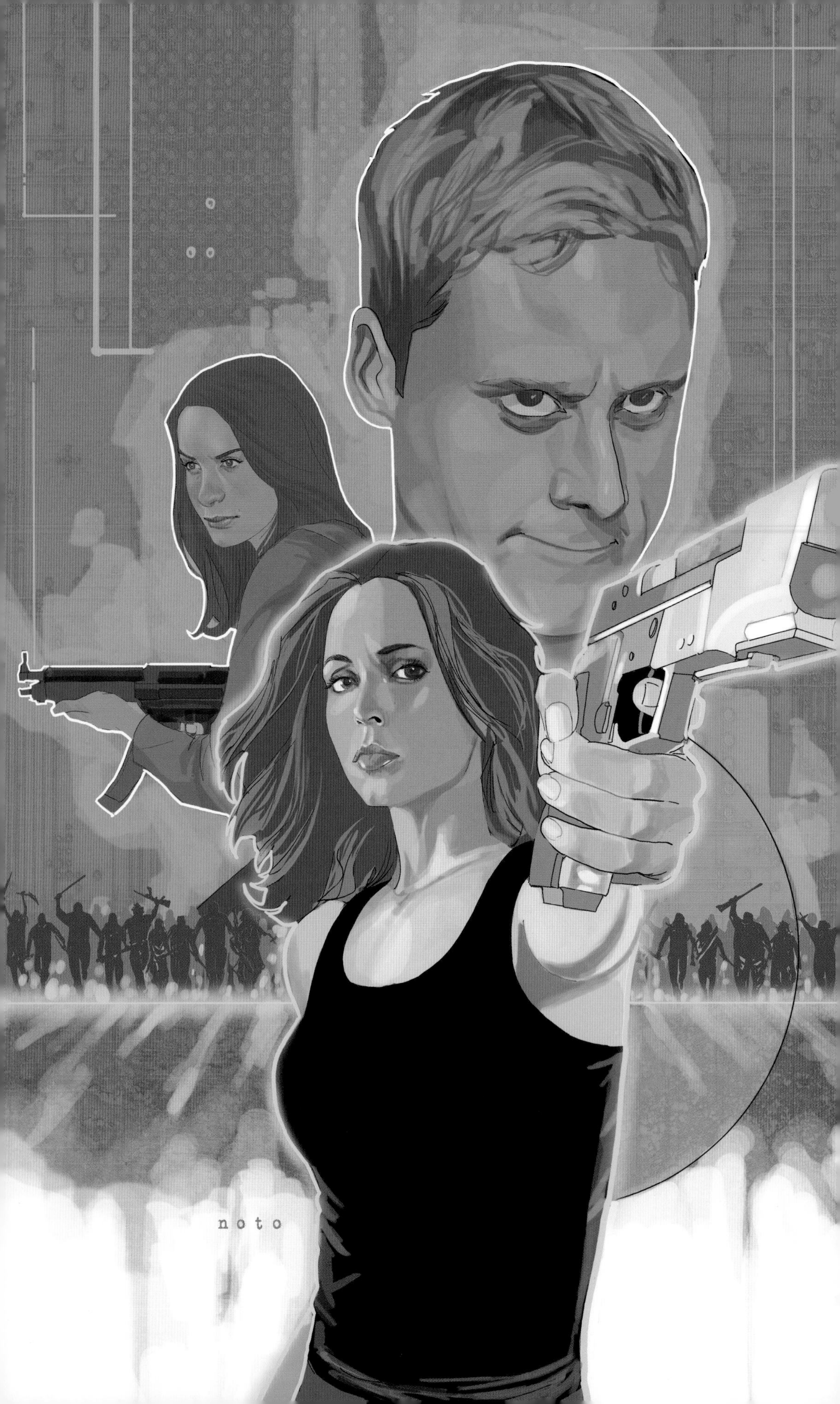
noto

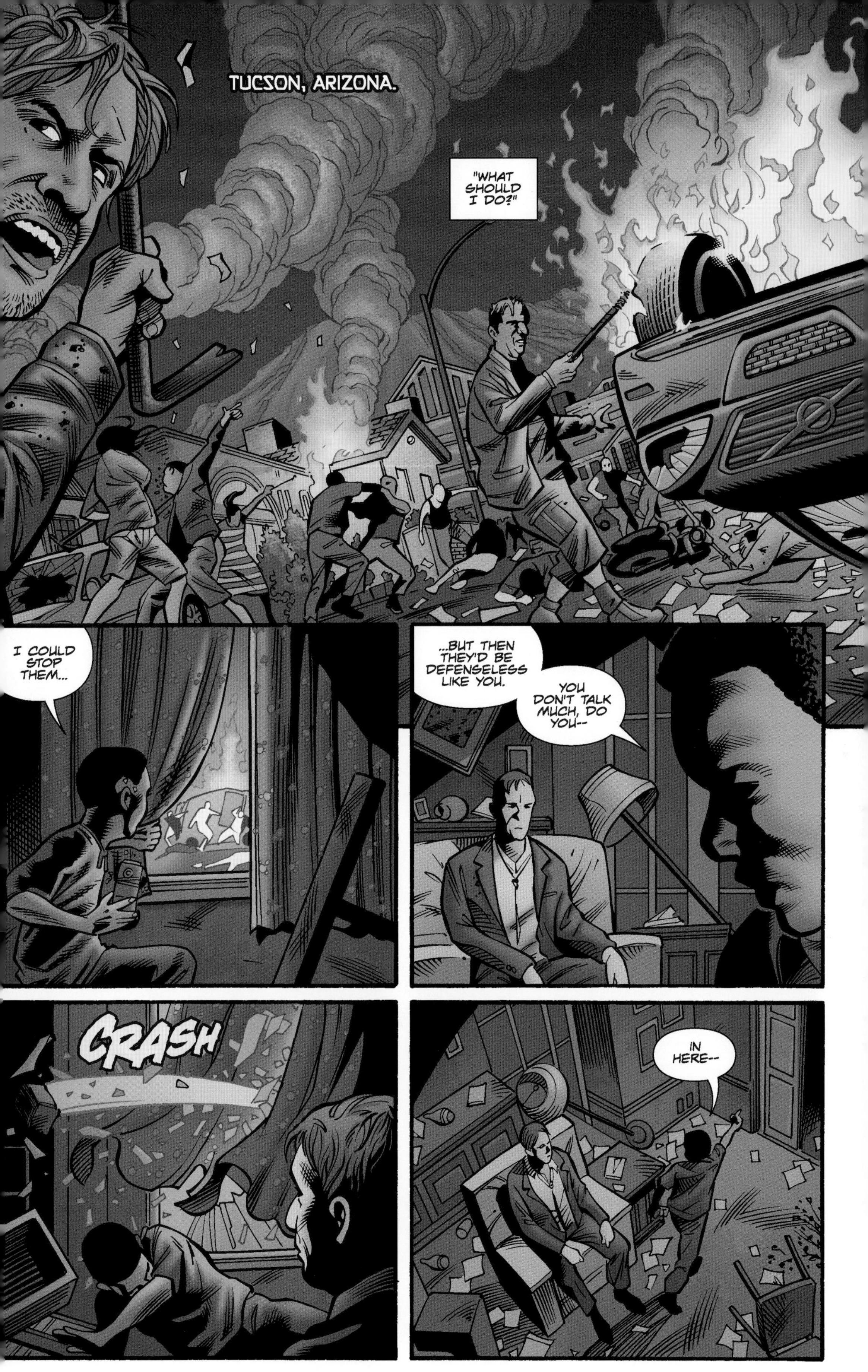
TUCSON, ARIZONA.
"WHAT SHOULD I DO?"
I COULD STOP THEM...
...BUT THEN THEY'D BE DEFENSELESS LIKE YOU.
YOU DON'T TALK MUCH, DO YOU--
CRASH
IN HERE--

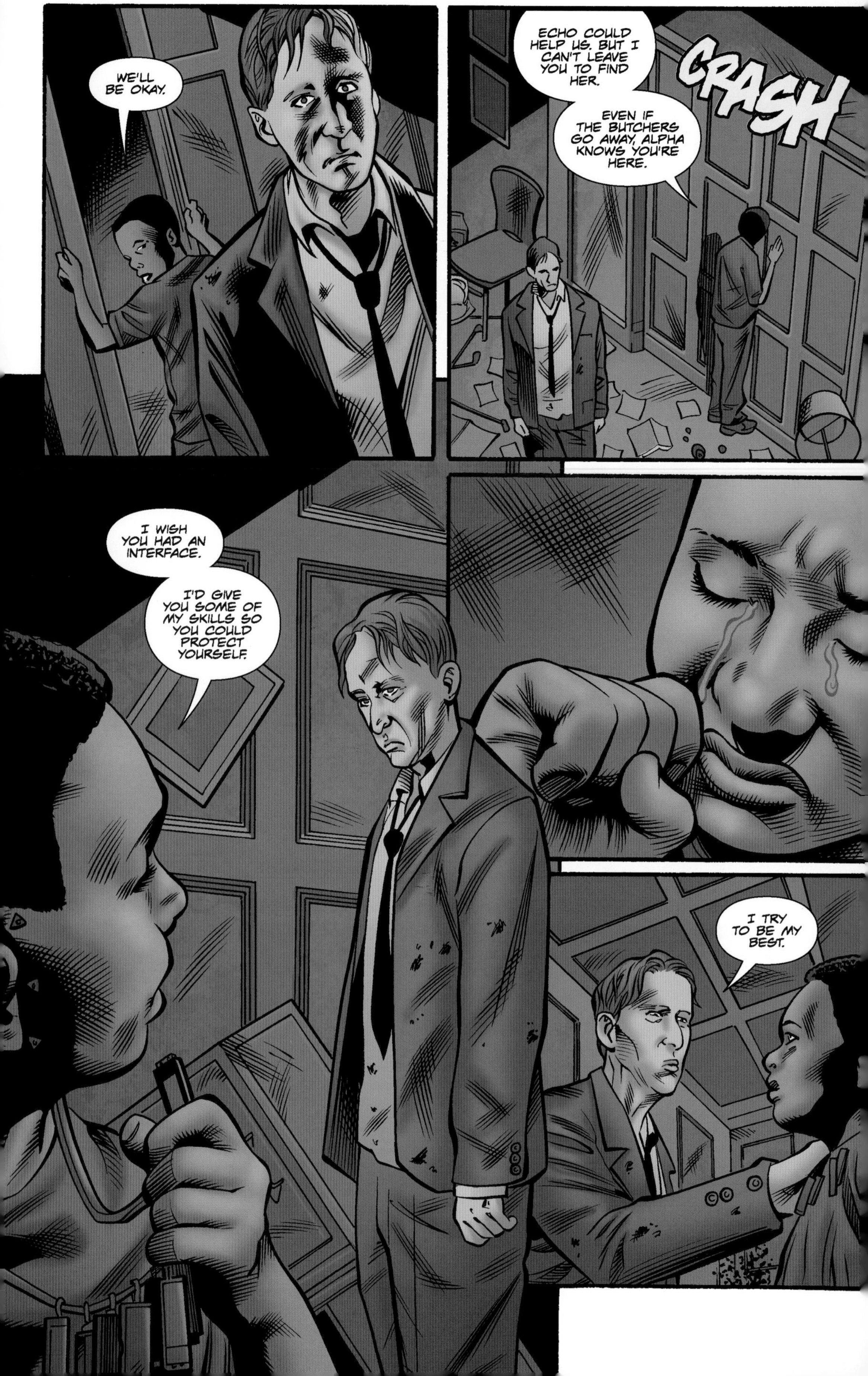

WE'LL BE OKAY.
ECHO COULD HELP US. BUT I CAN'T LEAVE YOU TO FIND HER.
EVEN IF THE BUTCHERS GO AWAY, ALPHA KNOWS YOU'RE HERE.
CRASH
I WISH YOU HAD AN INTERFACE.
I'D GIVE YOU SOME OF MY SKILLS SO YOU COULD PROTECT YOURSELF.
I TRY TO BE MY BEST.

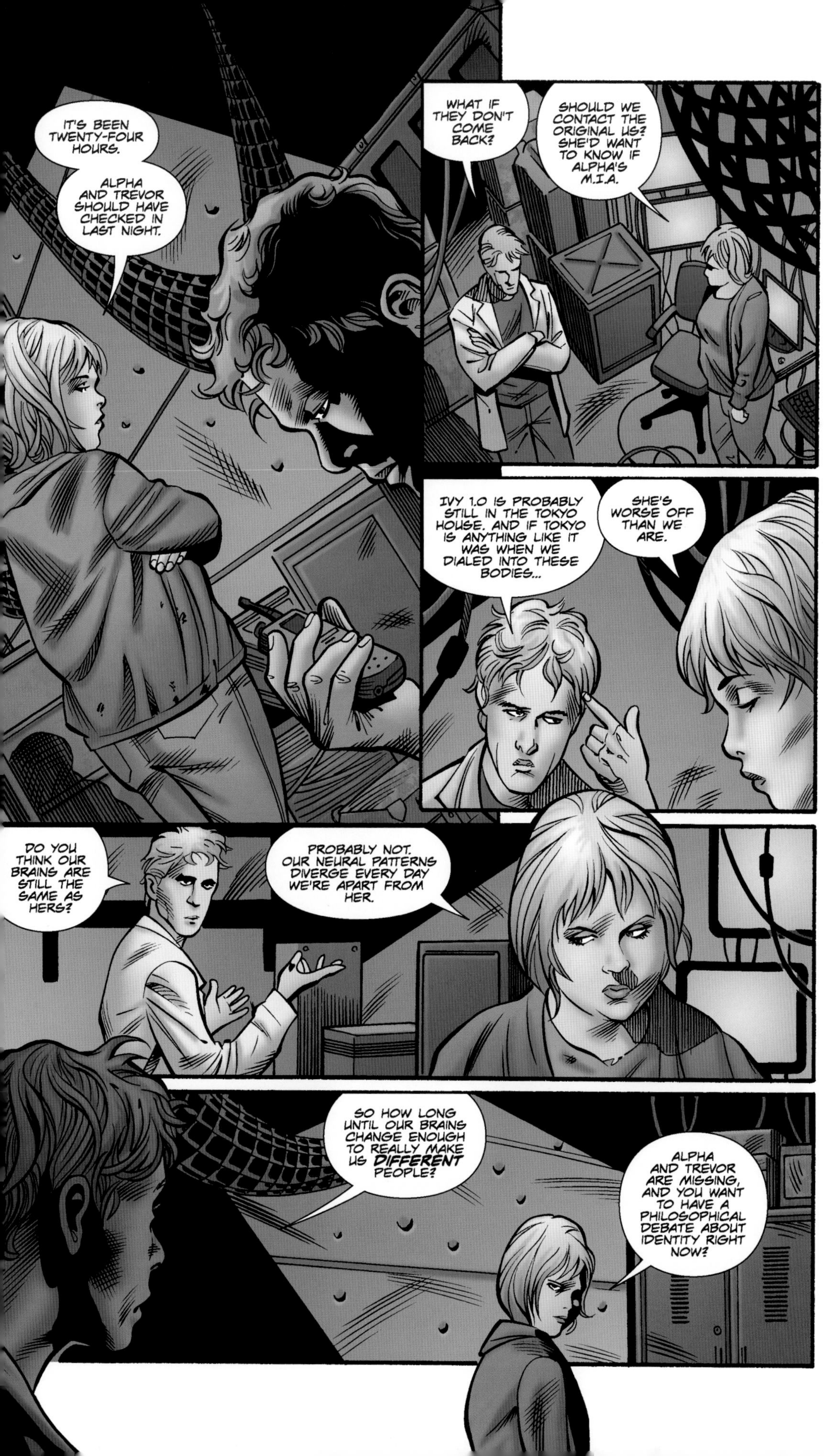
IT'S BEEN TWENTY-FOUR HOURS.
ALPHA AND TREVOR SHOULD HAVE CHECKED IN LAST NIGHT.
WHAT IF THEY DON'T COME BACK?
SHOULD WE CONTACT THE ORIGINAL US? SHE'D WANT TO KNOW IF ALPHA'S M.I.A.
IVY 1.0 IS PROBABLY STILL IN THE TOKYO HOUSE. AND IF TOKYO IS ANYTHING LIKE IT WAS WHEN WE DIALED INTO THESE BODIES...
SHE'S WORSE OFF THAN WE ARE.
DO YOU THINK OUR BRAINS ARE STILL THE SAME AS HERS?
PROBABLY NOT. OUR NEURAL PATTERNS DIVERGE EVERY DAY WE'RE APART FROM HER.
SO HOW LONG UNTIL OUR BRAINS CHANGE ENOUGH TO REALLY MAKE US ***DIFFERENT*** PEOPLE?
ALPHA AND TREVOR ARE MISSING, AND YOU WANT TO HAVE A PHILOSOPHICAL DEBATE ABOUT IDENTITY RIGHT NOW?

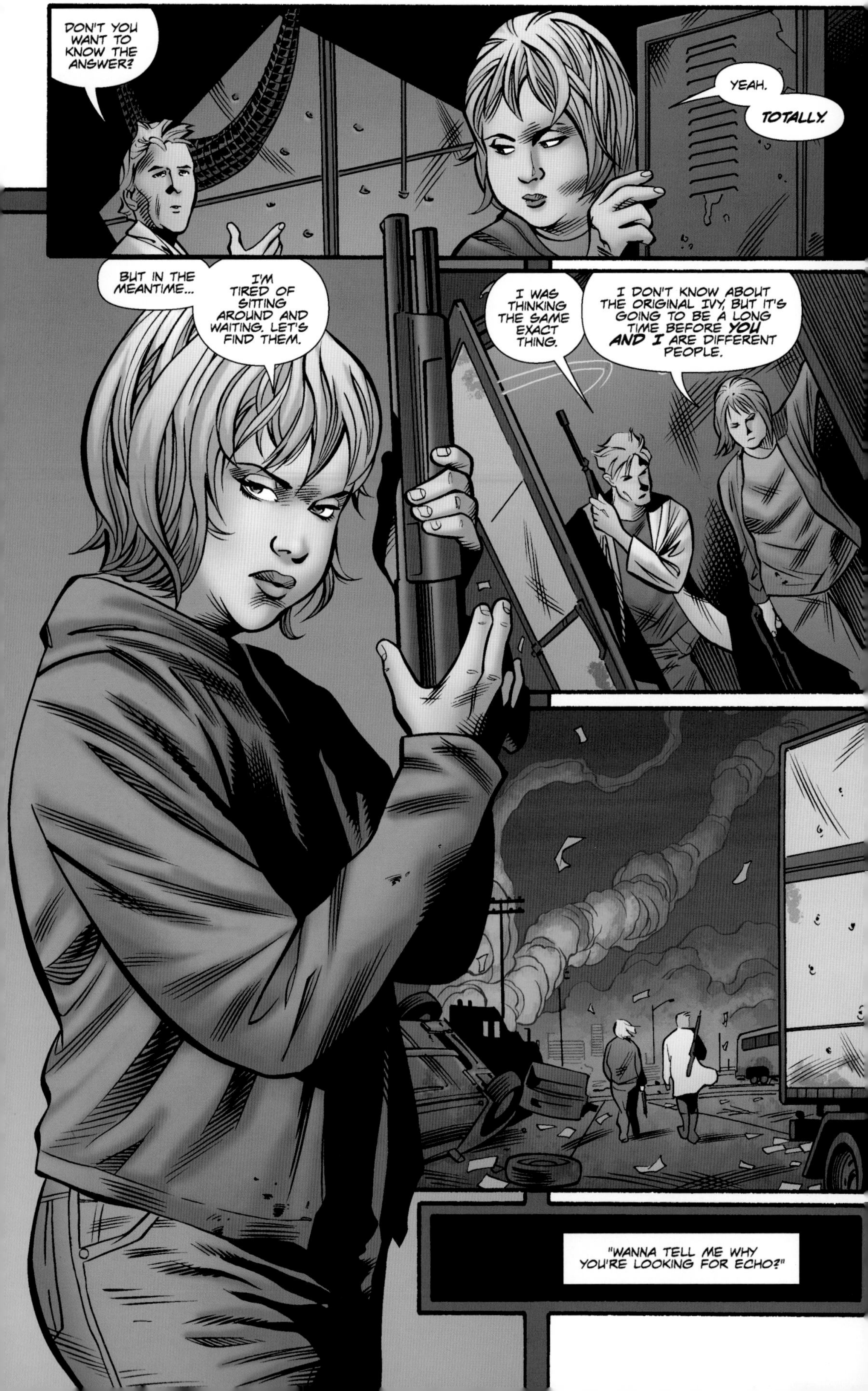

DON'T YOU WANT TO KNOW THE ANSWER?
YEAH.
TOTALLY.
BUT IN THE MEANTIME...
I'M TIRED OF SITTING AROUND AND WAITING. LET'S FIND THEM.
I WAS THINKING THE SAME EXACT THING.
I DON'T KNOW ABOUT THE ORIGINAL IVY, BUT IT'S GOING TO BE A LONG TIME BEFORE YOU AND I ARE DIFFERENT PEOPLE.
"WANNA TELL ME WHY YOU'RE LOOKING FOR ECHO?"

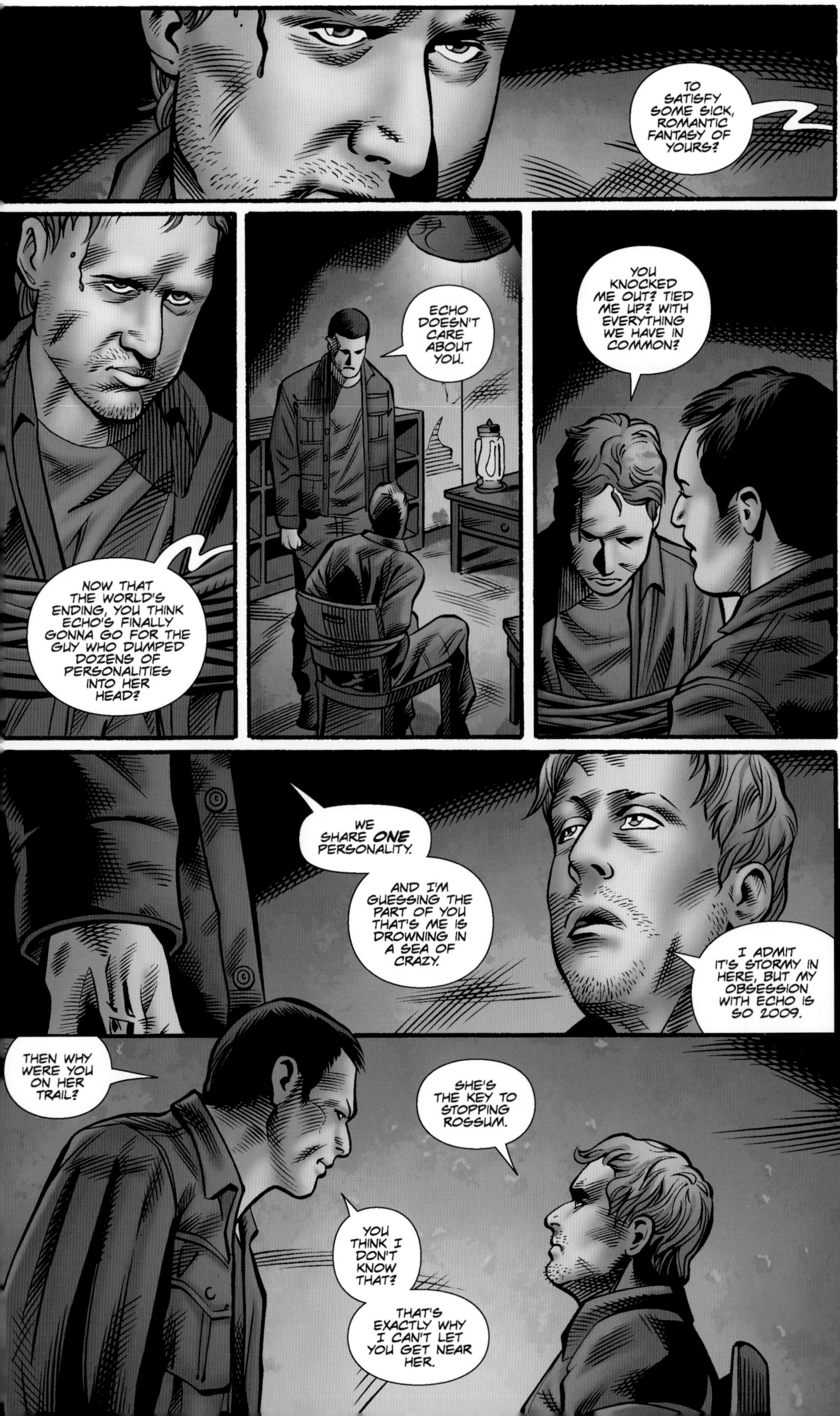
TO SATISFY SOME SICK, ROMANTIC FANTASY OF YOURS?
NOW THAT THE WORLD'S ENDING, YOU THINK ECHO'S FINALLY GONNA GO FOR THE GUY WHO DUMPED DOZENS OF PERSONALITIES INTO HER HEAD?
ECHO DOESN'T CARE ABOUT YOU.
YOU KNOCKED ME OUT? TIED ME UP? WITH EVERYTHING WE HAVE IN COMMON?
WE SHARE ***ONE*** PERSONALITY.
AND I'M GUESSING THE PART OF YOU THAT'S ME IS DROWNING IN A SEA OF CRAZY.
I ADMIT IT'S STORMY IN HERE, BUT MY OBSESSION WITH ECHO IS SO 2009.
THEN WHY WERE YOU ON HER TRAIL?
SHE'S THE KEY TO STOPPING ROSSUM.
YOU THINK I DON'T KNOW THAT?
THAT'S EXACTLY WHY I CAN'T LET YOU GET NEAR HER.

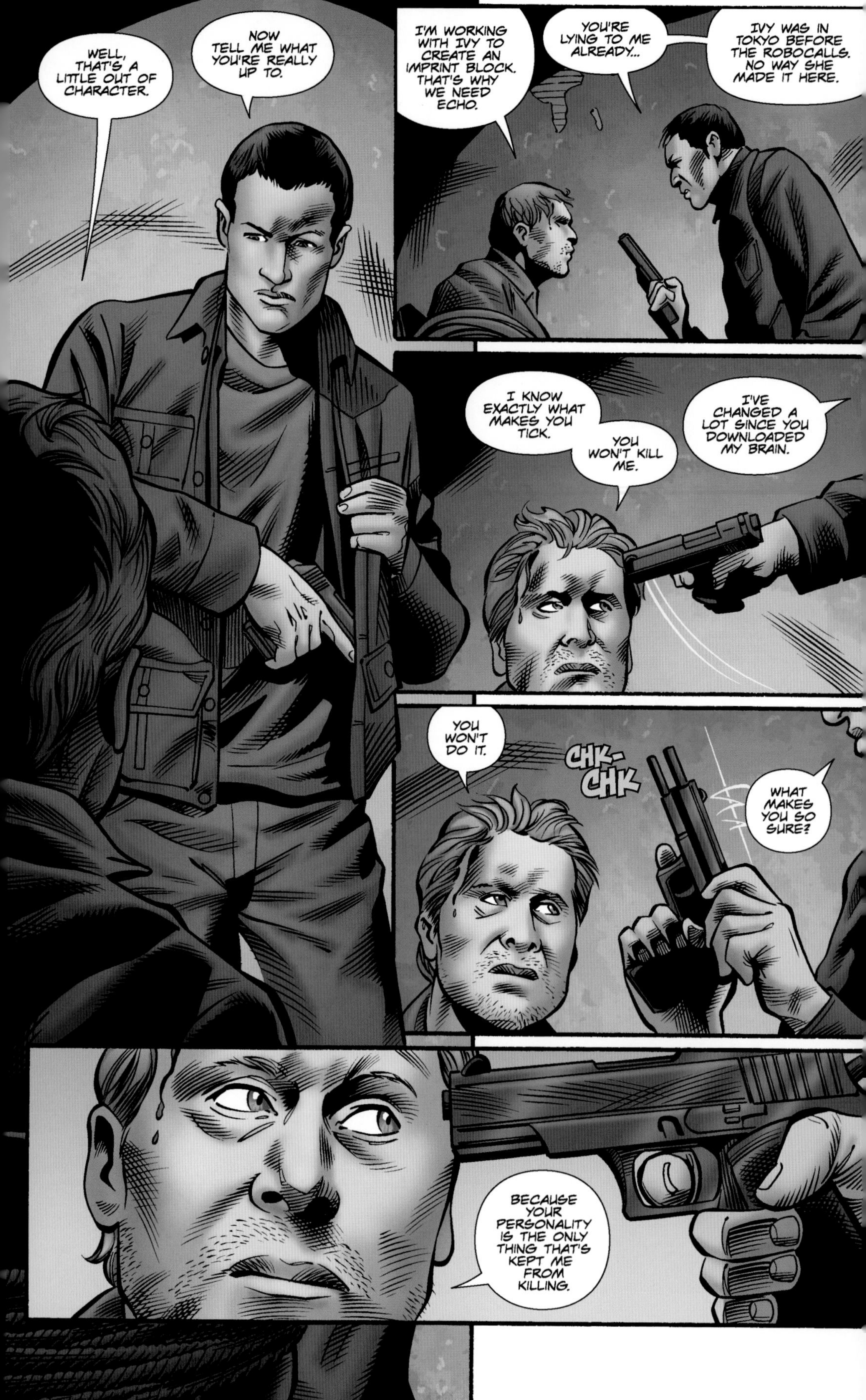
WELL, THAT'S A LITTLE OUT OF CHARACTER.
NOW TELL ME WHAT YOU'RE REALLY UP TO.
I'M WORKING WITH IVY TO CREATE AN IMPRINT BLOCK. THAT'S WHY WE NEED ECHO.
YOU'RE LYING TO ME ALREADY...
IVY WAS IN TOKYO BEFORE THE ROBOCALLS. NO WAY SHE MADE IT HERE.
I KNOW EXACTLY WHAT MAKES YOU TICK.
YOU WON'T KILL ME.
I'VE CHANGED A LOT SINCE YOU DOWNLOADED MY BRAIN.
YOU WON'T DO IT.
CHK-CHK
WHAT MAKES YOU SO SURE?
BECAUSE YOUR PERSONALITY IS THE ONLY THING THAT'S KEPT ME FROM KILLING.

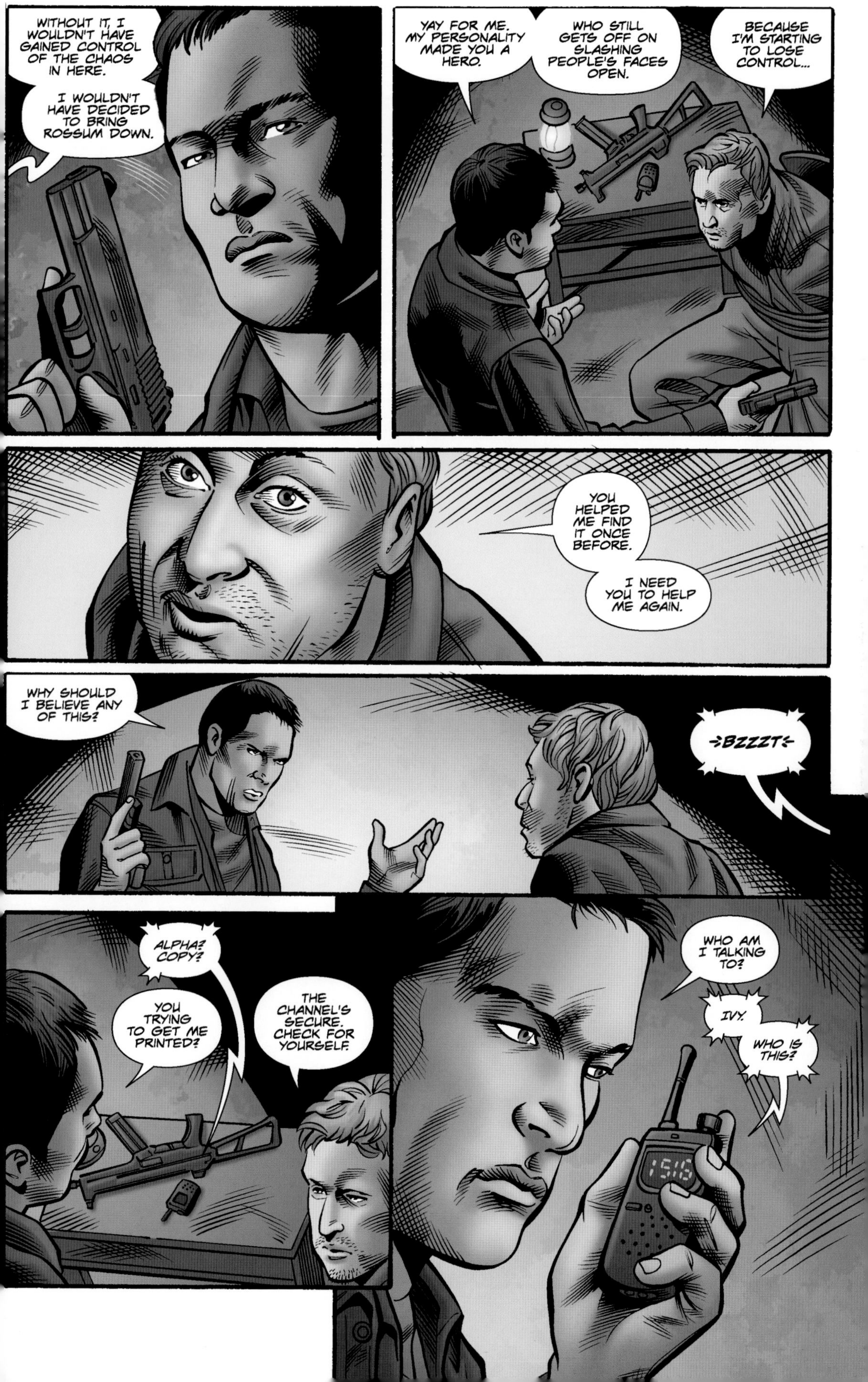
WITHOUT IT, I WOULDN'T HAVE GAINED CONTROL OF THE CHAOS IN HERE.
I WOULDN'T HAVE DECIDED TO BRING ROSSUM DOWN.
YAY FOR ME. MY PERSONALITY MADE YOU A HERO.
WHO STILL GETS OFF ON SLASHING PEOPLE'S FACES OPEN.
BECAUSE I'M STARTING TO LOSE CONTROL...
YOU HELPED ME FIND IT ONCE BEFORE.
I NEED YOU TO HELP ME AGAIN.
WHY SHOULD I BELIEVE ANY OF THIS?
BZZZT
ALPHA? COPY?
YOU TRYING TO GET ME PRINTED?
THE CHANNEL'S SECURE. CHECK FOR YOURSELF.
WHO AM I TALKING TO?
IVY.
WHO IS THIS?

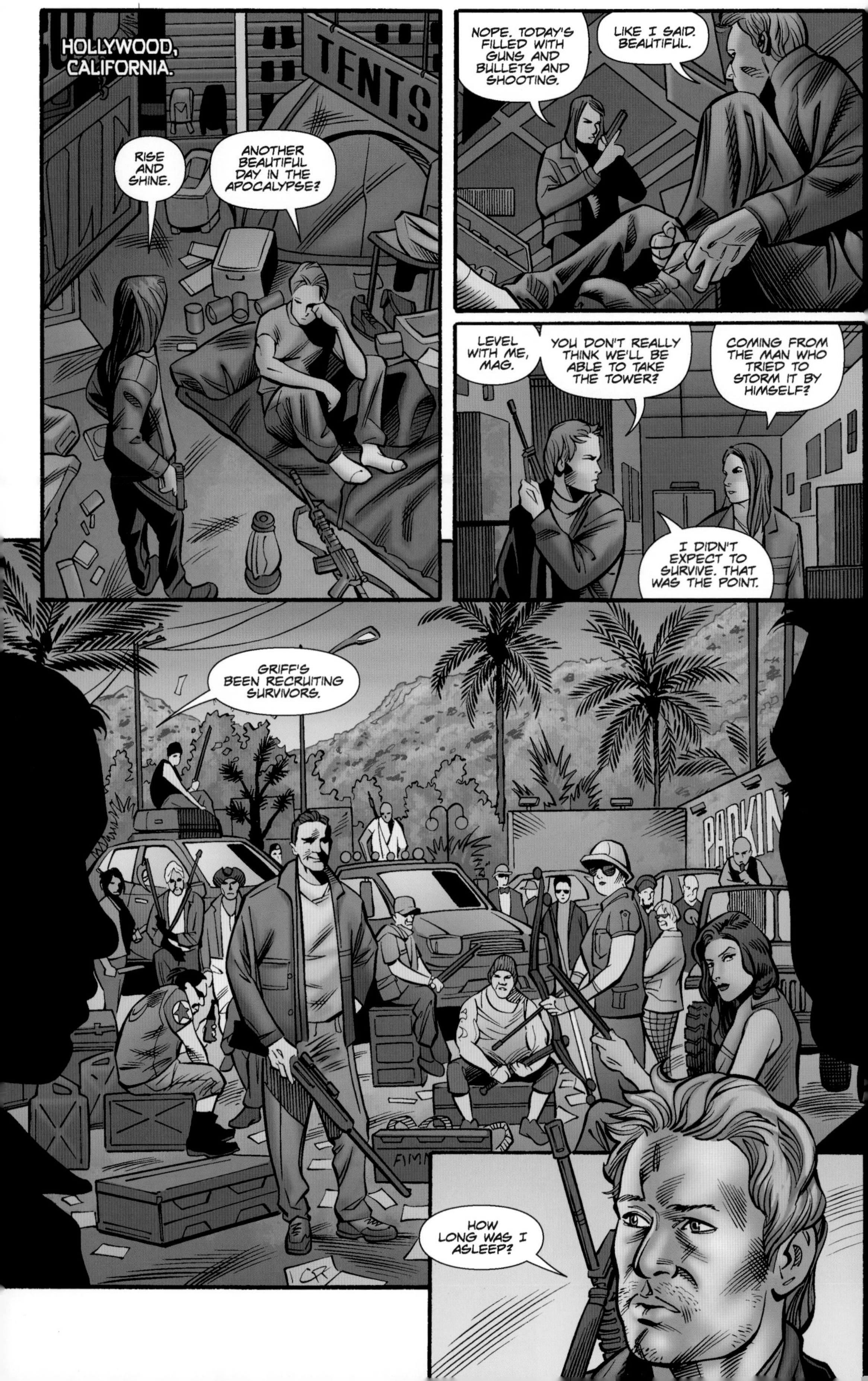
HOLLYWOOD, CALIFORNIA.
TENTS
RISE AND SHINE.
ANOTHER BEAUTIFUL DAY IN THE APOCALYPSE?
NOPE. TODAY'S FILLED WITH GUNS AND BULLETS AND SHOOTING.
LIKE I SAID. BEAUTIFUL.
LEVEL WITH ME, MAG.
YOU DON'T REALLY THINK WE'LL BE ABLE TO TAKE THE TOWER?
COMING FROM THE MAN WHO TRIED TO STORM IT BY HIMSELF?
I DIDN'T EXPECT TO SURVIVE. THAT WAS THE POINT.
GRIFF'S BEEN RECRUITING SURVIVORS.
HOW LONG WAS I ASLEEP?

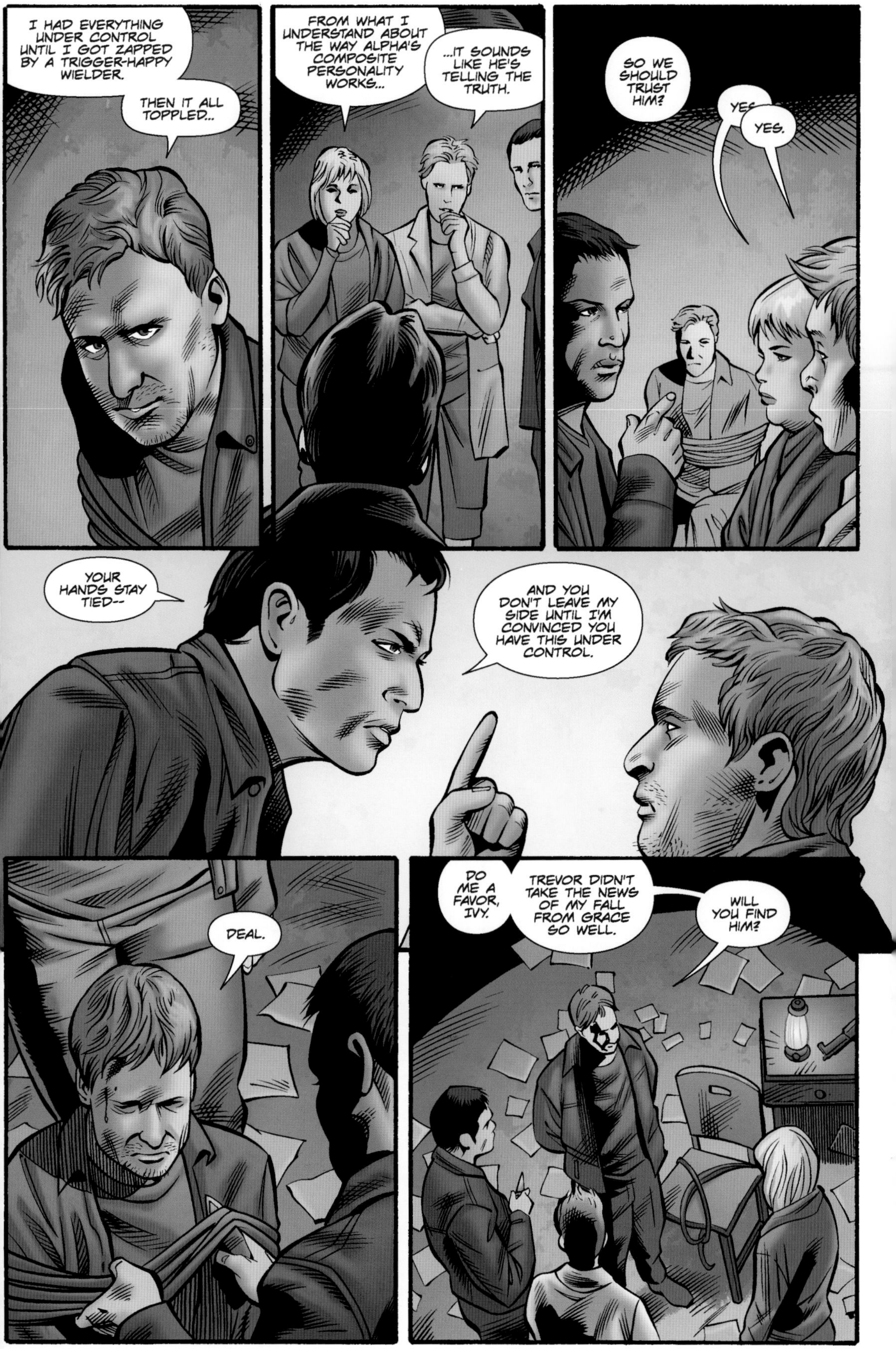
I HAD EVERYTHING UNDER CONTROL UNTIL I GOT ZAPPED BY A TRIGGER-HAPPY WIELDER.
THEN IT ALL TOPPLED...
FROM WHAT I UNDERSTAND ABOUT THE WAY ALPHA'S COMPOSITE PERSONALITY WORKS...
...IT SOUNDS LIKE HE'S TELLING THE TRUTH.
SO WE SHOULD TRUST HIM?
YES
YES.
YOUR HANDS STAY TIED--
AND YOU DON'T LEAVE MY SIDE UNTIL I'M CONVINCED YOU HAVE THIS UNDER CONTROL.
DEAL.
DO ME A FAVOR, IVY.
TREVOR DIDN'T TAKE THE NEWS OF MY FALL FROM GRACE SO WELL.
WILL YOU FIND HIM?

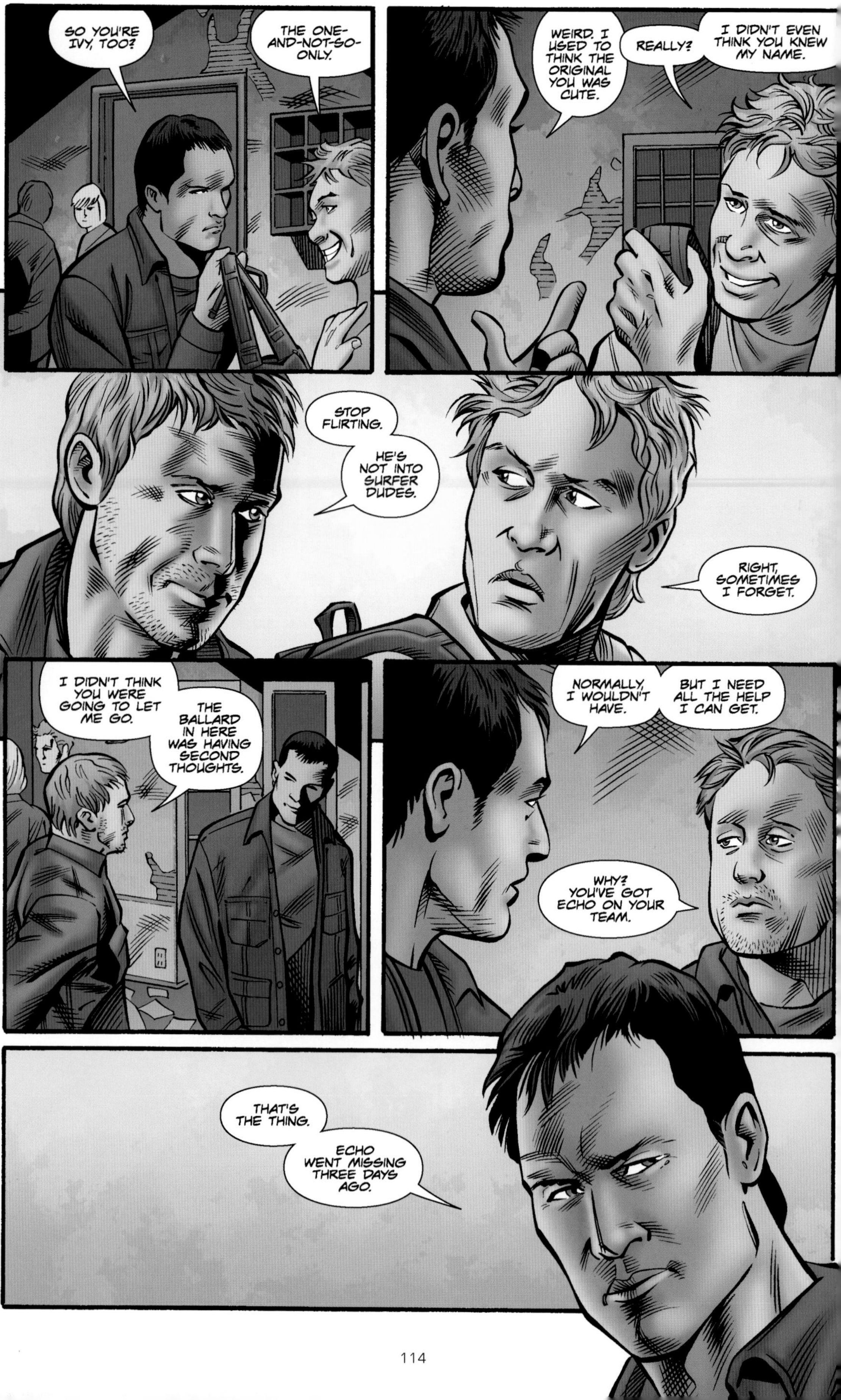
SO YOU'RE IVY, TOO?
THE ONE-AND-NOT-SO-ONLY.
WEIRD. I USED TO THINK THE ORIGINAL YOU WAS CUTE.
REALLY?
I DIDN'T EVEN THINK YOU KNEW MY NAME.
STOP FLIRTING.
HE'S NOT INTO SURFER DUDES.
RIGHT, SOMETIMES I FORGET.
I DIDN'T THINK YOU WERE GOING TO LET ME GO.
THE BALLARD IN HERE WAS HAVING SECOND THOUGHTS.
NORMALLY, I WOULDN'T HAVE.
BUT I NEED ALL THE HELP I CAN GET.
WHY? YOU'VE GOT ECHO ON YOUR TEAM.
THAT'S THE THING.
ECHO WENT MISSING THREE DAYS AGO.

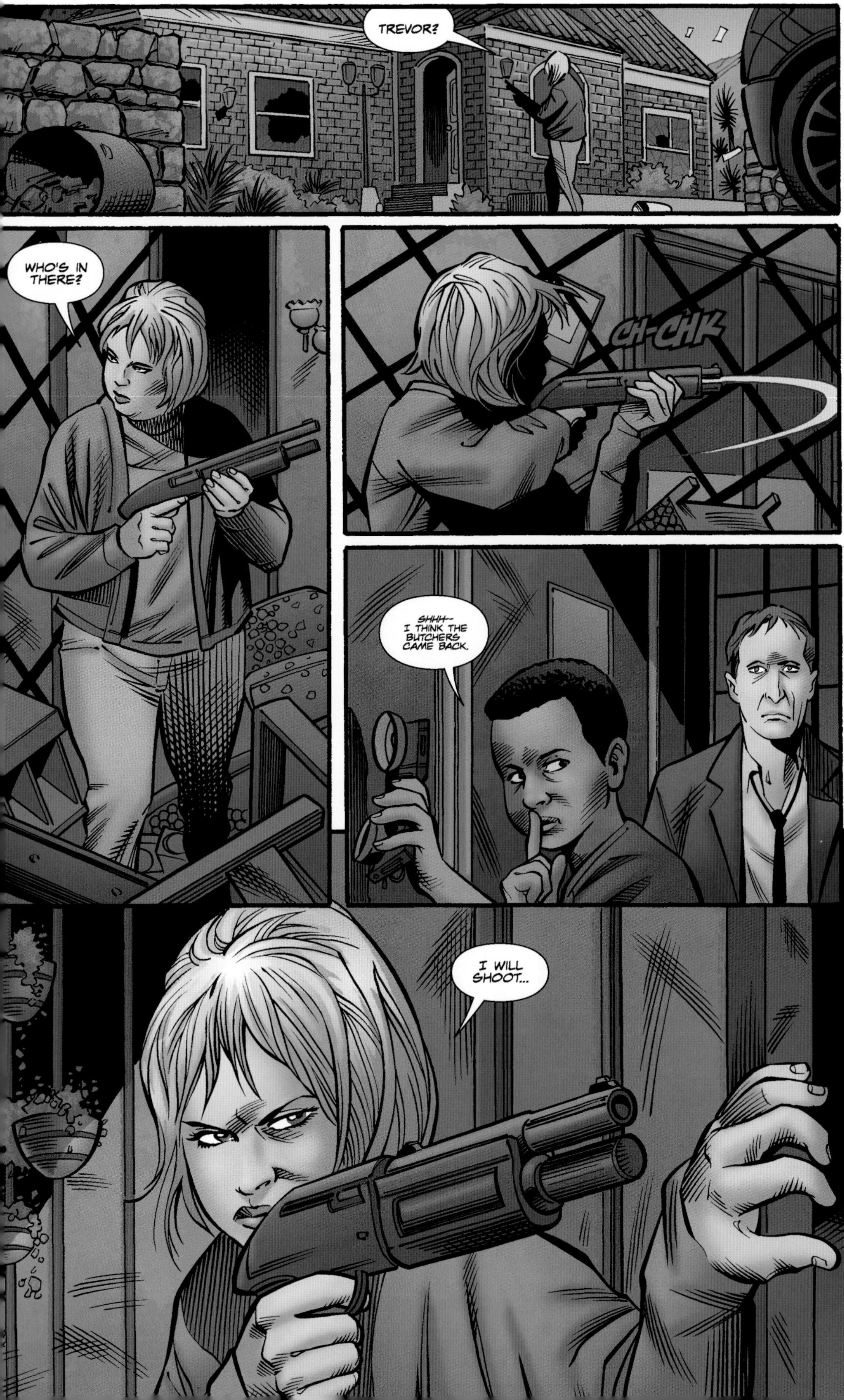
TREVOR?
WHO'S IN THERE?
CH-CHK
SHHH-- I THINK THE BUTCHERS CAME BACK.
I WILL SHOOT...

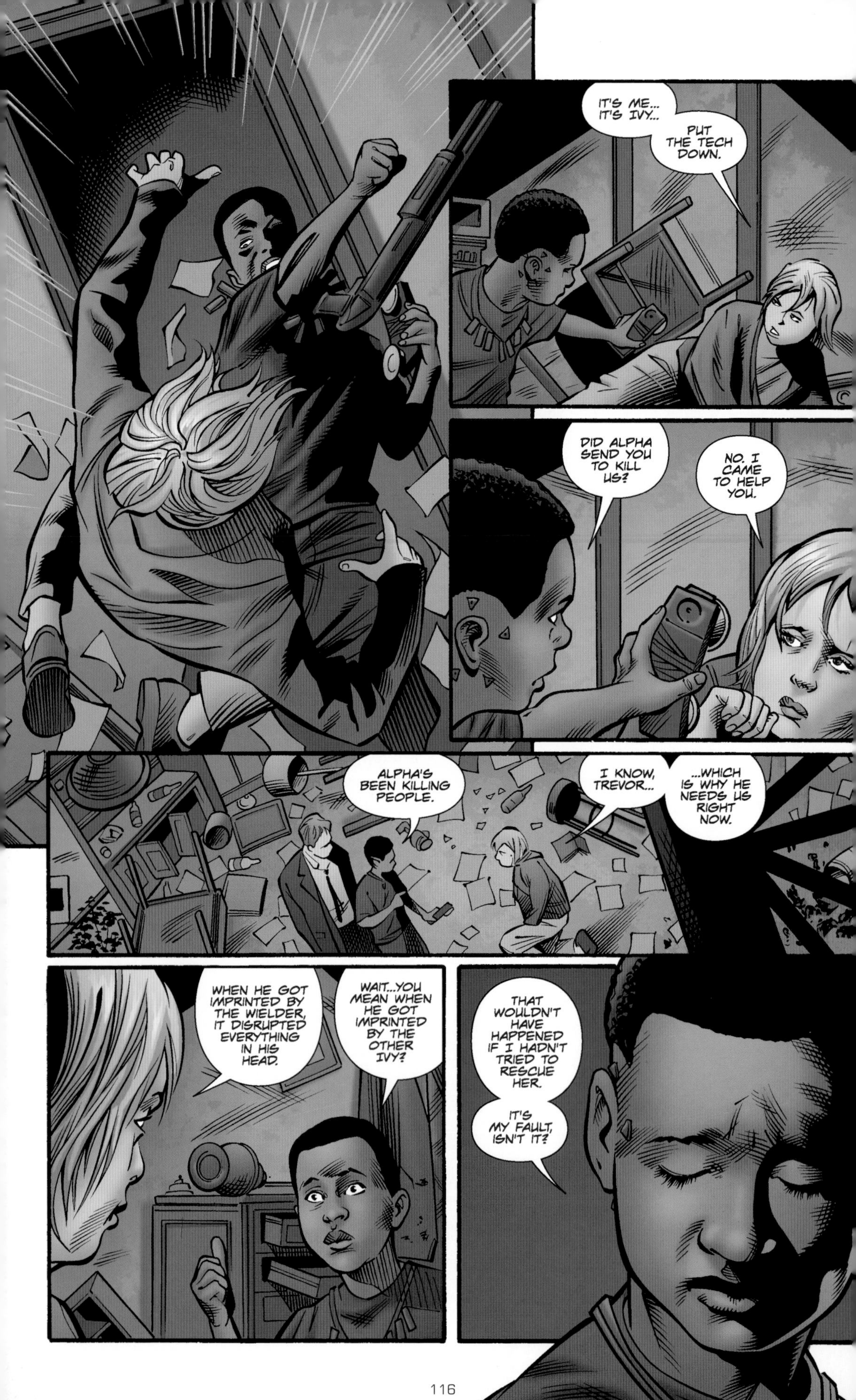

IT'S ME... IT'S IVY...
PUT THE TECH DOWN.
DID ALPHA SEND YOU TO KILL US?
NO. I CAME TO HELP YOU.
ALPHA'S BEEN KILLING PEOPLE.
I KNOW, TREVOR...
...WHICH IS WHY HE NEEDS US RIGHT NOW.
WHEN HE GOT IMPRINTED BY THE WIELDER, IT DISRUPTED EVERYTHING IN HIS HEAD.
WAIT...YOU MEAN WHEN HE GOT IMPRINTED BY THE OTHER IVY?
THAT WOULDN'T HAVE HAPPENED IF I HADN'T TRIED TO RESCUE HER.
IT'S MY FAULT, ISN'T IT?

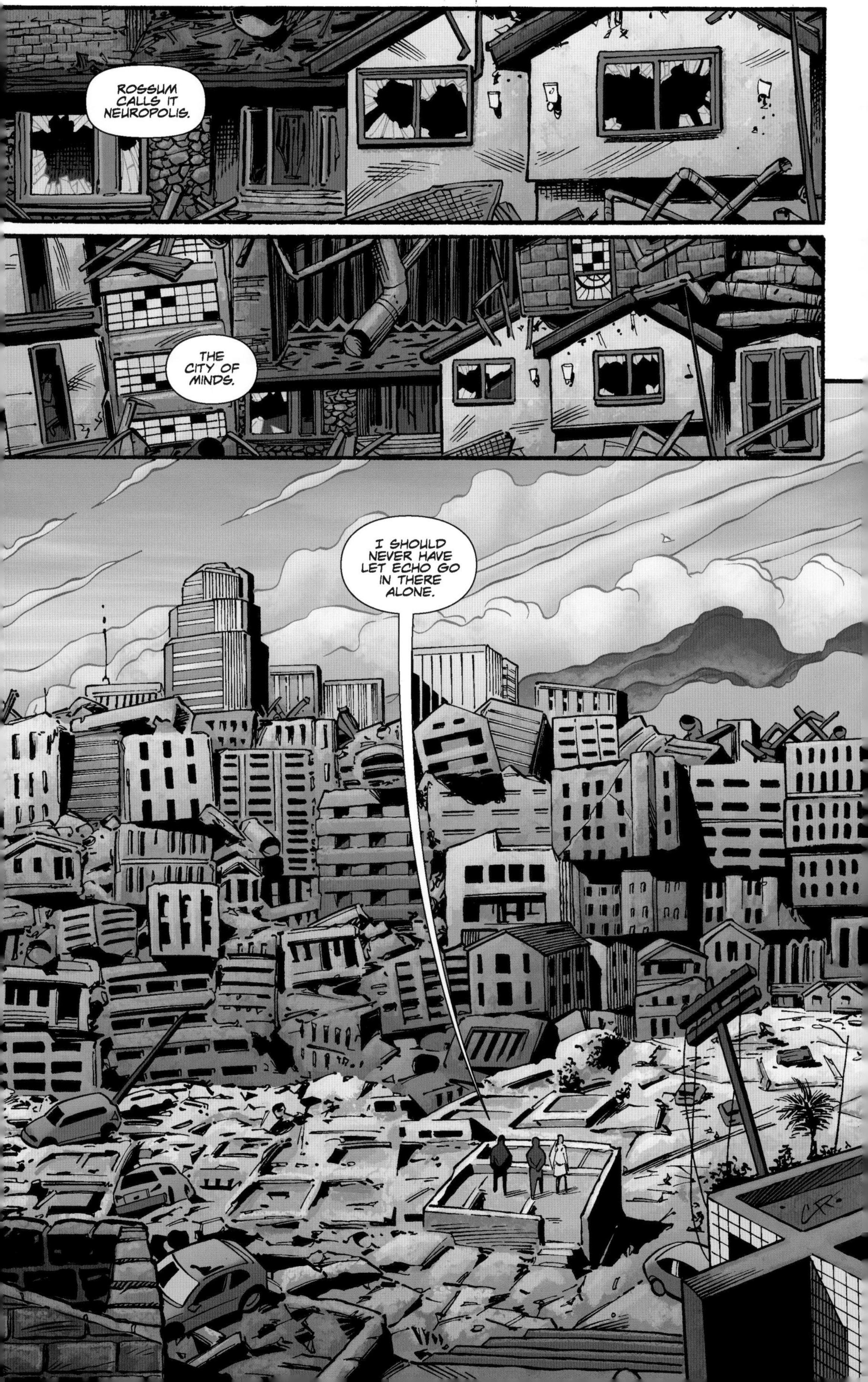
ROSSUM CALLS IT NEUROPOLIS.
THE CITY OF MINDS.
I SHOULD NEVER HAVE LET ECHO GO IN THERE ALONE.

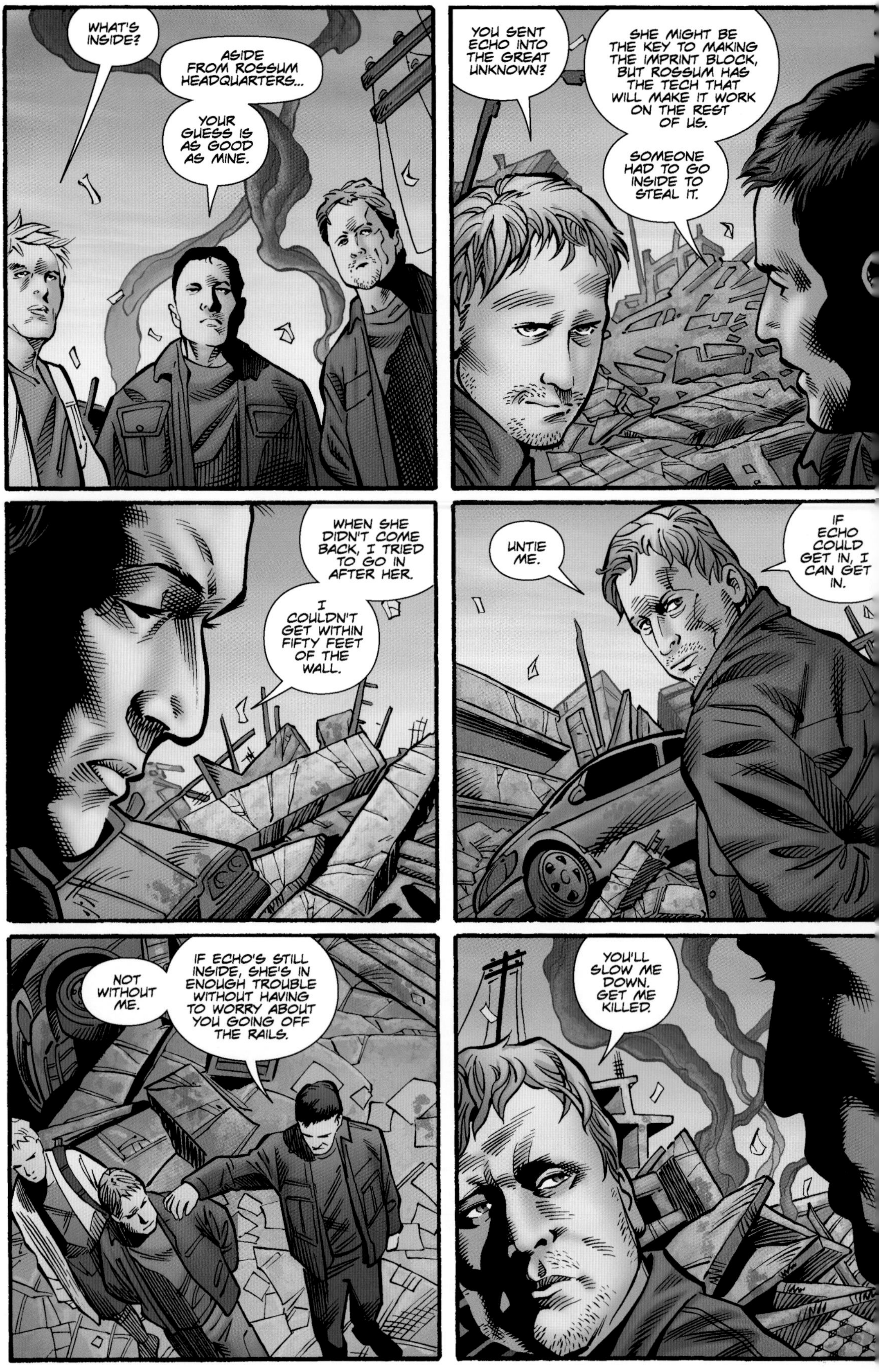
WHAT'S INSIDE?
ASIDE FROM ROSSUM HEADQUARTERS...
YOUR GUESS IS AS GOOD AS MINE.
YOU SENT ECHO INTO THE GREAT UNKNOWN?
SHE MIGHT BE THE KEY TO MAKING THE IMPRINT BLOCK, BUT ROSSUM HAS THE TECH THAT WILL MAKE IT WORK ON THE REST OF US.
SOMEONE HAD TO GO INSIDE TO STEAL IT.
WHEN SHE DIDN'T COME BACK, I TRIED TO GO IN AFTER HER.
I COULDN'T GET WITHIN FIFTY FEET OF THE WALL.
UNTIE ME.
IF ECHO COULD GET IN, I CAN GET IN.
NOT WITHOUT ME.
IF ECHO'S STILL INSIDE, SHE'S IN ENOUGH TROUBLE WITHOUT HAVING TO WORRY ABOUT YOU GOING OFF THE RAILS.
YOU'LL SLOW ME DOWN. GET ME KILLED.

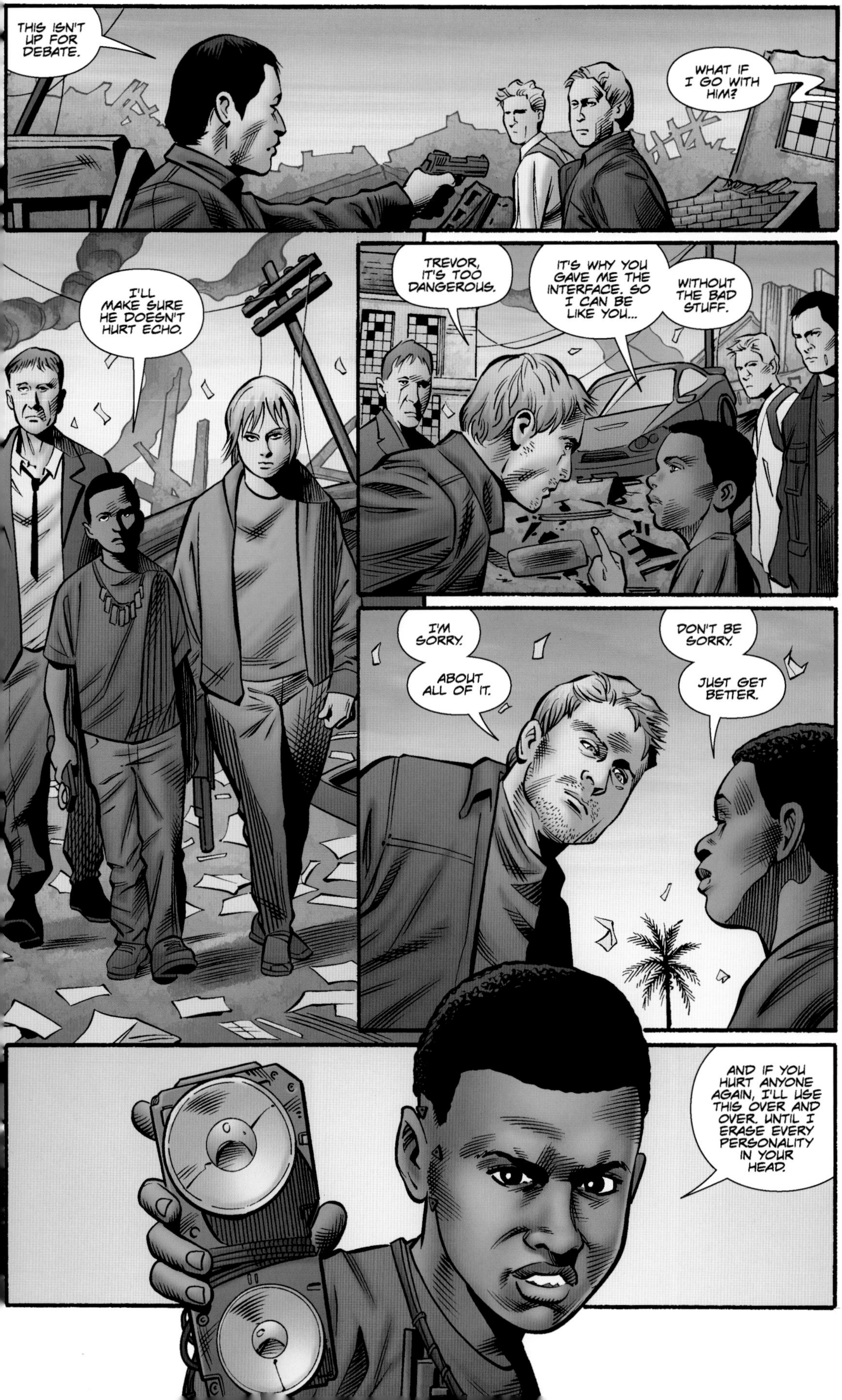
THIS ISN'T UP FOR DEBATE.
WHAT IF I GO WITH HIM?
I'LL MAKE SURE HE DOESN'T HURT ECHO.
TREVOR, IT'S TOO DANGEROUS.
IT'S WHY YOU GAVE ME THE INTERFACE. SO I CAN BE LIKE YOU...
WITHOUT THE BAD STUFF.
I'M SORRY.
ABOUT ALL OF IT.
DON'T BE SORRY.
JUST GET BETTER.
AND IF YOU HURT ANYONE AGAIN, I'LL USE THIS OVER AND OVER. UNTIL I ERASE EVERY PERSONALITY IN YOUR HEAD.

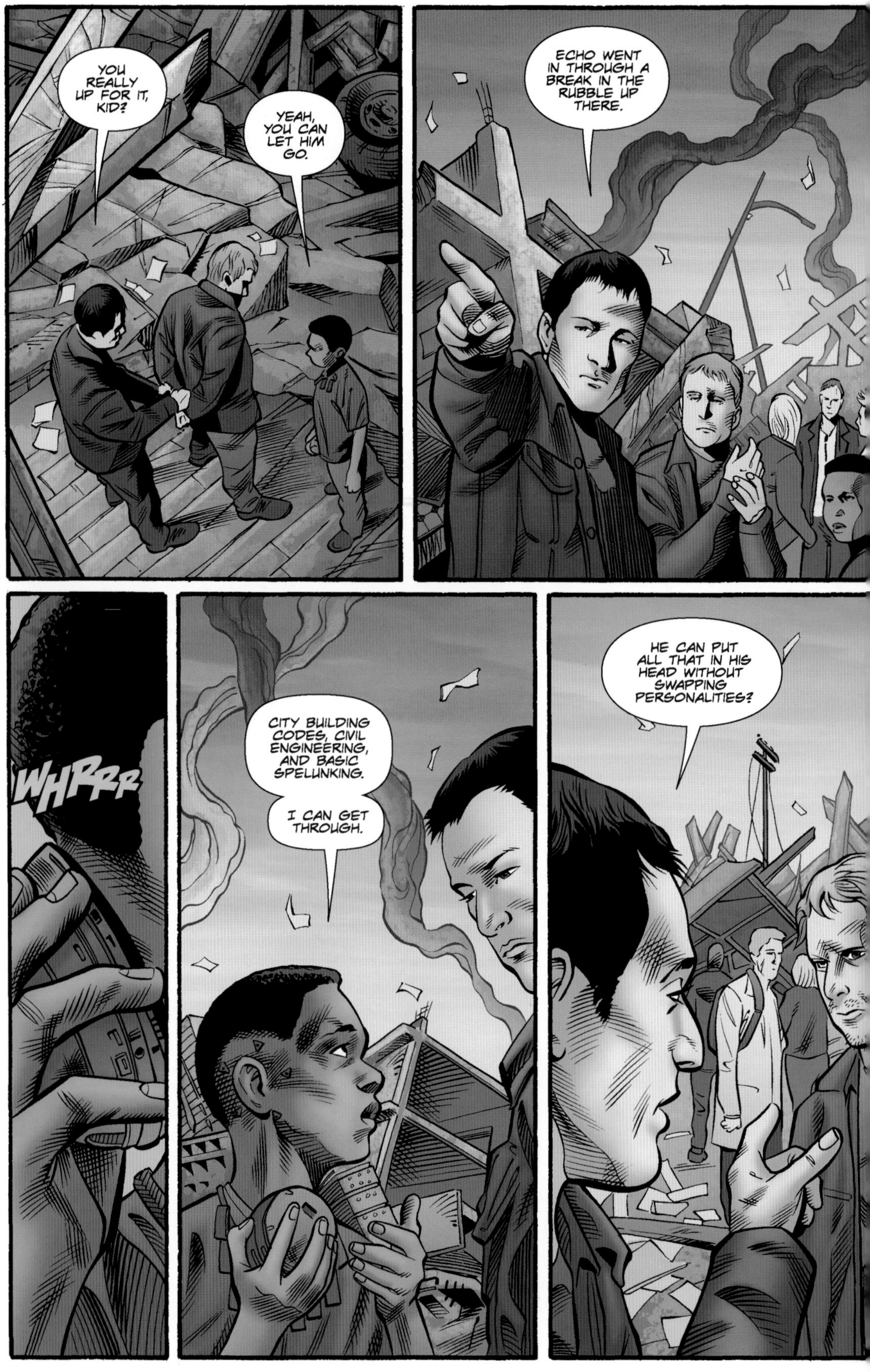
YOU REALLY UP FOR IT, KID?
YEAH, YOU CAN LET HIM GO.
ECHO WENT IN THROUGH A BREAK IN THE RUBBLE UP THERE.
WHRRR
CITY BUILDING CODES, CIVIL ENGINEERING, AND BASIC SPELUNKING.
I CAN GET THROUGH.
HE CAN PUT ALL THAT IN HIS HEAD WITHOUT SWAPPING PERSONALITIES?

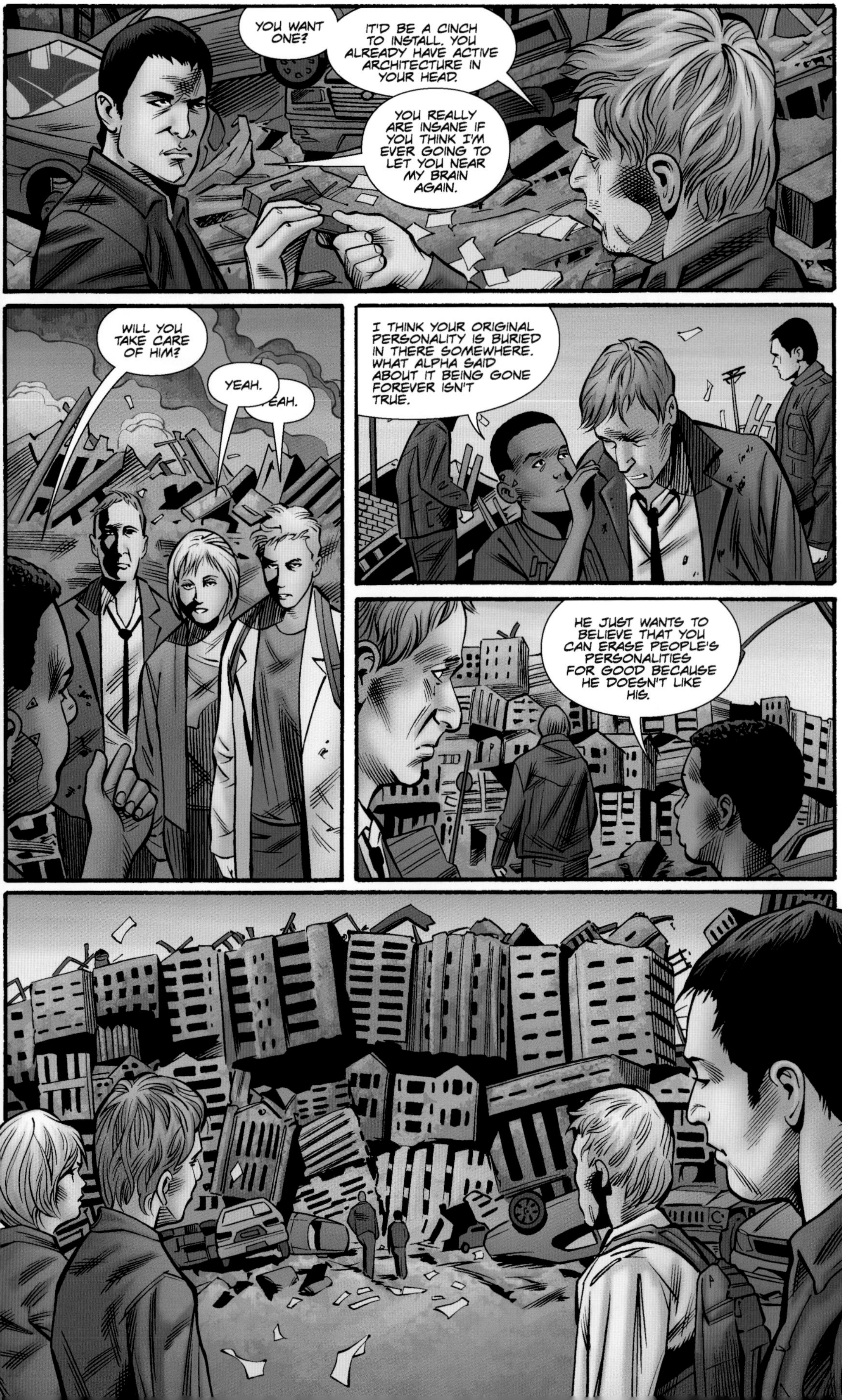
YOU WANT ONE?
IT'D BE A CINCH TO INSTALL. YOU ALREADY HAVE ACTIVE ARCHITECTURE IN YOUR HEAD.
YOU REALLY ARE INSANE IF YOU THINK I'M EVER GOING TO LET YOU NEAR MY BRAIN AGAIN.
WILL YOU TAKE CARE OF HIM?
YEAH.
EAH.
I THINK YOUR ORIGINAL PERSONALITY IS BURIED IN THERE SOMEWHERE. WHAT ALPHA SAID ABOUT IT BEING GONE FOREVER ISN'T TRUE.
HE JUST WANTS TO BELIEVE THAT YOU CAN ERASE PEOPLE'S PERSONALITIES FOR GOOD BECAUSE HE DOESN'T LIKE HIS.

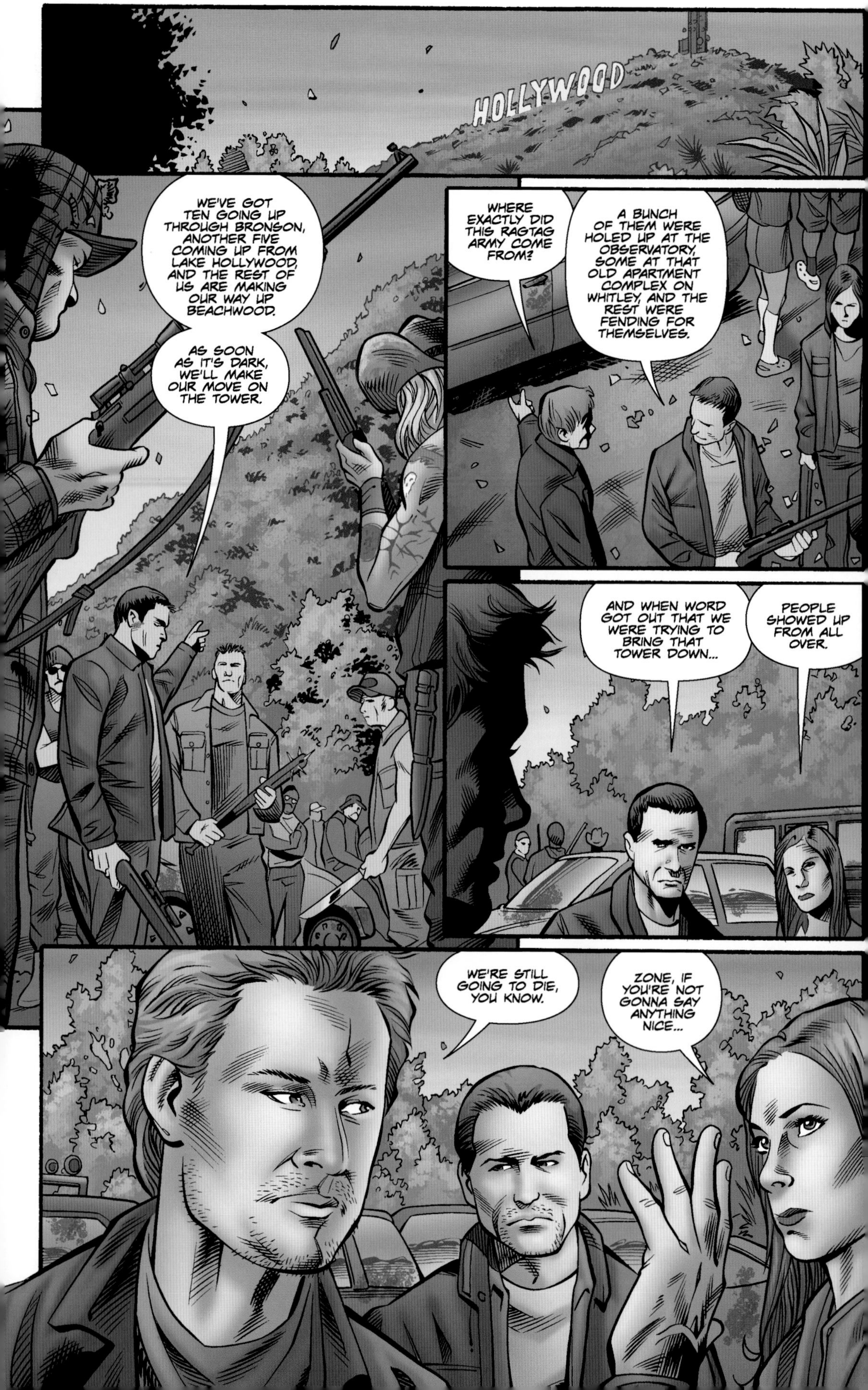
HOLLYWOOD
WE'VE GOT TEN GOING UP THROUGH BRONSON, ANOTHER FIVE COMING UP FROM LAKE HOLLYWOOD, AND THE REST OF US ARE MAKING OUR WAY UP BEACHWOOD.
AS SOON AS IT'S DARK, WE'LL MAKE OUR MOVE ON THE TOWER.
WHERE EXACTLY DID THIS RAGTAG ARMY COME FROM?
A BUNCH OF THEM WERE HOLED UP AT THE OBSERVATORY, SOME AT THAT OLD APARTMENT COMPLEX ON WHITLEY, AND THE REST WERE FENDING FOR THEMSELVES.
AND WHEN WORD GOT OUT THAT WE WERE TRYING TO BRING THAT TOWER DOWN...
PEOPLE SHOWED UP FROM ALL OVER.
WE'RE STILL GOING TO DIE, YOU KNOW.
ZONE, IF YOU'RE NOT GONNA SAY ANYTHING NICE...

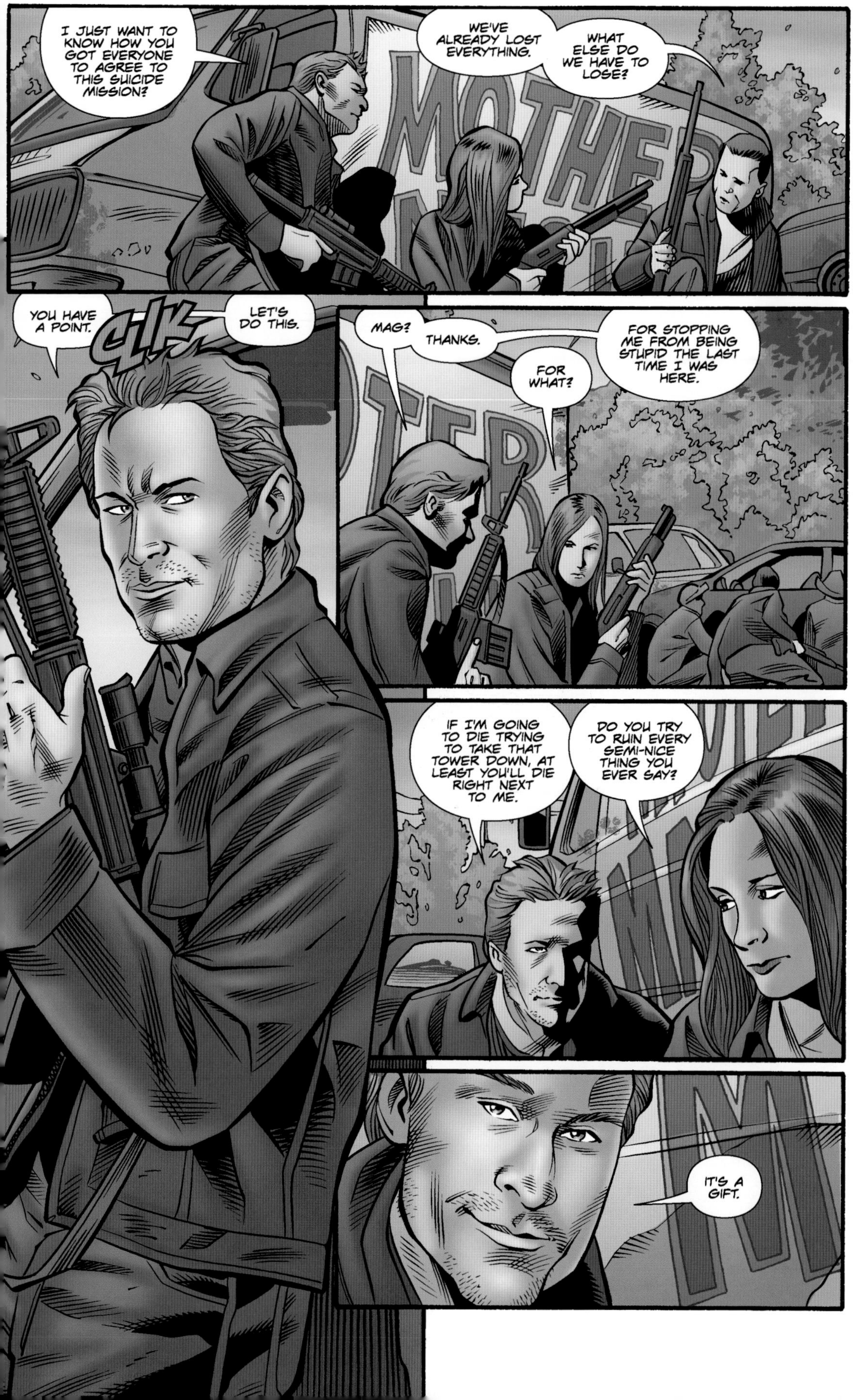

I JUST WANT TO KNOW HOW YOU GOT EVERYONE TO AGREE TO THIS SUICIDE MISSION?
WE'VE ALREADY LOST EVERYTHING.
WHAT ELSE DO WE HAVE TO LOSE?
MOTHER
YOU HAVE A POINT.
CLIK
LET'S DO THIS.
MAG?
THANKS.
FOR WHAT?
FOR STOPPING ME FROM BEING STUPID THE LAST TIME I WAS HERE.
IF I'M GOING TO DIE TRYING TO TAKE THAT TOWER DOWN, AT LEAST YOU'LL DIE RIGHT NEXT TO ME.
DO YOU TRY TO RUIN EVERY SEMI-NICE THING YOU EVER SAY?
IT'S A GIFT.

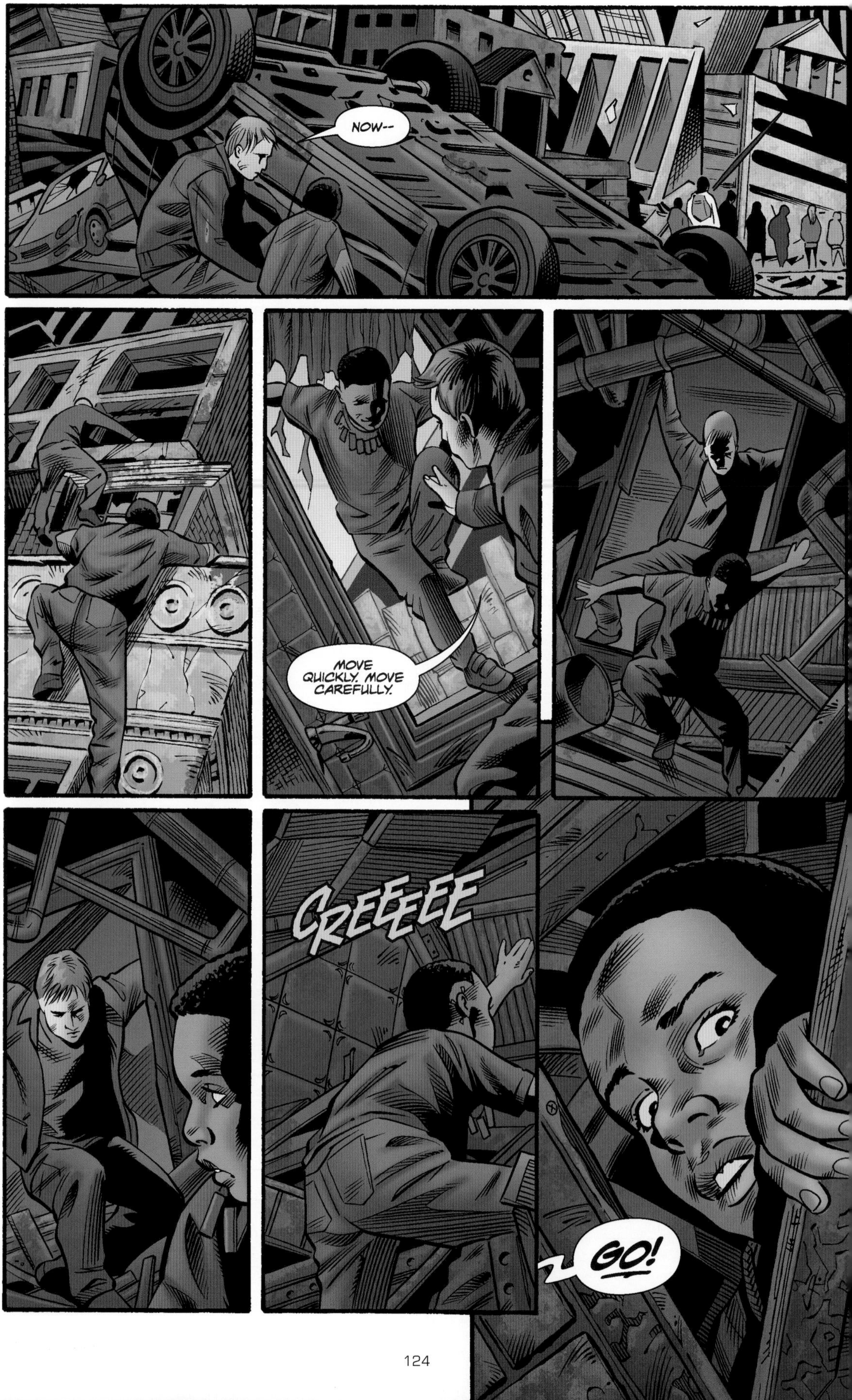
NOW--
MOVE QUICKLY. MOVE CAREFULLY.
CREEEEEE
GO!

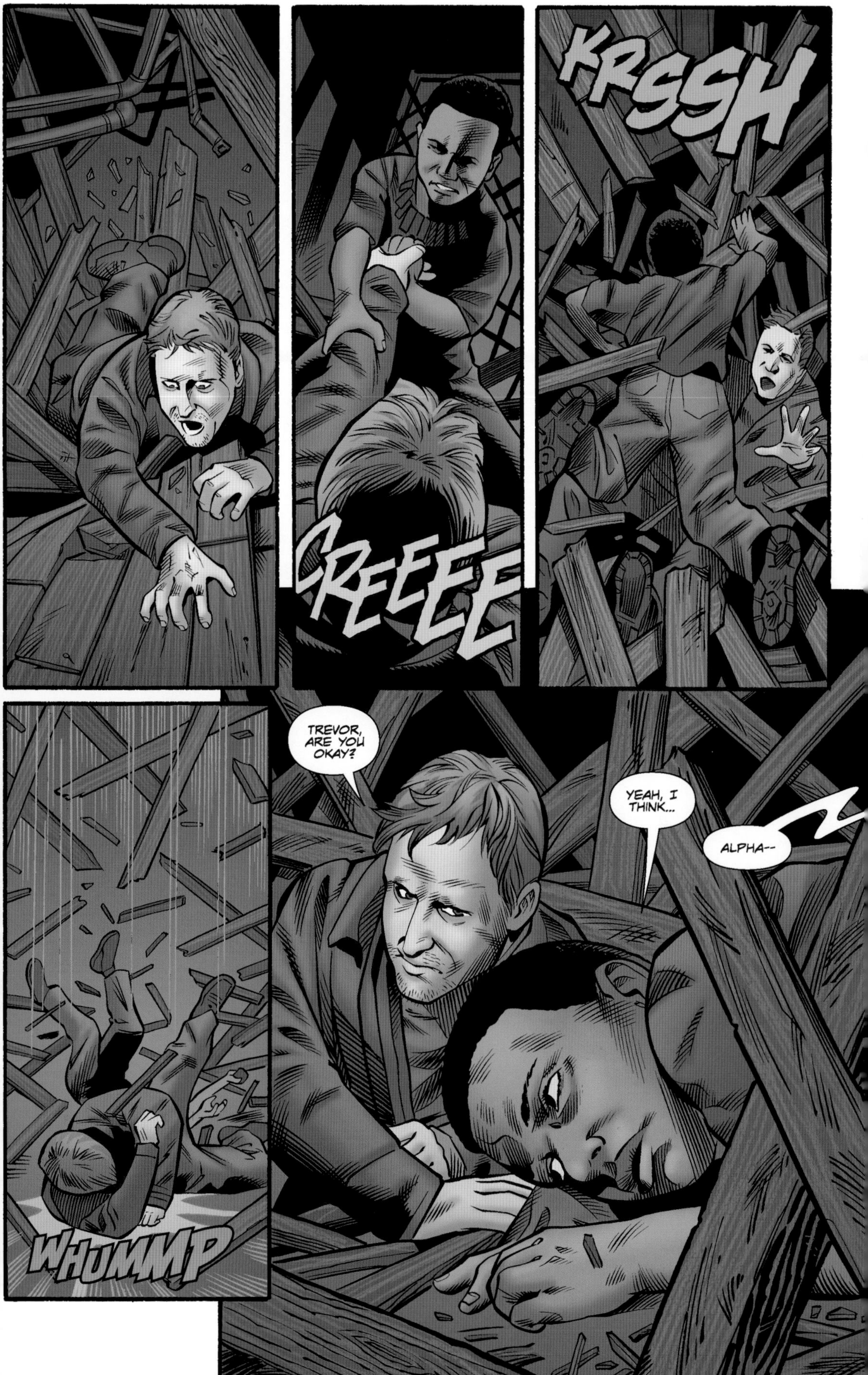
CREEEE
KRSSH
WHUMMP
TREVOR, ARE YOU OKAY?
YEAH, I THINK...
ALPHA--

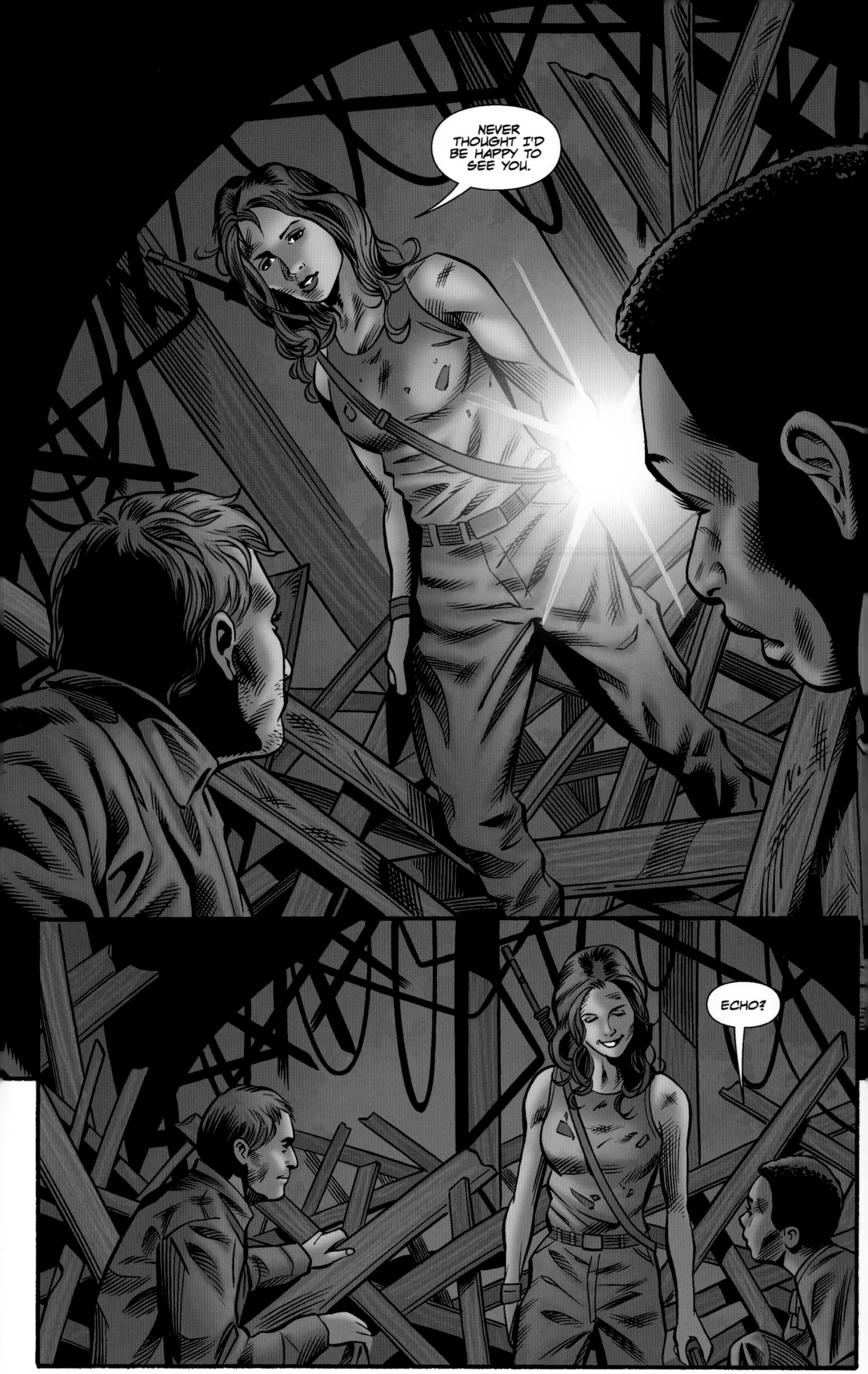
NEVER THOUGHT I'D BE HAPPY TO SEE YOU.
ECHO?

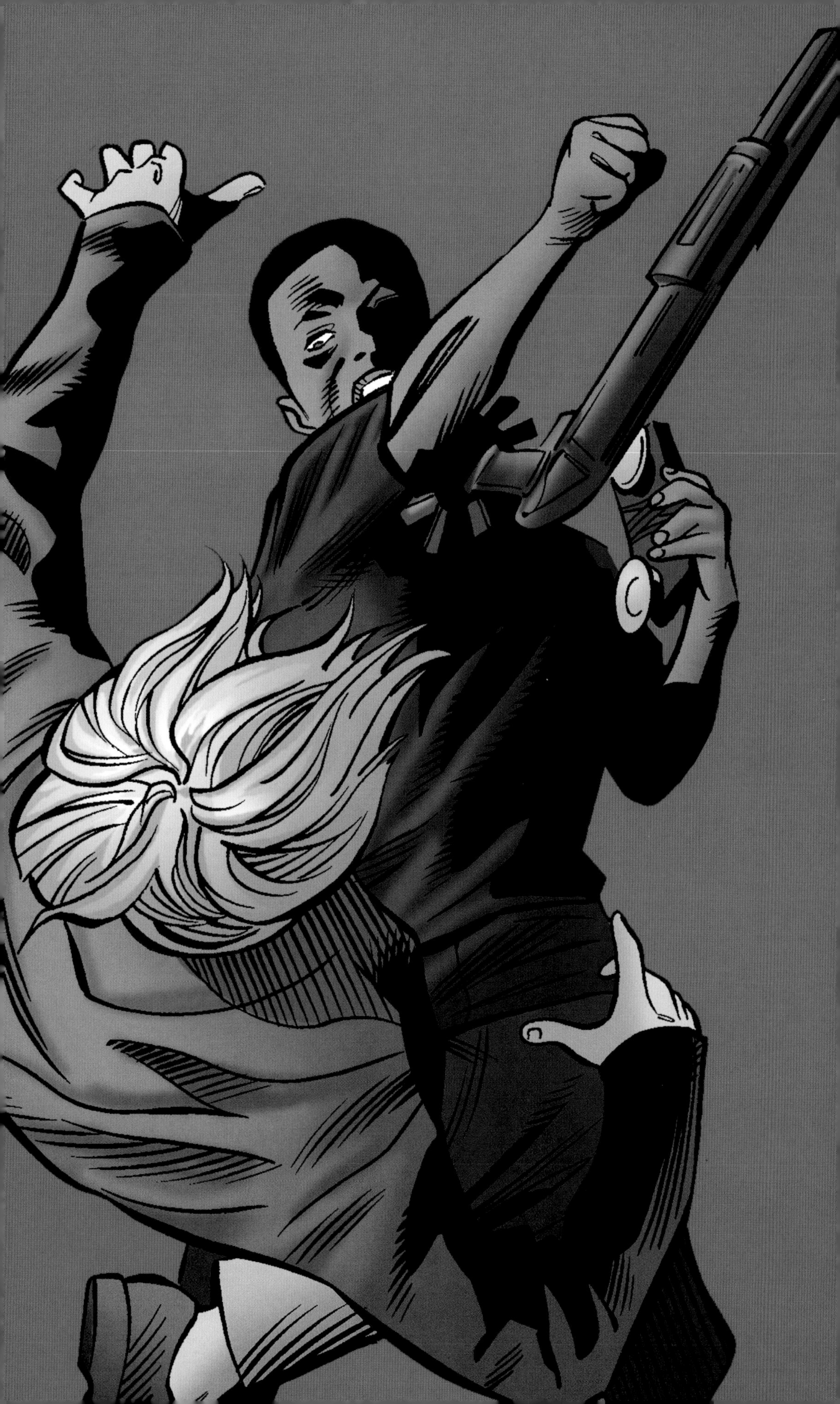

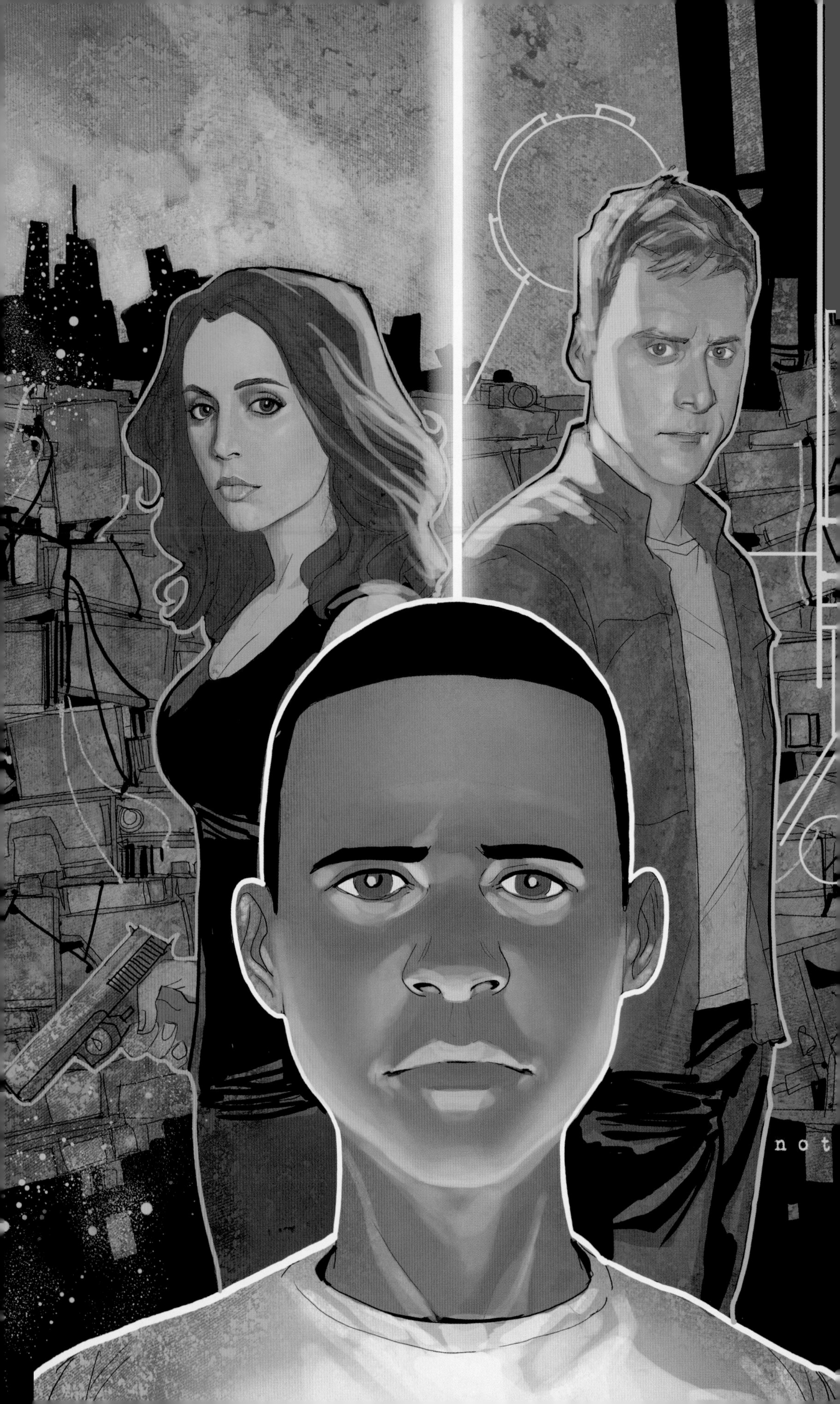
not

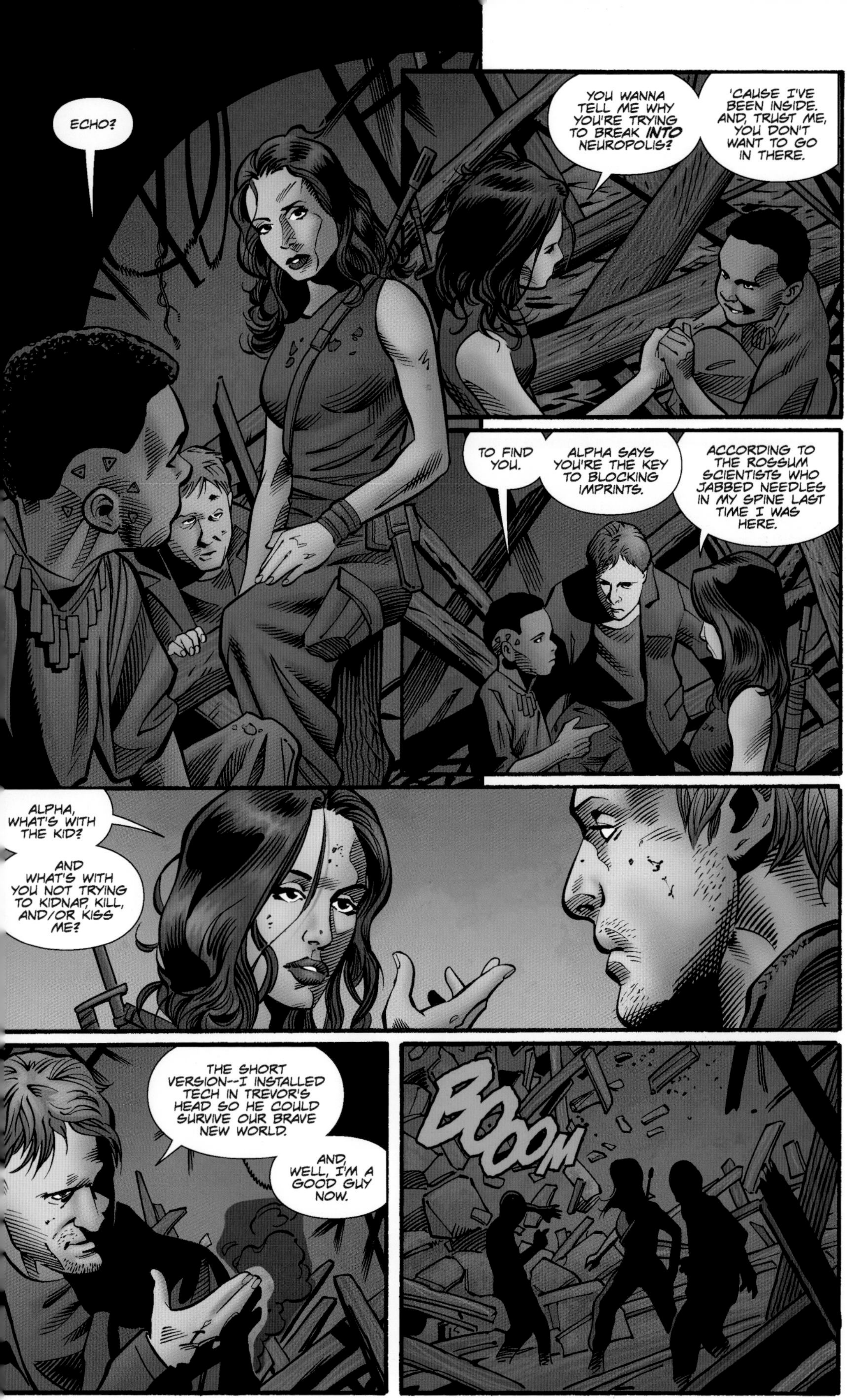
ECHO?
YOU WANNA TELL ME WHY YOU'RE TRYING TO BREAK INTO NEUROPOLIS?
'CAUSE I'VE BEEN INSIDE. AND, TRUST ME, YOU DON'T WANT TO GO IN THERE.
TO FIND YOU.
ALPHA SAYS YOU'RE THE KEY TO BLOCKING IMPRINTS.
ACCORDING TO THE ROSSUM SCIENTISTS WHO JABBED NEEDLES IN MY SPINE LAST TIME I WAS HERE.
ALPHA, WHAT'S WITH THE KID?
AND WHAT'S WITH YOU NOT TRYING TO KIDNAP, KILL, AND/OR KISS ME?
THE SHORT VERSION--I INSTALLED TECH IN TREVOR'S HEAD SO HE COULD SURVIVE OUR BRAVE NEW WORLD.
AND, WELL, I'M A GOOD GUY NOW.
BOOOM

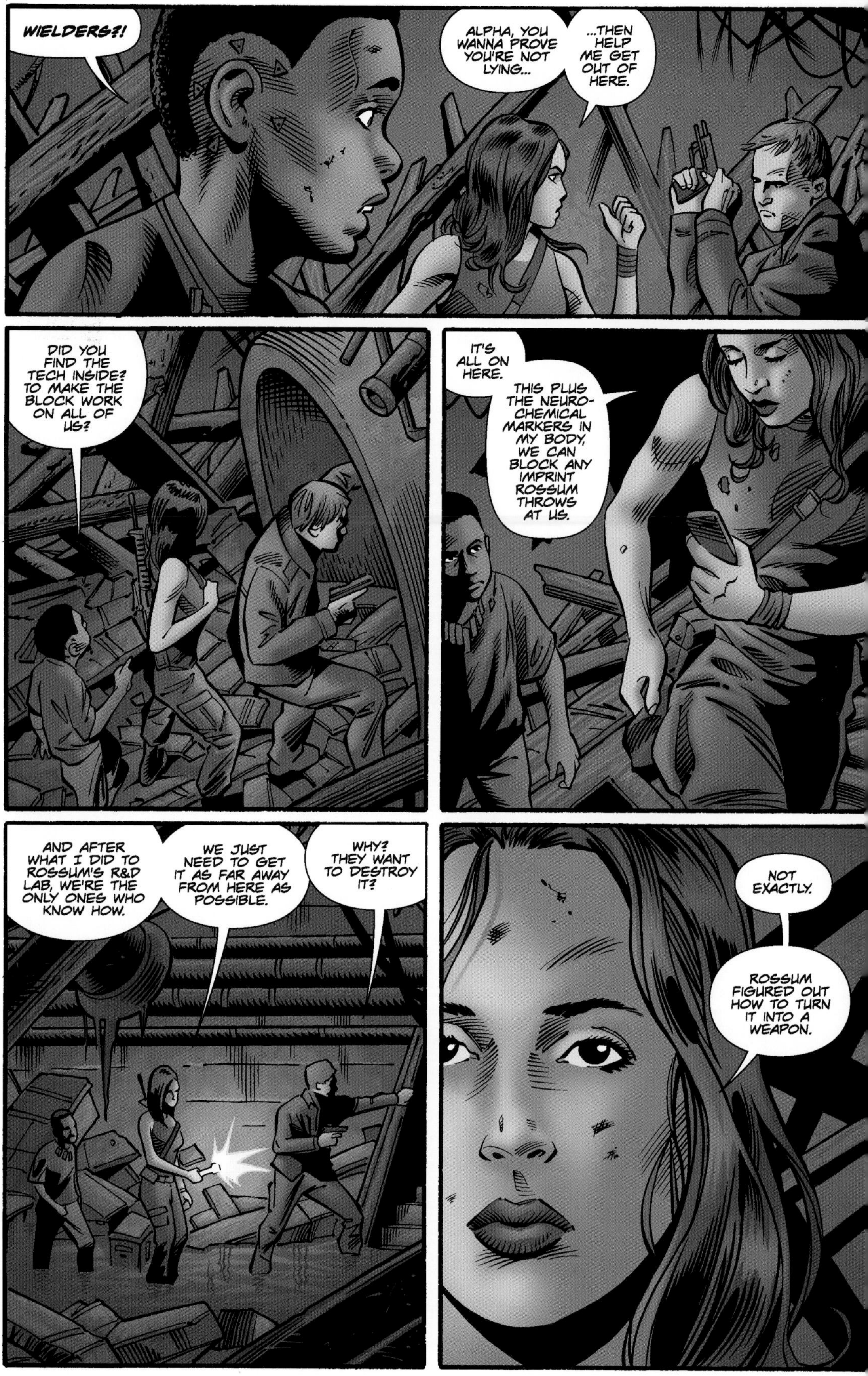
WIELDERS?!
ALPHA, YOU WANNA PROVE YOU'RE NOT LYING...
...THEN HELP ME GET OUT OF HERE.
DID YOU FIND THE TECH INSIDE? TO MAKE THE BLOCK WORK ON ALL OF US?
IT'S ALL ON HERE.
THIS PLUS THE NEURO-CHEMICAL MARKERS IN MY BODY, WE CAN BLOCK ANY IMPRINT ROSSUM THROWS AT US.
AND AFTER WHAT I DID TO ROSSUM'S R&D LAB, WE'RE THE ONLY ONES WHO KNOW HOW.
WE JUST NEED TO GET IT AS FAR AWAY FROM HERE AS POSSIBLE.
WHY? THEY WANT TO DESTROY IT?
NOT EXACTLY.
ROSSUM FIGURED OUT HOW TO TURN IT INTO A WEAPON.

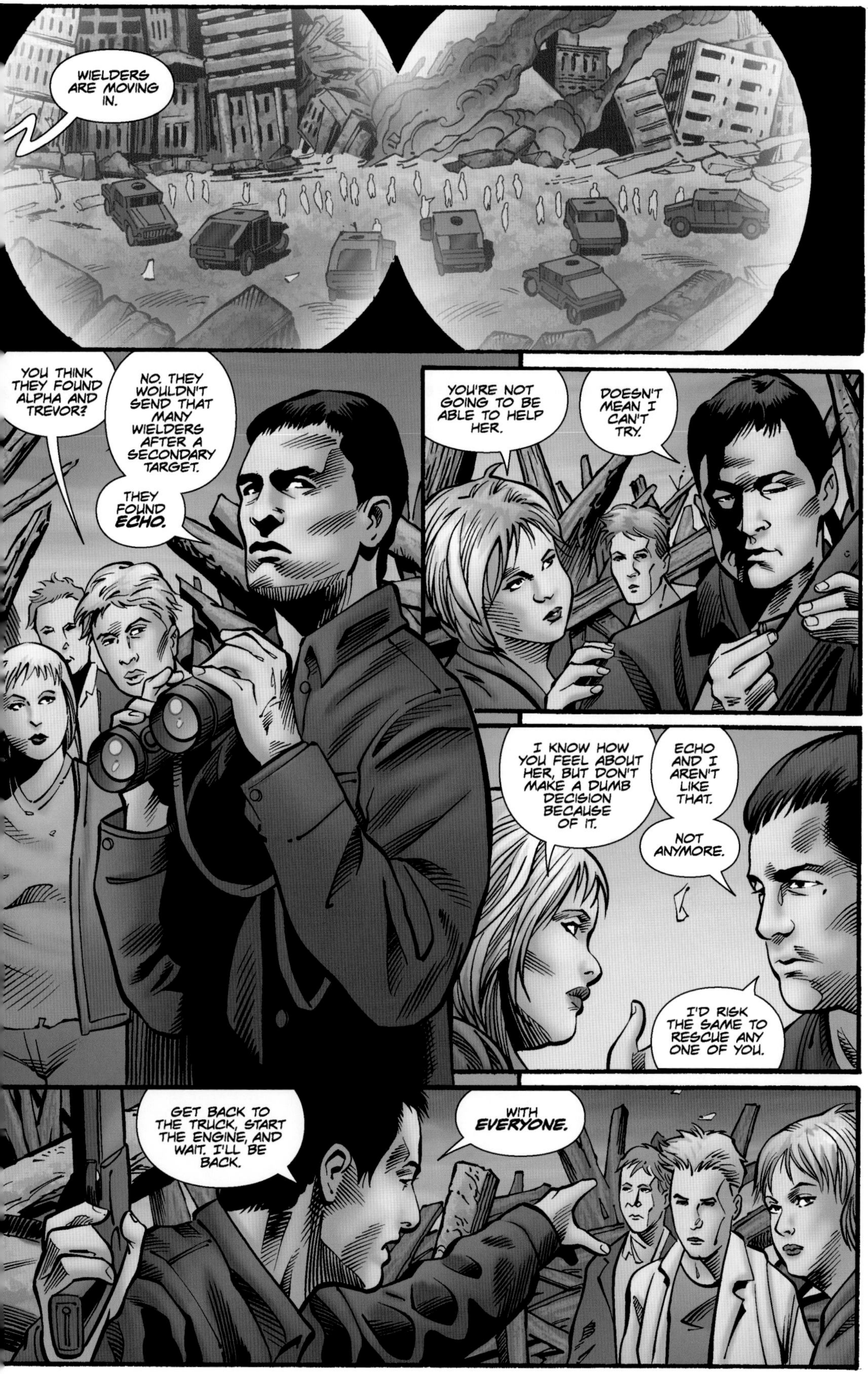
WIELDERS ARE MOVING IN.
YOU THINK THEY FOUND ALPHA AND TREVOR?
NO. THEY WOULDN'T SEND THAT MANY WIELDERS AFTER A SECONDARY TARGET.
THEY FOUND **ECHO.**
YOU'RE NOT GOING TO BE ABLE TO HELP HER.
DOESN'T MEAN I CAN'T TRY.
I KNOW HOW YOU FEEL ABOUT HER, BUT DON'T MAKE A DUMB DECISION BECAUSE OF IT.
ECHO AND I AREN'T LIKE THAT.
NOT ANYMORE.
I'D RISK THE SAME TO RESCUE ANY ONE OF YOU.
GET BACK TO THE TRUCK, START THE ENGINE, AND WAIT. I'LL BE BACK.
WITH **EVERYONE.**

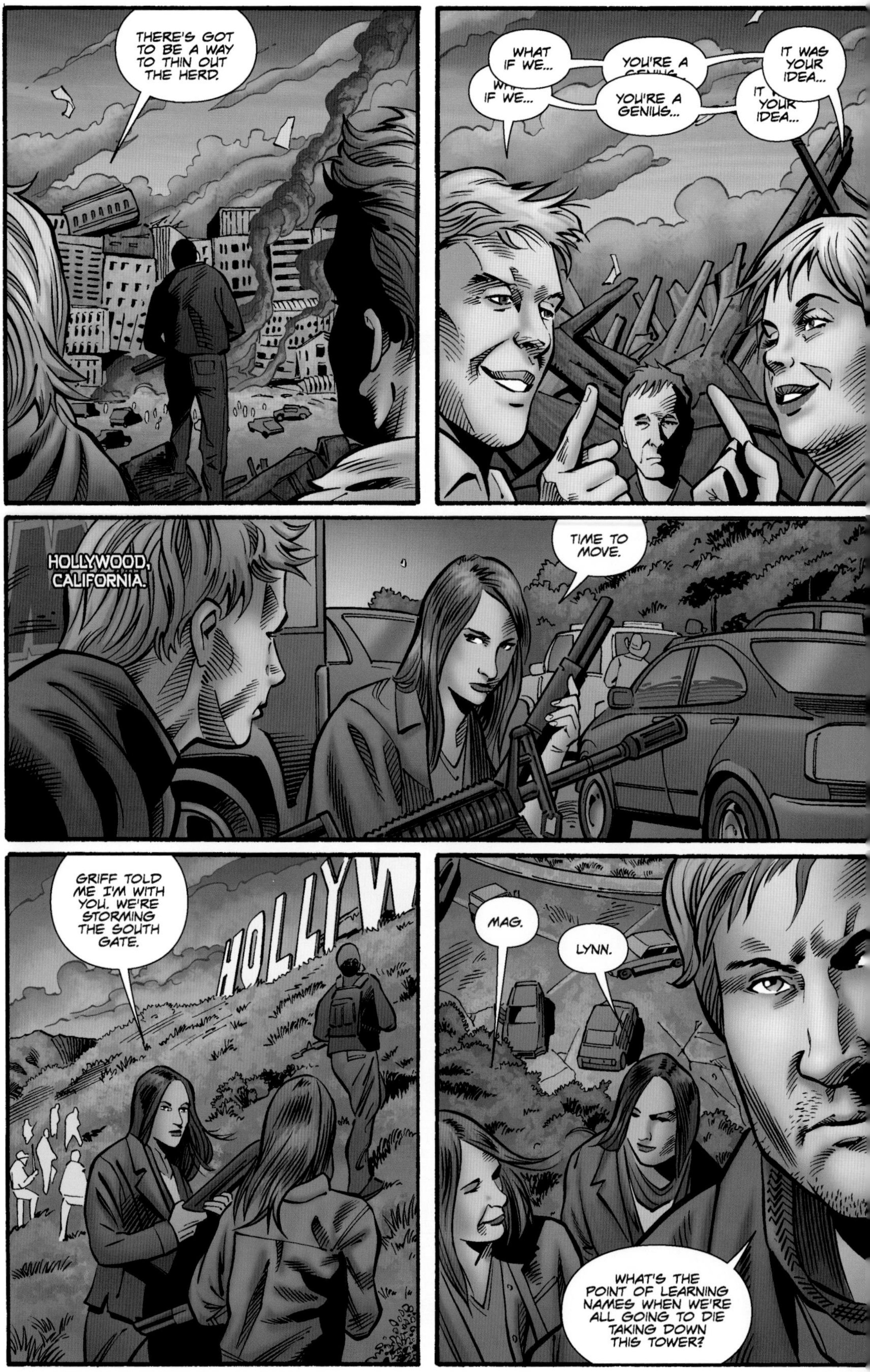

THERE'S GOT TO BE A WAY TO THIN OUT THE HERD.
WHAT IF WE...
IF WE...
YOU'RE A
YOU'RE A GENIUS...
IT WAS YOUR IDEA...
YOUR IDEA...
HOLLYWOOD, CALIFORNIA.
TIME TO MOVE.
GRIFF TOLD ME I'M WITH YOU. WE'RE STORMING THE SOUTH GATE.
HOLLYW
MAG.
LYNN.
WHAT'S THE POINT OF LEARNING NAMES WHEN WE'RE ALL GOING TO DIE TAKING DOWN THIS TOWER?

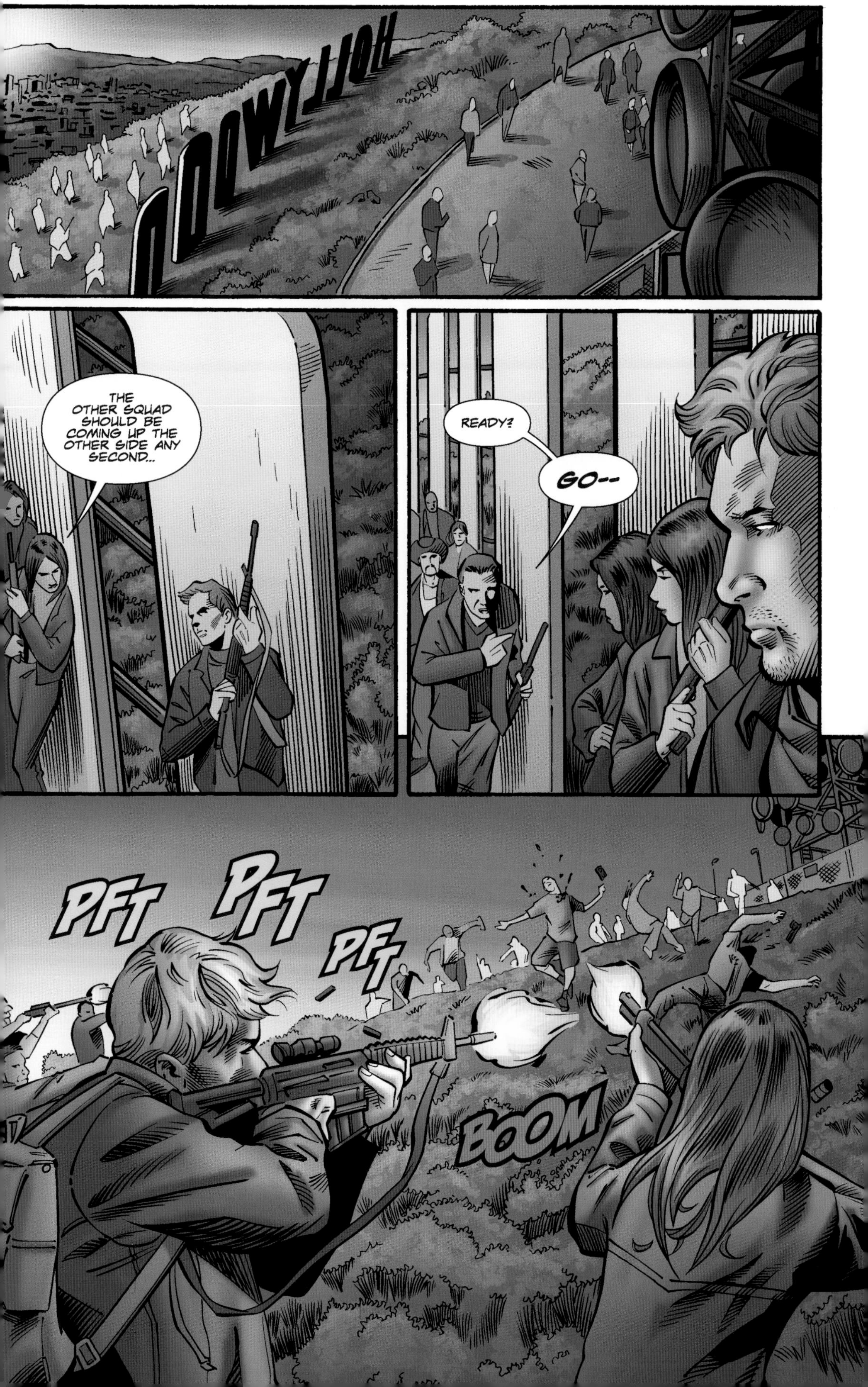
HOLLYWOOD
THE OTHER SQUAD SHOULD BE COMING UP THE OTHER SIDE ANY SECOND...
READY?
GO--
PFT
PFT
PFT
BOOM

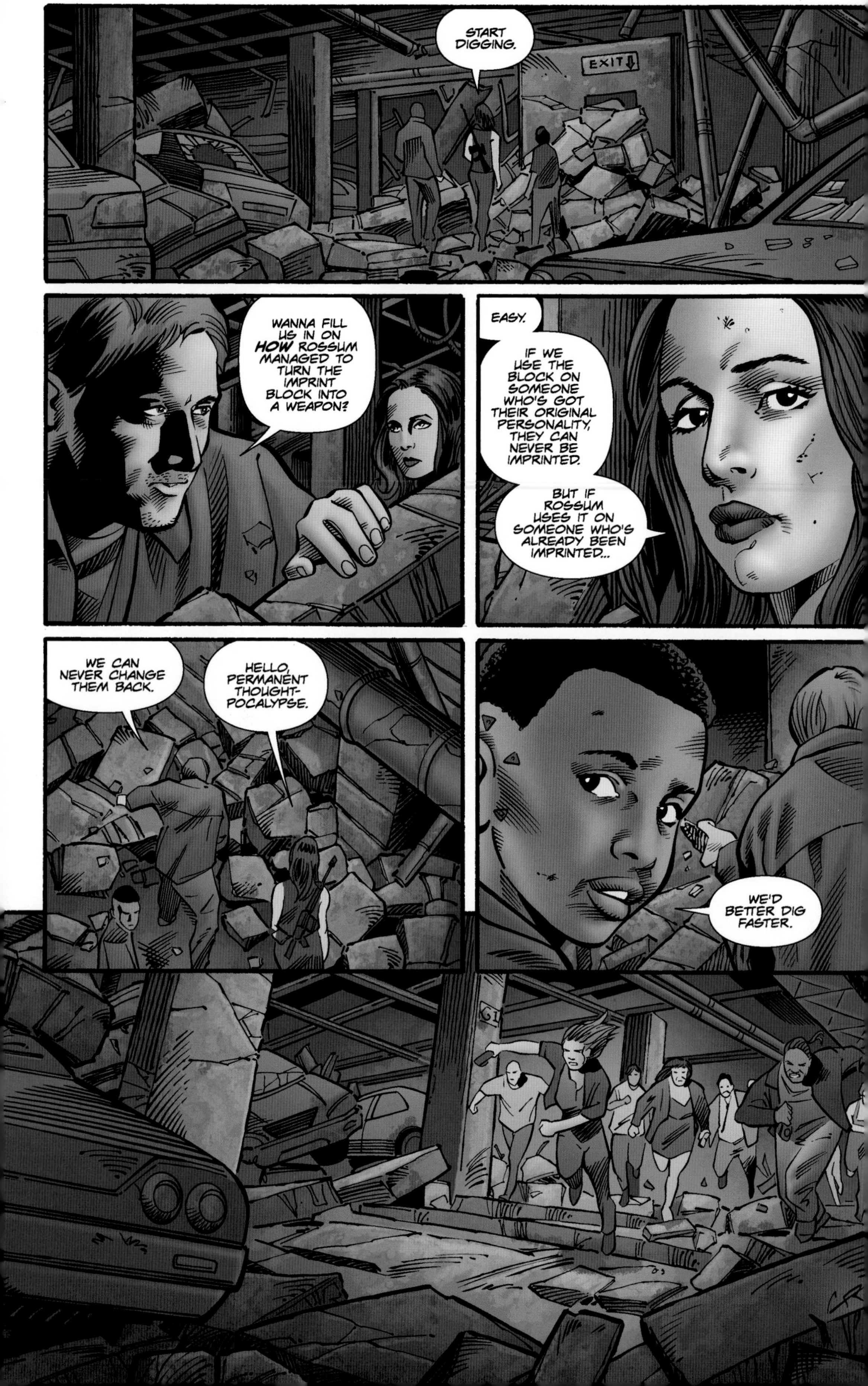
START DIGGING.
WANNA FILL US IN ON HOW ROSSUM MANAGED TO TURN THE IMPRINT BLOCK INTO A WEAPON?
EASY.
IF WE USE THE BLOCK ON SOMEONE WHO'S GOT THEIR ORIGINAL PERSONALITY, THEY CAN NEVER BE IMPRINTED.
BUT IF ROSSUM USES IT ON SOMEONE WHO'S ALREADY BEEN IMPRINTED...
WE CAN NEVER CHANGE THEM BACK.
HELLO, PERMANENT THOUGHT-POCALYPSE.
WE'D BETTER DIG FASTER.

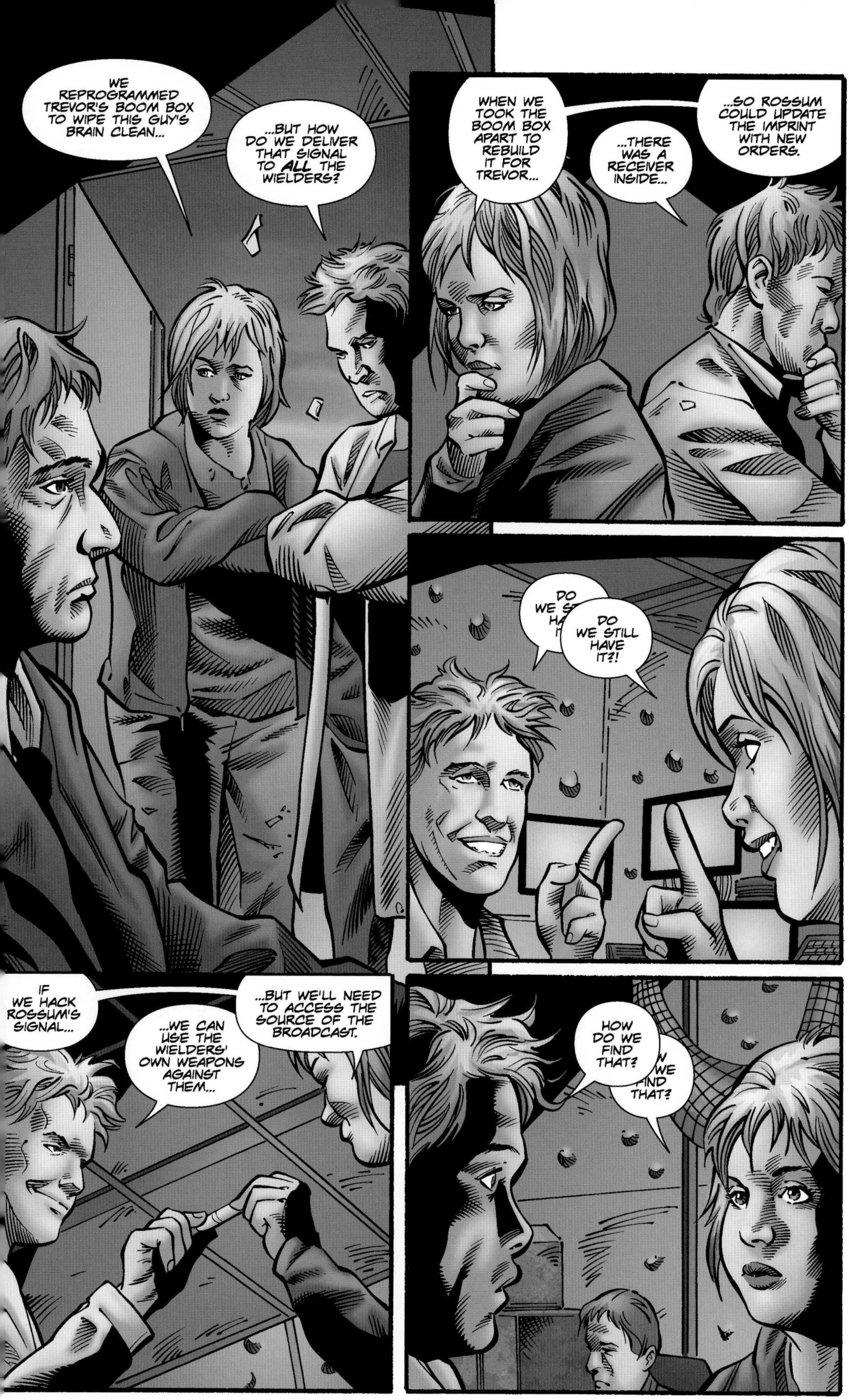
WE REPROGRAMMED TREVOR'S BOOM BOX TO WIPE THIS GUY'S BRAIN CLEAN...
...BUT HOW DO WE DELIVER THAT SIGNAL TO ALL THE WIELDERS?
WHEN WE TOOK THE BOOM BOX APART TO REBUILD IT FOR TREVOR...
...THERE WAS A RECEIVER INSIDE...
...SO ROSSUM COULD UPDATE THE IMPRINT WITH NEW ORDERS.
DO WE STILL HAVE IT?!
IF WE HACK ROSSUM'S SIGNAL...
...WE CAN USE THE WIELDERS' OWN WEAPONS AGAINST THEM...
...BUT WE'LL NEED TO ACCESS THE SOURCE OF THE BROADCAST.
HOW DO WE FIND THAT?

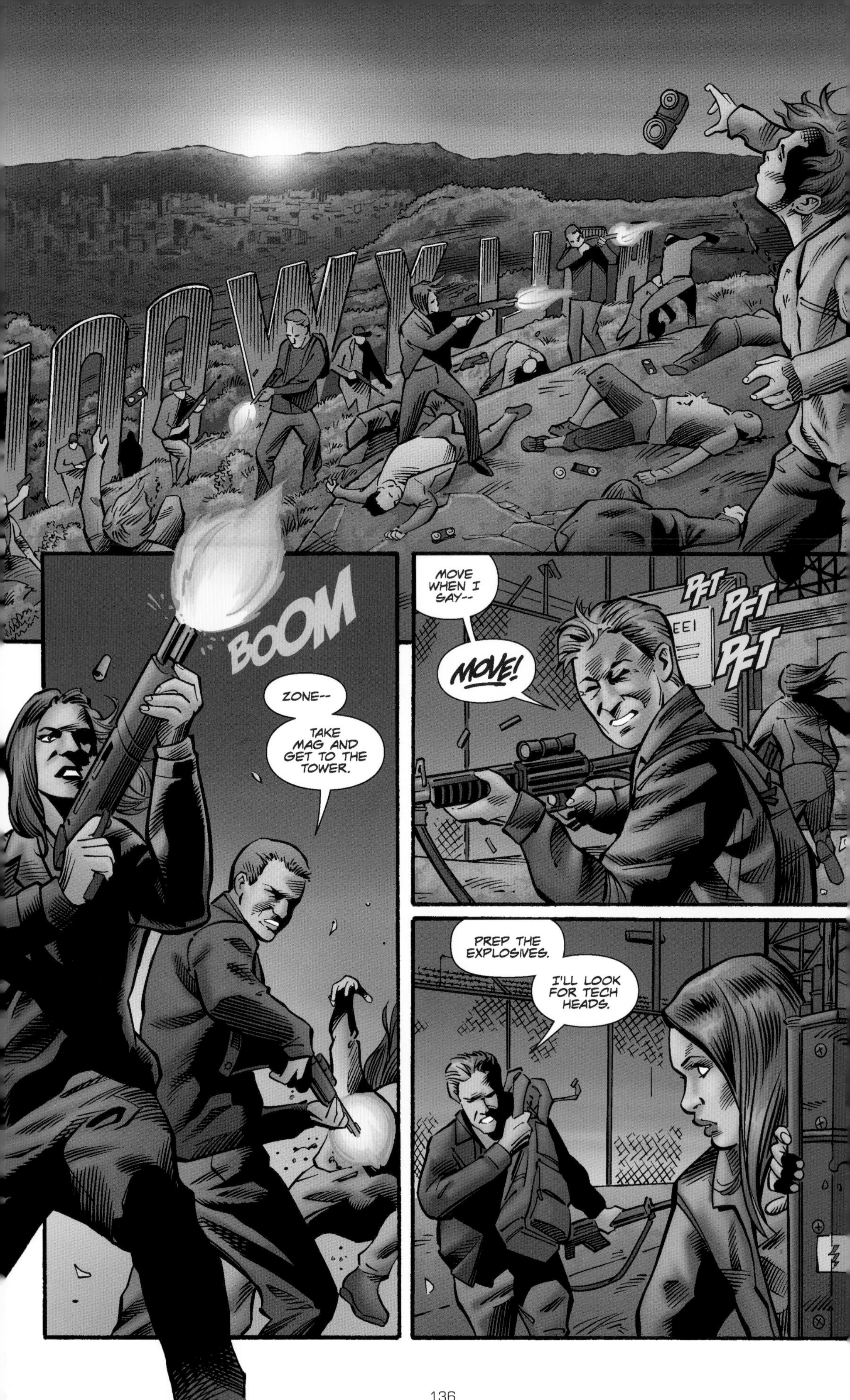
BOOM
ZONE--
TAKE MAG AND GET TO THE TOWER.
MOVE WHEN I SAY--
MOVE!
PFT
PFT
PFT
PREP THE EXPLOSIVES.
I'LL LOOK FOR TECH HEADS.

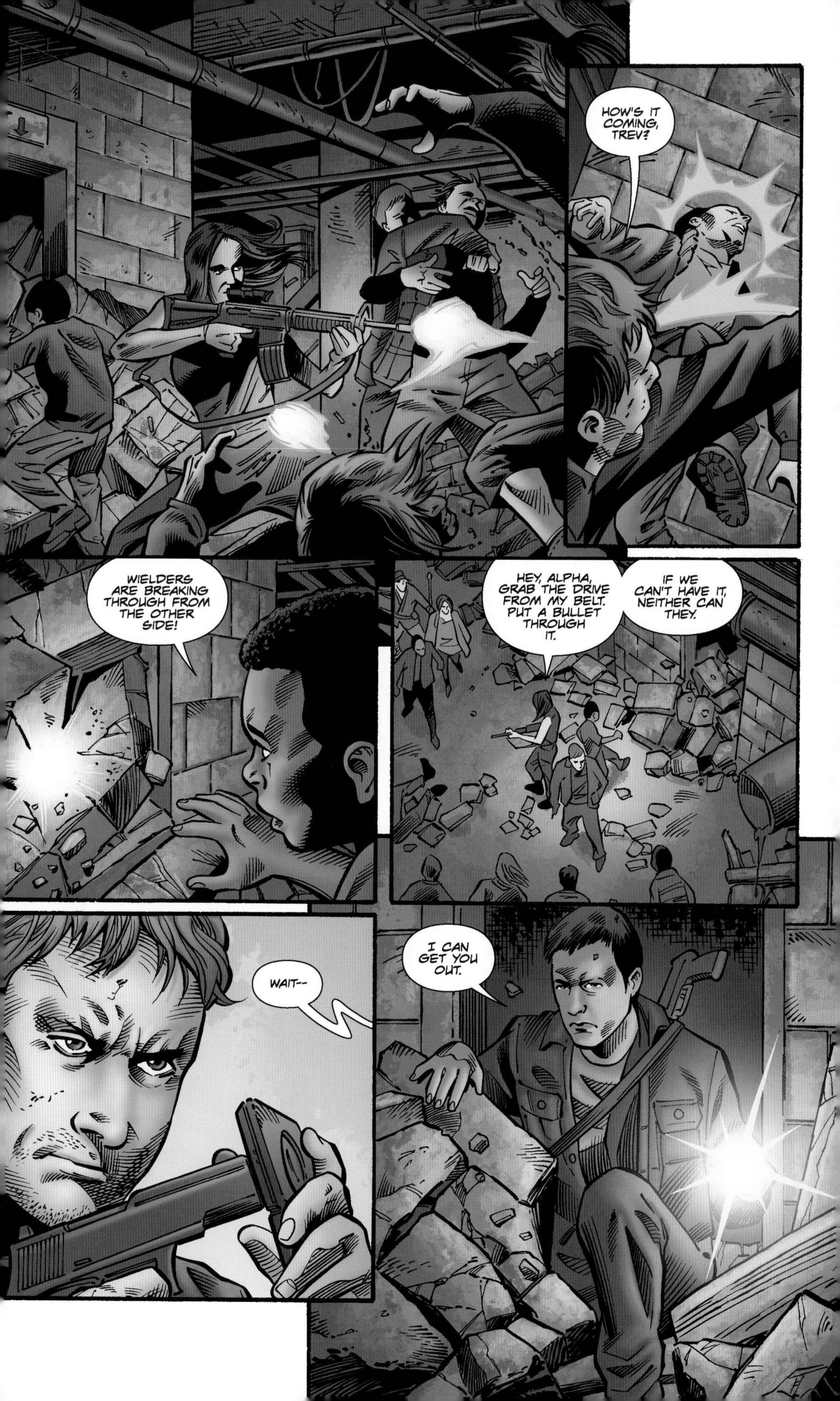
HOW'S IT COMING, TREV?
WIELDERS ARE BREAKING THROUGH FROM THE OTHER SIDE!
HEY, ALPHA, GRAB THE DRIVE FROM MY BELT. PUT A BULLET THROUGH IT.
IF WE CAN'T HAVE IT, NEITHER CAN THEY.
WAIT--
I CAN GET YOU OUT.

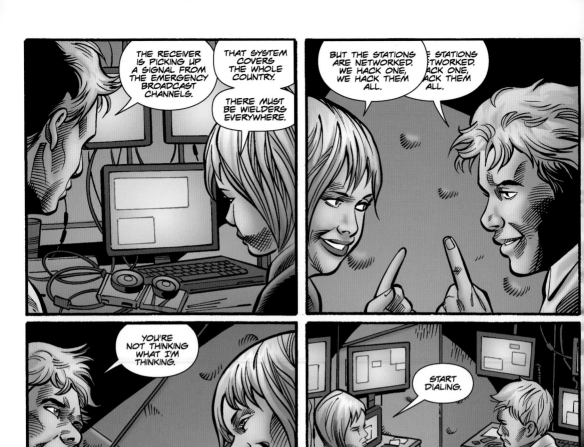

THE RECEIVER IS PICKING UP A SIGNAL FROM THE EMERGENCY BROADCAST CHANNELS.

THAT SYSTEM COVERS THE WHOLE COUNTRY.

THERE MUST BE WIELDERS EVERYWHERE.

BUT THE STATIONS ARE NETWORKED. WE HACK ONE, WE HACK THEM ALL.

YOU'RE NOT THINKING WHAT I'M THINKING.

OF COURSE I AM.

START DIALING.

THE IVIES SHOULD BE ABLE TO BUILD THE TECH ON THIS DRIVE.

IF THEY DON'T MIND THE COMPANY.

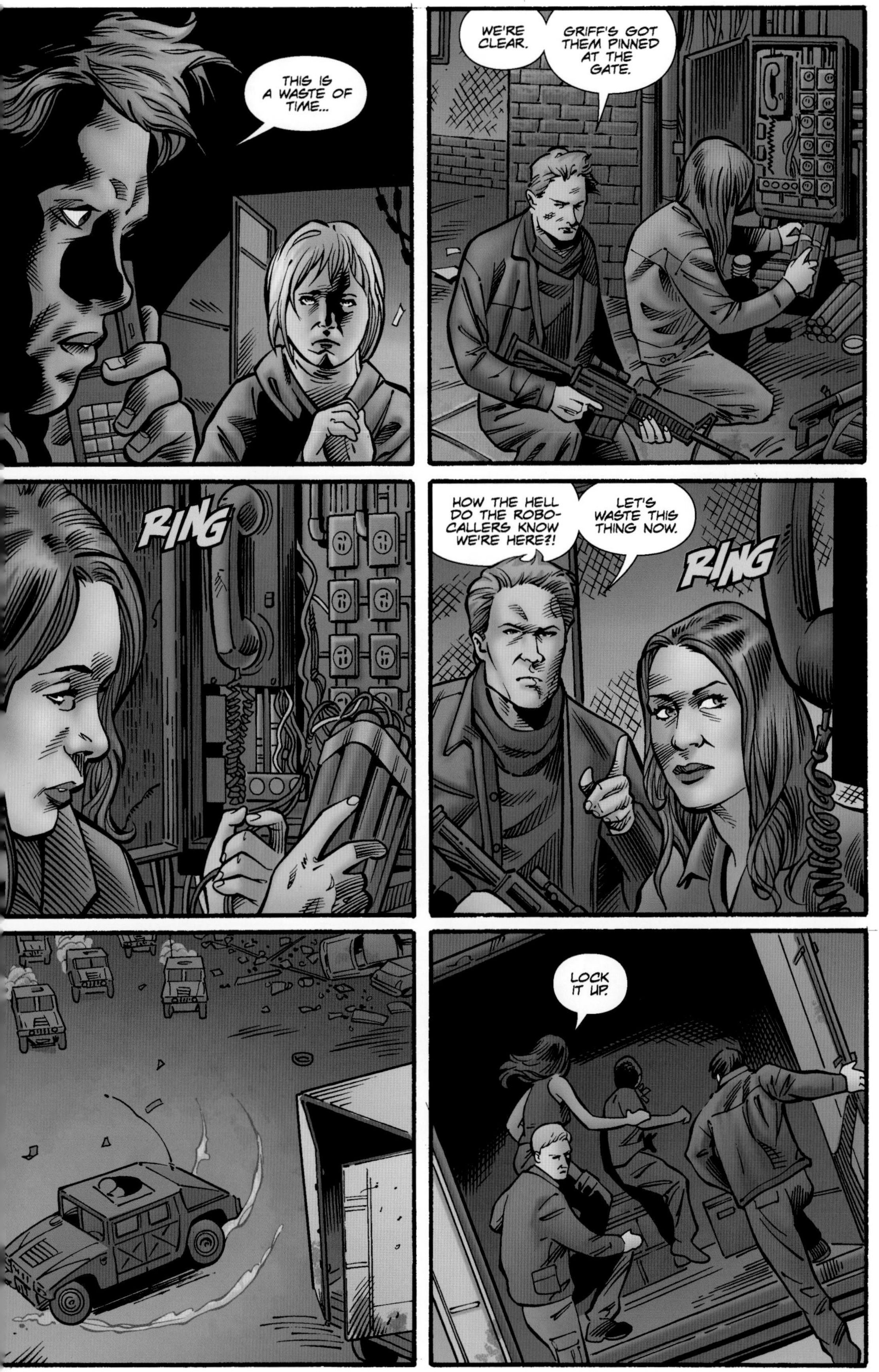

THIS IS A WASTE OF TIME...
WE'RE CLEAR.
GRIFF'S GOT THEM PINNED AT THE GATE.
RING
HOW THE HELL DO THE ROBO-CALLERS KNOW WE'RE HERE?!
LET'S WASTE THIS THING NOW.
RING
LOCK IT UP.

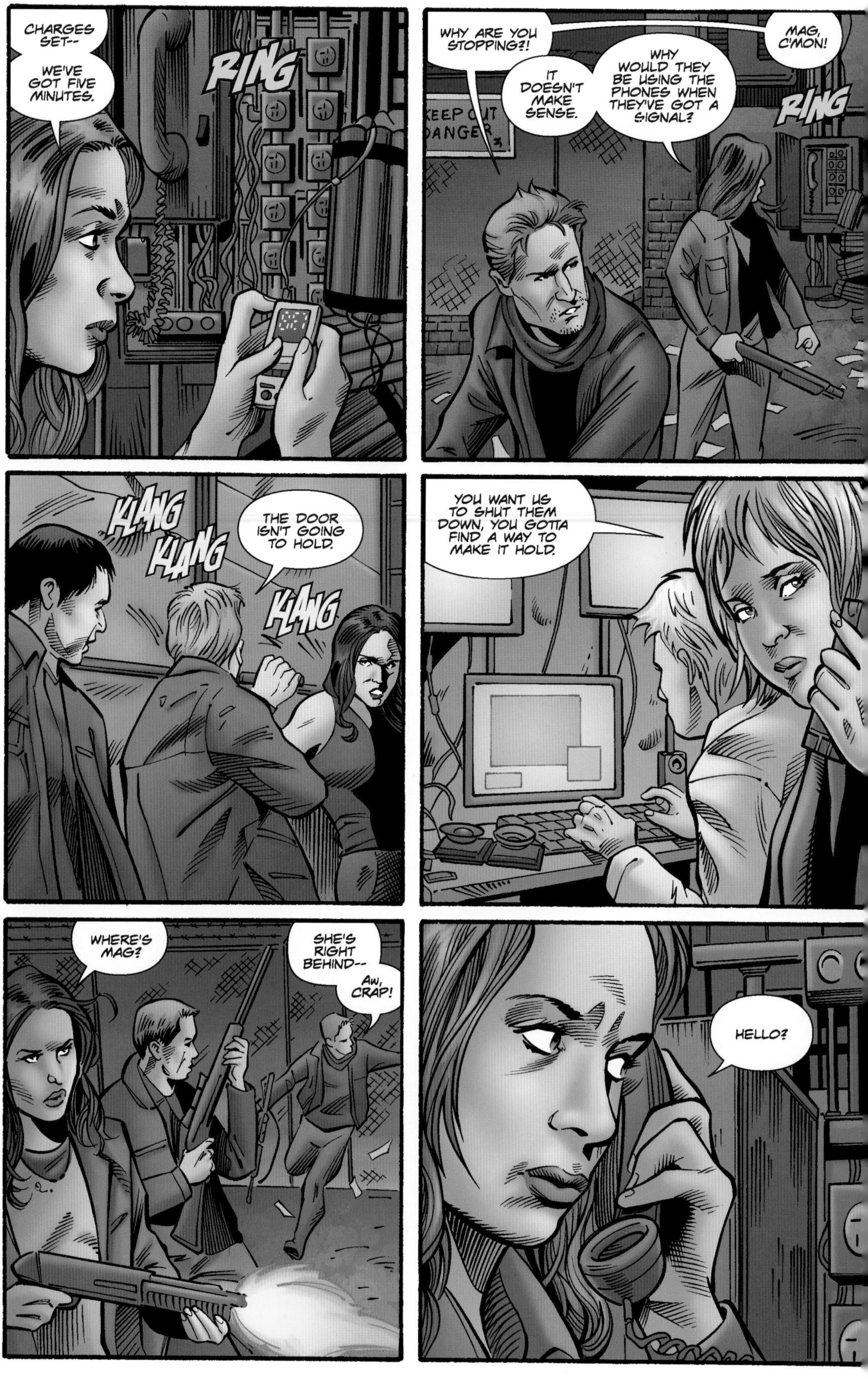
CHARGES SET--
WE'VE GOT FIVE MINUTES.
RING
WHY ARE YOU STOPPING?!
IT DOESN'T MAKE SENSE.
WHY WOULD THEY BE USING THE PHONES WHEN THEY'VE GOT A SIGNAL?
MAG, C'MON!
KEEP OUT DANGER
RING
KLANG
KLANG
THE DOOR ISN'T GOING TO HOLD.
KLANG
YOU WANT US TO SHUT THEM DOWN, YOU GOTTA FIND A WAY TO MAKE IT HOLD.
WHERE'S MAG?
SHE'S RIGHT BEHIND--
AW, CRAP!
HELLO?

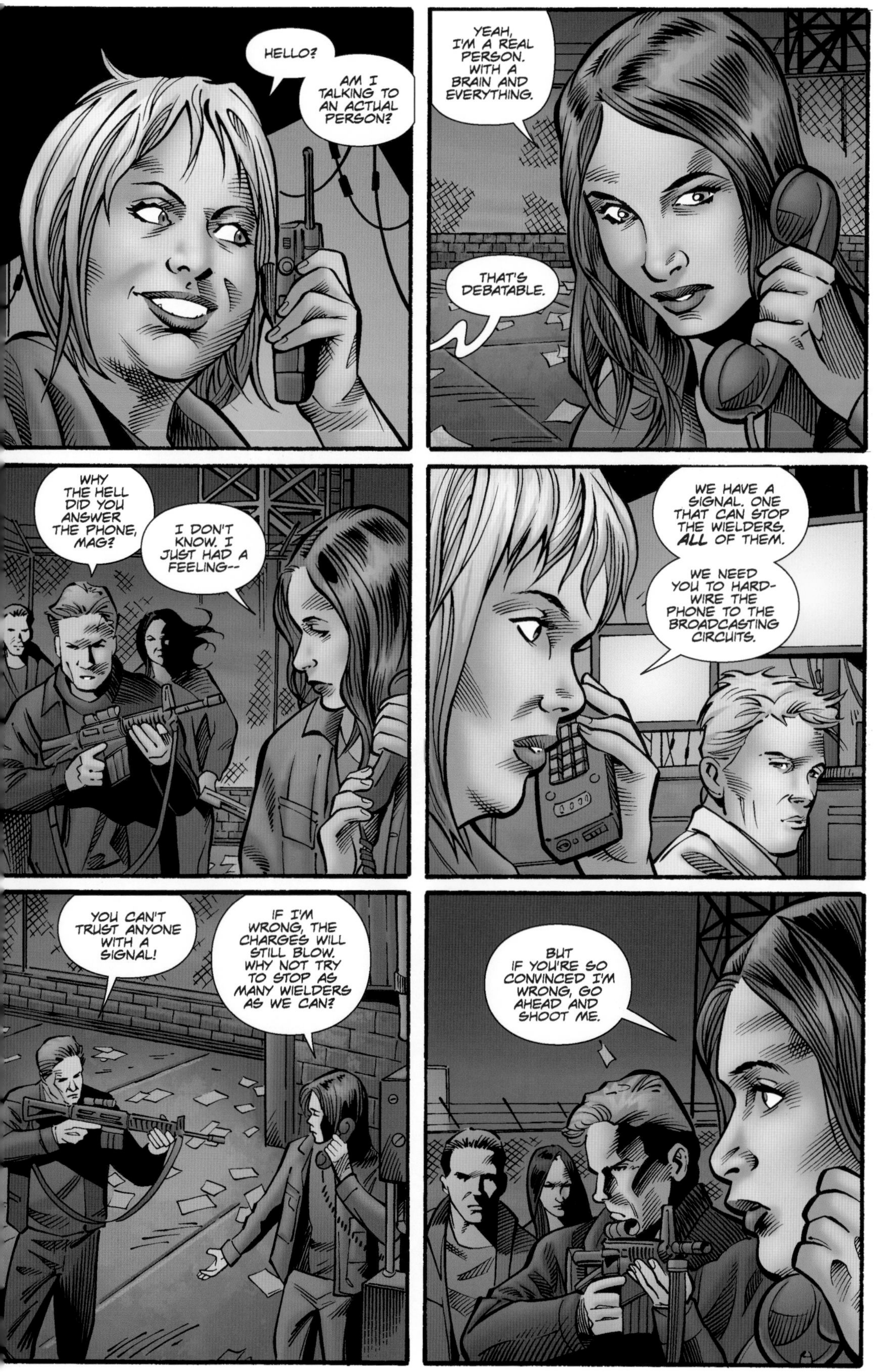
HELLO?
AM I TALKING TO AN ACTUAL PERSON?
YEAH, I'M A REAL PERSON. WITH A BRAIN AND EVERYTHING.
THAT'S DEBATABLE.
WHY THE HELL DID YOU ANSWER THE PHONE, MAG?
I DON'T KNOW. I JUST HAD A FEELING--
WE HAVE A SIGNAL. ONE THAT CAN STOP THE WIELDERS. ALL OF THEM.
WE NEED YOU TO HARD-WIRE THE PHONE TO THE BROADCASTING CIRCUITS.
YOU CAN'T TRUST ANYONE WITH A SIGNAL!
IF I'M WRONG, THE CHARGES WILL STILL BLOW. WHY NOT TRY TO STOP AS MANY WIELDERS AS WE CAN?
BUT IF YOU'RE SO CONVINCED I'M WRONG, GO AHEAD AND SHOOT ME.

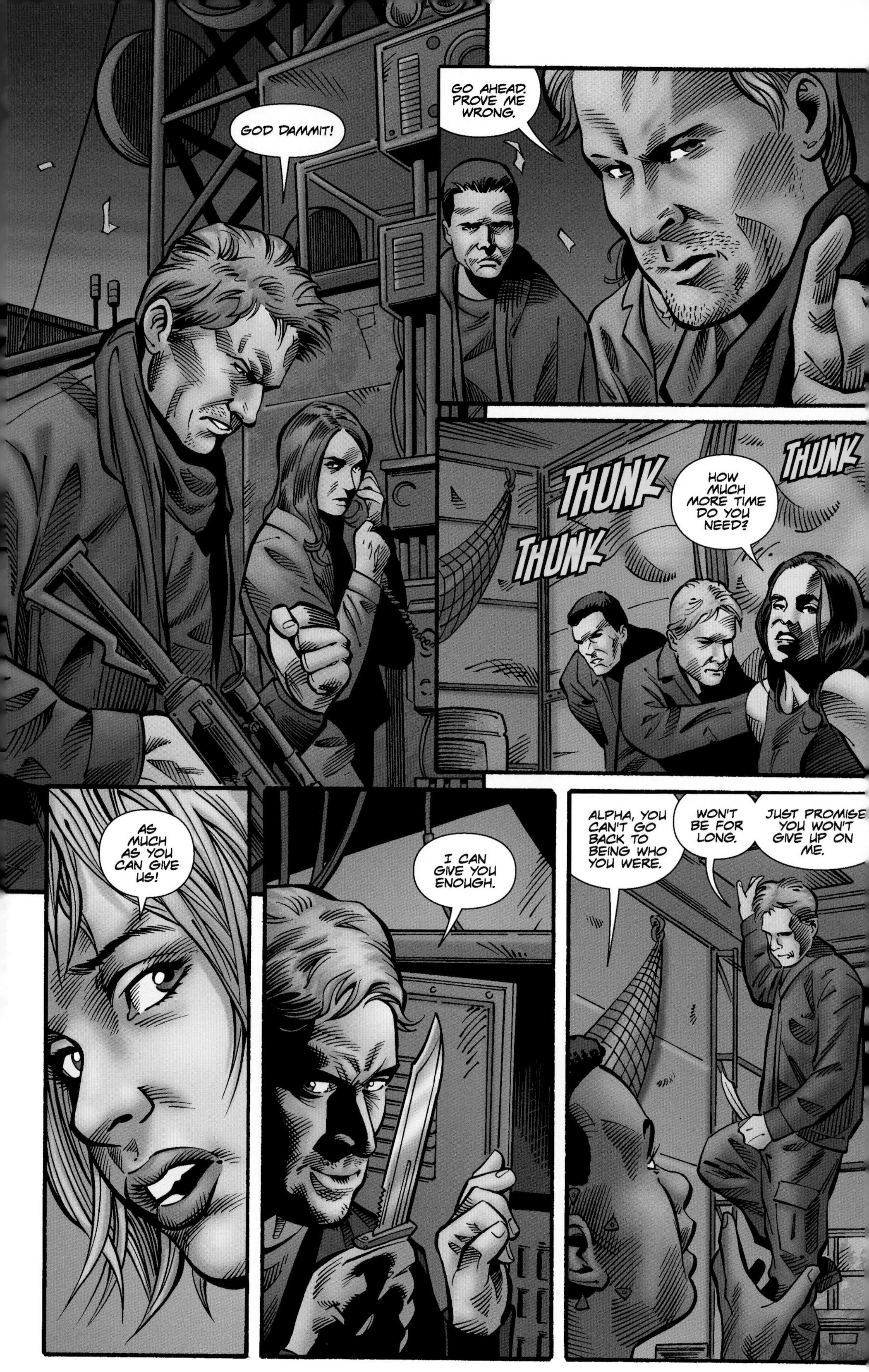
GOD DAMMIT!
GO AHEAD. PROVE ME WRONG.
THUNK
THUNK
HOW MUCH MORE TIME DO YOU NEED?
THUNK
AS MUCH AS YOU CAN GIVE US!
I CAN GIVE YOU ENOUGH.
ALPHA, YOU CAN'T GO BACK TO BEING WHO YOU WERE.
WON'T BE FOR LONG.
JUST PROMISE YOU WON'T GIVE UP ON ME.

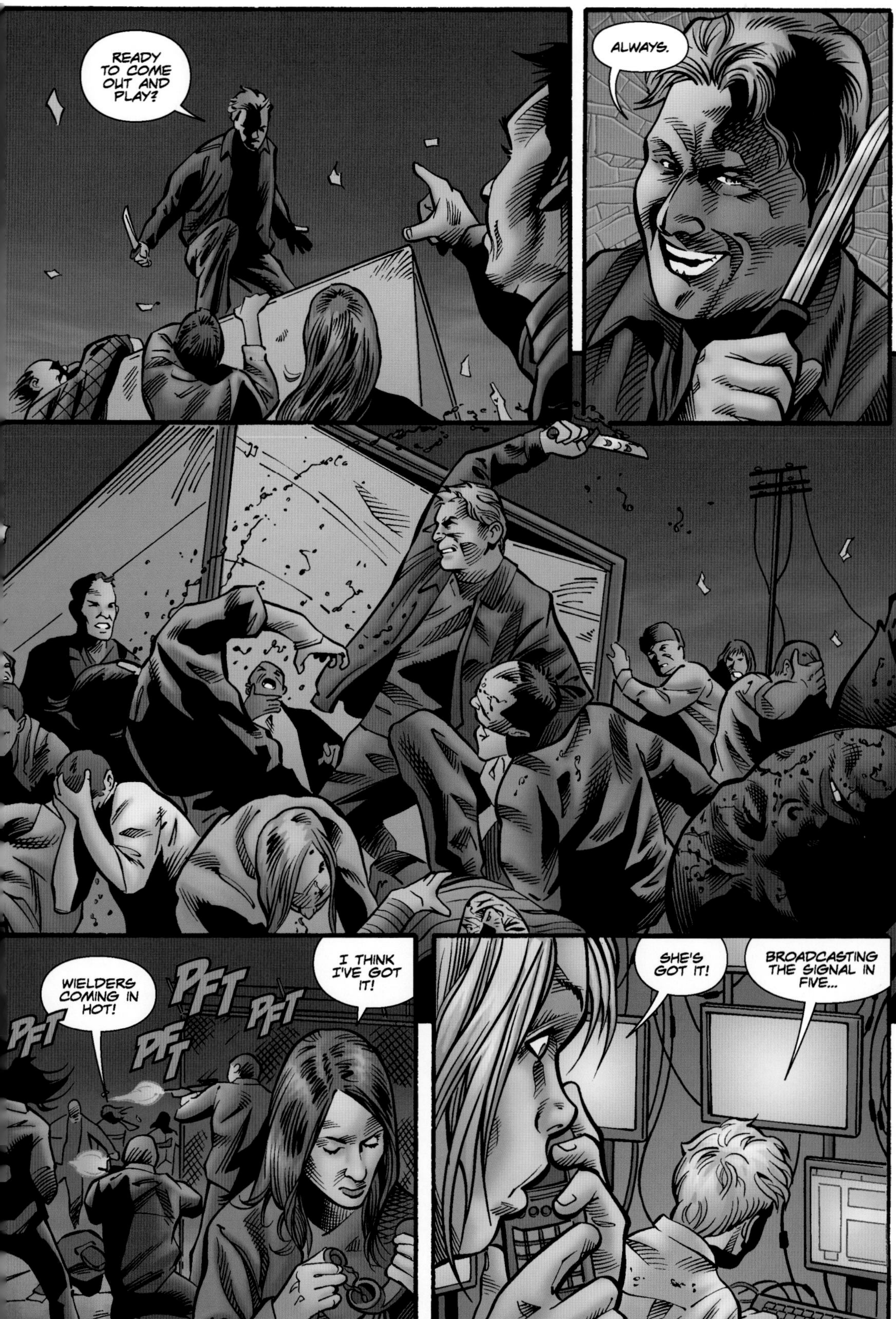
READY TO COME OUT AND PLAY?
ALWAYS.
WIELDERS COMING IN HOT!
PFT
PFT
PFT
PFT
I THINK I'VE GOT IT!
SHE'S GOT IT!
BROADCASTING THE SIGNAL IN FIVE...

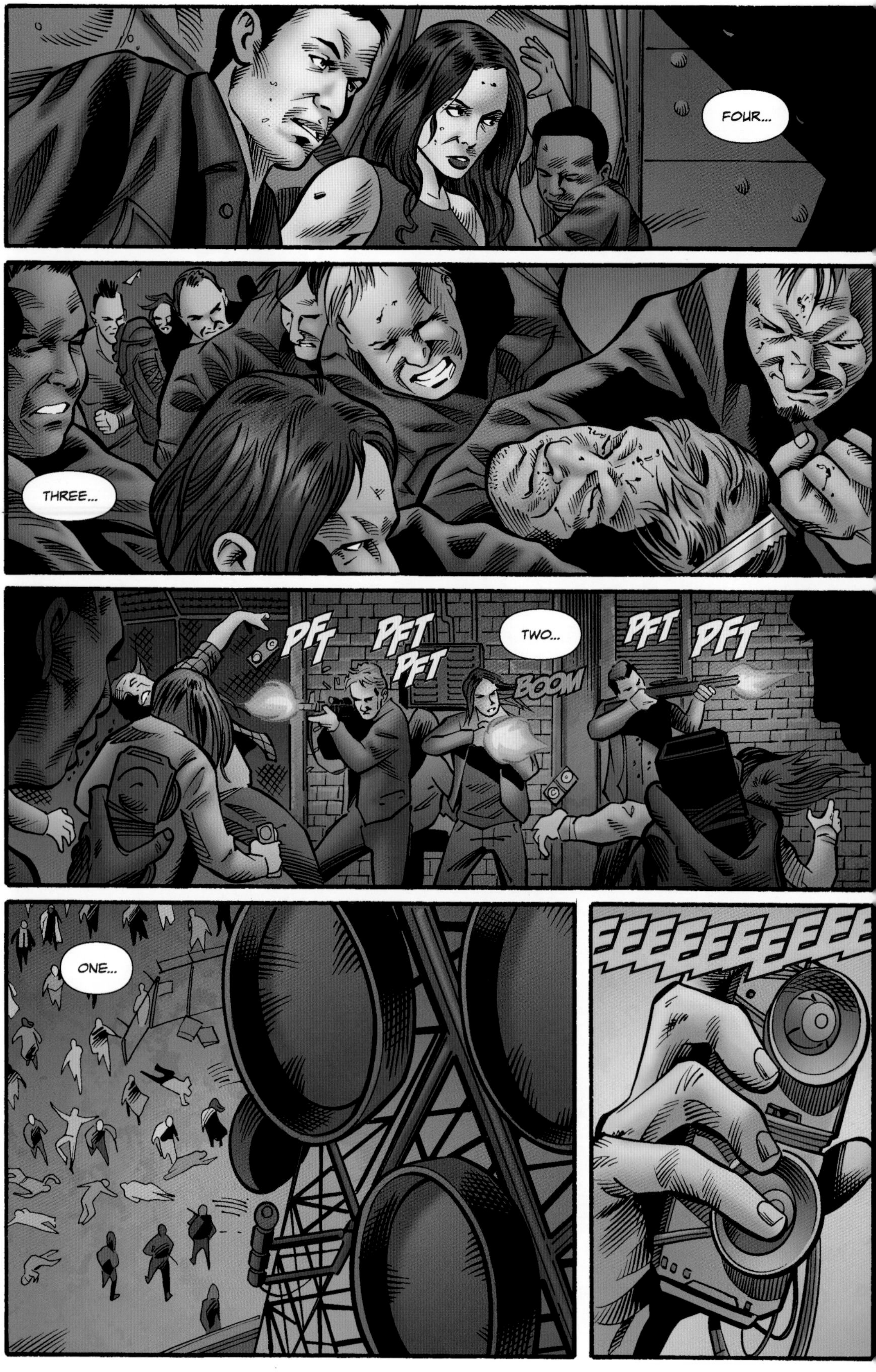
FOUR...
THREE...
PFT
PFT
PFT
TWO...
PFT
PFT
BOOM
ONE...
EEEEEEEEEEE

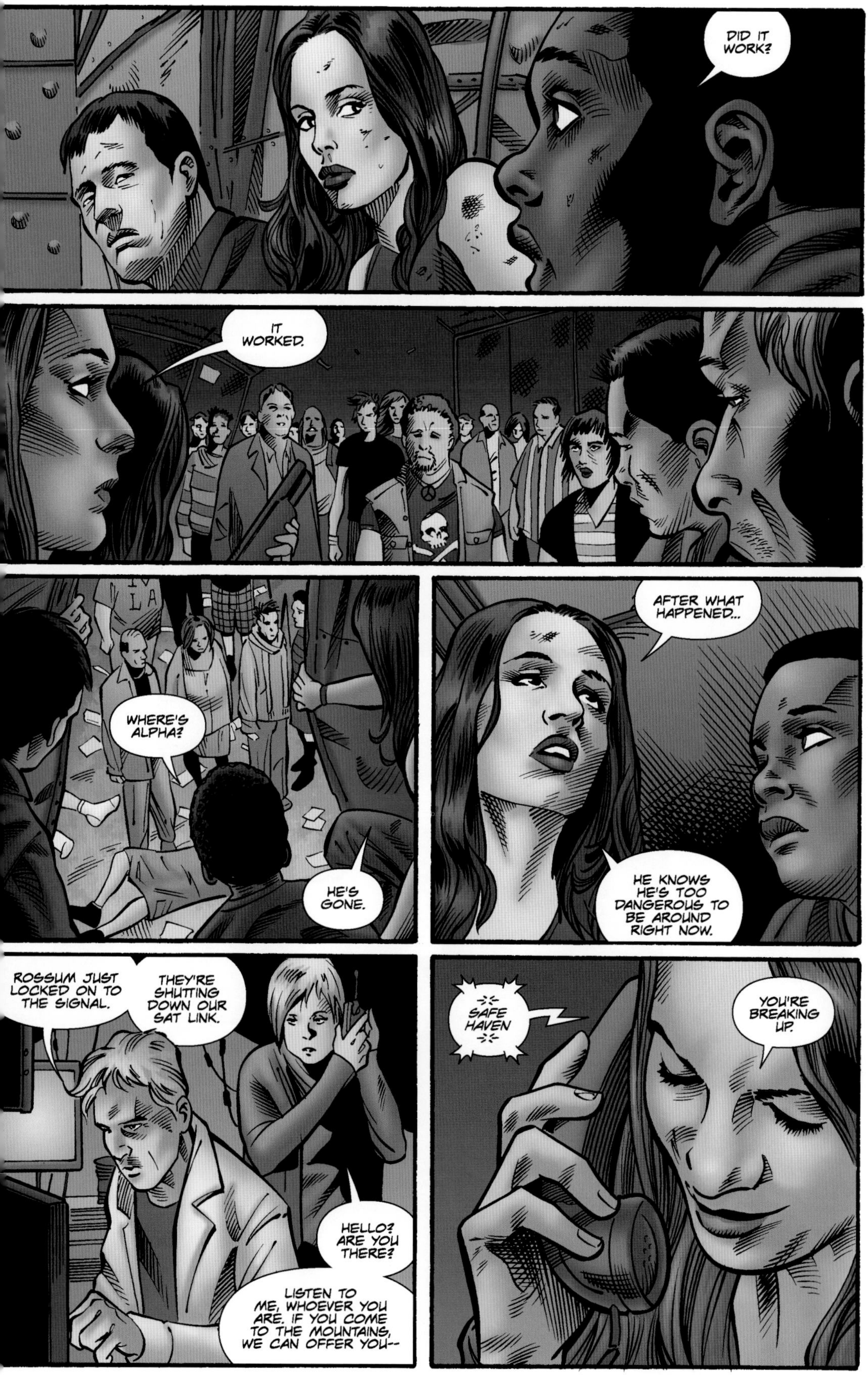
DID IT WORK?
IT WORKED.
WHERE'S ALPHA?
HE'S GONE.
AFTER WHAT HAPPENED...
HE KNOWS HE'S TOO DANGEROUS TO BE AROUND RIGHT NOW.
ROSSUM JUST LOCKED ON TO THE SIGNAL.
THEY'RE SHUTTING DOWN OUR SAT LINK.
HELLO? ARE YOU THERE?
LISTEN TO ME, WHOEVER YOU ARE. IF YOU COME TO THE MOUNTAINS, WE CAN OFFER YOU--
SAFE HAVEN
YOU'RE BREAKING UP.

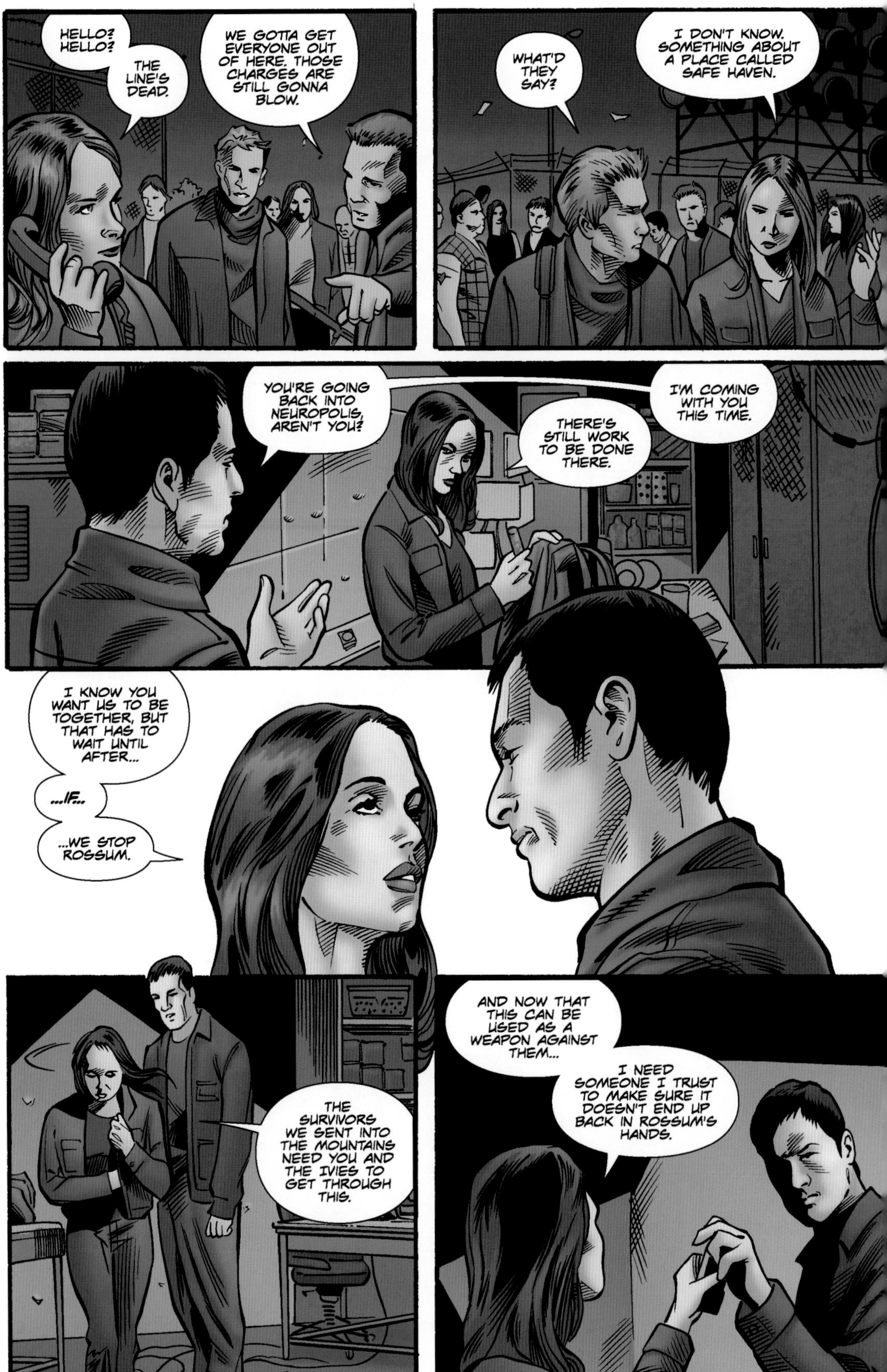
HELLO? HELLO?
THE LINE'S DEAD.
WE GOTTA GET EVERYONE OUT OF HERE. THOSE CHARGES ARE STILL GONNA BLOW.
WHAT'D THEY SAY?
I DON'T KNOW. SOMETHING ABOUT A PLACE CALLED SAFE HAVEN.
YOU'RE GOING BACK INTO NEUROPOLIS, AREN'T YOU?
THERE'S STILL WORK TO BE DONE THERE.
I'M COMING WITH YOU THIS TIME.
I KNOW YOU WANT US TO BE TOGETHER, BUT THAT HAS TO WAIT UNTIL AFTER...
...IF...
...WE STOP ROSSUM.
THE SURVIVORS WE SENT INTO THE MOUNTAINS NEED YOU AND THE IVIES TO GET THROUGH THIS.
AND NOW THAT THIS CAN BE USED AS A WEAPON AGAINST THEM...
I NEED SOMEONE I TRUST TO MAKE SURE IT DOESN'T END UP BACK IN ROSSUM'S HANDS.

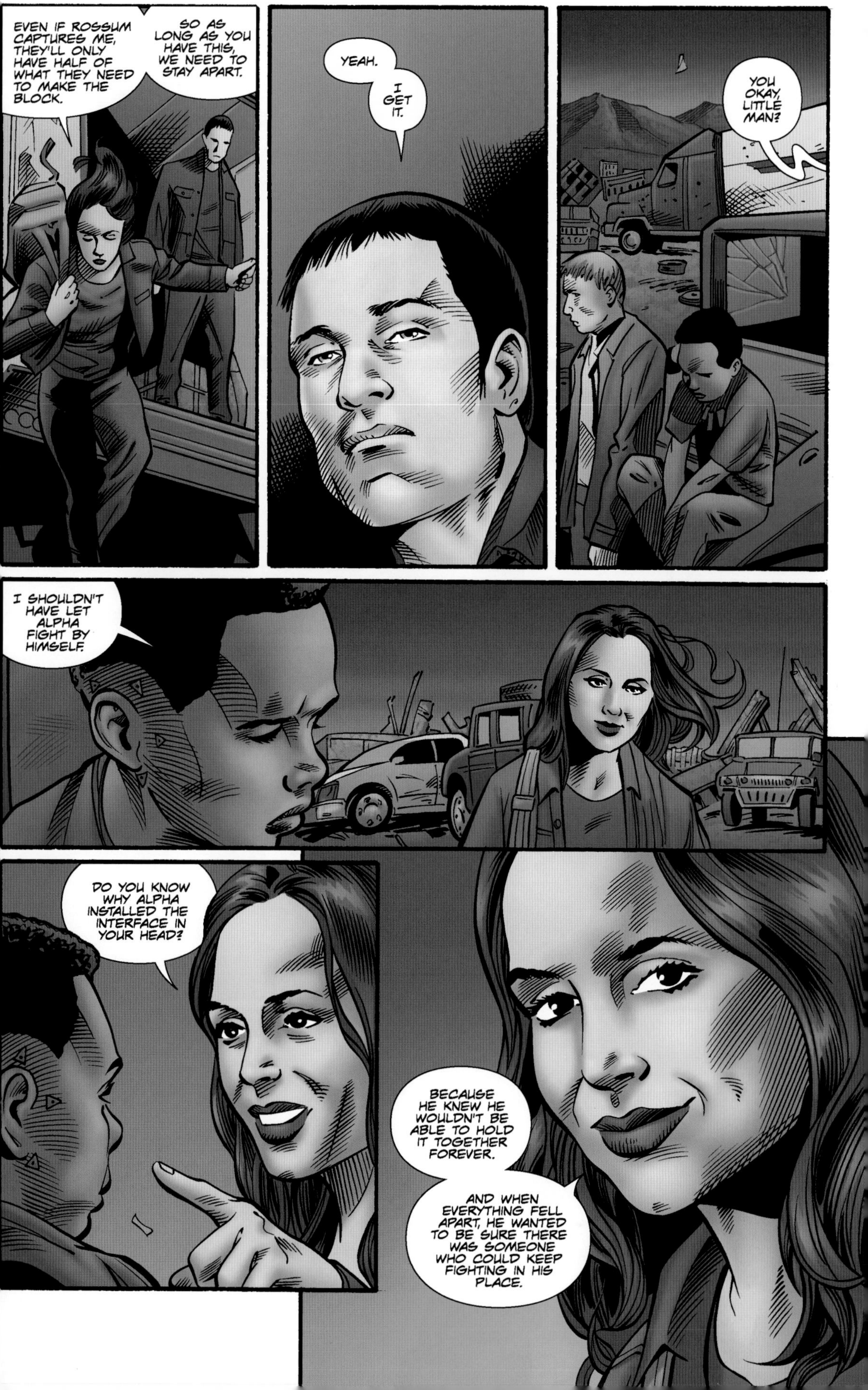
EVEN IF ROSSUM CAPTURES ME, THEY'LL ONLY HAVE HALF OF WHAT THEY NEED TO MAKE THE BLOCK.
SO AS LONG AS YOU HAVE THIS, WE NEED TO STAY APART.
YEAH.
I GET IT.
YOU OKAY, LITTLE MAN?
I SHOULDN'T HAVE LET ALPHA FIGHT BY HIMSELF.
DO YOU KNOW WHY ALPHA INSTALLED THE INTERFACE IN YOUR HEAD?
BECAUSE HE KNEW HE WOULDN'T BE ABLE TO HOLD IT TOGETHER FOREVER.
AND WHEN EVERYTHING FELL APART, HE WANTED TO BE SURE THERE WAS SOMEONE WHO COULD KEEP FIGHTING IN HIS PLACE.

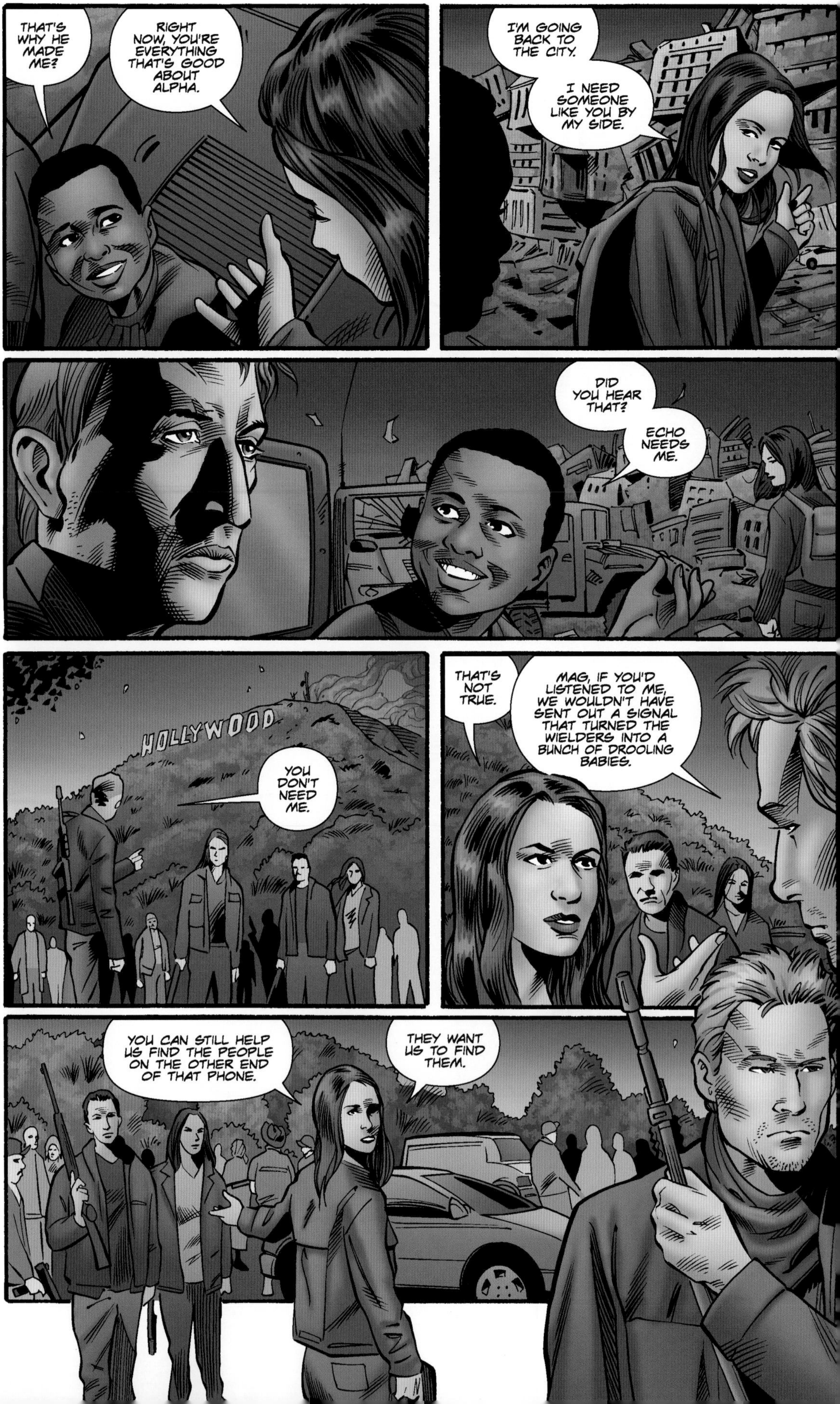

THAT'S WHY HE MADE ME?
RIGHT NOW, YOU'RE EVERYTHING THAT'S GOOD ABOUT ALPHA.
I'M GOING BACK TO THE CITY.
I NEED SOMEONE LIKE YOU BY MY SIDE.
DID YOU HEAR THAT?
ECHO NEEDS ME.
HOLLYWOOD
YOU DON'T NEED ME.
THAT'S NOT TRUE.
MAG, IF YOU'D LISTENED TO ME, WE WOULDN'T HAVE SENT OUT A SIGNAL THAT TURNED THE WIELDERS INTO A BUNCH OF DROOLING BABIES.
YOU CAN STILL HELP US FIND THE PEOPLE ON THE OTHER END OF THAT PHONE.
THEY WANT US TO FIND THEM.

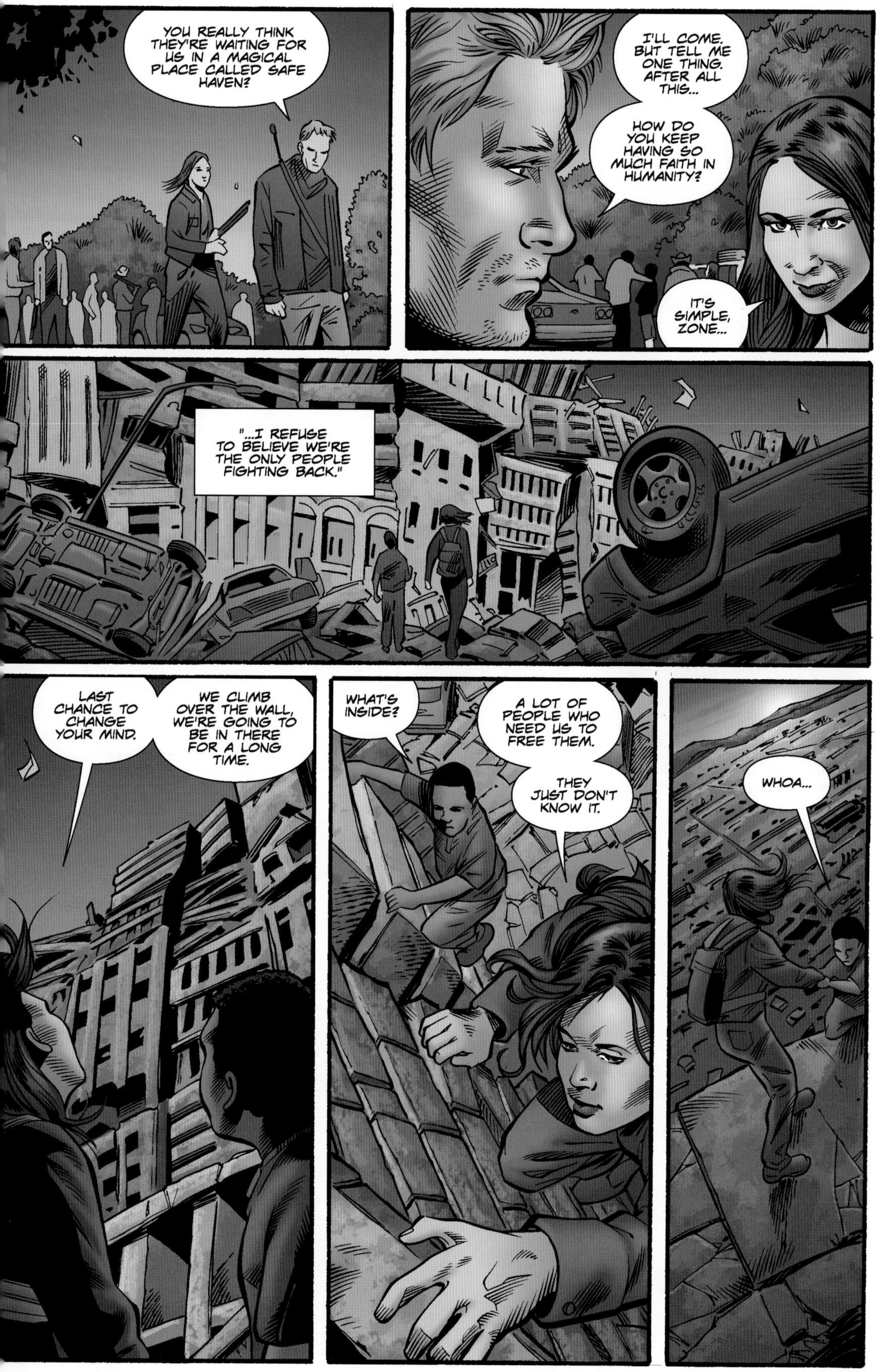
YOU REALLY THINK THEY'RE WAITING FOR US IN A MAGICAL PLACE CALLED SAFE HAVEN?
I'LL COME. BUT TELL ME ONE THING. AFTER ALL THIS...
HOW DO YOU KEEP HAVING SO MUCH FAITH IN HUMANITY?
IT'S SIMPLE, ZONE...
"...I REFUSE TO BELIEVE WE'RE THE ONLY PEOPLE FIGHTING BACK."
LAST CHANCE TO CHANGE YOUR MIND.
WE CLIMB OVER THE WALL, WE'RE GOING TO BE IN THERE FOR A LONG TIME.
WHAT'S INSIDE?
A LOT OF PEOPLE WHO NEED US TO FREE THEM.
THEY JUST DON'T KNOW IT.
WHOA...

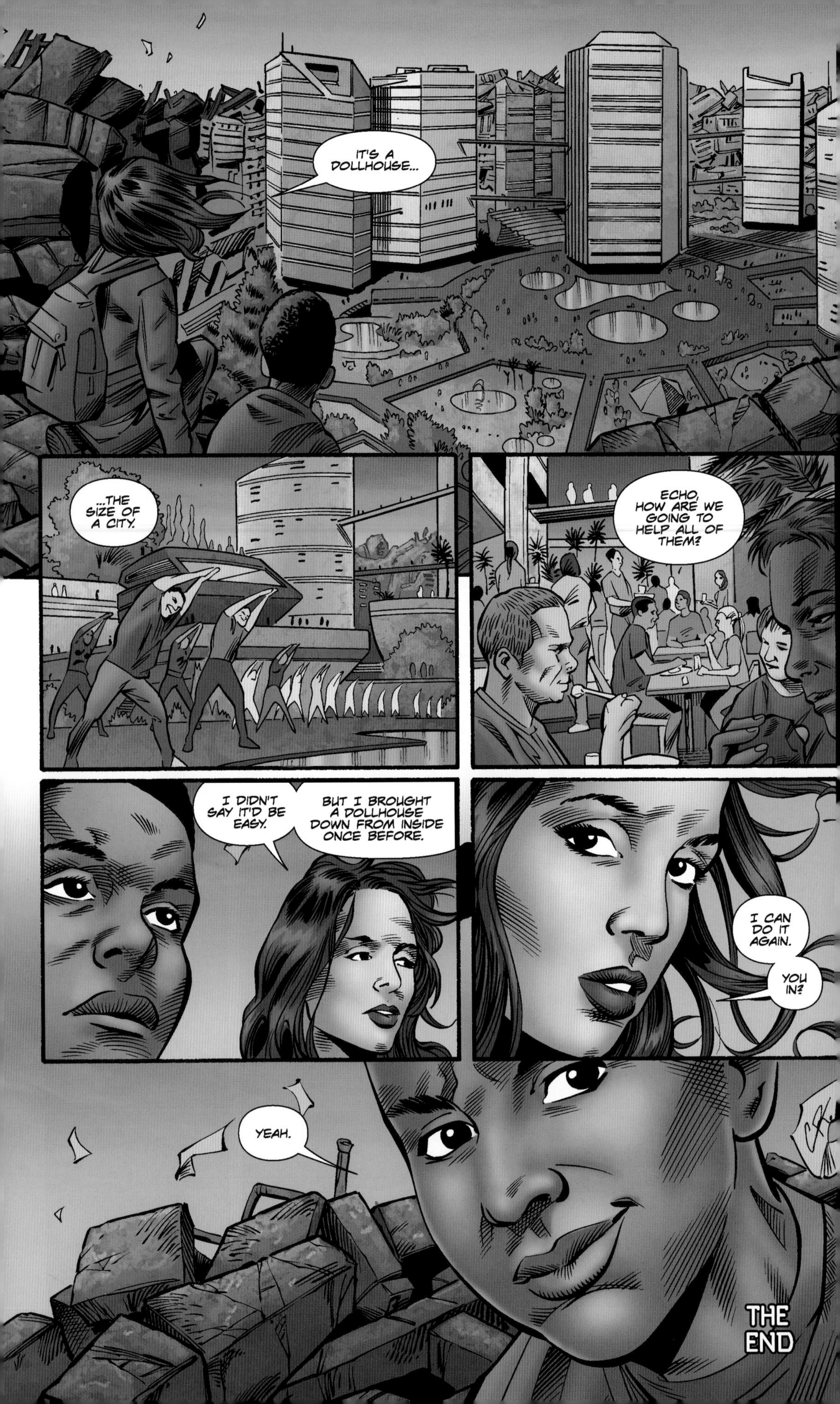
IT'S A DOLLHOUSE...
...THE SIZE OF A CITY.
ECHO, HOW ARE WE GOING TO HELP ALL OF THEM?
I DIDN'T SAY IT'D BE EASY.
BUT I BROUGHT A DOLLHOUSE DOWN FROM INSIDE ONCE BEFORE.
I CAN DO IT AGAIN.
YOU IN?
YEAH.
THE END

COVER GALLERY

THE FOLLOWING PAGES SHOWCASE the variant covers that were commissioned for the *Dollhouse* one-shot and the *Dollhouse* series, as well as a few sketches from the artists. Usually when each comic in a series has a variant cover, a single artist draws all of them (often the interior artist). But on *Dollhouse* we took an unusual route, deciding to have a different artist for each variant cover. With these covers, we added some new talent to the Dark Horse stables, and we were able to show the characters from *Dollhouse* in several diverse artistic styles.

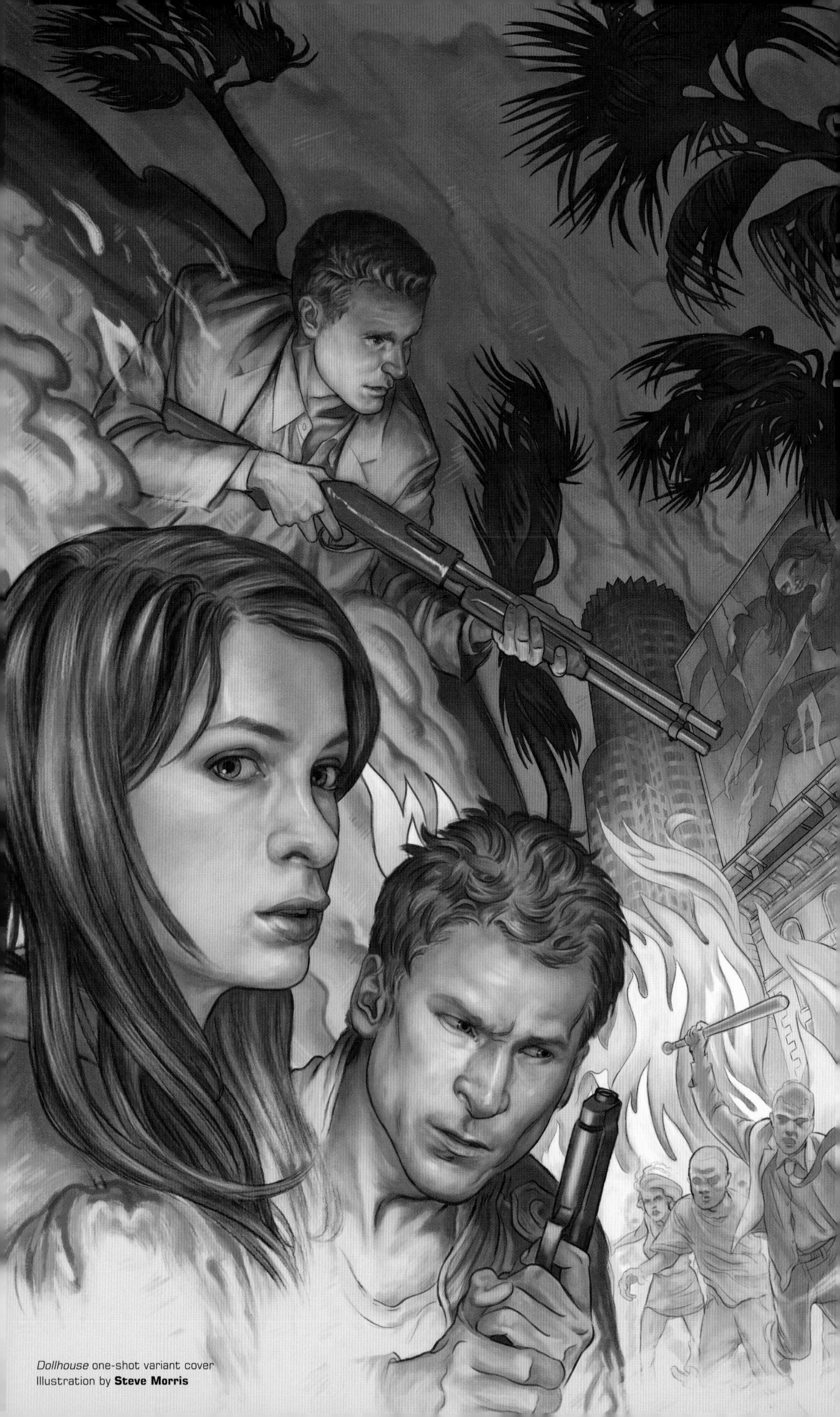

Dollhouse one-shot variant cover
Illustration by **Steve Morris**

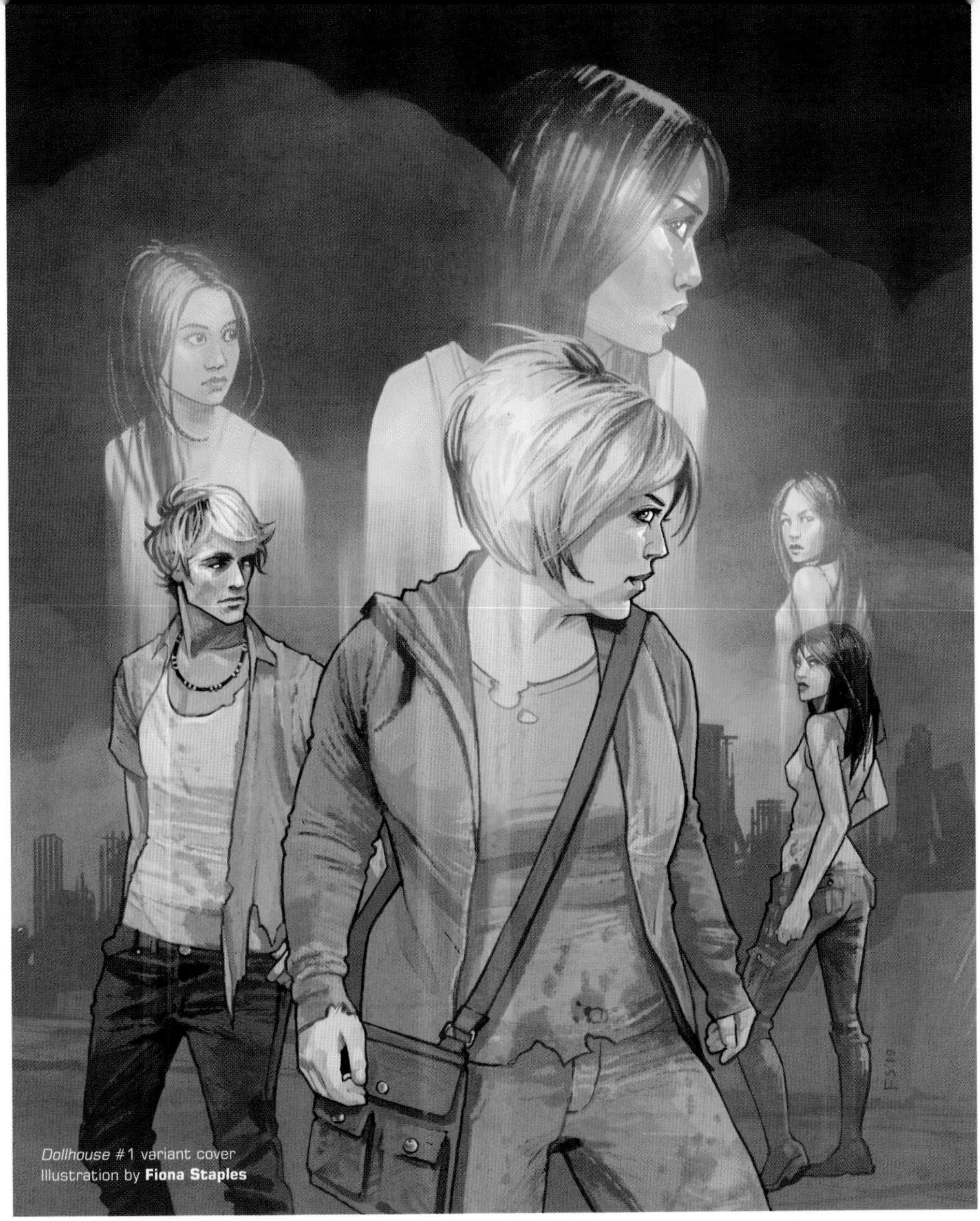

FS10

Dollhouse #1 variant cover
Illustration by **Fiona Staples**

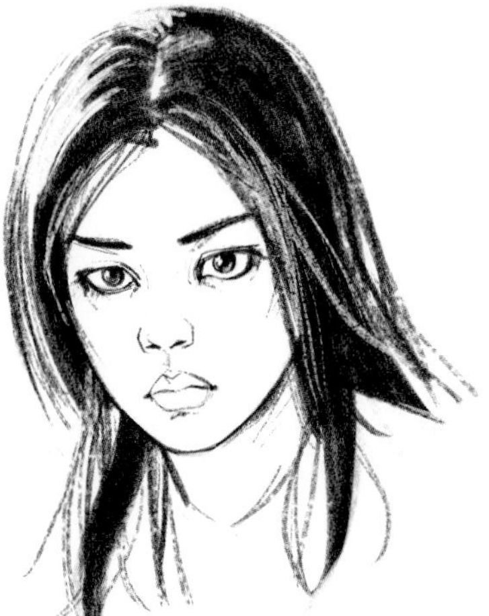

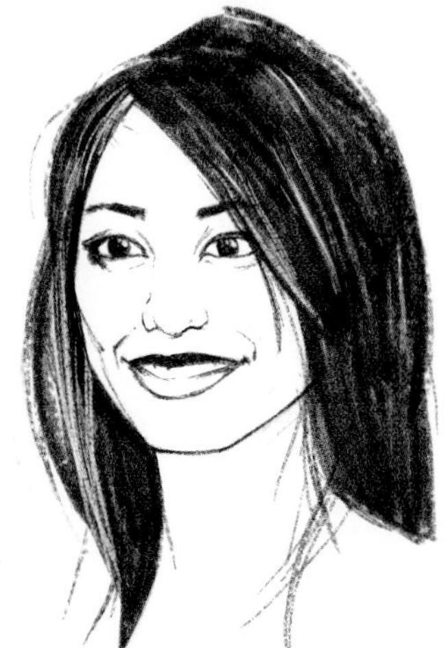

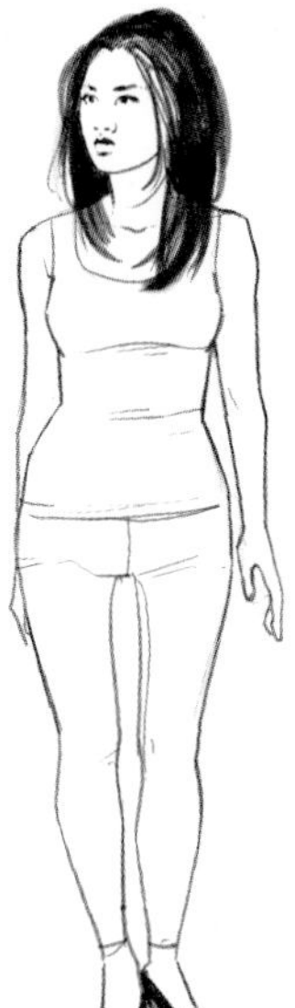

Sketches of actress Liza Lapira, the original Ivy. Fiona created these before drawing the ghostly images of Ivy on her final cover.

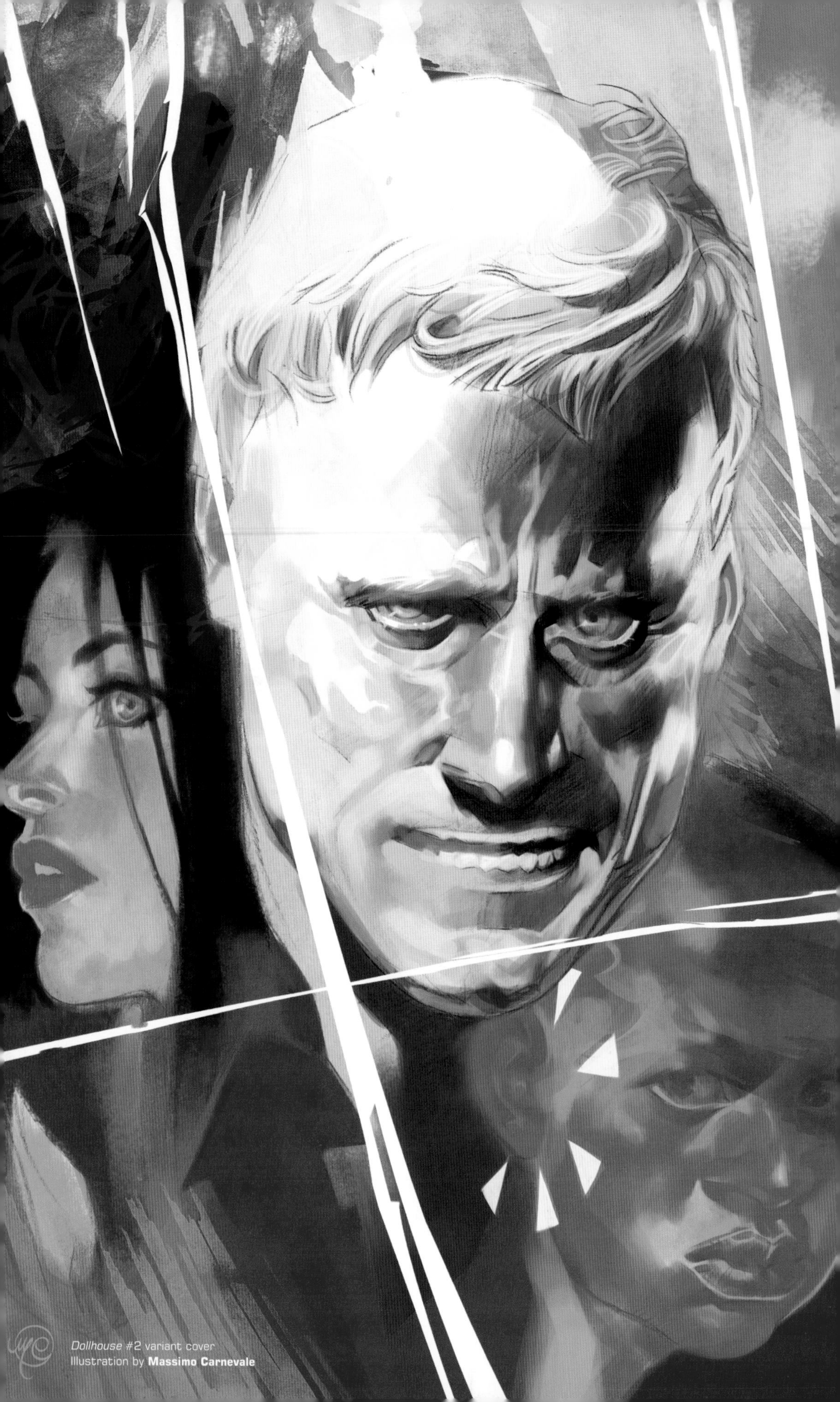

Dollhouse #2 variant cover
Illustration by **Massimo Carnevale**

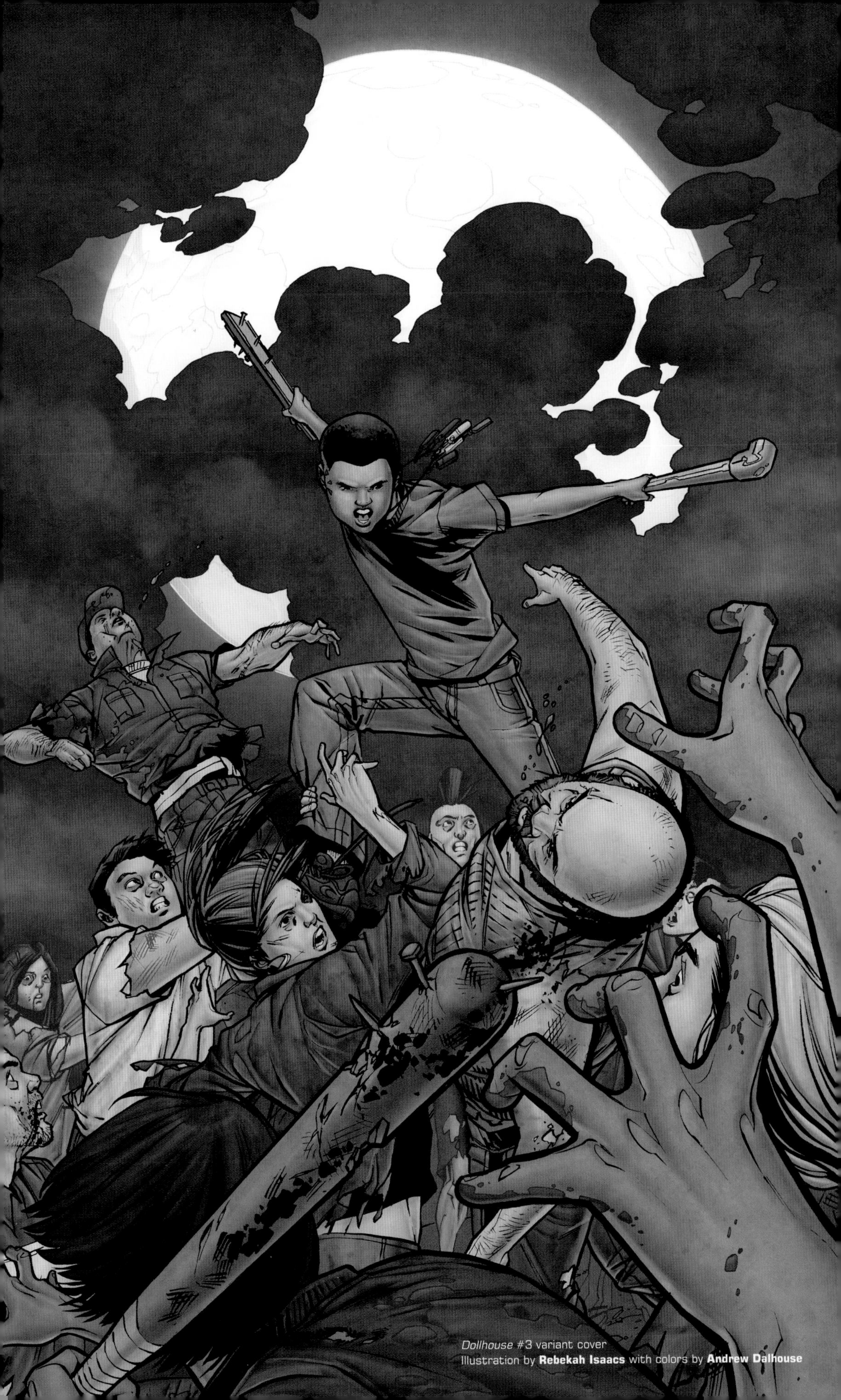

Dollhouse #3 variant cover
Illustration by **Rebekah Isaacs** with colors by **Andrew Dalhouse**

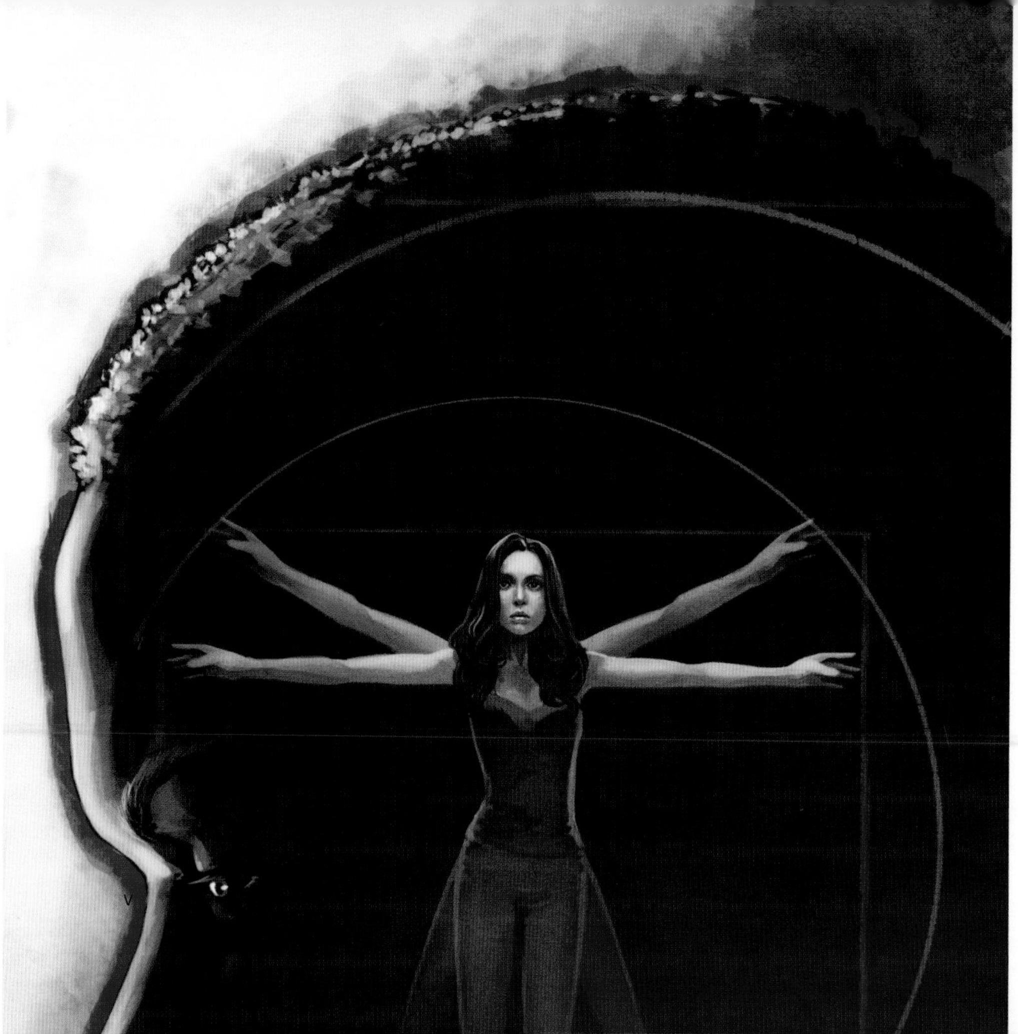

Dollhouse #4 variant cover
Illustration by **Stephanie Hans**

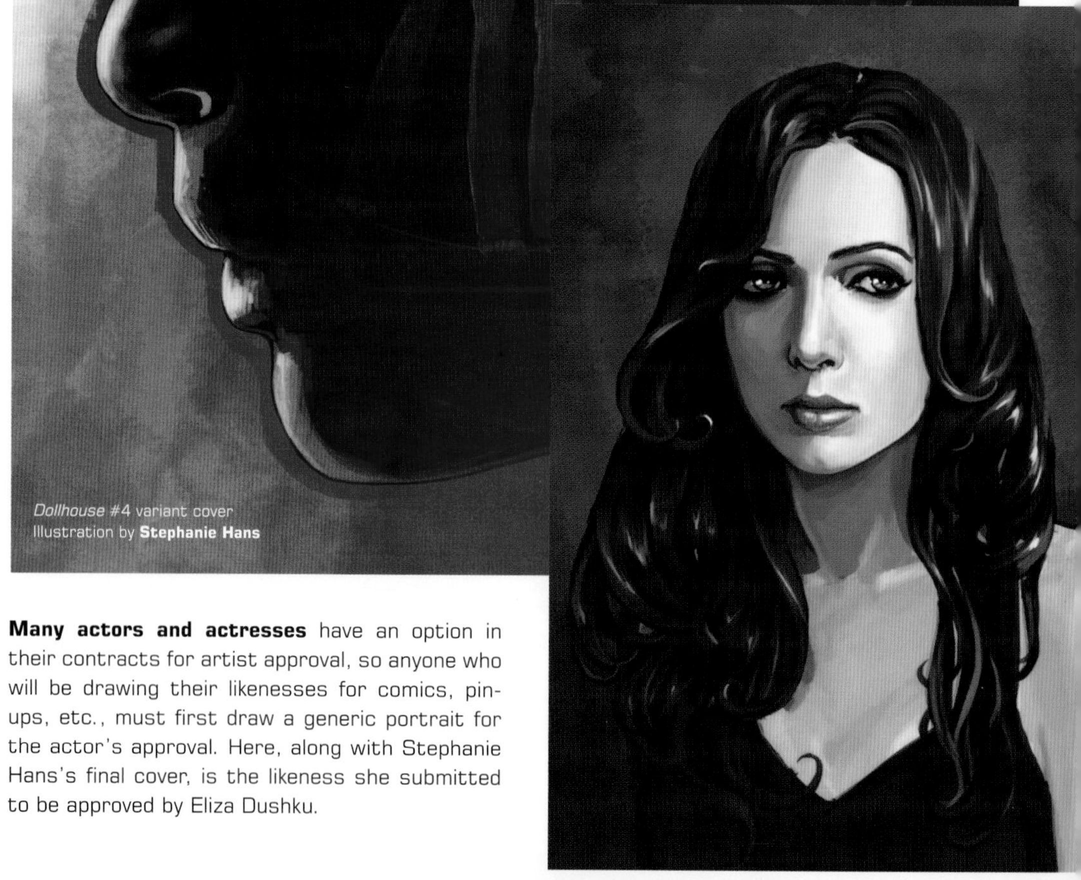

Many actors and actresses have an option in their contracts for artist approval, so anyone who will be drawing their likenesses for comics, pin-ups, etc., must first draw a generic portrait for the actor's approval. Here, along with Stephanie Hans's final cover, is the likeness she submitted to be approved by Eliza Dushku.

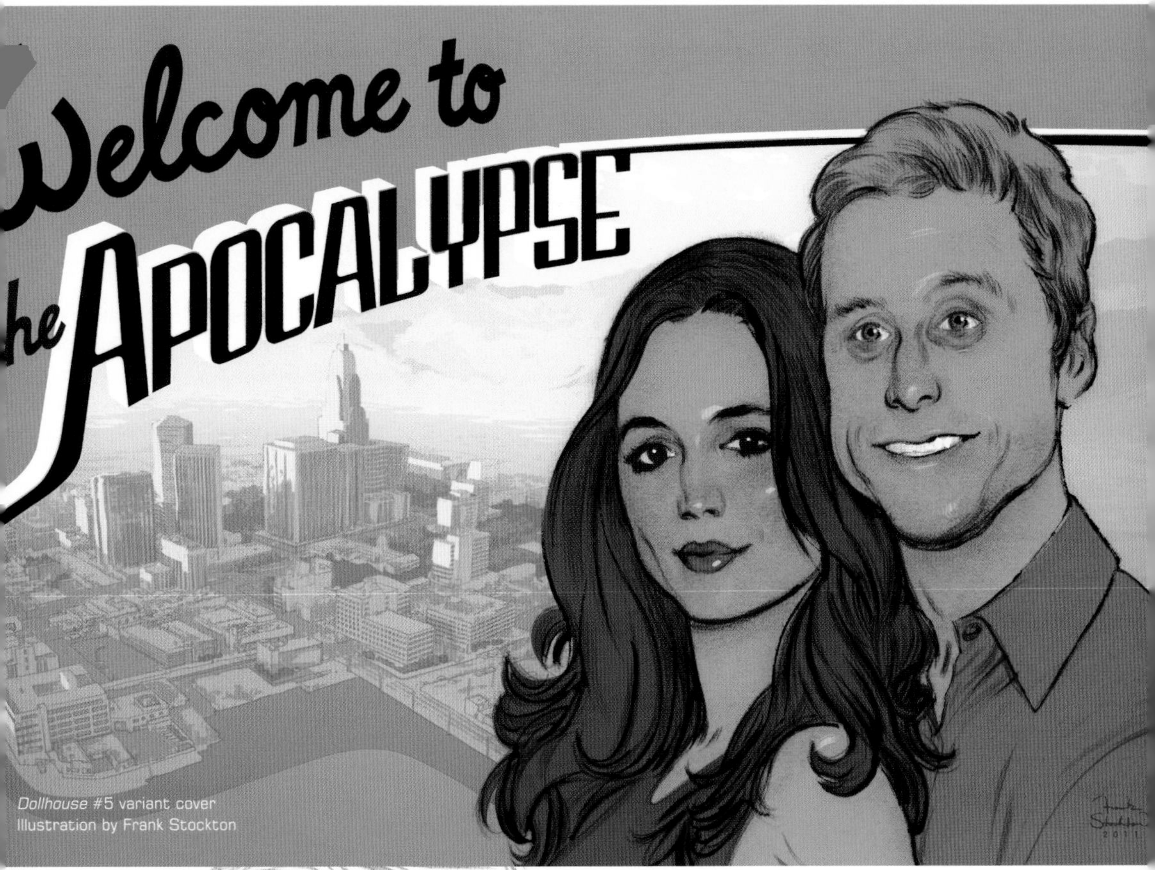
Welcome to
the APOCALYPSE

Dollhouse #5 variant cover
Illustration by Frank Stockton

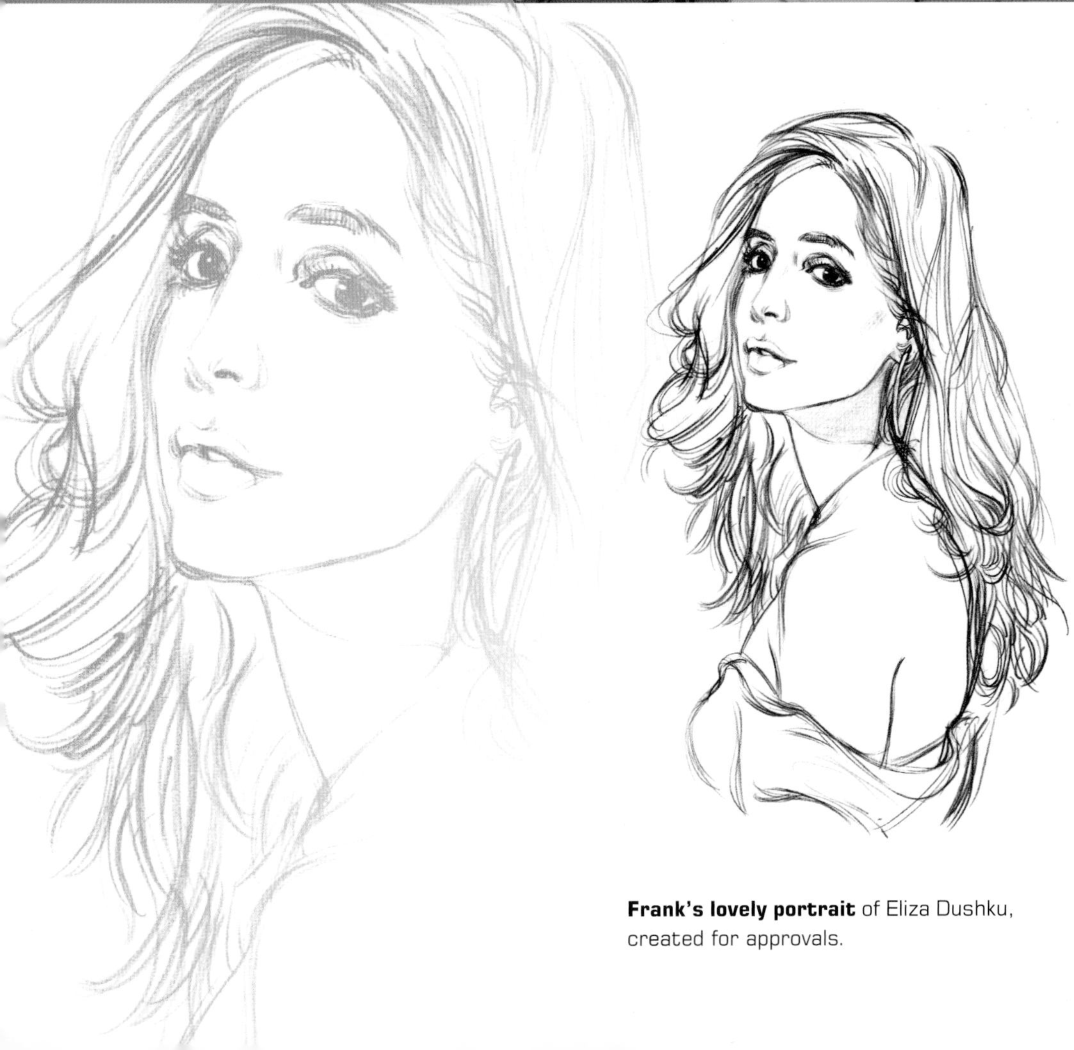

Frank's lovely portrait of Eliza Dushku, created for approvals.

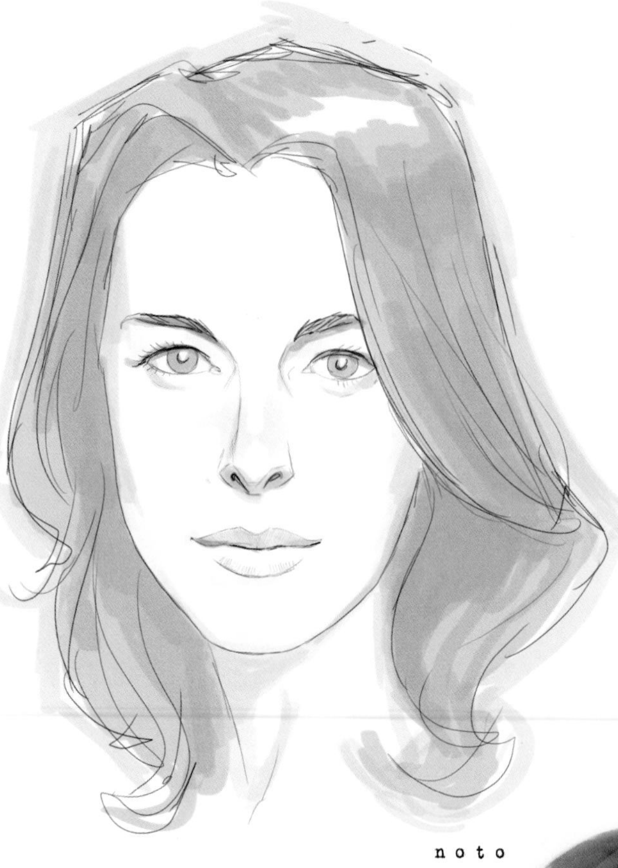
noto

This is a likeness tryout that regular *Dollhouse* cover artist Phil Noto created when we believed that Olivia Williams's character, Adelle DeWitt, would be appearing in the comic series. Sadly, her part was cut from the story—but Phil's tryout was enthusiastically approved! Olivia actually loved his drawing so much that she asked if Phil would let her have it. Phil was happy to let her have the drawing, but since his tryout had been created digitally, he hand drew another portrait. Score!

Cover artist Steve Morris also did a likeness of Eliza Dushku for his variant cover on the one-shot. Echo ended up being quite a bit smaller in his painting than we initially planned—but this early likeness also got him ready to be our regular cover artist on the then-upcoming *Angel & Faith*.

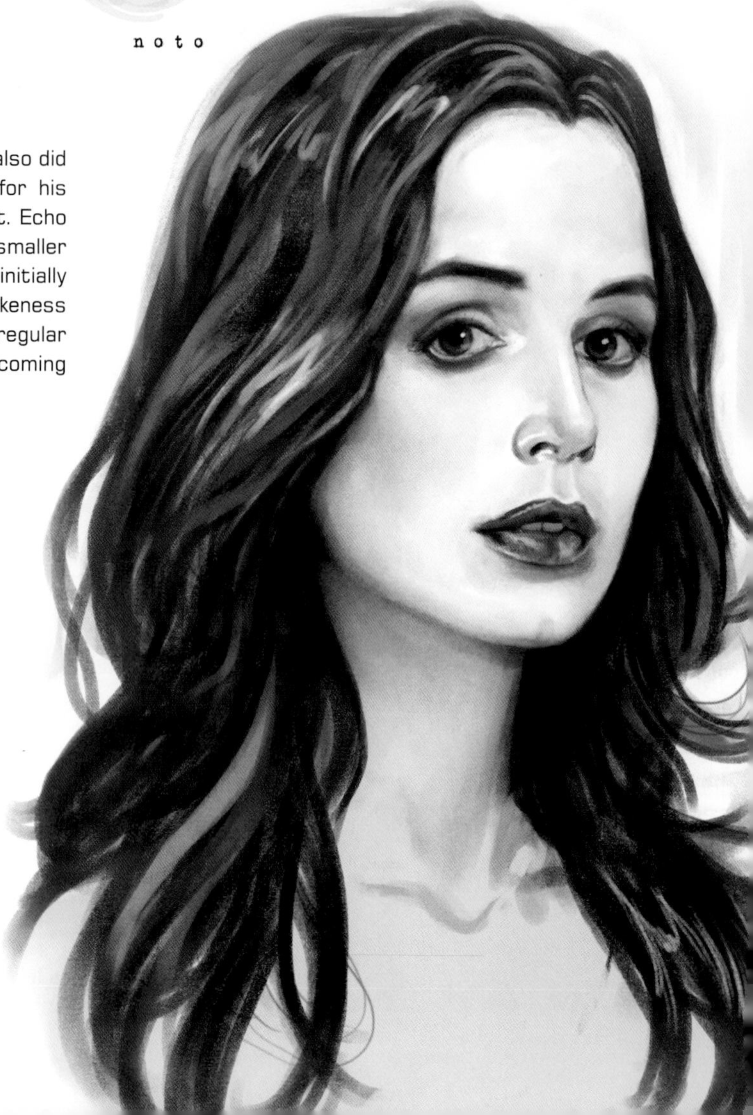

ALSO FROM JOSS WHEDON

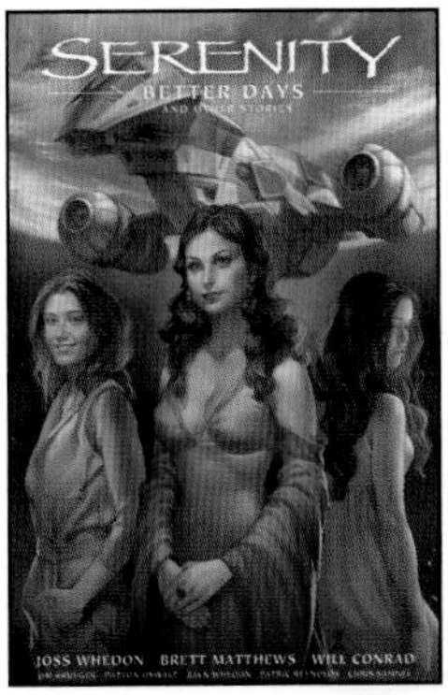
SERENITY
BETTER DAYS
JOSS WHEDON BRETT MATTHEWS WILL CONRAD

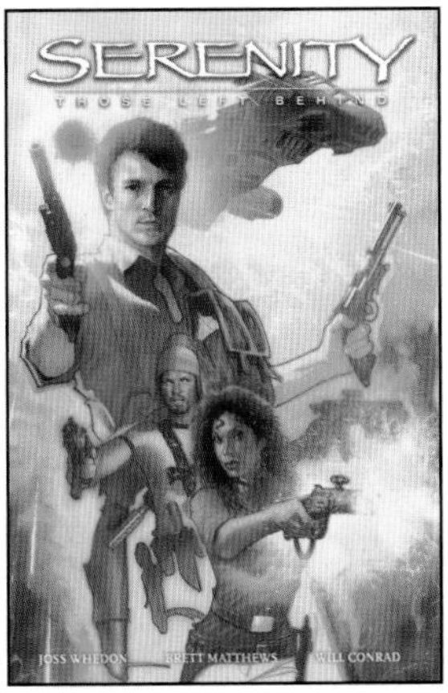
SERENITY
THOSE LEFT BEHIND
JOSS WHEDON BRETT MATTHEWS WILL CONRAD

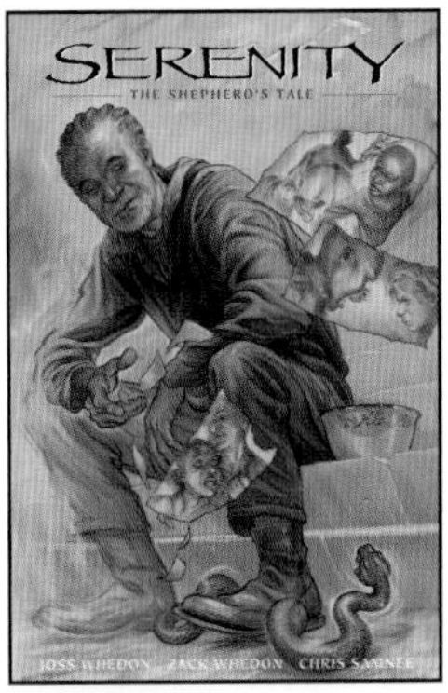
SERENITY
THE SHEPHERD'S TALE
JOSS WHEDON ZACK WHEDON CHRIS SAMNEE

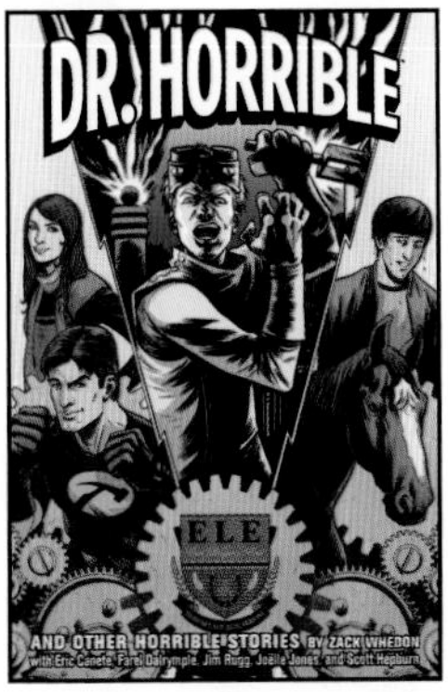
DR. HORRIBLE
ELE
AND OTHER HORRIBLE STORIES BY ZACK WHEDON

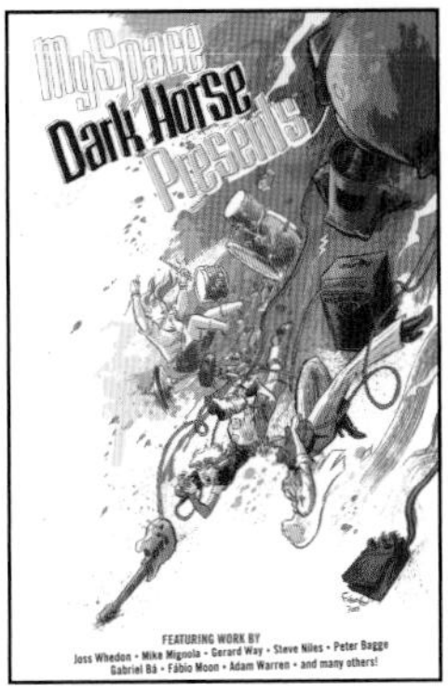
MySpace
Dark Horse
Presents
FEATURING WORK BY

SERENITY VOLUME 1: THOSE LEFT BEHIND SECOND EDITION HARDCOVER
Joss Whedon, Brett Matthews, and Will Conrad
ISBN 978-1-59307-846-1 $17.99

SERENITY VOLUME 2: BETTER DAYS AND OTHER STORIES HARDCOVER
Joss Whedon, Patton Oswalt, Zack Whedon, Patric Reynolds and others
ISBN 978-1-59582-739-5 $19.99

SERENITY VOLUME 3: THE SHEPHERD'S TALE HARDCOVER
Joss Whedon, Zack Whedon, and Chris Samnee
ISBN 978-1-59582-561-2 $14.99

DR. HORRIBLE AND OTHER HORRIBLE STORIES
Joss Whedon, Zack Whedon, Joëlle Jones, and others
ISBN 978-1-59582-577-3 $9.99

MYSPACE DARK HORSE PRESENTS VOLUME 1
Featuring Sugarshock *by Joss Whedon and Fábio Moon*
ISBN 978-1-59307-998-7 $19.99

DOLLHOUSE VOLUME 1: EPITAPHS
Andrew Chambliss, Jed Whedon, Maurissa Tancharoen, and Cliff Richards
ISBN 978-1-59582-863-7 $18.99

FROM JOSS WHEDON

BUFFY THE VAMPIRE SLAYER SEASON 8:

VOLUME 1: THE LONG WAY HOME
Joss Whedon and Georges Jeanty
ISBN 978-1-59307-822-5 | $15.99

VOLUME 2: NO FUTURE FOR YOU
Brian K. Vaughan, Georges Jeanty, and Joss Whedon
ISBN 978-1-59307-963-5 | $15.99

VOLUME 3: WOLVES AT THE GATE
Drew Goddard, Georges Jeanty, and Joss Whedon
ISBN 978-1-59582-165-2 | $15.99

VOLUME 4: TIME OF YOUR LIFE
Joss Whedon, Jeph Loeb, Georges Jeanty, and others
ISBN 978-1-59582-310-6 | $15.99

VOLUME 5: PREDATORS AND PREY
Joss Whedon, Jane Espenson, Cliff Richards, Georges Jeanty, and others
ISBN 978-1-59582-342-7 | $15.99

VOLUME 6: RETREAT
Joss Whedon, Jane Espenson, Cliff Richards, Georges Jeanty, and others
ISBN 978-1-59582-415-8 | $15.99

VOLUME 7: TWILIGHT
Joss Whedon, Brad Meltzer, and Georges Jeanty
ISBN 978-1-59582-558-2 | $16.99

VOLUME 8: LAST GLEAMING
Joss Whedon, Scott Allie, and Georges Jeanty
ISBN 978-1-59582-610-7 | $16.99

TALES OF THE SLAYERS
Joss Whedon, Amber Benson, Gene Colan, P. Craig Russell, Tim Sale, and others
ISBN 978-1-56971-605-2 | $14.99

TALES OF THE VAMPIRES
Joss Whedon, Brett Matthews, Cameron Stewart, and others
ISBN 978-1-56971-749-3 | $15.99

BUFFY THE VAMPIRE SLAYER: TALES
ISBN 978-1-59582-644-2 | $29.99

FRAY: FUTURE SLAYER
Joss Whedon and Karl Moline
ISBN 978-1-56971-751-6 | $19.99

ALSO FROM DARK HORSE . . .

BUFFY THE VAMPIRE SLAYER OMNIBUS

VOLUME 1
ISBN 978-1-59307-784-6 | $24.99

VOLUME 2
ISBN 978-1-59307-826-3 | $24.99

VOLUME 3
ISBN 978-1-59307-885-0 | $24.99

VOLUME 4
ISBN 978-1-59307-968-0 | $24.99

VOLUME 5
ISBN 978-1-59582-225-3 | $24.99

VOLUME 6
ISBN 978-1-59582-242-0 | $24.99

VOLUME 7
ISBN 978-1-59582-331-1 | $24.99

ANGEL OMNIBUS
Christopher Golden, Eric Powell, and others
ISBN 978-1-59582-706-7 | $24.99

BUFFY THE VAMPIRE SLAYER: PANEL TO PANEL
ISBN 978-1-59307-836-2 | $19.99

DARK HORSE BOOKS®
DarkHorse.com

Buffy the vampire slayer™

GEORGE
OWENS

AVAILABLE AT YOUR LOCAL COMICS SHOP OR BOOKSTORE!
To find a comics shop in your area, call 1-888-266-4226.
For more information or to order direct: • On the web: DarkHorse.com • E-mail: mailorder@darkhorse.com • Phone: 1-800-862-0052
Mon.–Fri. 9 AM to 5 PM Pacific Time.
*Prices and availability subject to change without notice